Archaeology of Ancient Australia

Australia has been inhabited for 50,000 years. This clear and compelling book shows how it is possible to unearth this country's long human history when our historical records are limited to the few hundred years since its European discovery.

Beginning with the first human colonization and ending with European contact in the eighteenth century, Peter Hiscock traces the ever-changing and sometimes turbulent history of the Australian Aboriginal peoples and their ancestors. While they remained hunters and gatherers throughout this time, their culture continually evolved, with their changes in economics, technology, cosmology, beliefs and social life.

Hiscock shows how this human past can be reconstructed from archaeological evidence in easy-to-read style and without unnecessary jargon or detail, yet reflecting the weight of scientific research. Including information from genetics, environmental sciences, anthropology and history, this book encompasses the wide variety of disciplines in the sciences and humanities which contribute to an archaeological investigation.

World-renowned discoveries such as the human bodies at Lake Mungo, the ice-age art sites of Arnhem Land, the deformed human skulls from Kow Swamp, the early ornaments and paintings from remote desert caves, and the puzzling giant shell mounds of the north coast, are discussed and extensively illustrated.

The result is not only a comprehensive and understandable introduction for beginners in archaeology, but also a challenging and absorbing view about the richness and variety of ancient human civilization.

Peter Hiscock is a Reader at the Australian National University where he teaches the archaeology of Australia. His work on Australian sites has concentrated on ancient technology but has also explored human exploitation of coastal and desert landscapes.

Archaeology of Ancient Australia

Peter Hiscock

Routledge
Taylor & Francis Group

LONDON AND NEW YORK

First published 2008
by Routledge
2 Park Square, Milton Park, Abingdon, Oxon OX14 4RN

Simultaneously published in the USA and Canada
by Routledge
270 Madison Ave, New York, NY 10016

Reprinted 2008, 2010

Routledge is an imprint of the Taylor & Francis Group, an informa business

© 2008 Peter Hiscock

Typeset in Joanna
by Keystroke, 28 High Street, Tettenhall, Wolverhampton
Printed and bound in Great Britain
by Antony Rowe Ltd, Chippenham, Wiltshire

British Library Cataloguing in Publication Data
A catalogue record for this book is available from the British Library

Library of Congress Cataloging in Publication Data
A catalog record for this book has been requested

ISBN 978–0–415–33810–3 (hbk)
ISBN 978–0–415–33811–0 (pbk)

Contents

Figures

Preface

Popular texts are needed for teaching the next generation of researchers what is known, stimulating them to overturn that knowledge and build more substantial understandings of the world as their own contribution. Teetering on the edge of the hard sciences and the humanities, archaeology has sometimes seen texts that are scientifically detailed but technical rather than intellectual in nature, while at other times texts have embraced concerns about the complexity of understanding human society but have not engaged with the scientific nature of the evidence of archaeology. Luckily there have always been archaeologists, from Gordon Childe to Peter White, who sought to balance the sciences and humanities in such a way that limitations and ambiguity of archaeological methods were acknowledged but an entertaining story of the human past could still be told. Such was my goal here. I brought to this book the conviction that an introductory text on the science of archaeology could be written without much jargon and still convey the essential logic and evidence of the discipline. The *Archaeology of Ancient Australia* reflects this approach and my perspectives as an archaeologist. Many traits in this book reflect my premise that archaeology is at its best when it is simultaneously easily read, without unnecessary jargon and detail, yet reflects the weight of scientific research; when archaeology tells the stories of our ancestors by developing inferences about their lives, without pretending that our ancestors were like ourselves or presenting fiction in the place of reasoned inference; when archaeology conveys the excitement of what we know and may learn about early people while understanding that scientific research is never diminished by acknowledging the limits of evidence and leaving those things beyond existing evidence as uncertain and mysterious.

Note about the case studies

Answers to many questions about human existence in pre-historic Australia have been offered by scientists studying materials preserved from the past; there is room for only some of them in this book. In *Archaeology of Ancient Australia* a selection of questions that have puzzled researchers are presented – questions that exemplify discoveries about the dynamic and ever-changing human past in the Australian landmass.

No book discussing the human past in a continent can be exhaustive; there are too many pieces of evidence, too many sites with interpretive difficulties, too many studies that repeat the same general interpretation. To give a clear and accessible explanation of the complex and diverse evidence that exists, and of the nature of competing interpretations of the evidence, this book focuses on a small number of outstanding examples to illustrate the archaeological investigations and the understanding of pre-history that has resulted. Places described in this book are a small proportion of the millions of archaeological sites that exist in Australia, but they exemplify the kinds of material that record past human lives in ancient Australia. Similarly the activities of pre-historic people who created this archaeological debris are examples of the many different economic and social lives that were led by ancient humans. Additionally, the few researchers featured here serve as representatives of the many hard-working scientists who have studied archaeological material on the Australian continent. Consequently, this book uses a selection of examples to deliver an account of the archaeology of the ancient Australian people, revealing some of the most remarkable and most thoroughly studied archaeological sites and objects as a way to present an understanding of the pre-historic life of this land.

Note on terminology

Choice of language not only is important for clarity, but also conveys theoretical frameworks with which we describe the world. In this book I made two choices about the use of labels. The first is that it will be clearer for readers without training in archaeology to have as few technical terms as possible, and to have complex ideas distilled to their essential meaning. Of course simplification inherent in this approach alters the content and implications of terms and concepts, and for my professional colleagues who correctly observe that, for example, my use of El Niño is not as technically accurate as ENSO (El Niño – Southern Oscillation) or that the word 'preservation' is not quite the same as 'taphonomy'; I ask only for tolerance. Second, and more importantly, I have been particular with my use of labels that designate the identity of people and groups of people. For example, while I have adopted convention in using 'Aboriginal people', 'Aboriginal' or 'Aborigines' when specifically referring to historical indigenous peoples of Australia, I have seldom used such terms for much earlier humans, despite the wealth of evidence that they were the ancestors of historic Aboriginal people, preferring instead a number of less specific phrases such as 'humans', 'foragers', 'pre-historic people', 'ancient Australians' or even occasionally 'ancient Aboriginal people'. This was done explicitly to give readers a linguistic device to distance their mental images of pre-historic Aboriginal people in this land from the depictions of Aborigines in historical records. This is a response to the concerns voiced in Chapter 1 that the application to archaeological investigations of ethnographic pictures of Aboriginal people has often created the unnecessary view that Aboriginal people of the past and present were unchanging, a static culture uniform across space and time, a culture which had always been as it was in the nineteenth century. I recognize that such an academic distinction brings with it the danger that some readers may misinterpret this as language that denies the Aboriginality of the past inhabitants of Australia or alternatively denies present-day Aboriginal people their long cultural history. In answer I can only point to the arguments presented in this book, that archaeological investigations challenge stereotypes of Aboriginal people as timeless and unchanging, and that archaeological reconstructions of ongoing transformations in language, cosmology, perceptions of land and self, settlement, technology and economy will inevitably raise confronting questions about identity.

Acknowledgements

Errors found in this work, and in any book this size they can be expected, will, I hope, be judged fairly by readers and corrected by the next generation of Australian archaeologists. Those future archaeologists, and current readers, whatever they may think of the approach taken in this book, will, I hope, also appreciate and applaud the commitment and effort of archaeologists whose labour I have drawn on. The work of scientists, archaeological and other flavours, is exhausting and often unheralded. Fame and wealth come to few in the field of archaeology; toil and even danger have come to many. What I would like readers to take from this book, beyond an insight into the dynamism of past human life in Australia, is an understanding of the lives of so many archaeologists, often supported and aided by local Aboriginal people and interested amateurs, that have worked hard to yield the evidence I summarize here. So many have helped me directly, and deserve to be named as small compensation for their help.

I thank Richard Stoneman from Routledge for his initial enthusiasm for the project, his patience while I completed it, and his final efforts in producing the book. Many thanks also to Amy Laurens for her work in making the book happen.

Conversations with many people shaped my thinking about Australian pre-history and aided in the development of the arguments found in this volume. A list of those I can recall and to whom I offer thanks is as follows: Kim Akerman, Harry Allen, Jim Allen, Ken Aplin, Brit Asmussen, Val Attenbrow, Geoff Bailey, Bryce Barker, Peter Bellwood, Patricia Bourke, Greg Bowen, David Bowman, Sally Brockwell, Peter Brown, Chris Chippindale, Anne Clarke, Peter Clarke, Chris Clarkson, Sophie Collins, Richard Cosgrove, Barry Cundy, Bruno David, Iain Davidson, Charlie Dortch, Pat Faulkner, Judith Field, Jeff Flenniken, Richard Fullagar, Colin Groves, Jay Hall, Simon Holdaway, Phil Holden, Geoff Hope, Philip Hughes, Ian Johnson, Rhys Jones, Ian Keen, Boone Law, Matthew Leavesley, Ian Lilley, Judith Littleton, Harry Lourandos, Isabel McBryde, Pat McConvell, Jo McDonald, Oliver McGregor, Alex MacKay, Ian McNiven, Fiona Mowat, John Mulvaney, Jim O'Connell, Sue O'Connor, Marc Oxenham, Colin Pardoe, David Pearson, Nicolas Peterson, Norma Richardson, Gail Robertson, Sarah Robertson, Richard Robins, Andre Rosenfeld, Wilfred Shawcross, Robin Sim, Mike Smith, the remarkable Marjorie Sullivan, Paul Taçon, Peter Thorley, Lorna Tilley, Robin

Torrence, Sean Ulm, Bruce Veitch, Peter Veth, Lynley Wallis, Ian Walters, Peter White, and Richard Wright.

I want to specifically mention six of the most remarkable archaeologists, and nicest humans, I ever met: the sweet-natured doyen of Australian archaeology, Val Attenbrow; the utterly remarkable Barry Cundy; the ever-encouraging Philip Hughes, true master of the two cultures; the uniquely astute Jim O'Connell; the insightful Wilfred Shawcross, who trained me in archaeological thought; and the amazing, dynamic and discipline-shaping Peter White. Both my professional perspectives and my adult personality evolved through interaction with them, and it is with delight that I recognize them as friends as well as mentors.

Thanks are also due to my colleagues and students in the School of Archaeology and Anthropology, at the Australian National University. Conversations and kindnesses in our hallways assisted in immeasurable ways. I single out Sue Fraser for particular acknowledgement over many years. No matter what other burdens she carried, and they were many, she found many ways to assist me; they did not go unnoticed, Sue!

I owe a debt to the people and institutions that provided permission to use illustrations found throughout the book. I take this opportunity to thank them as follows, for the images listed in parentheses (figure numbers): Brit Asmussen (10.5), Val Attenbrow (12.8), Peter Brown (5.7), Giovanni Caselli (1.1), Christopher Chippindale (6.9), Richard Cosgrove (6.11), Bruno David (14.2), Judith Field (4.4, 4.5), Simon Holdaway (12.11), Harry Lourandos (7.2, 7.3, 7.6, 10.2, 10.3), Campbell Macknight (14.6), Scott Mitchell (14.5), Kate Morse (6.16), Fiona Mowat (14.7), National Museum of Health and Medicine, Armed Forces Institute of Pathology, Washington DC (1.3), Marc Oxenham (12.2), Wilfred Shawcross (2.7, 5.4, 6.15), Mike Smith (3.2, 3.3), and the Trustees of the Board of the Australian Museum (8.5).

More pressing still I owe thanks to all of the scholars who read one or more draft chapters and generously provided me with comments to improve the volume. I selected these people as the experts in each subject, and it is astonishing that they agreed to give their time to this task. Each one could have written the chapter I sent them with more authority than I can offer, and if I have not digested their suggestions the failing is mine. In alphabetical order these helpful experts were Brit Asmussen, Val Attenbrow, Peter Brown, Christopher Clarkson, Richard Cosgrove, Barry Cundy, Pat Faulkner, Judith Field, Simon Holdaway, Ian Keen, Judith Littleton, Jo McDonald, Colin Pardoe, Sarah Robertson, Robin Sim, Mike Smith, Lorna Tilley and Peter Veth. In addition, Barry Cundy read and critiqued a draft of the entire book. Since all those who know Barry recognize his unrivalled scholarship and thoughtfulness, it is not necessary to admit that the quality of this book was enhanced in many ways by his contributions.

Finally, it is my pleasure to thank my mother and father, and my sister, Jill, for their kindnesses and support. Last and most importantly, to Alison, my wife and wonderful companion, I offer this book with gratitude and love.

1 The veil of Antipodean pre-history

In the late decades of the nineteenth century European scientists arrived at a startling conclusion. They realized that not only had the earth existed for a vast length of time, but also humans had lived in that ancient world. The realization that people had existed in a period so remote it was long before the invention of writing brought with it the puzzle of how modern researchers could learn of those ancient lives. Nineteenth century archaeologists sometimes wrote poetically about their concern that we may never have detailed knowledge about the ancient human past before written records. For example, the Scandinavian scientist Sven Nilsson (1868), one of the founders of archaeology, described the lives of ancient people, prior to the advent of written records, as being enveloped in obscurity, while Victorian politician and scientist Sir John Lubbock (1872) employed a similar metaphor, saying the past is hidden from the present by a veil so thick that it cannot be penetrated by either history or tradition. Nowadays the task of seeing beyond this veil of obscurity, to reveal something of the unwritten past, falls mainly on archaeology, a distinctive scientific discipline. By studying the material remains of past human activities archaeologists make statements about the lives of people long dead, and reconstruct an image of their economy, social interactions and perceptions of the world.

Archaeologists now think that Australia was inhabited more than 50,000 years ago by humans who were ancestors of modern Australian Aboriginal people; but we have written records of their lives for only the final centuries of that long occupation. European sailors left written impressions of coastal dwelling Aborigines from the seventeenth century onwards, British settlers wrote of Aboriginal people and their land at the end of the eighteenth century, while in isolated parts of the continent European explorers did not glimpse Aboriginal people until late in the nineteenth century. Their documents form the foundations of many interpretations of Australian Aboriginal life during the historic period. Of the humans who lived in Australia thousands of years earlier, those historical records tell us little or nothing. For knowledge of the long passage of human occupation prior to written records, called the pre-historic period because it precedes the first written or historical documents, we must turn to other kinds of records. Archaeological investigations of the buildings, artefacts, food debris, quarries, art works and skeletons of ancient Aboriginal people who lived in Australia during pre-historic times form the primary source of information with which we can tell the story of those people. Additional studies of genetics, reconstructions of past environments, physical and chemical information about the ages of objects, supplement archaeological information and help answer questions about the human occupation of ancient Australia.

The quest to see through the 'veil' that separates us from a view of the human past in Australia must begin with an explanation of why archaeologists find it difficult to interpret ancient materials. One process creating ambiguity is the preservation of only some residues of cultural activities and the subsequent destruction and disturbance of archaeological objects, making it hard for archaeologists to develop detailed anthropological-like reconstructions of ancient events. Another way in which the past is obscured is when the methods used to study it actually prevent ancient activities from being recognized. For example, researchers often used written descriptions of Aboriginal ways of life in the historical period to create detailed stories about the pre-historic past, a practice which imposed images of recent cultures on the lives of ancient people, thereby overlaying the past with reproductions of recent life ways. To the surprise of many people first studying archaeology, the principal complication confronting archaeologists is how our knowledge of the modern, historical world can and should be used to reconstruct stories about the ancient, pre-historic world!

How and why archaeologists used historic records

In precisely the same period that European exploration and settlement of Australia began, the seventeenth through nineteenth centuries, archaeological thinking was emerging in the scientific traditions of Western Europe. At that time people became interested in incorporating ruins and relics into their understanding of the past. Initially it was thought that the age of the world was recorded in biblical genealogies, that it was only about 6,000 years old, and that much of human history was accurately recorded in historical documents such as the Bible (Grayson 1983; Trigger 1990). With those attitudes early archaeologists thought all archaeological ruins were the work of historically known tribes, and their investigations focused on questions of which tribe was responsible for each ruin. This interpretation reflected widely held views that scriptures, classical poems and early histories contained all that could be known about the past, and that ancient monuments or remains alone taught us little of the past. Such an understanding was based on the idea that archaeological and written records documented the same events, and that humans had not existed before the invention of writing.

Gradually, as archaeologists such as Lubbock and Nilsson demonstrated that many of the archaeological objects in Europe were truly pre-historic, it became necessary to find ways of thinking about archaeological discoveries without using the historic records from Europe. In the second half of the nineteenth century European archaeologists such as John Lubbock frequently used observations of indigenous peoples around the world as a source of inspiration in creating their stories of the European past. In Britain this approach, now termed 'cultural evolutionism', was derived from enlightenment ideas that humans had gradually progressed as past generations had used their reasoning capacities to improve their lives. It was commonly believed that organisms, including humans, had an 'internal drive' propelling them to higher levels of complexity. For archaeologists and historians this encouraged the idea that human cultures around the world inevitably developed in the same direction, progressing through a number of stages until modern civilizations appeared. Sven Nilsson, for example, believed that all civilizations started as hunters and gatherers, became nomadic herds-folk before becoming sedentary farmers, which enabled them to develop a political state with military and bureaucratic organizations. In the nineteenth century this proposition helped to make sense of the archaeological sequence then being discovered in Europe. Researchers such as Edward Tylor (1871) and Lewis Morgan (1877) suggested that if different cultures around the world progressed from one stage to another at different times observations of less 'advanced' societies in remote places could supply details about pre-historic life in Europe.

This intellectual journey of nineteenth century European archaeologists, with their story that all humans developed along the same pathway, had important consequences for how scientists explored the pre-history of Aboriginal people in Australia. Although the idea that all societies must develop in the same way has now been shown to be untrue, these consequences shaped perceptions of Aborigines and their past among early archaeologists, and continue to subtly influence the theory and practice of Australian archaeology.

One consequence of cultural evolutionary views was the establishment of a tradition of archaeological interpretation that relied on the use of information about recent indigenous people. Use of written, historical records about recent societies to provide details about the lives of pre-historic peoples represents an 'analogy'. Using this analogical argument involved identifying features in a historical society which archaeological debris shows also existed in an ancient society, then inferring both societies shared further similarities not demonstrated by archaeological evidence (Salmon 1982). Although analogies can be potentially helpful to archaeologists they can also be dangerous, because they can produce narratives of pre-historic life that merely borrow from stories of recent life, implying that little has altered over time. Archaeologists therefore need to be careful that their use of analogies from history does not hide change in the nature of human life during pre-history.

Because pre-historic humans lived differently from the way present-day scientists live, it is important to recognize that some stories created about the past reflect modern perspectives on the world rather than the behaviour and attitudes possessed by ancient people. For this reason archaeologists have used historical accounts of non-European societies to give them insights into other cultures, and assist them to imagine societies unlike their own. With a greater understanding of subsistence strategies, technology, and social systems foreign to their own socio-economic lives, archaeologists believed they could interpret the archaeological record without imposing inappropriate European images on ancient peoples. Using this argument, generations of Australian archaeologists sought to avoid 'Eurocentric' interpretations of evidence for the ancient Aboriginal past by immersing themselves in historical descriptions of Aboriginal life. Of course this approach never really avoided European visions: depictions of historical Aboriginal people were still interpretations by Europeans of what they saw. Furthermore, as cultural outsiders, early European explorers and settlers altered the way Aboriginal people behaved and often recorded situations that they themselves were responsible for creating. Even worse, it would be curious if archaeologists had such limited imaginations that they relied on historical descriptions of recent societies, such as the ethnographies compiled by anthropologists, as their sole source of inspiration. Societies which existed in the historic period probably represented only a fraction of the cultural diversity that existed throughout pre-history; recent societies do not necessarily resemble all societies which existed in the distant past (Wobst 1978; Bailey 1983; Murray 1988). Nevertheless, the idea that understanding of Aboriginal life in historic times helps archaeologists reconstruct Aboriginal life in ancient times has been very popular in Australia.

A second consequence of the cultural evolutionist idea that all human societies passed through the same stages of development was the belief that Australian Aborigines had progressed only a small distance along the evolutionary path, and had therefore changed little during their occupation of Australia. Adam Kuper (1988) pointed out that images of naked, black, hunters and gatherers, combined with the recentness of European discovery of the continent and the notion that Australia had been isolated, led to the thought that nineteenth century Australian Aborigines represented the kind of early society that had died out elsewhere. This perception promoted notions of Aborigines as a simple, unchanging society. Late nineteenth century anthropologists were convinced that Australia reflected 'primitive' society, and important observers of Aboriginal society were influenced by the interpretation of Aborigines as the epitome of the unchanged primitive. This shaped the nature of the diverse nineteenth century observations of Aborigines; from the focus on religion (Kuper 1988) to the search for rigid concepts about stone tools (Wright 1977) many of the early records of Aboriginal life reflected these attitudes. Since historical observers expected that Aborigines had lived since the earliest periods without substantial change it was easy to think that descriptions of Aboriginal life and society during the eighteenth and nineteenth centuries could give archaeologists an insight into how Aborigines lived in more ancient times.

Australian archaeology was therefore considered privileged to have a large number of historical records of eighteenth, nineteenth and twentieth century Aboriginal life; many researchers made use of those records to imagine how the past might have been. Australia is also frequently cited as an outstanding example of long-term continuity of economy, ideology and social life; an idea that promoted rhetoric of Aboriginal society as the longest continuous culture in existence. These propositions are not separate but are actually two parts of a single idea, each sustaining the other: if the culture has not changed, historical Aboriginal practices tell us of the operation of pre-historic society, while using historical records helped create an image of the past that looks like the present and invites us to think there has been little or no change. How pervasive and hazardous is this tradition of incorporating historical images of Aboriginal people into archaeological reconstructions of ancient human life in Australia? Let us take, as an example, stories offered by archaeologists about one well-known archaeological site.

Lake Mungo and the historic image

The acclaimed World Heritage site of Lake Mungo, a dry inland lake in the southeast of Australia, is one of the oldest archaeological sites in the continent. Discovered early in the archaeological exploration of Australia, the interpretations of this site influenced not only generations of archaeological thinking but also the public understanding of Australia's human past. Food debris, artefacts, fireplaces and human skeletons preserved in the sands and clays at the side of the lake are some of the most significant and well-studied archaeological materials in the continent. Surprisingly, many interpretations offered by archaeologists were more strongly influenced by images of historical Aboriginal life than by the archaeological material. Ethnographic images can be seen in Figure 1.1, Giovanni Caselli's remarkable reconstruction of life at Lake Mungo published by Bernard Wood (1977) as an aide to depicting daily life there more than 30,000 years ago. As Stephanie Moser (1992) has pointed out, this figure reveals the pervasive influence of ethnography on thinking about the past. While some objects and activities in the painting are similar to those that are known to have occurred at ancient Lake Mungo, others do not reflect the archaeological record. For example, the species of animals being captured and cooked by people in the painting are the same as those species whose bones were found in the archaeological deposits. However, some stone artefacts shown in the painting, such as the stone axe being ground by the man in the lower left, are not known in the excavations of Lake Mungo. When the lake existed, axes were used only in distant regions, thousands of kilometres away; they were recovered from sites near by Lake Mungo but only tens of thousands of years after the time represented in the painted scene. Evidence for many things shown in the painting, such as the nature of clothing, existence of jewellery, kinds of fishing gear, construction of huts, sexual division of labour and 'initiation' scars on the bodies of men, have never been found in the archaeological deposits at Lake Mungo. All those details in the painting reflect a generalized, even stereotyped, scene of Aboriginal life as presented in historical ethnographies of Australian deserts rather than a reconstruction of the past from the archaeological evidence. The image of ethnographic life contained within the picture has merely been given the veneer of antiquity by the addition of archaeological objects acting as props.

This subtle yet powerful use of ethnographic information, not to assist archaeological interpretations but to supplant them, is not confined to pictorial representations of ancient Lake Mungo; it is also found in many texts written by archaeologists. The idea revealed in Caselli's painting, that Aboriginal life in the past was much the same as it was in the historic period, reflects interpretations of archaeological evidence from Lake Mungo. For example, as a youthful field archaeologist Harry Allen (1974) interpreted the sparse archaeological evidence in the light of his knowledge of the seed collecting and consumption of Bagundji Aboriginal group,

Figure 1.1 Artistic image of life at Lake Mungo by Giovanni Caselli. Is it ancient past or historical Aboriginal life? (Courtesy of G.Caselli.)

who lived in the area during the historic period. He concluded that in the nineteenth century Bagundji relied on cereals as a seasonal food, their cereal processing used grindstones, and that grinding stones found in archaeological sites more than 15,000 years old had similarly been used to process cereals. He therefore argued that seed consumption was part of the subsistence pattern for much or all of the last 15,000 years. By filling 'gaps' in his archaeological evidence with details obtained from historical observations of Bagundji life, Allen created a vision of the ancient past at Lake Mungo which implied very little change during long periods of time. Allen and others have now shown that this and many other interpretations of unchanging behaviour were wrong. Archaeological evidence at Lake Mungo documents a series of economic and social changes, but many archaeologists imposed ethnographic images on the past instead of 'reading' the material evidence recovered by archaeological fieldwork.

A quarter of a century after his initial, ethnographically loaded interpretations of Lake Mungo, it was a more mature and reflective Harry Allen (1998) who recognized that his reconstruction of long-term cultural continuity at Lake Mungo arose from the projection of recent ethnographic relationships onto the archaeological data rather than detailed interpretations of the archaeological evidence itself. Allen's revised vision emphasized archaeological evidence and acknowledged the dangers of placing ethnographic details within archaeological interpretations. However, the presentation of the human past in Australia as corresponding to historical Aboriginal life remained entrenched in interpretations of many other archaeologists, resulting in implicit or explicit claims for relentless cultural continuity and changelessness in Aboriginal life.

Connections between the uncritical use of ethnographic information and the development of ethnographic-scale reconstructions and statements of long-term cultural continuity can be seen in the writings of archaeologists who relied on detailed analogy with historical observations to build images of the pre-historic period. For example, claiming historical records of post-contact Aboriginal life were a major asset, John Mulvaney and Johan Kamminga (1999) based many interpretations of archaeological materials from Lake Mungo on ethnographic information. They compared each piece of archaeological evidence with objects from the historical period to build a story of similarity between past and present. They wrote that freshwater molluscs and fish were eaten by nineteenth century Bagundji people, and that bones and shells of these creatures are found in archaeological sites at Lake Mungo; Aboriginal people speared and netted fish in the historic period, and one sharpened bone found in the archaeological deposits may be a prong from a fish-spear of the historic type; historical Aborigines hunted land animals such as wallabies, bandicoots and wombats, and archaeologists find the bones of these animals at Lake Mungo; Bagundji people lived on the Darling River during the summer but dispersed into the dry hinterland during the winter. Interpreting emu egg shells at Lake Mungo as a seasonal indicator Mulvaney and Kamminga (1999) suggested that ancient people had a seasonal settlement pattern similar to the historical people.

By juxtaposing interpretations of historical reports and archaeological objects in this way, the archaeologists subtly suggested that the lives of ancient people at Lake Mungo were the same or very similar to the lives of Aboriginal people in nearby regions nearly two thousand generations later. Like the earlier approach of Allen, the way Mulvaney and Kamminga (1999) intertwined ethnography with archaeological props led them to a vision of the static society painted by Caselli. By assuming continuity from pre-historic to present times, what is termed 'direct historical analogy', archaeologists created a story of the past that was embedded within and repeated European understandings of Aboriginal life during the historical period. Archaeologists have often made their idea of the past conform to their idea of the historic period.

The pervasive idea of an unchanging Aboriginal society is also observed in the way ethnographic images are the foundation of interpretations of ancient human ideology at Lake Mungo. Take for example Alan Thorne's assertion that, because Aboriginal people in the historic period sometimes buried males with their hands placed over their groin, protecting their penis, the similar body position of a human buried at Lake Mungo nearly 45,000 years ago revealed that the person was a male (Thorne et al. 1999). Biological evidence for the sex of this person, known as WLH3 to archaeologists, is actually ambiguous, and during pre-history women as well as men were sometimes buried with their hands over the pubic region (Brown 2000a). Thorne's interpretation assumed there had been no cultural changes throughout the human occupation of Australia; his conclusion that this particular burial practice and ideology has a long history is therefore a circular argument built on ideas of an unchanging Aboriginal past.

Another ethnographically augmented interpretation of ancient life at Lake Mungo is Josephine Flood's (1989) discussion of the burned bones of a woman called WLH1 by archaeologists. Drawing on images of historical Aboriginal societies, implying that social norms were not only the same in all Aboriginal groups but were also identical from the colonization of Australia until the historical period, Flood (1989) made four extraordinary statements about WLH1. First, she suggested that because in the nineteenth century gathering food was often women's work, only women collected the molluscs discarded in archaeological sites at Lake Mungo more than 30,000 years earlier. Next, Flood (1989) asserted that women had always provided the staple foods for human groups in Australia and had therefore always been 'respected'. Then, interpreting the burned bones of WLH1 as a cremation, Flood hypothesized that this was evidence of complex rituals symbolizing respect for women. Flood concluded that the evidence demonstrated cultural continuity in Aboriginal society from the earliest times to the present day. Of course this conclusion, that archaeology showed pre-historic people had similar social beliefs and activities to those observed in historic times, is untrustworthy because in using historical patterns to interpret archaeological evidence Flood had already assumed continuity. Her method did not investigate the nature of ancient life but instead developed interpretations of the past that merely recreated the format of Aboriginal life in the historic period.

These examples of archaeological interpretations at Lake Mungo clarify the way assumptions of cultural continuity and completing reconstructions of pre-history with details of daily life borrowed from historical Aboriginal lives can construct images of a changeless Aboriginal society. When this happens archaeologists are not assisting us to understand what life was like for pre-historic people in Australia. Instead, they are reproducing images of what life might have been like during European colonization. If Aboriginal societies were not changeless, if in reality they had been regularly altering, then embedding archaeological objects within stories built around the experience of Aborigines after European contact not only fails to illuminate the pre-historic past, but also actively constructs a veil that obscures the past and misleads us into thinking it must have been like the present.

As discussed throughout this book, scientists have abundant evidence demonstrating that Aboriginal lifestyles and societies were not fixed in a format recorded for the period after contact with Europeans. Subsequent chapters discuss archaeological evidence for changes in social life, beliefs, economy and technology throughout pre-history. Written records from the historical period also offer evidence that activities and social life represented in the ethnography of the eighteenth, nineteenth and twentieth centuries are not reliable indicators of the details of human life during Australian pre-history.

Diversity of Aboriginal people in the historic period

It was easy for Western thinkers to imagine the lives of Aboriginal people were unchanged during pre-history because of a common impression that Aboriginal societies were all the same. Stereotypes of Aborigines everywhere leading lives as mobile hunters, stalking kangaroos, congregating in small, independent tribes without leadership, and having a religion based on the notion of a 'Dreamtime', were prevalent and contributed to the idea that uniformity of Aboriginal societies across the continent reflected a uniformity of social and economic systems through time. In fact historical records of Aboriginal life in the eighteenth, nineteenth and early twentieth centuries provide abundant evidence for different beliefs, politics, customs, technologies and resource use across the continent.

Aboriginal people in the early historical period were often depicted as hunters and gatherers who collected plants and captured animals without a systematic process of domesticating those creatures. While women collected vegetables and fruits and caught small animals using digging sticks and bowls or bags, men typically concentrated on killing larger animals. However, these generalized descriptions do not reveal how procurement of foods, and associated processing of the plants and animals for cooking and consumption, involved many different types of activities. Hunters searched for game as individuals, in groups, and in cooperative communal events where animals were driven into nets. Individual and cooperative hunting occurred in many situations: on land, on beaches and in the open ocean, even with the help of other animals such as dolphins (Hall 1985). The image of a lone Aboriginal hunter stalking kangaroos in a barren landscape derived from life in the deserts; in the tropical north historical hunters harpooned large marine animals such as dugong and turtle from boats; in the south hunters clubbed seals and caught mutton birds; in the freshwater wetlands of Arnhem Land people wrestled snakes from lagoons; in the woodlands of the east men struck possums from tree branches; and in the southeastern highlands people feasted on moths during the summer. When Europeans entered the continent and made these observations in the nineteenth and twentieth centuries they were recording the Aboriginal exploitation of diverse resources in different environments.

The historical evidence also reveals the diversity and sophistication of recent Aboriginal hunting and collecting. Some hunting was 'passive', using artificial barriers in rivers or tidal traps on shorelines. Hunting and collecting were sometimes enhanced by artificially altering the landscape, setting fire to the vegetation, digging ditches to change drainage and regulate water animals, and so on. Careful management of resources to enhance future productivity, even tending of plants in ways that have similarities with agriculture, was common. Once plants and animals were caught they were sometimes eaten immediately, but in other situations they were prepared in complex ways, and in some instances stored for future consumption. The diversity of food procurement and processing observed historically in Australia is so large that anthropologists and archaeologists prefer the term *foraging* rather than hunting and gathering for the complex ways that Aboriginal foragers obtained a living. The plants and animals exploited in each region, the techniques foragers used to capture and process them, and the ways foragers organized themselves, are all components of the economy that varied across Australia during the historic period (Keen 2004).

Of course the economy of historic Aboriginal foragers involved not only their acquisition and consumption of food, but also procurement and use of other materials as tools. Tools varied regionally: spears, traps and grinding stones all differed in construction between environments (D. S. Davidson 1934; Anell 1960; Dickson 1981; Cundy 1989). Even tools that are seen to be emblematic of Aboriginal people were absent from or distinctly different between regions. For instance, boomerangs were not used in Tasmania, spear throwers were not used in the Lake Eyre region, while edge-ground stone axes were not used in southwestern Australia or Tasmania. Tools varied across the continent for many reasons; toolkits were matched to the resources that people were procuring and reflected the materials from which the tools were made. Toolkits were also articulated with the ways people organized the procurement and processing of resources and the size of territory over which they ranged.

In the historic period the number of people also varied regionally, reflecting the productivity of each group's territory as well as the strategies for extracting resources from the landscape. The geographic pattern of population density was complex; in historic times densities were generally higher near coasts and in major river corridors, and least in arid and semi-arid landscapes. Differences in the density of people were related to territory size, as showed by Joseph Birdsell (1953), who offered an iconic illustration of the connection of population density and environmental characteristics, comparing the recorded territory of 123 'tribes' living away from the coast or major rivers with the mean annual rainfall for each territory (Figure 1.2). Groups in higher rainfall environments had smaller territories; those living in drier environments had larger territories, partly because in less productive landscapes foragers required far greater areas in which to obtain resources. Despite uncertainties involved in Birdsell's calculations, the clear relationship between landscape productivity and number of people occupying the land during the historic period hints at fundamental connections between environments and the organization of human societies.

These relationships were linked to the diversity of social lives observed in nineteenth and twentieth century Aboriginal groups by Ian Keen (2004), who demonstrated that in a number of historical groups access to territory and resources was regulated through social convention. Rules differed across the continent in response to the abundance and predictability of resources: in rich environments social conventions often restricted who could access resources, while in uncertain environments, such as deserts, diversified social affiliations enhanced people's access to essential resources.

One of the ways that social practice provided or denied access to resources was through kinship. In every society kinship systems described socially acknowledged relationships and obligations, but the nature and complexity of kinship rules varied. Some groups simply distinguished generations, others emphasized the different lines of descent by distinguishing two or four categories of descent into which

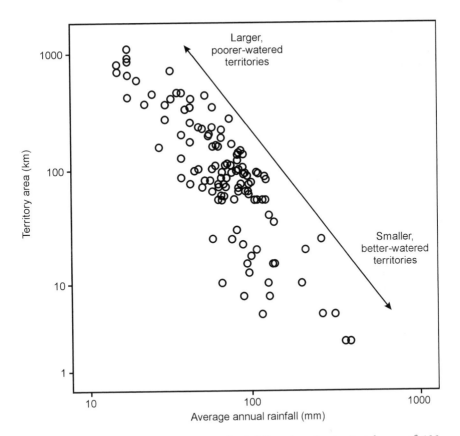

Figure 1.2 A graph plotting average annual rainfall against the territorial area of 123 historically recorded Aboriginal 'tribes' with relatively uniform environments. When rainfall was high, Aboriginal groups used smaller territories, but when rainfall was low, groups had larger territories. (Data in the graph comes from Birdsell (1953) with rainfall re-expressed in mm and territory in km, and both axes plotted using a logarithmic scale.)

individuals of any generation were classified. These different kinship classifications were related to differences in marriage patterns, often because socially acceptable partners were defined through the kinship position assigned to an individual. In some parts of Australia historical marriage systems involved fathers or brothers bestowing their daughters or sisters for political reasons or for compensation. In other regions more elaborate systems involved arranging marriage partners through 'asymmetrical' social rules, such as a long chain of matrilineal relationships leading to young women being married to men up to 50 or 60 years (three or four generations) older than them. Another dimension to marriage patterns was the level of polygyny (the marriage of a man to more than one woman concurrently). While in some regions it was uncommon for many men to have been married to more than two wives at one time, in other regions multiple wives were common, and among Yolŋu who lived on the northern coast some men married more than twenty women. Keen (2004) suggests that the level of polygyny displayed by different historical groups was related to whether or not they had particular social practices, such as asymmetrical marriage rules, but that it was also indirectly related to population density which in turn probably reflected environmental productivity.

It is no surprise that during historic times, Aboriginal people had many social and economic practices. They occupied many different environments, and only a limited range of foraging and social patterns would be suited to each environment. Across the continent each Aboriginal group's response to its environment was shaped by its social organization, which was conditioned by their past economic and social trajectories. The adjustment of each group to the natural and social environment in which it lived ensured that in a large, environmentally diverse continent difference in lifestyles and customs would have emerged. As significant environment changes occurred through time the economy and social life of Australian foragers would have been modified in response. Consequently the practices of historical Aboriginal groups were different from those of human groups occupying the same regions in pre-historic times. Historically documented differences between Aboriginal groups were the outcome of this long process of social and economic change; by acknowledging those differences archaeologists are forced to recognize that the historical cultural diversity of Aboriginal people cannot have existed throughout pre-history. Furthermore, accepting that there were dynamic, significant adaptations of economic, social and ideological systems to the changing physical environment makes it appropriate to situate archaeological interpretations of past human life in a framework of the ancient environments reconstructed for each time and place, rather than in a framework of much later cultural systems recorded in historical records. For this reason archaeological interpretations in this book are embedded in descriptions of the ever-changing environments of ancient Australia.

The recognition that historic records of Aboriginal life cannot simply be imposed on archaeological residues of earlier lives is amplified by the realization that many Aboriginal societies observed during the historic period were not 'pristine' examples of pre-historic life; they were actually highly modified by the process of contact with Europeans. One of the most dramatic examples of the rapid, complex and far-reaching nature of post-contact change is the response of Aboriginal people to the introduction of diseases such as smallpox.

Smallpox: a mark of contact

Shortly after British colonists arrived in Sydney in 1788 they witnessed the coming of smallpox to Aborigines of the east coast. Smallpox was then a feared and deadly disease, caused by the *variola* virus and spread directly from person-to-person or indirectly through contact with clothing contaminated by an infected person. Symptoms emerged between one and three weeks after the virus was contracted, and infected people travelled, meeting other humans, before anyone else realized they carried the illness. The disease began with a dangerous, extremely high fever followed immediately with headaches, muscle aches, convulsions, vomiting and delirium (Fenner et al. 1988). Most infected people survived for several days,

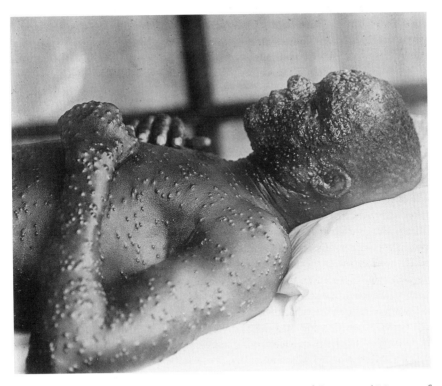

Figure 1.3 Smallpox pustules on the face and body. (Courtesy of the National Museum of Health and Medicine, Armed Forces Institute of Pathology, Washington, DC [Reeve 48135].) This man is not an Aborigine.

developing ugly and painful lesions all over the body, including the mouth and throat (Figure 1.3). These lesions erupted to form leaking pustules, releasing large amounts of virus-filled mucous. Body temperature then increased and the pustules grew. At this stage many people succumbed to these awful torments. Other people survived the fevers and gradually recovered, although they often suffered ongoing afflictions such as blindness and respiratory problems. In survivors the lesions formed scabs and healed, leaving depigmented and pitted scars on the face or limbs which marked them for life. These 'pock marks' visibly altered survivors, revealing to all who saw them that they had once been infected with smallpox. Pock marks were often observed on Aboriginal people by European explorers and settlers, long after the active form of the disease had passed.

Although the origin of smallpox in Sydney in 1789 puzzled the British, we now know that it was contracted by Aborigines living on the coast of Arnhem Land after contact with fishermen from island southeast Asia (Butlin 1985; Macknight 1986; Campbell 2002). The disease spread across Australia, unobserved by any Europeans, but the face of smallpox, those pock marks on survivors, was a record of the epidemic seen by explorers and settlers who traversed inland southeastern

Australia in the early 1800s. Except around Sydney, this was a hidden epidemic, concealed from historic records by its transmission across the vast inland areas, beyond the gaze of the coastal hugging European settlers. Nevertheless, we know it was widespread and devastating in its effects on Aboriginal people.

Smallpox caused a shocking number of Aboriginal people to die. Medical knowledge of smallpox epidemics in other parts of the world, in populations without a long history of previous exposure to smallpox, demonstrates that mortality rates were catastrophically high (Butlin 1983; Hopkins 1983; Campbell 2002). The death toll in isolated parts of Africa during the eighteenth and nineteenth centuries was more than 70 per cent, sometimes as high as 90 per cent. Similarly, in North American Indian peoples, mortality greater than 60 per cent was common, and in some cases 98 per cent of people died. Noel Butlin (1983) argued that prior to the 1780s Aboriginal people had been previously unexposed; he estimated that in 1789 more than 80 per cent of them died. Of course we shall never know the actual number of Aboriginal people who died from smallpox, and some groups may have had lower death rates, but the magnitude of Butlin's estimate is plausible.

The consequences of this smallpox epidemic are difficult to envision, but imagine, if you can, four out of every five people you have ever known dying within a few weeks. The social and psychological toll on Aboriginal people cannot be underestimated, and historic documents from the early Sydney settlement demonstrate this. Governor Arthur Phillip (1789) described finding elderly people and young children dead around Sydney harbour. He estimated that half of the local Aboriginal people had died, and noted that many others walked inland away from the settlement in the hope of escaping the disease. We might speculate that this retreat from the smallpox onslaught was a common response across the continent, and that it often did little except spread the disease to neighbours.

A similarly sombre image of the impact of smallpox was presented by Lieutenant-Governor David Collins (1798) in his memoirs. Collins recalled finding a lone Aboriginal man, unable to find another living member of his group, despairing on a beach, and another 'tribe', being reduced to three survivors, negotiated a merger with a different Aboriginal group for their mutual survival. It is clear that the consequence of the 1789 smallpox epidemic on Aboriginal people near Sydney was disastrous.

Shortly after the arrival of English observers on the east coast of Australia in 1789, smallpox altered the operation of Aboriginal life. Near Sydney the massive death toll radically changed the functioning of Aboriginal society. The immediate alteration to social life was obvious: people mourning the dead, caring for the ill, fleeing to distant places to avoid disease, depopulation of areas, mergers between groups, invasion of abandoned lands, and so on. In the years that followed, after the smallpox epidemic had run its course and vanished from the territory of a forager group, the consequences continued. Aboriginal societies needed to respond to the political and knowledge vacuums created by the deaths of many high status elders. Survivors were obliged to consider the meaning of the apocalypse within the framework of existing cosmologies, a process that might have been associated with the emergence and spread of new ideologies. Conventions of obtaining marriage partners might have changed following demographic shifts. Land use patterns probably altered as survivors remembered the places where people died or were buried. Foraging strategies may also have been modified in light of lost knowledge or reduced pools of labour. In the Sydney region, where we have historical observations of some of these processes, the effects of smallpox were combined with the direct impacts of contact with European settlers themselves, such as the disruption of hunting, dispossession of land, and the economic and social effects of new foods, technologies and ideologies.

Because smallpox spread rapidly, changes in Aboriginal society caused by the epidemic preceded the arrival of European observers in areas beyond Sydney, and for most parts of Australia we have no historic records of the process of change. Across the continent most historic records describe Aboriginal societies that had already been transformed, not only by the 1789 smallpox outbreak but also by the effects of subsequent smallpox epidemics and a spate of many other diseases. A further three smallpox outbreaks occurred during the nineteenth century, in 1829–30, 1858 and 1869, and the first of these was probably as widespread and devastating as the 1789 epidemic. Other diseases also spread ahead of European observation. Deadly and infectious tuberculosis was probably introduced by the English. Nowadays it continues to be one of the world's greatest killers and the effects of tuberculosis on Aboriginal people might have rivalled those of smallpox. Influenza also spread rapidly across the land, probably severely affecting Aboriginal health. Venereal infections, such as syphilis and gonorrhoea, were very common among English settlers and spread to the Aboriginal population, not only causing ill-health but also reducing fertility (Littleton 2005). These, and other ripples of change, spread out to many parts of the continent, altering Aboriginal life before Europeans recorded it.

The consequences of smallpox were magnified by its uneven impact on members of a society. We know from records of the disease in many parts of the world that there was an age- and sex-related pattern to the frequency of deaths from smallpox (Butlin 1983; Campbell 2002). Older people, over 45 or 50 years, had very high rates of death. Children less than about 4 years old and adults older than 20–25 years also had high mortality rates. Even among young adults mortality rates were not the same: women were more likely to die than men, pregnant women more likely to die than non-pregnant women, and so on. Differing patterns of death within a community added to the disruption of disease by creating power, status and knowledge imbalances.

One estimate of disease-induced changes in Aboriginal society comes from central Australia, where European accounts of Aboriginal life date only from 1860 onwards, decades after the two major smallpox epidemics. Dick Kimber (1988, 1990, 1996) speculated that in this region smallpox started a cascade of social changes. The deaths of more women than men would have created a sex imbalance, leaving many men without marriage partners. Increased fighting between men within the group, perhaps raids on other groups, resulted. Laws resolving conflicts between men over women were developed, resulting in the rules requiring lending of wives observed by Europeans at the end of the nineteenth century. The shortage of women also led to the adoption of new, more complex kinship systems from people to the north as a way of restructuring the rules of relationships and marriage. Reciprocal exchange systems also expanded and intensified during the eighteenth and nineteenth centuries, not only facilitating negotiations that brought wives, ceremonies and goods into any community but also providing ways for new magic to spread to central Australia, as people sought magic to combat the disease and its aftermath. For example, distinctive incised pearl shells were brought to central Australia from the northwest coast for use in men's love magic, only after the middle of the nineteenth century (Akerman and Stanton 1993), and the popularity of such magic was only one of many responses to men's increased difficulty of obtaining wives after smallpox.

The deaths of so many women had ramifications beyond the search for wives. With fewer mouths to feed people probably targeted their preferred foods (Kimber 1996), and perhaps with fewer women to gather reliable plant foods, men's success in hunting became more valued. With greater reliance on hunting, people altered their use of the central Australian landscape, focusing on areas with higher densities of game and other preferred foods. Land management practices, such as where and when fires were started, may also have altered. Since an emphasis on hunting facilitated movement into unfamiliar localities, the territorial boundaries of groups may have shifted. Kimber pointed out that altered foraging patterns might have been accompanied by a changed emphasis on toolkits.

Smallpox even triggered changes in politics and ritual. The deaths of many elderly people probably meant a reduction in conservative tendencies within many central Australian groups. Kimber (1996) suggested that in the new situation some men acquired status and power by persuading others that their sorcery had the capacity to evoke or ward off disease. There may even have been changes in the ideologies of male and female powers, as men were increasingly seen to possess greater metaphysical power than women, a mystical explanation for the imbalance in male and female deaths. Combined with the drastic reduction in senior women, those altered social conceptions of women's powers led to a reduction in women's ritual roles and the ownership of sacred objects, resulting in the male domination of those spheres noted by historical observers. Because women were more severely affected by smallpox there was an increase in the political and religious power of males, reflected in their dominant roles in intensified magical, ritual and cere-monial activities. Kimber (1996) argued that transformations of social practice could explain many aspects of the historical use of the sacred objects called *tjurunga*: the relatively young age of many objects, the association of women in the mythology of these objects even though women were not allowed to see them, and the role of *tjurunga* exchange in developing and maintaining gift-giving relationships with others.

Kimber's (1996) interpretations of the social transformations in central Australia suggest that while the spread of disease hastened the deaths of many people, and reduced the birthrates with which another generation could be created, these were merely the start of a prolonged period of social and political change. Land use and foraging territory changed; political and kinship systems were substantially altered;

trade networks intensified and new trade goods were sought; all of which initiated changes in myth, ritual and ideology. The outcome was a reshaping of Aboriginal culture before European observers reached the area.

Social and economic changes caused by highly infectious diseases in the eighteenth and nineteenth centuries do not represent the 'destruction' of traditional Aboriginal societies. On the contrary, as the example of central Australia illustrates, many changes in Aboriginal society were ways of dealing with, even limiting, the enormity of social damage wrought by disease. The magnitude of social and economic change during this period is an indication of the capacity of Aboriginal societies to adjust to new circumstances; transformation rather than stability was the means by which these societies continued. Concepts of traditional society being destroyed merely give credibility to the notion that before these diseases, and European contact in general, Aboriginal society had changed little for vast stretches of time. In reality, as this book demonstrates, ancient societies of Australia were repeatedly transformed in response to altered cultural and environmental circumstances. Consequently the nature of Aboriginal economies, social organizations and beliefs immediately before smallpox hit is no more a record of the earliest human life in the continent than the historic records of post-smallpox societies are a record of the functioning of societies in the centuries before the disease. The dynamic, changing past of humans in Australia leaves no value in the proposition that there was ever a single, permanent, unchanging Aboriginal way of life. This fundamental revelation of archaeological research in Australia is revisited in Chapter 14. What matters here, at the start of the book, is the implication of this conclusion for the archaeological investigation of ancient Australia.

How the present helps us understand the past

It is a chilling coincidence that at almost the same time British colonists in Sydney observed the devastating spread of smallpox among Aboriginal people on the east coast, the foundations of historical sciences were being created by a British thinker, James Hutton (1788: 66), who wrote that 'In examining things present we have data from which to reason with regard to what has been'. Present-day scientists still accept his notion that we can reconstruct the past only because of our knowledge of how the world operates at the moment. It is inevitable that we will use knowledge of the present in our archaeological interpretations. What we must decide is *how* we should use our understanding of the present. As described above, some ways of using historic records will be misleading, including the use of post-smallpox observations of Aboriginal society to reconstruct details of Aboriginal life during pre-history.

Evidence that Aboriginal lifestyles and social systems have changed in even recent times makes it obvious that archaeologists should avoid building stories about pre-historic Australian society through simple analogies that suggest ancient societies were almost identical with societies observed historically. Instead, this book seeks to use evidence from archaeological research and investigations in related disciplines to describe the timing and nature of social change in the past, without inserting details of ethnographic events which would imply that people in Australia were changeless. Reconstructions of the human past that are focused on archaeological evidence operate through a number of rules, one of which involves 'uniformitarianism'.

Scientists have long differentiated between two ways of using information about the present. Both are 'uniformitarian' arguments, in which a researcher acts as though the past is in some way like the present in order to make the past more comprehensible. One form of argument, called 'substantive uniformitarianism', is based on the idea that the nature of our world, including the past operation of human societies was little different from that which can be observed in historical times. This argument usually leads to stories in which pre-historic people and their societies are described as either being the same as historic people and societies, or else changing at the same speed and in the same ways as in history (Bailey 1983). This was the basis for the interpretations of ancient Lake Mungo discussed above, in which details of nineteenth and twentieth century Aboriginal life were used to reconstruct the lives of people tens of thousands of years earlier. This kind of argument, drawing on historic patterns of Aboriginal society and then proceeding to use the reconstructions obtained to study the emergence of those historical societies, is circular in structure and unsatisfactory because it often hides differences in pre-historic life.

The alternative kind of argument, called 'methodological uniformitarianism', is based on the idea that we should make only one assumption about the past: that during pre-historic times the 'laws' established for physics, chemistry, geology, biology and other sciences were the same as they are now (Bailey 1983). Regularity in the operation of the world structures the processes of human behaviour and provides a basis for identifying the ancient physical environments in which humans operated. The advantage of this approach is that archaeologists can reconstruct a story about humans in ancient times without making assumptions about whether people and societies in the pre-historic past were the same as those recorded historically. As a result archaeologists are able to develop conclusions about the extent and nature of economic, technological and social change over time, without creating the problematic circular arguments that result from telling stories of the ancient past using details simply borrowed from ethnographic records. For example, medical knowledge of modern diseases can be used to estimate their spread and impact in past societies, as illustrated by the discussion of smallpox provided above. In the following chapters there are descriptions of how archaeologists study the antiquity of objects, the manufacture and use of ancient artefacts, the sex of human skeletons and the environmental contexts of past economic systems through the application of this form of methodological uniformitarianism. Reconstructions of environments in which ancient foragers lived and constructed their social and economic activities form the foundation of statements about past human activities throughout the book.

This and other principles are regularly employed by many archaeologists to reduce the degree to which their methods obscure the pre-historic past, to avoid imposing familiar images from the historical period on the debris that survives from ancient times. These approaches are used in this book to peer through the veil of obscurity that Victorian archaeologists felt separated them from the ancient lives that created archaeological debris, with the goal of summarizing what archaeological investigations have now revealed about human life in ancient Australia.

2   The colonization of Australia

When Europeans first visited the shores of Australia, they pondered the origin of Aborigines already in that land. Archaeologists have searched for evidence of how and when humans reached the continent, and their conclusions are a very different understanding of origins to the mythology and stories held by Aboriginal people. Lack of correspondence between indigenous oral traditions about the origins of humans and scientific investigations of human colonization is hardly surprising. Questions of ethnographic continuity and myth construction are revisited in Chapter 14; this chapter explores the colonization of Australia from a scientific perspective.

Environmental context of human colonization

At the time humans entered Australia the world was a place of rapid environmental changes; it was a period of global cooling characterized by marked environmental instability. Humans sometimes endured declining resources, perhaps struggled to survive unpredictable environments with which they were confronted; while in other places and times abundant resources and good conditions facilitated the movement of forager groups into new lands, providing them with novel opportunities. Oscillations in the fortunes of ancestral foragers mirrored oscillations in the climates in which they lived.

Climate change can be measured in many ways. One of the most powerful involves studying shifts in the composition of the world's ocean. Marine sediments formed from the skeletons of small animals called foraminifera preserve the chemistry of the skeletons, which in turn reflect the condition of oceans in which they lived. Foraminifera absorb two kinds of oxygen isotopes from the marine environment: ^{16}O and ^{18}O. During cold periods lighter ^{16}O was more readily removed from the oceans and stored in ice sheets, leaving marine environments relatively enriched in ^{18}O. When ice sheets melted during warmer phases the oceans were replenished with ^{16}O. In this way a measurement of the $^{16}O:^{18}O$ ratio in foraminifera-rich sediment indicates the temperature at one point in time. A low concentration of ^{18}O reflects warm, interglacial conditions; high concentrations of ^{18}O reflect cold, glacial periods. Deep cores in ocean sediments yield a continuous sequence of ratios which reveal chronological changes in climate and ice cap size.

Fluctuations in the ^{16}O:^{18}O ratio display alternating phases with high or low values, indicating changes in temperature (Figure 2.1). The last glacial cycle covered 120,000 years, stretching from the last interglacial when climate was similar to the present day, through the last ice-age, to the warmer conditions of recent millennia. Scientists divide this cycle into five Oxygen Isotope Stages (labelled OIS5 to OIS1). The earliest is OIS5, a warm period rather like the present day. OIS4 was a short, cold period marking the initiation of more severe ice-age conditions. OIS3 was a period beginning with slightly less cold temperatures but deteriorating to more cold conditions. The harshest, coldest period of the last ice-age is OIS2. Finally, the much warmer climatic conditions of our times, beginning between 10,000 and 12,000 years ago, is called OIS1 or the 'Holocene'.

Oscillations in the global sea-level curve match trends displayed in the oxygen isotope curve because both curves track alterations in global temperatures. During colder phases greater amounts of water became trapped in polar ice caps or large glaciers in the northern hemisphere and so the level of oceans around the world dropped. For much of the past 100,000 years, reduced sea exposed land which is now hidden under oceans.

Colonists arriving during times of lower sea level landed on the now submerged continental shelf of an enlarged landmass called 'Sahul' or 'Greater Australia' which incorporated mainland Australia, Tasmania and New Guinea (Figure 2.2). About 70,000 years ago oceans dropped to more than 60 metres below their current level, exposing land in the Arafura Sea and joining northern Australia with New Guinea. Greater Australia then stretched hundreds of kilometres to the north. Large tracts of land in what is now the Gulf of Carpentaria, Arafura Sea and Joseph Bonaparte Gulf were then tropical lands containing savannas and woodlands. Lower sea levels reduced the ocean distance required to reach Australia, making it a larger, closer target.

Pathways that people may have travelled from Asia to Australia were identified by Joseph Birdsell (1977), who suggested that colonists arrived by island hopping either along a southern route through the islands of Flores and Timor or a northern one via Sulawesi (Figure 2.3). These hypothetical paths trace the shortest water crossings possible, but we lack knowledge of the maritime abilities of colonizing humans, who perhaps did not need to take the easiest route. Nor do Birdsell's pathways reflect the distribution of resources that may have attracted moving foragers away from the shortest route. Furthermore, suggestions that colonizers took the shortest routes do not consider the possible complications caused by the presence of other hominid species who lived on islands to Australia's northwest and who may have represented competition for resources in those areas (Brown et al. 2004; Morwood et al. 2004). Although foragers colonizing Australia came from lands to the northwest we may never know how they came.

The demographic context of human colonization

Genetic and archaeological evidence demonstrates that modern humans descended from anatomically modern *Homo sapiens* who evolved in Africa and spread across the

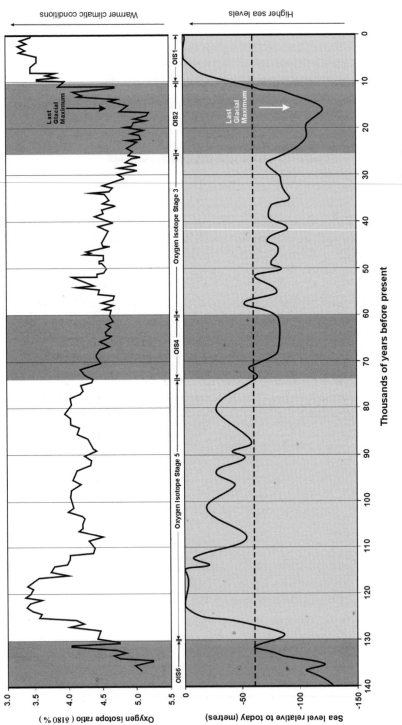

Figure 2.1 Indications of climatic change over the past 140,000 years, showing the Oxygen Isotope Stages discussed in the text. Top = oxygen isotope curve (data from Shackleton and Pisias 1985; see also Shackleton 1987; Grootes et al. 1993). Bottom = global sea-level curve for the past 140,000 years (data from Chivas et al. 2001): the dashed line represents 60–65 metres below modern sea level.

Figure 2.2 Greater Australia (at sea level of −130 metres) shown in grey, and its relationship to modern Australia, New Guinea and parts of Melanesia and southeast Asia. Locations are places mentioned in Chapter 2.

world, replacing other kinds of hominids where they existed and colonizing vacant lands where they did not (Lahr and Foley 1994, 1998; Chen et al. 1995; Watson et al. 1997; Relethford 1998, 2001; Quintana-Murci 1999; Ingman et al. 2000; Cooper et al. 2001; Forster et al. 2001; Henshilwood et al. 2002; Macauley et al. 2005; Rose 2006). This spread of Homo sapiens probably occurred between 50,000 and 100,000 years ago (Watson et al. 1997; Forster 2004; Palanichamy et al. 2004; Forster and Matsumura 2005; Merriwether et al. 2005), when modern humans occupied India and Asia, bringing them into regions adjacent to Australia.

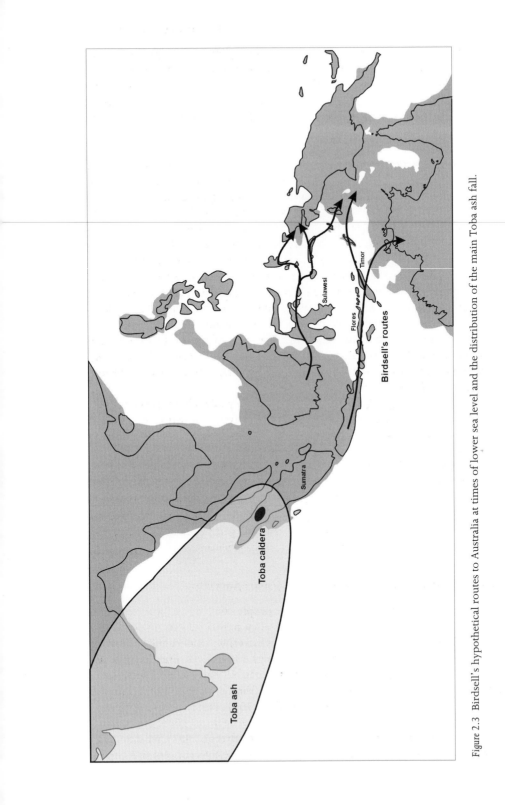

Figure 2.3 Birdsell's hypothetical routes to Australia at times of lower sea level and the distribution of the main Toba ash fall.

Colonization of Australia may have occurred shortly after Homo sapiens arrived in southeast Asia, perhaps an extension of the global dispersion of a language-using species who could solve many problems, including technical difficulties of large water crossings (Davidson and Noble 1992). However, arrival of Homo sapiens in southeast Asia has not been accurately dated (Barker et al. 2007); their movement to Australia was perhaps delayed, by the difficulty of the maritime voyage or by regional environmental events.

One event that may have interfered with the movement of humans was the catastrophic eruption of Mt Toba in Sumatra between 75,000 and 71,000 years ago (Chesner et al. 1991; Zielinski et al. 1996; see also Figure 2.3). Large areas of southeast Asia were partially or completely deforested by lava flows, dust and tephra ejected from the volcano (Rampino et al. 1988; Rose and Chesner 1990; Rampino and Self 1992, 1993; Flenley 1996). Foragers migrating eastward may have found regions devoid of food and tool resources they needed. Some researchers suggested that populations around the earth were killed, allowing the colonization of a mostly empty Asia by modern humans moving out refuge areas such as Africa (Rampino and Self 1992; Ambrose 1998, 2003; Rampino and Ambrose 2000; Rampino 2002). However, a world-wide near-extinction of humans is not supported evidence: no mass extinctions in other parts of the world are recorded (Oppenheimer 2002; Gathorne-Hardy and Harcourt-Smith 2003). Consequently the effects of the Toba eruption were regional, but they may still have influenced the migration of humans to Australia.

If humans were east of Toba when it exploded, they might have moved towards Australia in search of less affected landscapes. Alternatively if dispersing humans had not yet reached peninsula southeast Asia, Toba's destruction of resources may have presented them with a barrier of ecosystem destruction. One suggestion is that population growth following the explosion caused groups to migrate away from the recovering region, towards Australia, in the period between 65,000 and 45,000 years ago (Lahr and Foley 1994; Lahr 1996). By linking environmental change in southeast Asia with the spread of foragers to Australia, this idea perhaps explains why the estimated antiquity of common (maternal) genetic ancestors of all living Aboriginal people is similar to the date of the Toba explosion.

Genetic evidence for human colonization of Australia

Biological samples from modern Aboriginal people contain genetic information about historical distance between individuals. Each person inherits mitochondrial DNA (mtDNA) from their mother but not their father; it is abundant in many cells and has a high mutation rate, offering researchers a relatively simple way to study the recent evolutionary history of human lineages. All humans share a common mtDNA ancestor; within any population, such as Aborigines, the distance from the common ancestor can be calculated (Relethford 2001; Forster 2004). Assuming a constant rate of mutation it is also possible to estimate the length of time that has passed since that ancestor (Ingman et al. 2000). Analyses of this kind sometimes suggested that 74,000 years have passed since the most recent common female ancestor of Aboriginal people (Ingman and Gyllensten 2003; Merriwether et al. 2005; van Holst Pellekaan and Harding 2006). Other studies indicate more recent, rapid dispersals of people through South Asia towards Australia approximately 60,000–65,000 years ago (Macaulay et al. 2005; van Holst Pellekaan et al. 2006), and a dispersal towards New Guinea 42,000–66,000 years ago (Forster et al. 2001). These time estimates are not precise, they often have an uncertainty of 20 per cent or more, and they all point towards the common ancestor living sometime between 50,000 and 90,000 years ago. Furthermore, we do not know where this woman lived: it may have been outside Australia, hence mtDNA estimates do not date the colonization of Australia. Consequently any association of the Toba eruption and human migration towards Australia is ill defined.

The cultural context of human colonization

Modern humans who colonized the globe in the past 100,000 years had abilities similar to modern people. Archaeological discoveries in Africa show ancestral humans had elaborate toolkits that included spears and spear throwers, composite tools with stone artefacts hafted on handles, bone and ivory tools such as harpoons and needles, as well as clothing, basketry and ropes (Ambrose 2001). More importantly, these foragers also had diverse cultural practices still found in all human societies, such as the use of art ornamentation, and symbolism, burial of the dead, and the formulation of long-distance social networks (McBrearty and Brooks 2000; Henshilwood et al. 2002). Human groups entering Australia also possessed these cultural practices (Chapter 6).

Technological and social capacities of migrating groups probably assisted their movement into Australia. While some archaeologists employed the simple water-craft technology of historic Aborigines as an analogy for the craft of initial colonists (Jones 1979), it is likely that Pleistocene ocean voyages to Australia and Melanesia may have involved more sophisticated sea-craft (Birdsell 1977; White and O'Connell 1979). There is little archaeological evidence of the nature of early craft, although the expansion of people into Australia and Melanesia shows that images of colonists as small groups of technologically and culturally unsophisticated foragers is probably incorrect (Chapters 3 and 6). In considering the capacities of humans colonizing Australia, it is valuable to remember that they were descendants of adaptable foragers who had successfully and rapidly migrated from Africa through many environments to reach this distant region.

However, while speculation about the context and nature of human dispersals towards Australia is intriguing, it cannot be used to predict when the first humans arrived. To answer the question of when Australia was colonized we must rely on archaeological evidence from Australia itself.

The archaeology of Australian colonization

Dating human migrations has been the primary pursuit of investigations into the colonization of Australia. This involved archaeologists excavating caves, rock shelters, or occasionally lakeshore sediments, and estimating the age of the lowest levels containing what are termed 'cultural objects': skeletons, artefacts, fires and food debris; things made or used by humans. The oldest sites identified have been used as indicators of when people entered the continent or any region within it. This search for the antiquity of colonization sounds straightforward, but investigations of very ancient events have proved to be troublesome.

False leads: claims for very early occupation of Australia

Claims have been made for very early occupation of Australia, in excess of 80,000–100,000 years ago. In view of theories that modern humans spread from Africa at later times, these claims raise questions about the connection of colonizers and modern humans elsewhere in the world (Foley and Lahr 1997, 2003; Forster et al. 2001; Forster 2004; O'Connell and Allen 2004). Consequently, claims for early occupation were carefully and critically evaluated by scientists, and each appears unfounded. These mistaken interpretations taught archaeologists valuable lessons about the complexities and dangers of interpreting the ancient archaeological record. Two examples illustrate problems confronting archaeologists searching for the oldest signs of human occupation in Australia.

Lake George is a basin in southeastern Australia where more than 8 metres of sediment had accumulated. Pollen preserved in the sediments records vegetation change over hundreds of thousands of years. During cold periods the landscape was dominated by herbaceous plants; in warmer periods woodland and forest was present. Unexpectedly, in one level, called zone F, there was a dramatic change in vegetation: *Eucalyptus* woodland replaced *Casuarina* woodland, while fragments of charcoal increased, indicating that fires were more common. Singh and Geissler (1985) proposed that humans had been present, lighting fires, and this caused the vegetation to change. Since they thought zone F was about 130,000 years old their claim implied an extraordinary age for humans in Australia. Other scientists questioned the actual age of zone F, suggesting it was only 60,000 years old (Wright 1986), but the real difficulty was the interpretation of charcoal as having been produced by humans.

The idea that charcoal came from fires started by people emerged from observations of systematic Aboriginal fire-lighting in the twentieth century, a use of flames Rhys Jones (1969) poetically named 'fire stick farming'. However, while Jones assumed that Aboriginal people had always intensively and systematically burned vegetation, this may not be true; perhaps foragers began to employ fire well after they entered Australia (Chapter 4). Fire always occurred naturally in the Australian landscape and the presence of charcoal does not necessarily mean humans were present or responsible. Charcoal concentrations in pollen cores hundreds of thousands of years old are evidence of naturally intensified burning regimes (White 1994; Kershaw et al. 2006). Many factors can affect charcoal deposition: the nature of vegetation, amount of fuel, extent and intensity of fires, and amount and timing of erosion that washed charcoal into lakes (Head 1994a). At the time of zone F at Lake George there were larger fuel loads and warmer conditions; perhaps this increased the frequencies of natural fires. By themselves charcoal concentrations are not compelling indications of a human presence; scientists therefore seek archaeological sites with indisputable signs of human occupation in the form of cultural material: artefacts, hearths or even human remains.

However, even in sites rich with cultural objects archaeologists sometimes fail to understand what they excavate and incorrectly assert that humans colonized Australia at very early times. For example, in the mid-1990s Richard Fullagar, David Price and Leslie Head claimed that humans had occupied the tiny shelter of Jinmium for more than 100,000 years. Excavating at this overhang beneath a sandstone boulder protruding from a sand sheet they recovered stone artefacts more than a metre below the present ground surface. The age of artefacts was estimated with two techniques discussed later in the chapter. Radiocarbon analysis indicated that the artefacts were only 5,000–10,000 years old. Thermoluminescence (TL) analysis, which measures the length of time since sand grains had been exposed to sunlight, gave surprisingly different estimates, leading Fullagar et al. (1996) to conclude that the artefacts were between 115,000 and 175,000 years old.

This extraordinary claim was re-examined by dating experts. A fundamental flaw was revealed almost immediately. Thermoluminescence was a crude method; it used nearly 3,000 sand grains to measure the time since last exposure to sunlight. Physicist Nigel Spooner concluded that at Jinmium some quartz grains had not received sufficient exposure to sunlight and so retained an old signal which did not indicate when they were deposited (Spooner 1998). Geologically ancient sand grains falling from the boulder into the shaded deposit of the shelter kept their ancient luminescence signal, giving readings that overestimated the sample age. Only more sophisticated methods yielded an accurate indication of the age of artefacts at Jinmium.

A team led by Bert Roberts re-examined sands at Jinmium using optically stimulated luminescence (OSL), a technique that allowed problematic 'old-signal' grains to be identified (Roberts et al. 1998). When old-signal grains were excluded, the site turned out to be less than 20,000 years old, perhaps much less! Furthermore, young grains were found in older layers, suggesting the deposit was disturbed. In disturbed archaeological deposits excavators cannot be certain that sediment samples are really associated with artefacts found at the same level. TL and OSL analyses merely reveal the age of quartz grains; they tell us nothing about the antiquity of humans if we are not confident of the association with cultural materials. At Jinmium neither the initial estimate of sediment age nor its association with cultural material was correct.

The original excavators of Jinmium proposed their claims in good faith, but the interpretations were based on superficial consideration of the evidence rather than on detailed research about how the site built up, what TL analyses meant, or how cultural material was associated with analysed samples. Concern for these issues underlies current knowledge and debates about the antiquity of colonization.

Complexities of estimating antiquity

Only in recent decades have archaeologists recognized the daunting nature of the quest for evidence of the first human colonists. In the large, little-explored Australian continent there is no reason to think archaeologists have found the footprints of colonization. There is a low probability that archaeologists will ever find the location where humans arrived. Relatively small colonizing populations would initially have inhabited only a small portion of the continent, near their landing place, and because sea levels were lower the first regions occupied were on the now submerged continental shelf. Evidence of the earliest humans in Australia is now hidden beneath the waves. What archaeologists discover therefore represents the expansion of colonists into higher areas away from the coast and still above sea level nowadays; these sites will establish a minimum age for human colonization.

Archaeologists may also encounter difficulties in identifying early human activities because they have repeatedly targeted specific kinds of site, such as large caves. The better preservation found in many caves makes them ideal for archaeological investigation, but they are only one kind of place that could have been used by ancient people. If ancient colonists made minimal use of caves the almost exclusive focus on them by archaeologists may create biases in our evidence.

One of the greatest complications in the search for the antiquity of colonization is the difficulty of precisely dating archaeological materials. This issue has two inseparable components: the complexity of age-estimation techniques and the difficulty of establishing cultural association.

Age-estimation techniques typically involve elaborate chemical or physical tests of the objects found in archaeological sites. Scientists who carry out these tests are in the habit of describing their results as 'dates', whereas the results are always only *estimates of antiquity* (Murray-Wallace 1996). Very often they are extremely sophisticated and reliable, but they are only estimates nonetheless. Their value depends on many factors including the techniques used to develop the age-estimate.

Age-estimates can be obtained from 'radiometric techniques', analyses that measure internal changes in an object which result from radioactive decay. Each age-estimate has a stated 'uncertainty' that expresses its imprecision. This uncertainty is not a reference to mistakes made in the calculation; it is a statistical expression of the precision of the estimate. Usually age-estimates are expressed as a combination of values, such as 40,000±6,000, where the first number (40,000) describes the average calculated age for a sample and the second number (6,000) describes the precision of the estimate. Uncertainty values should be used in thinking about the possible age of a sample. This can be done in a very simple way: by subtracting and adding the uncertainty value (or, for statistical reasons, double the uncertainty value) to the average age, to give a range for the possible antiquity of each sample. Hence it is best to stop thinking that an estimate of 40,000±6,000 tells us the sample is 40,000 years old; instead this estimate is a well-researched *suggestion* that the sample is between 34,000 and 46,000 years old. This is a more powerful understanding of the exactness of radiometric estimates. This kind of age-range format is employed throughout this book.

Statistical and theoretical manipulations of uncertainty values can be more sophisticated than this example conveys. The crucial point is that size of the uncertainty affects our estimate of the antiquity of analysed samples. The imprecision of age-estimation techniques is important in evaluating models of the antiquity of colonization.

Radiometric techniques express antiquity in 'years before present' (years bp), which actually means before 1950 AD, the date after which nuclear testing changed the composition of the earth's atmosphere. Age-estimates expressed as 'years before present' (bp) or 'years ago' represent the number of years before that date. This convention takes only a little practice before it can be used effortlessly, and employing it for historical events helps in this training: the British colony of Sydney was founded in 162 years bp, Columbus reached the Americas about 450 years bp, and Julius Caesar invaded Britain almost 2,000 years bp.

Age-estimates in this book often come from radiometric analyses; hence the 'years before present' convention is used extensively. Radiometric estimates are expressed as calendar (solar) years and rounded to the nearest 50, 100 or 500 years; the Appendix explains how this was calculated. Rounding highlights broad-scale trends and is commensurate with the low resolution available for radiometric estimates. When specific radiometric dates are mentioned, the age in calendar years is provided, followed in brackets by an age-range of the sample. More general ages established by multiple radiometric analyses, or inferred by researchers on some other basis, are usually presented with either a general age-estimate or the age-range, but not both.

A final feature of radiometric analyses is that ideal conditions, yielding reliable estimates, are different for each technique. Consequently, no technique is 'better' than another in all contexts. What matters is that conditions were suited to the technique used and the analysis was sophisticated. As Jinmium revealed, inappropriate techniques give poor results. Every age-estimate should be evaluated for appropriateness rather than uncritically accepted, a process that requires at least an introductory understanding of the techniques.

Almost all attempts to discover the age of a past event require archaeologists to understand the association between radiometric samples and the cultural materials of interest. Some cultural material can be 'directly dated' but this is rare; most samples are not indisputably a result of human activity. Samples are typically sand grains (in luminescence analyses), small fragments of charcoal (radiocarbon analyses) or pieces of bone (radiocarbon). Unless the bone is human none of these objects necessarily indicate the presence of humans. Sand grains accumulate naturally as they fall from rock walls, are washed into sites by streams or travel under gravity from surrounding slopes. Charcoal fragments can be created by human fires but they also wash or blow into site from bushfires. Bones can be the remains of human meals but they could also be the work of another carnivore or scavenger, have been washed into a deposit, or simply resulted from animals dying in the site. Analyses of these objects do not reveal humans were present, and archaeological interpretations rely on what is called the 'stratigraphic association' with a cultural object.

Establishing stratigraphic associations involves several steps. During excavations archaeologists distinguish sediments created in each depositional episode, called a stratum (strata for plural) or layer. Strata are identified by differences in the colour, texture and chemistry of sediments. The age of cultural objects deposited as sediments accumulated around them can be estimated by analyses of the sediments or fragments of charcoal or bones within them. Strata are not arranged horizontally, they sometimes slope, hence the angle and thickness of each stratum must be identified if the association of radiometric samples with cultural objects is to be correctly established. The accuracy of this stratigraphic association usually determines whether archaeologists can accurately infer the age of human occupation at any archaeological site (Harris 1989).

Careful excavation alone does not ensure that archaeologists can establish the antiquity of human activities; correct identification of objects as cultural material is also required. Some cultural objects, such as human remains or elaborate art works, are unambiguous. However, in the oldest Australian sites the objects most commonly preserved are stone artefacts. Rocks can be shaped by humans or splintered naturally, through heat or pressure, and it takes a trained eye to know whether a specimen is natural or an artefact. Archaeologists assess each piece of stone using characteristics such as the existence of features that reveal it was manufactured by humans (Figure 2.4). These features are patterns of conchoidal fracture caused by a blow to the outside of the rock, and/or striations caused by repeated and systematic abrasion of the rock (see Odell 2003; Andrefsky 2005). When these marks are found on pieces of rock, and cannot have been caused by natural processes, the specimens indicate that humans were present; the antiquity of human occupation can then be inferred through stratigraphic association with samples that have undergone radiometric analysis.

A final, critical step in defining a stratigraphic association is to reconstruct the formation of the archaeological deposit. Almost every archaeological site is 'disturbed' in some way, by cycles of erosion and deposition, human feet scuffing the earth, humans digging, animals burrowing, insects building nests, water percolating through the sediment, waves washing over the deposit, or sediments shrinking or expanding as they are dried and saturated (E. D. Stockton 1973; Cahen and Moeyersons 1977; Siirainen 1977; Wood and Johnson 1978; Villa 1982; Bocek 1986; Hofman 1986; Schiffer 1987; McBrearty 1990). These formation processes create interpretative difficulties because strata are not sealed and are modified by later events. Artefacts, bones, pieces of plant, charcoal fragments and sand grains can move upwards or downwards in an archaeological deposit, infiltrating strata and coming to rest in sediments older or younger than those into which they had been deposited. Apparent associations of cultural material would then be false and age-estimates in error.

Studies of archaeological deposits can determine if objects have been disturbed upwards or downwards. One way to do this is by piecing together fragments of a single bone or artefact, a method called 'conjoining', to determine if they have been vertically separated. Because they would usually have been deposited at a single time the separation between fragments reveals the amount of movement. Vertical

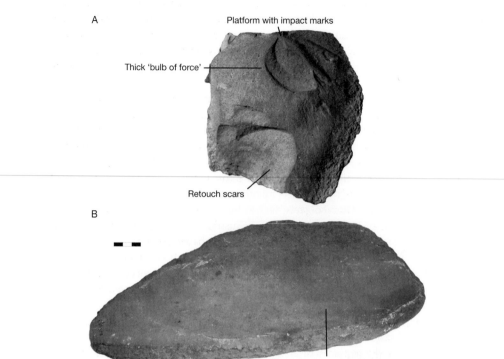

Figure 2.4 Photographs showing some of the distinctive features found on stone artefacts. A = a flake, with the conchoidal fracture, displaying marks such as the 'bulb of force' created by an external blow. The flake has been flaked again, or retouched, leaving additional flake scars. B = a grinding stone with a large shallow groove created by abrasion with another rock. Black bar is 1 cm long.

movement can be great in one site, minimal in the next, and this needs to be assessed for every site. Without studies of this kind the validity of age-estimates obtained through stratigraphic association is ambiguous.

Archaeological traces of colonization are faint, veiled after long periods of time, and these considerations make evidence for ancient human occupation hard to find and difficult to understand.

Radiocarbon and luminescence techniques

Two different radiometric methods have formed the basis for statements of human antiquity in Australia. The most widely used technique is radiocarbon analysis, which measures naturally occurring isotopes of carbon, Carbon-12 and Carbon-14 (written ^{12}C and ^{14}C). The first, ^{12}C, is 'stable' in the sense that it does not change of its own accord. But ^{14}C is 'unstable', or radioactive, because it naturally disintegrates to form nitrogen by emitting an electron; it is therefore called *radiocarbon*.

Radiocarbon is created in the upper atmosphere by the action of cosmic radiation on Nitrogen-14; it then combines with oxygen to form carbon dioxide, which is taken up by plants through photosynthesis, and by animals when they feed on plants. Although ^{14}C is constantly created, it also constantly disintegrates. Consequently the ratio between ^{14}C and ^{12}C remains nearly steady in the atmosphere and in living organisms taking new ^{14}C from the atmosphere. At death this balance is broken, because organisms no longer take up fresh carbon dioxide. The amount of ^{12}C in dead material remains unaltered, yet radiocarbon disintegrates, gradually changing the ratio of ^{14}C to ^{12}C. This ratio is measured in archaeological remains, such as charcoal from burned trees or bones. Because radiocarbon decays at a constant rate, the number of atoms is reduced by half every 5,730 years, the abundance of ^{14}C in these samples can be used to estimate time since the organism died (Libby 1952; Aitken 1990).

Radiocarbon analysis seems straightforward, but in practice it has many complications. One is that atmospheric ratios of ^{14}C to ^{12}C were not always the same, and organisms living in the past had higher or lower ratios than present-day organisms. In recognition of atmospheric fluctuations in radiocarbon scientists systematically alter age-estimates. This procedure is called 'calibration' because radiocarbon estimates are calibrated against an independent measure of time, such as a tree-ring record. By counting yearly growth rings on living and preserved trees, the exact age of each ring is established; its ^{14}C content is then measured to reveal the relationship between radiocarbon estimates and time.

Radiocarbon age-estimates can be greatly affected by sample contamination: when there is plant or bacterial activity within samples, when radiocarbon-enriched or -depleted water alters samples, or in a number of other ways. Addition of older carbon, with less ^{14}C, makes samples appear older than they actually are; addition of younger carbon, with more ^{14}C, raises radiocarbon concentrations samples, making them appear younger. The impact of contamination depends on the amount of contaminant and its age, but the consequence of contamination is far greater for older samples. Old samples retain little ^{14}C and small amounts of contaminant drastically change the estimated age. For example, a sample 60,000 years old requires the addition of only 1 per cent modern carbon to give a false age-estimate of 40,000 years bp. This sensitivity to contaminants makes it difficult to be confident of radiocarbon age-estimates in excess of about 40,000 years, because much older, contaminated samples cannot be recognized. Some researchers call 40,000 years bp a 'radiocarbon barrier', meaning that although it is possible to get older radiocarbon age-estimates, it is not possible to be convinced of their accuracy (Jones 1993; Roberts et al. 1994a; Chappell et al. 1996).

A different radiometric method, luminescence analysis, measures the abundance of electrons trapped in sediment particles to estimate the time since those grains were exposed to sunlight. Trapped electrons are released and measured in the laboratory when the sample is exposed to heat (thermoluminescence or TL) or light (optically stimulated luminescence or OSL). Those electrons accumulated over time as sediment received natural radiation, making age-estimates more reliable and sensitive on older samples. Luminescence analysis can provide accurate age-estimates on samples up to half a million years old; it can therefore identify occupation in Australia in time periods beyond the radiocarbon barrier.

There are many situations in which luminescence analyses may give incorrect age-estimates. The distribution and quantity of rocks in sediments can affect the number of electrons that accumulated and hence the age-estimates derived. Variation in water content and water deposition of uranium or thorium salts also affect age-estimates. Additionally, as at Jinmium, ancient sand grains can contaminate analysed samples and produce over-estimates of the antiquity.

Luminescence analysis can give accurate age-estimates if two conditions are met. There must be evidence that the electron signal was emptied, or 'zeroed', when last exposed to sunlight, leaving no electrons preserved from earlier time. OSL is a more sophisticated technique because it is capable of isolating and measuring only zeroed grains. The second condition is that radiation dosage received by the archaeological deposit in the past, called the 'palaeodose', is known. Since the palaeodose was different for each deposit it needs to be estimated by implanting a dosimeter in each site, measuring the rate being received nowadays and allowing past dosage rates to be calculated. Once zeroing and palaeodose are established the measured electron load can be used to calculate the time since the grains last saw sunlight. In favourable circumstances the resulting age-estimates are reliable but they are always imprecise.

Stratigraphic associations can be difficult to establish when employing luminescence estimates. Sand grains are not cultural; usually they define the antiquity of human occupation only through their stratigraphic association with cultural objects. Many crucial sites in debates about the antiquity of occupation are sandy deposits with few discernible strata and possibly with extensive vertical movement of objects within them. In these sites descriptions of stratigraphy have not always been published, investigations of disturbance not often undertaken, and stratigraphic associations not always determined. Demonstrations of association and formation or disturbance processes have not yet become routine, and consequently claims that luminescence analyses provide reliable age-estimates for the colonization of Australia have been repeatedly challenged (Hiscock 1990; O'Connell and Allen 2004).

Both radiocarbon and luminescence methods yield reliable age-estimates in some conditions, and the chronological structures of Australian pre-history are built upon these methods. However, radiometric age-estimates can be understood only when archaeologists have adequate knowledge about stratigraphy and formation processes. The need to integrate these kinds of information is clear in debates about a central question of colonization: when did humans arrive in the Australian landmass?

Did humans colonize Australia less than 50,000 years ago?

A wealth of evidence indicates that humans were present in Australia more than 40,000 years ago. Many sites have artefacts in levels estimated to be close to or more than 40,000 years old: Allen's Cave (Roberts et al. 1996), Carpenter's Gap

(O'Connor 1995; Fifield et al. 2001), Cuddie Springs (Roberts et al. 2001), Devil's Lair (Turney et al. 2001), GRE8 (O'Connell and Allen 2004), Lake Mungo (Bowler et al. 2003), Malakunanja (Roberts et al. 1990a, 1990b, 1990c, 1994a), Nauwalabila (Roberts et al. 1990a, 1993, 1994b), Ngarrabullgan (David et al. 1997), Parmerpar Meethaner (O'Connell and Allen 2004), Puritjarra (M. A. Smith et al. 1997, 2001) and Riwi (Balme 2000). These sites are spread across the landmass of Pleistocene Australia (Figure 2.2). This evidence is unambiguous: humans had occupied all or nearly all parts of the continent by at least 40,000 years ago. But how long before that date had people arrived in Australia?

For decades researchers debated whether humans colonized Australia shortly before 40,000 years bp, or long before, perhaps 50,000–65,000 years bp. The debate reflected not only difficulties of interpreting archaeological evidence but also theoretical predispositions of the researchers. It is no coincidence that scientists such as Alan Thorne and Rhys Jones who supported an early age for colonization also advocated the idea of multiple pre-historic migrations into Australia and attacked the reliability of radiocarbon, while supporters of a later date for colonization, such as Jim O'Connell and Jim Allen, argued for only a single human migration and/or defended the reliability of radiocarbon. However, views about the number of migrations or other matters are not critical to an assessment of the date of colonization.

The most conservative view, a 'late colonization model', states Australia was occupied about 45,000 years ago. In proposing this claim Jim Allen and Jim O'Connell evaluated and dismissed claims for older human occupation by questioning the stratigraphic associations of dated samples and cultural material (J. Allen 1989, 1994; O'Connell and Allen 1998, 2004; Allen and O'Connell 2003). They argued that age-estimates greater than 45,000 years bp could not be trusted, and that even if the 'date' was correct for samples of sand, charcoal or bone it was also necessary to demonstrate a real stratigraphic association with cultural objects such as artefacts and skeletons. Allen and O'Connell were unconvinced by claimed stratigraphic associations older than 45,000 years. An example of their evaluations shows how they argued their view.

When they excavated two rock shelters in northern Australia, Nauwalabila and Malakununja II, Rhys Jones and Mike Smith discovered artefacts far below the modern ground surface. At Nauwalabila excavations reached a depth of 3 metres, and artefacts were recovered in between sandstone rubble near the base of the trench (Figure 2.5). OSL analyses by Bert Roberts indicated the earliest sands were hidden from sunlight for about 60,000 (53,500–67,000) years, and he argued that stone artefacts below sands estimated to be 53,000 (47,500–57,500) years old demonstrated that humans arrived in the continent more than 53,000 years ago (Roberts et al. 1993, 1994b; Roberts and Jones 1994). The luminescence age-estimate was imprecise, and the inferred date for colonization is too specific: the last time the sands had been exposed to light could have been 47,500 years ago or more than 55,000 years ago. Nevertheless, Roberts claimed the Nauwalabila evidence revealed that people had been at the site for about 50,000 years or more.

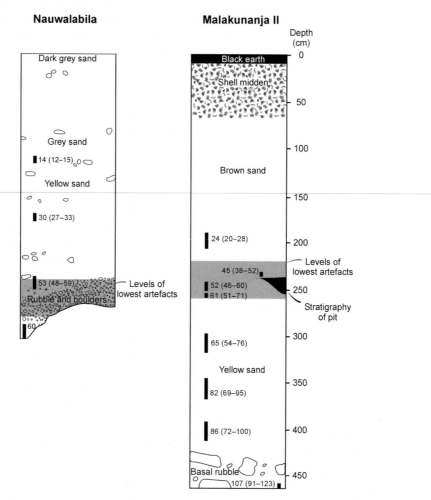

Figure 2.5 Schematic stratigraphic profiles of the excavations by Rhys Jones and Mike Smith at Nauwalabila and Malakunanja II, showing the reported stratigraphy, lowest artefacts' luminescence dates in thousands of years. The black bars represent the approximate location of the lower luminescence samples (with numbers giving age-estimate and age-range); the grey areas indicate the levels containing the lowest artefacts in each site (data from Roberts et al. 1994b; O'Connell and Allen 2004).

In response Allen and O'Connell argued that the Nauwalabila evidence was unreliable because no trustworthy stratigraphic association between the dated sands and the stone artefacts had been demonstrated. They suggested the stone artefacts may have moved vertically, creating a false association between dated sediments and artefacts (O'Connell and Allen 1998). This argument echoed the ideas of Eugene Stockton (1973), who, in the pioneering days of Australian archaeology, showed that in sandy sediments like that of Nauwalabila, artefacts could move more than 5 cm downwards in a single day when people walked in and used the shelter. In addition to human and animal traffic on the surface of Nauwalabila, earthquakes common in the region, as well as seasonal soaking and drying of the deposit, may have relocated objects. Over thousands of years artefacts in a deposit could have been repositioned (Cahen and Moeyersons 1977; Richardson 1992). At Nauwalabila modern glass fragments found 8 cm below the surface show the distance that objects moved in only a few decades.

It was the possibility of animal disturbance that concerned Allen and O'Connell. They suggested that over long periods termites tunnelling through the deposit brought ancient sand grains towards the surface while artefacts moved downwards when the tunnels collapsed, bringing younger artefacts into spurious associations with sand grains containing older luminescent signals. Young, well-preserved charcoal is present throughout the Nauwalabila deposit, a possible indication of extensive movement of material, by termites and other agents (O'Connell and Allen 2004). If artefacts and sand were relocated in Nauwalabila, the luminescence age-estimates would not indicate the antiquity of human occupation at the site: even a small downward movement of the lowest artefacts could mean they were actually 30,000–40,000 years old rather than 50,000 or more (Hiscock 1990). For this reason Allen and O'Connell argued against accepting information from Nauwalabila and similar sites as evidence for human presence in Australia more than 40,000 years ago.

This critique by Allen and O'Connell highlights the failure of twentieth century archaeologists to make investigations of site formation their highest research priority. Claims for human occupation more than 40,000 years ago relied on technically sophisticated analyses of non-cultural samples such as sand grains, but not a single cave or rock shelter with such claims has been subjected to an extensive study of its deposit formation. Without those sorely needed studies, the evidence for humans in Australia before 45,000 years ago is currently weak. Of course the absence of detailed studies of site formation does not mean that humans were absent from Australia prior to 50,000 years ago; merely that archaeologists have failed to adequately assess the possible evidence of early occupation.

Palaeoenvironmental evidence continues to be offered in support of the idea that human colonization took place less than 50,000 years ago. Peter Kershaw and his colleagues identified changes in vegetation and landscape burning that seemingly cannot be explained in terms of global climate change (Kershaw et al. 2002, 2006). At locations such as Lynchs Crater in northeast Australia, and the Banda Sea and Lombok Ridge off the northwest coast, increased quantities of charcoal particles were recovered from sediments 40,000–47,000 years old. This indication of altered fire frequency was interpreted by Kershaw as the initial human impact on Australian vegetation and hence the colonization of Australia. However, this argument is not compelling evidence for the arrival of humans; humanly induced vegetation change may say more about the nature of people's activities than about their presence. Even if greater charcoal abundance was a result of human burning, a claim that is still debatable, intensified fire frequencies might signal a time when humans began regularly using fire to burn their ecosystem, which could be long after the colonization of Australia (Flannery 1994; Chapter 4, this volume).

Lake Mungo: a test of the antiquity of occupation

Debates about colonization have focused on Lake Mungo, a dry inland lake in the southeast of Australia. On its eastern side an eroded dune of clay and sand records the history of the lake and of people who lived there. Called a 'lunette', this dune originally stood almost 40 metres high, but much of the sediment has since been eroded away, revealing parts of the oldest layers to archaeologists walking across the modern land surface (Figure 2.6). The story of the lake can be reconstructed from the sequence of strata because characteristics of sediments reflect the environ-mental conditions in which they accumulated. When lake levels were high, sands were blown from the sandy beaches of the lake, whereas at times of oscillating or low lake levels, layers of pelletal clays accumulated when fine sediments from the exposed lake floor were scoured out by the wind and mixed with sand on the lunette. The strata are named from oldest to youngest, as Golgol, Mungo (divided into Lower and Upper), Arumpo, Zanci and lastly modern, mobile white sands. Interspersed within and between those strata are thin layers of soils which formed during stable periods, when vegetation could grow on the lunette.

The stratum relevant to questions of colonization is the Lower Mungo unit. Below the Mungo sands, the Golgol stratum is clearly pre-human in age and is likely to be more than 100,000 years old (Bowler and Price 1998). Lower Mungo sediments began accumulating about 55,000 years ago, when the lake filled for the first time; it had stopped accumulating nearly 40,000 years ago. In sediments at the very top of the Lower Mungo unit there is abundant evidence of human activity in the form of hearths, burned bones, middens of mollusc shells, human skeletons, as well as stone artefacts. The question for archaeologists is: how much earlier were people present in the area?

Answers to this question are found in two pieces of evidence. One is the skeleton of a human known to archaeologists as WLH3 (Willandra Lakes Hominid 3).

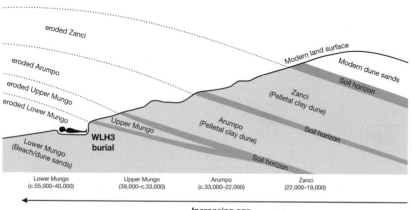

Figure 2.6 Schematic stratigraphic section through the Lake Mungo lunette along the Mungo III transect (based on Bowler 1998; Bowler and Price 1998: 160; Bowler et al. 2003).

Significant as one of the earliest burials known anywhere, and the earliest in Australia, this skeleton gained notoriety when a team of researchers estimated it was more than 60,000 years old (Thorne et al. 1999). This estimate was based on experimental methods not suited to the particular conditions: ESR (electron spin resonance), which measured radiation-induced changes in tooth enamel from the human skeleton, and U-series analysis, which measured the abundance of uranium and thorium in shavings from one of the skeleton's leg bones.

Estimating the age of WLH3 with these techniques was very difficult for a number of reasons. Bones of the skeleton may have been enriched with thorium and leached of uranium while it lay in the deposit, producing estimates that are older than the real age of the skeleton (Gillespie and Roberts 2000; Bowler et al. 2003). Additionally the ESR estimate, like luminescence analyses, required a measurement of the radioactivity of the sediments around the body. However, sediments covering the burial eroded away before it was found and the calculation of age was made with assumptions about the conditions that might have prevailed (Gillespie and Roberts 2000). While the team who obtained estimates of more than 60,000 years defended their analysis (Grün et al. 2000), their results were probably wrong.

Lake Mungo is one of the most studied landscapes in Australia; antiquity of strata has been established over many years of research. The WLH3 burial is located in the uppermost portion of the Lower Mungo stratum, at a period of soil formation (Bowler 1998). The grave for WLH3 was probably dug by people living on the stable land surface indicated by the soil formation (Figure 2.6), and WLH3 can be no older than the age of the top part of the Lower Mungo stratum in which it was found. These sediments are about 40,000 (38,000–42,000) years old and so the humans buried in them must also be that age (Bowler 1998; Bowler and Price 1998; Bowler and Magee 2000; Bowler et al. 2003).

A second, more powerful, piece of evidence for early human occupation at Lake Mungo comes in the form of stone artefacts meticulously excavated by Wilfred Shawcross in 1976. Shawcross (1998) dug a large pit into the Mungo unit (Figure 2.7), in sands below the stratigraphic level represented by the burial of WLH3 (Figure 2.8). He recovered hundreds of artefacts scattered throughout the deposit to a depth of almost 2 metres from the top of the strata. OSL analyses of sediments led Bowler and Shawcross to conclude that the lowest artefacts found in the excavations were 45,000–50,000 years old (Bowler et al. 2003).

Not all archaeologists accepted this conclusion. O'Connell and Allen (2004) rejected claims for human occupation at Lake Mungo prior to 45,000 bp with the same arguments they employed in their critiques of other sites. They hypothesized that the lowest artefacts might have been displaced downwards through the Mungo sands by burrowing animals or by rapid deposition or erosion indicated by the steep bedding of layers. Archaeological information gives little evidence of disturbance in the levels containing the oldest artefacts. Animal burrows were observed only in the overlying Zanci sediments and upper portion of the Mungo sediments. Shawcross (1998) argued that similar signs of burrows were not found at lower levels because they were rare or absent. His conclusion is consistent with

Figure 2.7 Base of the Shawcross trench at Lake Mungo. (Courtesy of W. Shawcross.)

the observation that below the beach gravels and lacustrine sediments found 1 metre down in Shawcross's excavation the history of sand deposition was different; hence there is no reason to think the same magnitude of vertical displacement occurred at all levels in the deposit.

O'Connell and Allen (2004) argued that conjoining of artefacts in the upper portion, which revealed vertical separations between pieces made at the same time, was evidence of vertical movement in the Mungo stratum. However, this is not a viable interpretation. Shawcross (1998) explained at length that vertical distance between the objects reflects their position on an irregular sloping land surface and does not indicate large movements. Thus there is no compelling reason to think that the lowest artefacts moved downwards from later sediments.

The final reason O'Connell and Allen offered for doubting the antiquity of the lowest artefacts in Shawcross's excavation was the inconsistencies in OSL age-estimates for nearby sand samples (Figure 2.8). Most samples yielded estimates of 38,000–55,000 years, but one gave a younger and another an older estimate. Allen and O'Connell argued that these anomalies make it impossible to assign precise dates to any of the archaeological materials in Shawcross's excavation. However, the stratigraphic position of the excavation is well below WLH3, a level in which there are many OSL estimates in excess of 43,000 years, giving little reason to doubt Jim Bowler's conclusion that some archaeological materials are more than 45,000 years old, although they need not be substantially older.

Furthermore, archaeologists may not have recovered the oldest artefacts in the Lake Mungo lunette. In the lower parts of the deposit, beneath the beach gravels,

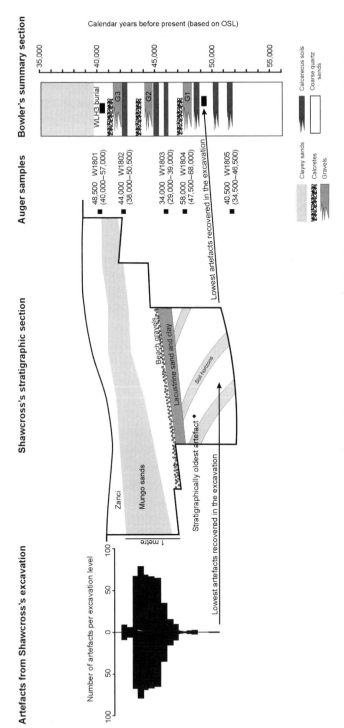

Figure 2.8 Shawcross's excavation B and its relationship to Bowler's summary stratigraphic section (luminescence age-estimates rounded to the nearest 500 years) (data from Bowler and Price 1998; Shawcross 1998; Bowler et al. 2003). Note that Shawcross's section is vertically exaggerated and not to the same scale as Bowler's summary section.

artefacts are rare and only a small volume of deposit was excavated; older specimens could exist, as yet undiscovered, within the dune (see Hiscock 2001). It is therefore premature to conclude that the oldest artefacts excavated at Lake Mungo are the oldest that exist there. This conclusion raises the question of whether evidence of human occupation substantially earlier than 45,000 bp might exist in Australia?

Were humans in Australia before 50,000 years ago?

Difficulties of dating human occupation in specific rock shelters or sand dunes exemplify the veil of obscurity that hides accurate knowledge of the pre-historic past from modern scientists. The dearth of investigations into site formation or disturbance leaves unanswered questions concerning the reliability of evidence for colonization about 50,000 years ago, but this is not grounds to reject those claims. Evidence used to claim that humans arrived in Australia 50,000–60,000 years ago has neither been demonstrated to the satisfaction of all archaeologists nor shown to be false. Contrary to the arguments of Allen and O'Connell, evidence consistent with colonization before 50,000 bp cannot be jettisoned merely because it has been poorly presented and is hard to evaluate. In fact, the evidence from a number of sites with artefacts in levels containing luminescence age-estimates greater than 45,000 years bp cannot easily be dismissed.

The foundations of an 'early colonization model', positing that humans arrived slightly before 50,000 years bp, was laid in the 1970s when Rhys Jones pointed out that radiocarbon analysis was inherently unsuited to the investigation of human colonization in Australia. He explained that the colonizing event had undoubtedly occurred before 40,000 years bp and even technically sophisticated radiocarbon analyses could not reliably date samples of greater age (Jones 1979, 1993; Chappell et al. 1996). Development of luminescence techniques made it possible to estimate the age of deposits that were older than the 'radiocarbon barrier'; the result was an announcement by Roberts, Jones and Smith (1990a) that at Malakunanja II artefacts were in sands estimated to be 50,000–60,000 years old. The discovery of sediments last exposed to light more than 50,000 years ago, and which contained artefacts, was hailed as evidence for an 'early' human colonization (Dayton and Woodford 1996). However, several archaeologists were wary of the stratigraphic associations inferred at Malakunanja II (Bowdler 1990, 1991; Hiscock 1990; J. Allen 1994; O'Connell and Allen 1998, 2004; Allen and O'Connell 2003). How should we regard the evidence from Malakunanja II and the nearby site of Nauwalabila?

At Nauwalabila vertical movement of artefacts may have occurred in the grey and yellow sand levels, as O'Connell and Allen (2004) hypothesized, but it is more difficult to understand how stone artefacts moved so far down into densely packed rubble at the base of the excavation (Figure 2.5). It seems likely that artefacts within the basal rubble had not moved much since they were deposited (Roberts et al. 1990a, 1990b). While the rubble and artefacts have not been adequately described, and might represent a palimpsest created by erosion, the accumulation of sands on top of the rubble about 53,000 (48,000–59,000) years ago probably indicates that artefacts have been trapped in the rubble for something like 50,000 years or more.

An even more convincing case for early colonization exists for Malakunanja II. In that deposit the lowest artefacts came from 230–260 cm below the surface (Figure 2.5). At those depths there were three luminescence age-estimates: sample KTL164 yielded an estimate of 45,000 (38,000–52,000) years bp for sediments 230–236 cm deep, KTL158 an estimate of 52,000 (46,000–60,000) years bp for sediments 241–254 cm deep, and KTL162 an estimate of 61,000 (51,000–71,000) years bp for sediments 254–259 cm deep (Roberts et al. 1990a). Artefacts were found at all of these depths, but do they result from disturbance? The excavators noted that artefact size and raw material did not suggest their wholesale displacement (Roberts et al. 1990b), but sceptical researchers conjectured that the artefacts moved downwards to enter sands of a pre-human age (Hiscock 1990; O'Connell and Allen 2004). It is now clear that vertical displacement of artefacts cannot explain away the apparent associations.

In Malakunanja II there was stratigraphic evidence of a small pit approximately 20 cm deep, dug from an old land surface that was covered by sands analysed in the KTL164 sample. This ancient pit was a fragile feature, preserved only as a subtle and delicate difference in the sediments; it was not disturbed or displaced. It was dug sometime between the deposition of sand estimated to be 45,000 (38,000–52,000) years old and 52,000 (46,000–60,000) years old. These highly imprecise luminescence estimates would be consistent with the pit being slightly younger than 40,000 years bp or substantially more than 50,000 years old, but archaeologists agree that it is consistent with the presence of humans at Malakunanja before 45,000 years ago.

Evidence from Malakunanja and Lake Mungo raises a final, little discussed, point in favour of an 'early colonization' model. At these sites archaeologists have unambiguously demonstrated a human presence at least 43,000–45,000 years ago, and uncovered evidence that hints at the existence of human occupation close to or before 50,000 years ago. If we conclude that humans lived at these sites 45,000–50,000 years ago, it is clear this was the *latest* period in which colonization could have occurred. The earliest reliable archaeological evidence found in Australia represents the minimum age for the arrival of people on the continental shelf. Colonization probably occurred long before the earliest residues identified by archaeologists. Very little is preserved of the initial period of human life in Australia; of the first settlements on the now submerged continental shelf it is likely that nothing has been preserved. Consequently, archaeologists have not found the earliest traces of human activities. Even if the pit at Malakunanja was dug about 45,000 years ago, and not earlier, it might not represent the earliest human use of the shelter, and it was certainly not evidence of the arrival of humans in Australia. It would be astonishing luck if in excavating one small area of sites that were a long way from the Pleistocene coast, Jones and Smith had even found evidence of human occupation that was within a few thousand years of the first landfall! We have almost no knowledge of where or how many people first landed on the Greater Australian coast and there are no reliable estimates of how long it took foragers to settle the area around Malakunanja and use the site with enough intensity to leave an archaeological signature. For the same kinds of reasons we cannot be sure how long it took people to spread from landing points in the north across the continent to places in the southeast such as Lake Mungo (Chapter 3). It is likely that there was a temporal gap of unknown duration between the first arrival of people on the now drowned coast and their occupation of places that archaeologists have studied. Since archaeologists can demonstrate occupation in the southeast of the landmass more than 45,000 years ago, even a conservative judge of the evidence might concede that colonization could have occurred 50,000 years ago or even earlier.

A balanced perspective on the antiquity of colonization?

Looking at the archaeological evidence from Malakunanja and Lake Mungo it is prudent to accept two points made by Peter Hiscock and Lynley Wallis (2005). First, it is currently impossible to determine the exact date of human colonization. Imprecision of dating techniques, combined with the distorting effects of disturbance, gives a chronological uncertainty of about 5,000–10,000 years for the lowest cultural evidence in early sites. Second, archaeological evidence provides us with a minimum age for the arrival of humans; the oldest undeniable evidence of people on this continent must represent a time *after* the colonization. Although the speed with which people spread across Australia is unknown, it can be conjectured that people became archaeologically visible at sites in the south, such as Devil's Lair and Lake Mungo, long after colonization.

The antiquity of human colonization of Australia can therefore be considered to be older than 45,000±5,000 years bp, an age that all archaeologists accept for sites like Malakunanja II and Lake Mungo. It is possible that *Homo sapiens* landed on the continental shelf of Greater Australia 45,000–50,000 years ago, but colonization of this landmass is more likely to have been between 50,000 and 60,000 years ago.

3 Early settlement across Australia

Between the arrival of humans 45,000–60,000 years ago and the historical period when Aborigines lived in all regions, people spread across Australia, discovering ways to survive in new environments. How quickly did they explore and settle the diverse landscapes? One idea, a 'marginal settlement' model, proposed that people spread around the continental margins, preferring familiar coastal habitats. The alternative idea, a 'saturated settlement' model, depicted settlers spreading uniformly and rapidly across all landscapes. A major distinction between these models is the time difference between when humans entered the continent, itself subject to debate, and when they occupied each landscape. The saturated settlement model predicts a short time difference; the marginal settlement model predicts a long delay before people occupied the inland. Archaeologists tested these competing models by examining evidence for the antiquity of human settlement in each part of the continent.

Inland Australia is the key place to evaluate these models. If early occupation is not found there, the marginal model may be correct, but early sites would indicate that the saturation model was correct. Early sites are difficult to find, they often have poorly preserved cultural materials and low chronological resolution, but the Pleistocene archaeology of inland Australia reveals remarkable stories of life and survival in extreme circumstances. The human settlement of harsh, unproductive environments was made possible by the flexible, effective economic and social systems of Pleistocene foragers. Archaeologists initially underestimated the dynamism of early settlement and economy.

Settlement restricted to the margins?

In the early 1970s Sandra Bowdler excavated in Cave Bay Cave, an immense cavern on Hunter Island, off the northwestern tip of Tasmania (Figure 3.1). She discovered an intriguing archaeological sequence extending back 27,000 years. The cave was occupied in some periods but abandoned in others. One layer with abundant hearths, artefacts and bones was created between 26,800 (26,300–27,300) years bp and about 21,000–24,000 years bp. After that time little archaeological material was deposited until about 7,000 years ago, when regular human occupation of the cave recommenced because the sea levels rose and the coast returned to its present

Figure 3.1 Map of the Sahul landmass (at −150 metres) and its relationship to modern Australia, showing the sites discussed in Chapter 3. Sites in bold are those employed by Hiscock and Wallis (2005) in their desert transformation model.

position. Perhaps foragers visited the site between 7,000 and 21,000 years bp but Bowdler thought they were brief visits by people based near the then distant coast. The cold, windswept Bassian Plain was resource poor during and immediately after the glacial period, but Bowdler (1977) speculated that it could have been exploited if foragers had suitable economic strategies. She hypothesized that the absence of intense occupation in Cave Bay Cave between 7,000 and 21,000 years ago indicated that Pleistocene foragers chose to stay close to the coast when the sea level was low, because they had a 'marine-oriented' economy.

Rather than depict this coastal focus of late-Pleistocene foragers as a local one, Bowdler thought it reflected the continent-wide settlement strategy. She speculated that people had moved through southeast Asia by living on islands and coastlines, exploiting coastal foods, and when they reached Australia they continued their traditional economic practices, settling only coastal landscapes. She thought hunters caught terrestrial mammals unsystematically and that the economy of early foragers depended on marine foods, especially fish and molluscs. Bowdler conjectured that while local economic adjustments sometimes occurred, when people hunted freshwater fish and molluscs rather than marine ones, the 'coastal economy' of early foragers was inflexible and unchanging. This was a model of conservative people who continued their marine focus until the end of the glaciation, when rising sea levels drowned coastal plains and forced them into non-coastal landscapes.

Bowdler's marginal settlement model predicted that sites of Pleistocene age would be found only near the coast and at inland water bodies linked to the coast by major rivers. When it was proposed, this model appeared plausible because many Pleistocene-aged sites discovered in the 1960s and 1970s were close to the present coastline. However, even then a handful of Pleistocene sites were known from inland landscapes and could not have been made by coastally focused foragers. For example, there was Pleistocene occupation at Kenniff Cave (Mulvaney and Joyce 1965), located on the inland side of the eastern line of mountains. There were no nearby marine or permanent riverine resources; only terrestrial plants and animals were available. Kenniff Cave and similar sites demonstrated that people living there subsisted on local terrestrial plants and animals and were able to settle areas away from the coast and large rivers; they were not the 'marine-oriented' foragers of Bowdler's vision.

The absence of early sites away from the coast was merely a product of the lack of archaeological fieldwork in many remote locations. During the 1980s detailed studies of isolated inland areas demonstrated that humans had occupied many environments during the Pleistocene and were not tethered to the continental margins by a coastal economy. Ironically an outstanding example of this came from the highlands of Tasmania, not far from the location that had stimulated Bowdler to think of the marginal settlement model. There archaeological sites such as Parmerpar Meethaner and Warreen, in remote upland valleys, have been dated to nearly 40,000 years bp, indicating that foragers were at that time already living in purely terrestrial environments (Cosgrove 1999).

The most powerful demonstration of the settlement of people away from the continental margins came when Mike Smith discovered and excavated a site in remote central Australia. The site he found was an ideal test of the marginal settlement model because it was located in the very heart of central Australia.

Occupation at Puritjarra in the heart of Australia

Puritjarra, a large rock shelter in the Cleland Hills of central Australia, illustrates long-term human occupation of the arid interior. Set amidst broken sandstone scarps, surrounded by sandy plains and dune fields (Figure 3.2), the shelter is near Murantji Rockhole, a deep, aquifer-fed water body. The conjunction of a large, sandy-floored shelter and a large reliable water source is unique in the region today and provided a refuge for foragers in the past.

Mike Smith's excavations revealed that Puritjarra contained a deposit that was deep and old (Figure 3.3). He dug more than 250 cm deep and radiometric analyses indicate the lowest artefacts came from a level that was 39,000 (36,500–42,500) years old (Smith et al. 1997). Stone artefacts were recovered from almost every level of the deposit although only a few were found from the Pleistocene. Smith (1989c) argued that vertical movement of objects was uncommon and the existence of

Figure 3.2 View of Puritjarra during Mike Smith's 1988 excavation. (Courtesy of M.A. Smith.)

Figure 3.3 Deep excavation of the main trench at Puritjarra rock shelter. This revealed human occupation in central Australia during the Pleistocene. (Courtesy of M.A. Smith.)

artefacts throughout the deposit indicates repeated, intermittent, human visits from approximately 40,000 years ago until the Holocene. Persistent human use of resource-rich, water-rich refuges embedded within desert landscapes, such as Puritjarra, is a feature of early occupation across the inland.

Settlement of the dry interior

Evidence from Puritjarra and other sites proves that humans occupied the dry interior more than 40,000 years ago. How people spread across different landscapes of the continental interior, especially arid and semi-arid environments, has been a puzzle. In the middle of the twentieth century Joseph Birdsell (1957) predicted it took humans between 1,300 and 2,200 years to settle the entire continent. His estimates did not consider the implications of different environments, simply the distance to be settled. But the difficulties that humans face settling a landmass cannot be measured by its size alone; the nature and distribution of resources and the suitability of technology and economic strategies in those environments should be considered as well. Consequently models of the initial settlement of inland Australia now take account of environmental differences through time and space.

The initial movement of people into the interior has been portrayed in two ways. The first is through biogeographic descriptions of regional differences in environment and their effects on early human settlement. This approach is exemplified by Peter Veth's (1989) 'refuge, corridor and barrier' model. A second approach describes chronological changes in conditions confronting foragers, typified by Peter Hiscock and Lynley Wallis's (2005) 'desert transformation' model. These two approaches are complementary and together offer an insight into the timing and nature of early settlement across the interior.

Looking first at a biogeographic framework, Veth's (1989) model of barrier environments proposed that early foragers occupied much of the inland, but avoided sand-ridge landscapes. Veth employed ecological principles to define three landscape categories: uplands, sand-ridge deserts and corridors (Figure 3.4). He argued that major sand-ridge deserts (the Great Sandy Desert, Great Victoria Desert and the Simpson Desert) were not easy for people to occupy, being resource-poor and often without well-defined drainage patterns. Because no archaeological evidence dating to the Last Glacial Maximum (LGM) had been found in these sandy deserts, Veth (1989) argued they had been barriers to human movement and settlement. Piedmont/montane uplands and riverine/gorge systems, he contended, provided networks of reliable water sources with coordinated drainage systems which were less sensitive to climatic changes. These landscapes were easier for foragers to inhabit, even in times of low and irregular precipitation, and Veth hypothesized that they served as refuges for Pleistocene human groups. A third biogeographic category, termed 'corridors', incorporated all other areas, such as gibber plains. These corridors may have been passageways for settlement in some periods and have acted as barriers in others, depending on climatic conditions.

While these ecological categories provide coarse-grained descriptions of environmental differences, their large scale obscures environmental variation,

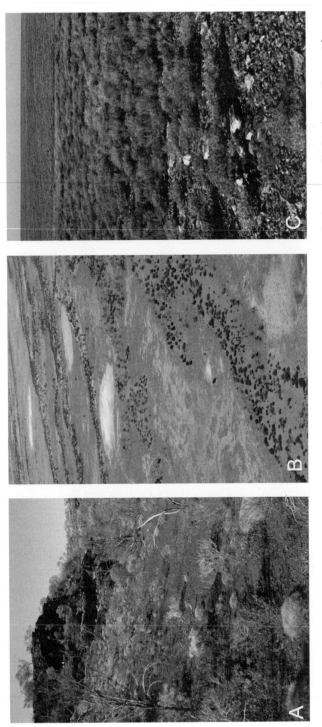

Figure 3.4 Photographs illustrating Veth's (1989) three landscape categories: A = piedmont/montane uplands; B = sand-ridge deserts; C = corridors.

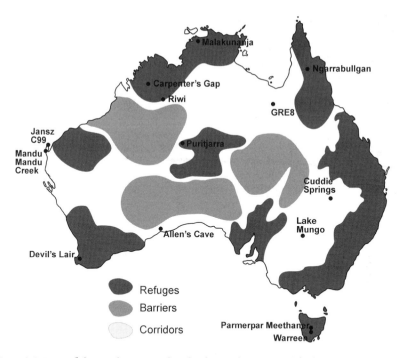

Figure 3.5 Map of the modern Australian landmass showing Veth's (1989) biogeographic zones and the locations of sites more than 35,000 years old (data points from Morse 1988; Turney et al. 2001; O'Connell and Allen 2004; Przywolnik 2005).

hiding water-poor localities within montane or upland zones or small refuge areas within corridors. An example of a refuge within a corridor zone is Lawn Hill, which is discussed further below. Nevertheless, on a continental scale Veth's model is congruent with evidence, and in Figure 3.5 the location of known archaeological sites older than 35,000 years reveals the pattern predicted in Veth's model (data from Smith and Sharp 1993; O'Connell and Allen 2004). Limited use of marginal sandy deserts occurred later in the Pleistocene, after 25,000 years bp (O'Connor et al. 1998), but evidence for use of sand-ridge deserts before 35,000 years bp is rare. At Puritjarra ochre was transported from distant sources across dune fields before 40,000 years bp, which may indicate occupation of the sandy landscape but might alternatively show that foragers were based in nearby montane environments rather than living entirely in sand-ridge deserts (M. A. Smith et al. 1998). In regions without montane environments, with only sand-ridge and flat stony deserts, archaeological evidence for early occupation has not been found; it is even suggested that Lake Eyre South was not occupied until the Holocene (Hughes and Hiscock 2005). Consequently, even in the earliest phase of settlement, sandy landscapes may have been obstacles to occupation. Hence, while settlement was widespread in the Pleistocene it appears not to have been uniform across the continent, with early foragers emphasizing the exploitation of specific environments and features.

This implies that Pleistocene foragers did not have a settlement system like twentieth century Aboriginal people in the sandy deserts. This reveals the paradox of using ethnographic information about recent desert dwellers to reconstruct initial settlement of arid and semi-arid lands. Images of historical Aboriginal desert life often emphasize the intensive use of vegetable foods such as seeds, and maintenance of long-distant social networks involving reciprocity and rights to territorial access (e.g. Gould 1977, 1980; Tonkinson 1991). Such strategies require neighbouring human groups and detailed knowledge of food resources. During the historical period Aboriginal desert dwellers were renowned for their intimate knowledge of landscapes and their reciprocal social arrangements with neighbours. However, these features cannot have been traits of the colonizers of the desert lands! Exploration of inland Australia was accomplished by foragers who did not know the terrain or the distribution of resources within it, and who were not surrounded by neighbours. Initial settlement of the deserts must have been undertaken by people who had economic and subsistence strategies different from those of the historic period.

One explanation of how humans settled the interior without the adaptive strategies used by historic desert peoples was offered by Hiscock and Wallis (2005), who argued that much of the interior was initially occupied during a period of higher rainfall and more abundant surface water and food resources. They hypothesize that Pleistocene people did not move into deserts fully equipped with a modern desert adaptation, but rather humans moved into many inland regions during a time when surface water was more plentiful and climatic conditions less harsh than nowadays. A foraging strategy which did not employ specific tools or detailed familiarity of local resources enabled early mobile forager groups to occupy regions across the inland, gradually refining their knowledge of resources available in each. Peter Veth (2005) suggested that by being highly mobile early settlers were able to explore and exploit unfamiliar environments, and Claire Smith (1992) hypothesized that if early settlers were not territorial it would be easier for them to disperse across new lands. Climate change subsequently made conditions within arid lands more extreme, and foragers who lived there had the opportunity to adjust their strategies to the new circumstances or move to other areas. Settlement of the interior during a favourable environmental period, followed by modification of economic systems as climate dried, is a model of 'desert transformation' (Hiscock and Wallis 2005).

Evidence of early inland occupation has steadily accumulated (Figure 3.4). In the northwest the lowest occupation level of Carpenter's Gap was estimated to be 45,000 (43,500–46,500) years ago (Fifield et al. 2001), while at Riwi it was 45,500 (44,000–47,500) years bp (Balme 2000). Puritjarra had occupation at 39,000 (36,500–42,500) years bp (M. A. Smith et al. 1997), and further south occupation of Allen's Cave was estimated to be 40,000 (37,000–43,000) years old (Roberts et al. 1996). The stratigraphically lowest artefacts in Lake Mungo are estimated to be at least 46,000–50,000 years (Bowler et al. 2003); Cuddie Springs has an age-estimate of 35,500 (32,500–38,500) years bp for artefacts (Roberts et al. 2001); the cave called GRE8 has a radiocarbon estimate of 41,500 (37,500–44,500) years for cultural material (O'Connell and Allen 2004). Hiscock and Wallis

(2005) argued that these sites show that humans lived in widely separated inland regions more than 40,000 years ago. Imprecise age-estimates make it impossible to say whether different inland regions were settled contemporaneously or sequentially, or to know how rapidly humans dispersed across inland Australia. However, widespread human settlement 40,000–50,000 years ago has been demonstrated and the desert transformation model suggests that people occupied inland landscapes because environmental conditions were very different at that time, allowing foragers to exploit dry inland regions without the kind of economic system observed historically (Thorley 1998; Hiscock and Wallis 2005). When humans moved into desert regions climatic and hydrological conditions were unlike those found now. Prior to 35,000–45,000 years bp conditions were cooler and in some regions surface freshwater was more available than in the past 10,000 years. Through time conditions in the interior became progressively more arid.

Evidence of greater water availability during the initial phase of human settlement comes from many studies. For example, near Carpenter's Gap marine cores, sedimentary sequences from lakes, and plant residues from archaeological sites all indicate greater precipitation and surface water until 38,000–40,000 years ago (van der Kaars 1991; Bowler et al. 1998; Wang et al. 1999; Wallis 2001; Bowler et al. 2003; Pack et al. 2003; Hiscock and Wallis 2005). The Lake Eyre Basin also received more summer rainfall, before 45,000 years bp (B. J. Johnson et al. 1999), and until about 30,000 years ago there was probably more winter rainfall (Miller et al. 1997; Magee and Miller 1998). In fact, greater winter rainfall, storms in the north, and reduced evaporation due to lower temperatures meant that until 30,000–35,000 years bp Lake Eyre was wetter than at any time since, and a low-level perennial lake was present 30,000–50,000 years ago (Hesse et al. 2004). In the Lake Mungo region of southeastern Australia, Bowler (1998) also documented a long-term trend towards dryer conditions. Prior to 42,000–45,000 years ago there was a prolonged lacustral phase with high water levels, but then lake levels reduced and fluctuated even though water bodies were present until 22,000 years ago.

This environmental information gives us a general image of the interior into which humans first moved: the landscapes were remarkable! In many regions characterized by Veth (1989) as corridors or uplands, seasonal floods and large standing water bodies were common and comparatively predictable prior to 40,000–45,000 years ago. These landscapes were still deserts, drier than many regions on the continental margins, but when humans first explored them they were significantly different from the desert environments observable at the present time, most noticeably in the presence of large permanent water bodies. In their desert transformation model Hiscock and Wallis (2005) proposed that availability and predictability of water and other resources in the 'lacustral phase' prior to 40,000 years ago facilitated exploration and exploitation of interior landscapes. They hypothesized that people moved into these lands with flexible foraging strategies focused on hunting a wide range of small- to medium-sized game such as marsupials, reptiles, fish and mussels. Although larger species of animal existed at that time there is no evidence that they were intensively hunted (Chapter 4). In several regions the exploitation of lacustrine and riverine resources was probably an important economic focus. As Peter Thorley (1998) observed, the image of early foragers of the inland focusing their economy on tropical gorges, reliable riverine environments and large, rich lake systems is remote from the characterization of recent desert dwellers in the modern arid landscape.

Movement of human groups into unfamiliar, relatively well-watered inland landscapes prior to 40,000 years ago probably provided a basis for the emergence of later Pleistocene arid zone economic systems. Following initial settlement of the interior a gradual desertification occurred, intensifying about 35,000 years ago. The amount and reliability of rainfall diminished and, in many areas, there was a decline in the availability of permanent surface water. Foraging and social strategies were able to be modified as new, more severe desert landscapes developed because people had established knowledge of their local environment. New economic and technological strategies were probably built on existing information and perceptions about the local environments. In this way pronounced late-Pleistocene drying assisted foraging groups already residing in inland Australia, employing flexible but unspecific terrestrial economies, to develop more desert-dedicated economic strategies. This process of economic transformation has not been traced in detail, partly because evidence for early desert occupation is scanty and partly because archaeologists focused on estimating the age of early sites rather than on interpreting life ways represented by material found in them. Nevertheless, the 'desert transformation' model removes the paradox of explaining how people were able to migrate into deserts in the Pleistocene: in important ways modern deserts of Australia came to inland dwelling people, rather than the reverse.

How fast was settlement?

The movement of people across the inland has sometimes been thought to have been gradual. Anne Ross suggests that people settled arid areas because their economic strategies had been successful in adjacent semi-arid regions and could therefore be slightly adjusted to suit the different, harsher conditions of a neighbouring desert (Ross et al. 1992). She thought that by becoming familiar with one kind of landscape, and developing economic and technological strategies to exploit it, foragers gradually acquired behaviours that enabled them to occupy other environments. In this view the harshest interior regions were occupied as the culmination of a series of settlement events.

Archaeologists such as Ross hypothesized that settlement of the south and centre of Australia was a gradual process because they assumed that human colonists were few in number and technologically and culturally unsophisticated. That idea formed the basis of arguments that humans had difficulties crossing water barriers to reach Australia and when they arrived were slow to increase the population size, adjust to new landscapes and develop technological and social complexity (e.g. Bowdler 1977; Jones 1979; Beaton 1983; Lourandos 1983a, 1997). Norma McArthur (1976) explored these views by constructing computer simulations of possible population growth from a founding population of only six to fourteen adults. She found that such small groups would probably have died out over a few generations,

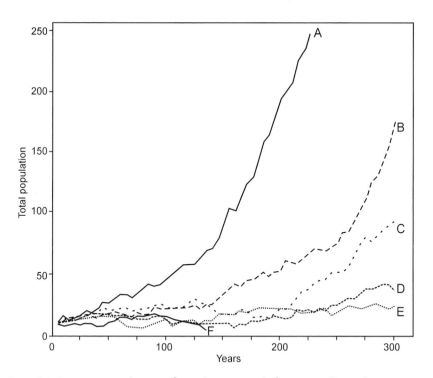

Figure 3.6 Computer simulations of population growth from a small initial group size, illustrating the potential variability in demographic trends (after McArthur 1976). Letters A–F label examples of the trends generated by different simulations.

but that if they survived there was no inevitable or predictable trend in growth of the total population; in some simulations population size barely changed over 300–500 years while in others dramatic increases in numbers occurred (Figure 3.6). Consequently, if colonization began with a small founding group the dispersal of people across the continent and growth of population could have been either rapid or slow.

It is difficult to use archaeological evidence to assess the speed of human settlement across Australia. As David Rindos and Esmee Webb (1992) observed, the low resolution of radiometric age-estimates makes it impossible to develop precise statements about the time humans took to settle the continent. However, evidence for early occupation of central Australia is consistent with relatively rapid dispersion and settlement events, which perhaps took only a few thousand years. Rapid settlement is also consistent with evidence that colonizers were more numerous and more capable than initially thought.

Genetic studies give evidence that the founding population was large. Max Ingman and Ulf Gyllensten (2003) argue that similar estimated age for several mtDNA sequences found in Australian Aborigines, and the genetic separations between modern Aborigines, is evidence of a large founding population which grew as people entered Australia (also Watson et al. 1997; Kayser et al. 2001). This possibility was also raised by Andrew Merriwether, who calculated that mtDNA diversity is consistent with a large initial population containing several hundred women (Merriwether et al. 2005). With males and children, the founding population was probably more than 1,000 people, and subsequent geographical and population expansions could have been relatively rapid.

Furthermore, people who reached Australia were descendants of humans who had expanded steadily through many different environments (Chapter 2). Genetic evidence suggests that humans spread from Africa to Australia, across southern and southeast Asia, at an average of 1–4 km per year (Forster 2004; Forster and Matsumura 2005; Macauley et al. 2005). This rate reveals the adaptability of early foragers and their capacity to colonize new landscapes. If foragers entering Australia expanded at similar rates human settlement of the continent would have taken only 1,000–4,000 years, an estimate very close to the one proposed by Birdsell (1957). Testing this hypothesis with archaeological evidence awaits the development of radiometric techniques with much higher resolution.

Climatic deterioration

While genetic and archaeological evidence indicates that early settlers were highly adaptable and spread rapidly across different environments, this does not mean that they were able to adapt to all the conditions they met. Minimal evidence for residence of sandy deserts during the initial phase of settlement reveals people successfully settled in many but not all niches. Existing evidence suggests that Pleistocene foragers were least able to occupy resource-poor environments, a conclusion reinforced by the profound difficulties encountered by humans as the climate deteriorated.

A trend to cool, dry climates began 45,000 years ago but the last glacial cycle intensified rapidly with the onset of the cold, dry period called OIS2 (Oxygen Isotope Stage 2) approximately 30,000 years ago. At that time oceans reduced dramatically, revealing the continental shelf to a depth of almost 150 metres below the present sea level (Figure 3.7), as moisture became locked up as ice or snow at high latitudes (Lambeck et al. 2002). The extensive exposure of the continental shelf greatly increased the landmass available to humans and changed environments in which they lived. Many inland areas were then located even further from the sea than they had been (Chappell 1991; Lambeck and Chappell 2001; Yokoyama et al. 2001; Lambeck et al. 2002). The increasingly dry, continental situation of inland areas compounded the effects of drying climates after 30,000 years bp.

Climatic deterioration can also be described in terms of increased evaporation and/or reduced precipitation in many regions. About 30,000 years ago monsoonal rain was much reduced; Lake Eyre become dry and remained so until around 10,000 years ago (Miller et al. 1997; Magee and Miller 1998; B. J. Johnson et al. 1999). At Lake Mungo and nearby lakes there were lower, fluctuating water levels and dune-building processes were activated (Bowler 1983, 1986, 1998). Other lake systems also had reduced water levels in this period, although the timing of drying

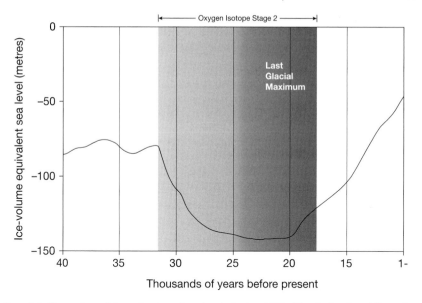

Figure 3.7 Illustration of the reduction of sea levels during OIS2. (Graph developed from data in Lambeck et al. 2002: Figure 11.)

varied locally (Harrison 1993). Reduced effective precipitation led to decreasing trees/shrubs in many regions and an increased distribution of grasslands (see review in Hiscock and Wallis 2005).

Average air temperatures also fell across the continent, affecting temperature-sensitive vegetation and lowering the altitude of snow-lines compared to today. In montane portions of Tasmania summer temperatures were 6–10°C cooler than today (Barrows et al. 2001). In central Australia, where chemical analysis of emu eggshell proteins preserves a record of temperature, it was at least 6°C cooler than at present between 20,000 and 30,000 years bp (Miller et al. 1997; B. J. Johnson et al. 1999).

Changes in precipitation, temperature and surface water availability acted together to enlarge desert landscapes. The semi-arid zone expanded laterally towards the continental margins, and previously semi-arid areas became arid (Jones and Bowler 1980). Deserts grew more inhospitable than they are today. During OIS2, not only did inland environments became drier, but also many of the large, reliable lacustrine ecosystems disappeared. However, the climate also became less variable and initially this probably assisted people to adapt to these drying landscapes.

Early in OIS2 many human groups continued to occupy drying inland regions, perhaps refining their economic strategies to suit the landscapes evolving around them. Localized adaptations to inland landscapes reflect the familiarity of people with their environments, and consequently different patterns of activities have been recorded in each region. For example, there were increased amounts of cultural material in some areas but decreasing amounts in other areas (Veth 1989; O'Connor et al. 1998; O'Connor et al. 1999; Hughes and Hiscock 2005). Social networks and regular use of resources are characteristics of this period (see Chapter 6). At several inland lakes large quantities of food debris indicate that sizeable groups of people were exploiting edible resources (Balme 1983, 1995). People living at Puritjarra continued to procure ochre from distant sources, as they had for more than ten millennia (M. A. Smith et al. 1998). Hiscock and Wallis (2005) interpreted this as evidence that initial economic strategies, partially dependent on reliable access to surface water and focused on riverine and lacustrine resources supplemented with nearby terrestrial resources, continued to be effective for many inland foragers in the period between 35,000 and 30,000 years ago. In deserts with those resources, containing uplands, major coordinated drainage and/or extant lake systems, archaeological evidence for human occupation is found at the start of OIS2; whereas many regions without those resources had little or no occupation. Current archaeological evidence indicates that during OIS2 sandy deserts without coordinated drainage and large permanent lakes were difficult environments for people to inhabit, as Veth (1989) had predicted. By the end of OIS2, following further climatic deterioration, there was a strong, widespread avoidance of dry, sandy environments (Hiscock and Wallis 2005).

The Last Glacial Maximum

Dry conditions were so extreme towards the end of OIS2, 17,000–25,000 years ago, that an exceptionally cold and dry phase is referred to as the Last Glacial Maximum (LGM). Lowest sea-surface temperatures occurred about 21,000 years bp and on land it was exceptionally cold and dry (Barrows et al. 2002). Evaporation and windiness were greater than today, a combination that reduced surface water availability (Chappell 1991; Hubbard 1995; Magee and Miller 1998). Consequently, in the LGM landscapes surrounding the arid core of Australia dried to such an extent that they too became deserts, expanding the arid interior. Rainfall was about half the amount received today, although water availability varied seasonally in some regions (Singh and Geissler 1985; Dodson and Wright 1989; Hubbard 1996). Glaciers formed in high altitude areas (Barrows et al. 2001; Barrows et al. 2004), and many upland areas became extremely cold, dry and treeless (Sweller 2001). Environmental conditions were more severe than any encountered since humans had arrived in Australia.

The LGM was perhaps the driest of all glacial cycles (Longmore and Heijnis 1999), and the consequences of these extreme conditions for people should not be underestimated. Reduced vegetation cover probably triggered a major phase of dune-building and aeolian dust storms were intense (Ash and Wasson 1983; Wasson 1983; Bowler and Wasson 1984; Bowler 1986; Nanson et al. 1992; Hesse 1994; Hesse and McTainsh 1999). The drying of lakes and reduced surface water was often linked to lowered water tables and the formation of salt crusts (Magee et al. 1995). The conditions at this time caused widespread environmental stress, creating massive, sometimes irreversible, changes to landscapes and to plant and animal resources found there. Foods sometimes disappeared, as was the case in lakes surrounding Lake Mungo where reduced temperature and water levels made fish and freshwater mussels locally extinct between 25,000 and 19,000 years ago (Bowler 1998). It also became harder to predict when rainfall would fill water sources, as good rains occurred less often and more irregularly. Climate during the LGM was highly variable compared to the initial portion of OIS2 (Lambeck et al. 2002); consequently this was a more difficult environmental context for people occupying many inland regions. Archaeological research has yielded evidence of the dramatic impact of these climatic conditions on humans attempting to live in drying landscapes. An example emerged from discoveries in an unusual area of northern Australia.

Last Glacial Maximum at Lawn Hill

South of the Gulf of Carpentaria, the massive river called Lawn Hill flows from artesian sources, and because it did not depend on surface runoff this river flowed all year round throughout the most arid conditions of the LGM. The river runs through limestone gorges containing deep, permanent lagoons that support fish, molluscs, turtles, crocodiles, water-rats and platypus (Figure 3.8). Outside these gorges water is available only after rainfall; the thin soils barely support scattered clumps of spinifex and eucalypts, and only a few desert-adapted animals such as Western Hare-Wallabies, Red Kangaroos and Common Wallaroos are found. During the LGM this gorge was a refuge for people, an oasis rich in water and food.

Figure 3.8 View of the oasis at Lawn Hill and the vegetation it supports.

Excavations at Colless Creek Cave, a site in Lawn Hill gorge, enabled Peter Hiscock and Philip Hughes to reconstruct how people had used the area. Once the LGM ended, over the past 17,000 years, people occasionally used the cave and brought to it food and artefacts obtained from all parts of the region, outside the gorge as well as inside. Foragers in recent millennia exploited all local environments, including dry non-gorge landscapes. However, during the LGM human occupation was radically different; it was more intensive than at any other time, as shown by the large numbers of artefacts, bones and shells left behind. Intensive use of the cave at that time mirrors the focus of foragers on resources in the gorge, with little or no use of the broader landscape. Most food came from animals living in the gorge, and the stone artefacts were made from nearby rocks; no food or artefacts were brought from areas away from the gorges. Hiscock (1988a) concludes that during the LGM people were unable or unwilling to regularly exploit the landscape outside the gorges, probably because hyper-arid conditions reduced returns in those areas but increased the risks of foraging there. Hiscock suggests that in the LGM people at Lawn Hill constricted their foraging range, avoided high-risk environments, and concentrated on exploiting relatively reliable resources. This strategy made it possible for small groups of people to reside in the gorges, at least periodically until resources were exhausted and the area abandoned. Without a refuge, humans at Lawn Hill may not have survived there during the LGM.

In regions without resource-rich gorges, refuges might have taken other forms, such as networks of ephemeral waterholes connected to permanent ones, which would allow people to exploit large tracts of resource-poor lands (Thorley 2001). However, many inland regions did not have refuges of any kind and Hiscock speculates that they were abandoned during the extreme aridity of the LGM.

Glacial abandonments and contractions

Archaeologists have identified many sites in which there is no cultural material during the LGM, signalling abandonment of the local area (Hiscock 1988a; Veth 1989; O'Connor et al. 1993, 1998, 1999). Examples of abandoned localities include the Lake Eyre Basin and Strzelecki Desert (Lampert and Hughes 1987), Nullarbor Plain near Allen's Cave (Hiscock 1988a), Central Australian Ranges near Kulpi Mara (Thorley 1998) and sandy desert regions (Veth 1989; O'Connor et al. 1993, 1998, 1999). The size of abandoned areas is unclear; evidence for abandonment of entire regions is equivocal where only one or two sites have been excavated, and only parts of those regions may have been unused during the LGM. When regions were completely deserted, the process may have been a gradual succession of local abandonments as people retreated from risky landscapes. For instance, abandonment of a long peninsula on the west coast is shown by a cultural hiatus in sites such as Mandu Mandu Creek (Morse 1988, 1996, 1999), Jansz and C99 (Przywolnik 2005), but while some of these sites ceased being used more than 30,000 years ago others continued to be visited until 25,000 years bp, revealing that human use of the region reduced over a prolonged period prior to abandonment at the LGM (Przywolnik 2005).

In a number of inland regions containing refuges, humans persisted through parts of the LGM. These refuges were typically uplands with aquifer-recharged water sources (Hiscock 1984, 1988a; M. A. Smith 1987; Lamb 1996). From these reliable bases people exploited broader territories, commonly contracting their activities to small, better-watered and more reliable resource zones while abandoning high-risk portions of their landscape. For example, at Fern Cave there was increased use of local rock in artefact manufacture during the LGM (Lamb 1996). Similarly, in the northwest, Ben Marwick's (2002) research at Milly's Cave identified an emphasis on manufacturing stone artefacts from local rocks during the LGM, indicating that foragers reduced their territorial range at that time, comparable to the response seen at Lawn Hill.

One of the best examples of territorial reorganization during the LGM comes from the central Australian rock shelter of Puritjarra. Mike Smith (1989c) concluded that in the LGM there had been a contraction of core foraging territory, as foragers exploited relatively predictable resources found in the springs and gorges there. Throughout pre-history people brought ochre to the shelter, and the origin of ochre at each time period informs us of their use of the surrounding landscape. Ochre from the Karrku source, 125 km to the northwest, had been used by humans living at Puritjarra since at least 39,000 years ago (Peterson and Lampert 1985; M. A. Smith et al. 1998). The pattern of ochre procurement changed when extreme LGM conditions began; people reduced their use of material from distant Karrku, substituting it with more local ochres (Figure 3.9). This indicates that people residing at Puritjarra reduced the distance and/or frequency with which they traversed across the sandy desert lands between them and Karrku, perhaps venturing into those environments only after rainfall made them less risky. During the LGM foragers at Puritjarra emphasized resources available in the local and more reliable upland landscape.

The response of inland inhabitants to the LGM tells us a great deal about the nature of hunter-gatherer life at that time. Abandonment of local areas, even entire regions, perhaps the extinction of human groups, demonstrates that Pleistocene foragers were subjected to severe stress in the extreme environmental conditions of the time. Water-abundant patches within ancient desert landscapes sometimes served as refuges which sustained groups through prolonged and unpredictable droughts, but where no adequate refuges existed groups perhaps abandoned their territories and moved to adjoining landscapes with more abundant and predictable resources, a process of inter-regional migration that may have precipitated untold social and economic disruption.

Settlement in Pleistocene Australia

Widespread alterations to the settlement systems of inland foragers during the LGM are an example of the dynamism of Pleistocene life. Although most landscapes were settled before 40,000 years bp, and people were not tethered to the coast for an extended period, human occupation of the continent was neither stable nor constant. Early settlement of inland tracts may have been facilitated by the relative

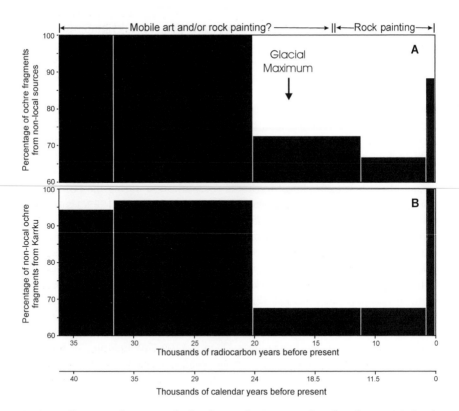

Figure 3.9 Changes in the origins of ochre deposited at Puritjarra (based on data in M. A. Smith et al. 1998: 279): A = percentage of ochre fragments transported from identifiable sources outside the local area (i.e. Smith's Group 1 = Karrku, Group 2 = Ulpunyali and Groups 4 and 5 = Puritjarra); B = percentage of non-local ochre from Karrku.

abundance of surface water. Growing understandings of their landscape led people to develop local economic strategies, which facilitated their adjustment to the gradual drying of inland Australia. Flexible foraging strategies, perhaps relying on lacustrine resources, initially enabled widespread occupation, until hyper-arid inland environments emerged at the LGM. In those harsh contexts people displayed a complex pattern of local abandonment or territorial contraction to refuges. Thorley (1998) argues that nothing in earlier adaptations of inland foragers prepared them for the hyper-arid conditions of the Last Glacial Maximum. This archaeological evidence indicates that early desert economies, subsistence and settlement transformed repeatedly and were different from those that existed in inland regions during the historic period. The nature of early life ways is explored further in the following chapters.

4 Extinction of Pleistocene fauna

When, in 1890, Robert Etheridge wrote a provocative article titled 'Has man a geological history in Australia?' he followed a well-established argument. Nineteenth century European archaeologists used the existence of skeletons or artefacts in layers containing bones of long-extinct animals as evidence that humans lived long ago, when the environment was very different. Some stratigraphic associations of animal bones and human skeletons or artefacts were dubious, better explained by post-depositional perturbations (Chapter 2), but by the 1860s the discovery of sites with little post-depositional disturbance had convinced scientists that, long ago, early humans had lived with animals that are now extinct (Grayson 1983).

This answered one question but raised another. Archaeologists pondered why the ancient animals had disappeared. Had they died out when the climate changed, leaving people to dominate the land, or had those curious animals been exterminated by ancient humans? In the twentieth century some archaeologists proposed a model of human 'overkill', hypothesizing that each time *Homo sapiens* colonized a landmass they had lived as big-game hunters, killing countless large animals until they pushed many species to extinction (Mosimann and Martin 1975; Grayson and Meltzer 2003). After the extinctions people were obliged to change their economic practices, to more sustainable kinds that were observed historically.

Initially proposed for the Americas, but subsequently applied elsewhere, this model stimulated debates about the nature of human impacts on the animals of Pleistocene Australia. While some scientists argued that the earliest humans in Australia were agents of destruction responsible for the extinction of many species of marsupials, others claimed climatic change and habitat loss were enough to explain the extinctions.

Complex categories: 'megafauna' and extinction

The evidence of fossil bones demonstrates that in ancient Australia there were many species that have not survived until the present. Some, like the giant kangaroos (such as *Macropus rufus* and *Macropus giganteus titan*) and wombat (*Phascolonus gigas*), resembled animals still seen in the Australian bush (Figure 4.1A). Other marsupials were similar yet oddly different from living ones (Figure 4.1B). For example, the genus *Sthenurus* contained large kangaroo-like animals which were browsers with

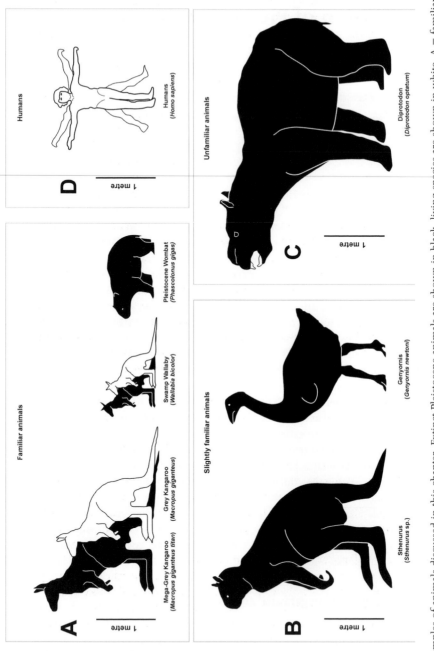

Figure 4.1 Examples of animals discussed in this chapter. Extinct Pleistocene animals are shown in black, living species are shown in white. A = familiar animals because they have descendants or counterparts alive nowadays; B = animals that are slightly familiar because they are similar to present-day animals; C = an example of animals that are unfamiliar because they are unlike any Australian animal now alive; D = an image of a human, one of the megafauna species surviving the Pleistocene. All animals are drawn to the same scale.

stocky bodies and short faces, while tall flightless birds called *Genyornis* were far larger than the emu, weighing up to 100 kg, and had different body and head shapes. Some extinct animals were unlike any living marsupials and these unfamiliar beasts are hard to visualize (Figure 4.1C). The largest was *Diprotodon optatum*, a four-legged browser living in inland areas. They were huge, up to 4 metres long and weighing over 2,500 kg, about the same size as some species of hippopotamus and rhinoceros (Wroe et al. 2003a, 2003b). Another giant marsupial, *Zygomaturus*, lived in southern Australia where it dug for plant foods. *Palorchestes*, a cow-sized quadruped, was probably a specialized browser with a short trunk. The distribution, behaviour and even biology of these species is still poorly known, but the complexity of Australia's ancient ecosystems and animal extinctions is gradually being established.

Late-Pleistocene extinctions of Australian animals have often been discussed as the extinction of 'megafauna', species whose adults were larger than 45 kg. This arbitrary weight was developed in the American context; when applied to Australia it has curious results. Smaller species of *Sthenurus* or *Protemnodon* are often classified as megafauna but may have been below the weight for megafauna; larger still living macropod species, such as red or grey kangaroos, are far heavier than 45 kg but are not conventionally described as megafauna. Additionally, substantial size differences between males and females in many marsupial species mean weight is an unsophisticated distinction. The term 'megafauna' also drew the attention of archaeologists to questions of why species of large animals had gone extinct, but the focus on animal size was misleading. Large body mass may not have made some species vulnerable to extinction through hunting or climatic change; it may have been other features such as their low reproductive rates. Furthermore, tiny terrestrial vertebrates also died out, prompting Tim Flannery (1990) to conclude that a wide variety of animals disappeared in the Pleistocene faunal extinctions, not only 'megafauna'. In fact a diversity of animals disappeared: large and small, marsupials and birds, desert and forest dwellers.

Species vanished from the Australian landscape in two different ways. 'Extinction' occurred when the genetic pattern of a species terminated, often when the last individuals died, leaving no descendants. Animals also disappeared when they evolved to such an extent that they became new species; in most cases distinctly smaller than previously. Many familiar marsupials are smaller versions of their Pleistocene ancestors: red and grey kangaroos become about a third smaller (as measured by tooth size), while swamp wallabies or koalas reduced by about an eighth. Ancestors of modern Australian animals were sometimes staggeringly large. For example, the largest grey kangaroos (*Macropus giganteus*) at Lancefield and Spring Creek were 3 metres tall and weighed nearly 200 kg, approximately twice as heavy as their descendants (Flannery 1994). Such extraordinary size reductions may indicate processes that caused extinctions in other animals. Extinctions and size reductions might have resulted from different processes, coincidentally occurring at the same time, but many researchers have thought that a single process probably explains both phenomena. The proposition that only one process is required to explain all faunal changes created protracted debates as some scientists argued that it was human hunting that affected Australia's animals while others advocated only environmental causes. This propensity to invoke a single cause is seen in models of human over-hunting, or 'overkill'.

Visions of big-game killers

The idea that large animal extinctions in Australia followed the same pattern as the rest of the world implied that extinctions everywhere had the same single cause. Some researchers even suggested that how humans killed megafauna on other continents or islands provided insights into what occurred in Pleistocene Australia (Burney and Flannery 2005; see Wroe and Field 2006); although what happened in other lands actually tells us nothing of the Australian situation. Whether or not any particular species survived initial human hunting depended on many factors, which differed for each species and landmass.

Nevertheless, visions of Australian faunal extinctions have been based on interpretations of the archaeology found in North America and New Zealand. It is not clear that pre-historic humans were responsible for extinctions in those foreign landmasses (Grayson 2001a, 2001b; Grayson and Meltzer 2002, 2003, 2004), but many scientists followed the lead of Paul Martin in advocating that human hunting was the primary cause (Martin 1973, 1984; Mosimann and Martin 1975; Martin and Steadman 1999; Haynes 2002; Fiedel and Haynes 2004). Martin's 'overkill' model claimed that humans were able to rapidly explore new territory by hunting large animals. Computer modelling of hunting patterns and population growth was used to conclude that extinctions occurred within 1,000 to 1,500 years of the arrival of humans in the Americas (Choquenot and Bowman 1998; Alroy 2001a, 2001b; Brook and Bowman 2002, 2004). In New Zealand there was also speedy extinction of large flightless bird species after human colonization (Anderson 1989, 2002; Grayson 2001a). Rapid extinctions following arrival of humans is a key test of the applicability of the overkill model. Such a test requires accurate age-estimates of both the appearance of humans and extinctions of species.

Martin's overkill model additionally predicted that megafauna became extinct because human hunting reduced animal numbers below a critical threshold. Consequently if the model is correct there should be evidence for human hunting and butchering of extinct species, and the targeting of larger individuals within a species. This might take the form of deposits containing bones of extinct animals, disarticulated by butchering, and cut by stone artefacts. Curiously, even in North America where the overkill model is popular, 'kill sites' of this kind are extremely rare (Grayson 2001b; Grayson and Meltzer 2004), and while computer simulations suggest hunting could exterminate species the lack of archaeological evidence for hunting may reveal the reality that, during pre-history and on vast landmasses, hunters were rarely so devastating (Wroe et al. 2004).

Overkill theorists assumed the density of hunters and their hunting success was great enough to have had significant impacts on the prey population. However, the number of hunters and their skills are not directly visible; archaeologists extrapolate from other observations. For instance, specialized stone-tipped weaponry has been used to infer hunting effectiveness, while butchered bones have been used to indicate targeted species. Proponents of overkill also assumed that extinct species were susceptible to hunting, making difficult-to-test assertions about animal density, their reproduction rate, and their 'naivety' towards new predators.

Visions of big-game killers invading new lands and hunting species to extinction are powerful and have influenced discussions of Australia's Pleistocene faunal extinctions. Although human colonists were new and clever predators who could have altered the dynamics of Australian ecosystems, their impacts on fauna, particularly megafauna, depended on many factors and the extinction or survival of any species was not inevitable. What knowledge do we have of Pleistocene hunters and their prey in Australia?

Images of Australian overkills

The idea of big-game hunting colonizers rapidly massacring Australian megafauna was given new impetus in the 1990s by Tim Flannery, who suggested that ecological perspectives on Australia's Pleistocene extinctions implicated humans (Flannery 1990, 1994, 1999; Flannery and Roberts 1999). He argued that each species responded differently to intense human hunting. In some species heavy culling of the largest adults resulted in extinction, but in other species human targeting of larger individuals gave a selective advantage to smaller animals which survived and reproduced, resulting in size reduction of that species. Flannery therefore hypothesized that human hunting of big game could explain both the extinction and size decreases of Pleistocene fauna. He suggested that extinctions occurred almost instantly across the continent following the coming of humans, a proposition that predicts not only a similar antiquity for colonization and mass extinctions but also evidence of kill sites and selective hunting of larger animals. Flannery and others sought this kind of evidence but none has emerged.

Australia's complete lack of megafauna kill sites is a major problem for Flannery's overkill model. None of the older archaeological sites has evidence for butchery and consumption of the large extinct species. If rapid expansion of big-game hunters was fed by the exploitation of megafauna archaeologists should find camp sites and kill sites containing the bones of extinct species. Preservation of bones in sites more than 40,000 years old is often poor, but there are archaeological deposits of that age with bone and they typically contain cultural debris but no bones of extinct species. There is no archaeological evidence of an initial phase of big-game hunting.

Flannery (1994) initially dealt with this lack of evidence by hypothesizing that human movement across the continent had been so quick that megafauna were exterminated without leaving archaeological traces. This desperate argument is unsatisfactory; it used an absence of information to suggest big-game hunting was systematic and intense, and Flannery offered no reason why kill sites in all environments have vanished, when other kinds of sites have survived.

Overkill advocates even claimed that archaeological evidence was unnecessary since modern hunters always target larger animals and ancient hunters would have used similar strategies (Flannery 1990). This analogy is weak. Many foragers now live in landscapes without large-sized species and only a small fraction of their meat comes from large animals, showing that targeting of big animals is not universal (Wroe and Field 2006). Furthermore, the present-day focus on meat, and on large animals, varies with climatic conditions including temperature, suggesting that hunting behaviour probably changed through time (Torrence 1983; Kelly 1995). Research in the Old World has shown that increasingly Pleistocene hunters targeted small, rapidly reproducing game rather than the largest animals available, and this might have been the pattern of hunting in Australia (Stiner et al. 1999; Stiner 2001). Ancient people colonizing Australia may not have made the same choices as modern hunters; researchers should be careful not to presume that ancient and modern hunters acted identically. Perhaps the earliest Australian foragers were not technologically equipped to hunt the largest of the extinct animals (Wroe et al. 2006), but if early hunters did not concentrate on megafauna it was probably not because of technological inadequacies but because the economic and social incentives for such a focus were not strong. Modern hunters sometimes target large game, not because of economic necessity, but to obtain social advantages (Hawkes 1991; Hawkes et al. 2001), and the situation of colonists need not have been the same. Evidence discussed in Chapter 6 shows that early hunters focused on reliable and abundant game rather than on scarce, large animals.

Another claim was that extinct species were easy to kill. For example, Diprotodons have been described as clumsy, lumbering and 'naive' to predators, making them easy targets for ancient hunters. This image of vulnerability has frequently been reinforced by comparisons between Australia's Pleistocene extinctions and the extinctions of flightless birds on islands such as New Zealand (Grayson 2001a). However, such images are based more on wishful thinking than on scientific investigations. Stephen Wroe and his colleagues have presented several kinds of evidence that indicate large, extinct marsupials should not be considered to be defenseless idiots (Wroe and Field 2006). Modern kangaroos display antipredator behaviours, even when they are exposed to a predator with which they are unfamiliar (Blumstein 2002; Blumstein and Daniel 2002; Blumstein et al. 2001, 2002). They can learn about and avoid new predators within a short time, even within a generation, making it unlikely that hunters could have exterminated species before they could respond. Furthermore, within Australia there have always been large and effective predators. Prior to, perhaps during, human colonization predators such as the 100 kg marsupial lion (*Thylacoleo carnifex*) and the 100–150 kg giant lizard *Megalania prisca* hunted in the Australian bush. Tooth marks on the bones of Diprotodons demonstrate that the marsupial lion attacked even the largest herbivores. Hence the large extinct marsupial herbivores were familiar with ferocious carnivores and equipped with anti-predator strategies long before human hunters entered the country.

Similarity in the antiquity of colonization and faunal extinctions is the most fundamental argument offered in support of the overkill model. When Flannery began advocating human overkill, the chronology of Australian extinctions and colonization was very poorly known. However, he had reason to believe that humans entered the continent when some of the now extinct species still roamed the land. For example, Ron Vanderwal and Richard Fullagar (1989) had shown that

Figure 4.2 Location of key sites in debates about the role of humans in the extinction of Australian megafauna. The dark area represents the Lake Eyre catchment.

a *Diprotodon* tooth found at Spring Creek had cut marks made when the bone was fresh, demonstrating that people coexisted with that species (Figure 4.2). By 1990 radiometric analyses suggested that some species of megafauna had survived until 35,000 years ago (Flannery 1990). However, this evidence was too imprecise to determine whether they became extinct immediately after the arrival of humans or whether humans had lived in Australia for a long period without having a substantial impact on species that later became extinct.

New dating techniques were applied at several sites, and the results revealed that the antiquity of extinctions is uncertain. For example, at Spring Creek Tim Flannery and Beth Gott (1984) initially thought that *Diprotodon*, *Protemnodon* and the mega-grey kangaroo (*Macropus giganteus titan*) survived until 23,750 (23,000–24,200) years bp. Additional research at the site revised its likely antiquity to 31,500–40,000 years ago (White and Flannery 1995). Similarly, radiocarbon analysis of the bone bed at Lancefield initially indicated an age of 24,000–30,000 years bp (Gillespie et al. 1978) but techniques such as ESR and amino-acid racemization later indicated that *Diprotodon* bones were substantially greater than 30,000 years bp (van Huet et al. 1998; J. Dortch 2004). These kinds of results encouraged the idea that extinctions occurred soon after the human colonization of Australia, just as Flannery had expected (e.g. van Huet et al. 1998; Pate et al. 2002).

However, the stratigraphic association of fossils was often ambiguous. This was obvious at some sites containing extraordinarily young age-estimates for megafauna bones. Such sites probably resulted from reworking of older deposits. Ancient bones eroded from one place and redeposited with recent archaeological material gave a false impression that extinct species survived until a few millennia ago. These deposits made researchers wary of accepting dates from sites with a few fragmentary bones; a concern that applies to sites from all time periods, not merely recent ones. For example, Devil's Lair cave contained bones from extinct species in layers that also contained artefacts. Examination of the bones revealed they had sand grains from another environment cemented onto their surfaces, demonstrating that they were reworked from a different deposit and were older than the archaeological levels in which they were found (Balme 1980). Those bones may have come from species already extinct when humans arrived in the region. At Devil's Lair the stratigraphic location of megafauna bone fragments was not a reliable indication of their age. Aware of this problem some researchers began their investigations by excluding sites they thought contained unreliable stratigraphic associations (Roberts et al. 2001; C. N. Johnson 2005).

Tim Flannery's persistent advocacy of the overkill model appeared to be rewarded when new age-estimates were published. In a detailed study at Lake Eyre, Gifford Miller and John Magee used the chemical composition of ancient eggshells to estimate when they had been laid. Two species of large birds laid eggs there: one was the emu, *Dromaius novaehollandiae*, which still lives in the region, and the other was the extinct flightless bird *Genyornis newtoni*. Emu shells were laid in all time periods during the past 120,000 years, but *Genyornis* shells stopped being laid about 45,000 years ago, indicating their local extinction at that time (Miller et al. 1999; M. I. Bird et al. 2003; Miller et al. 2005a). Miller and Magee believed that *Genyornis* extinction occurred during a mild environmental period shortly after the arrival of humans in Australia, and that human occupation of Lake Eyre led to the local extinction of *Genyornis*. This conclusion was striking but it dealt with only one extinct species in a single region.

A study of many species in many regions was completed in 2001 by a team of researchers led by Richard Roberts and Tim Flannery (Roberts et al. 2001). They concluded that all megafauna species died out 46,000 years ago in a continent-wide extinction. Their study of bones from 28 palaeontological and archaeological localities estimated the age of animals through optical luminescence analyses of sediments near or adhering to bones, supplemented by ^{230}Th/^{234}U studies of the crystallization of flowstones present in some localities. A wide range of age-estimates were obtained, but Roberts and Flannery argued that some were unreliable. In particular they dismissed deposits in which skeletons were not articulated in their anatomical position, on the assumption that disarticulated remains signalled disturbance. By excluding disarticulated samples, and any more than 55,000 years old, Roberts and Flannery argued that species such as Diprotodon, Procoptodon, Protemnodon and Simosthenurus became extinct between 40,000 and 51,000 years ago, most likely at 46,000 years bp.

While acknowledging that climate changed at that time, Roberts and Flannery argued that humans were primarily responsible for the extermination of megafauna. They presented two arguments blaming humans, similar to those previously offered by Flannery (1990, 1994). First, they thought an extinction event at 46,000 years bp occurred shortly after the arrival of humans, as predicted by the overkill model. Second, they believed that simultaneous continent-wide extinctions, before the extreme climatic conditions of the LGM, were not consistent with the idea that climate change alone caused the extinctions; instead it convinced them that widespread ecosystem disruption followed the appearance of people.

Was this announcement proof of the culpability of human hunting in the extermination of many Pleistocene terrestrial animal species? In reality the interpretations of Roberts and Flannery, and of Miller and Magee, provided evidence against an overkill model. If humans entered Australia before 50,000 years bp, and Roberts and Flannery accepted this, but widespread extinctions did not take place until 46,000 years ago, there was 5,000–10,000 years of coexistence between humans and the extinct species. This time span exceeds predicted periods of co-existence generated by proponents of the overkill model, indicating that megafauna extinctions at 46,000 years ago were probably not simply due to the colonization of humans.

More significantly, the claim that many species became extinct across Australia 46,000 years ago is not reliable; it was re-examined by independent teams of scientists, with devastating results (Field and Fullagar 2001; Wroe and Field 2001a, 2001b, 2006; Brook and Bowman 2002; Wroe et al. 2002). The sample used by Roberts and Flannery was too small to give them a good chance of identifying the last surviving individuals or groups, or variation between regions in the date of extinctions, or even the timing of declines in the population of any species. Furthermore, all sites younger than 46,000 years ago had some disarticulated skeletons and Roberts and Flannery arrived at their conclusion only by excluding those sites from their interpretation.

Roberts and Flannery reasoned that disarticulated skeletons indicated disturbance. However, dismembered skeletons also result from human butchering and consumption. If disarticulation at sites less than 46,000 years old resulted from human butchering the lack of complete skeletons merely indicates ongoing human exploitation of ancient species, not their extinction. This explanation for disarticulation is consistent with the available age-estimates for extinct species, as shown in Figure 4.3. Remains of extinct species have been found in many contexts younger than the period 40–60,000 years ago. Very recent dates probably result from disturbance within a site, but Stephen Wroe and his team carried out computer simulations, and discovered that the pattern in Figure 4.3 was very unlikely to have been produced if all extinctions took place between 40,000 and 50,000 years ago (Wroe et al. 2004). Pleistocene faunal extinctions did not occur at the same time everywhere, nor did they take place immediately after human colonization. In some

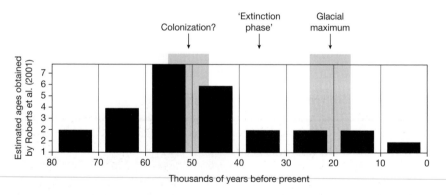

Figure 4.3 Number of age-estimates on samples of extinct megafauna per 10,000 years (data from Roberts et al. 2001, after Wroe et al. 2004).

regions species of large animals coexisted with humans for more than 20,000 years before they became extinct. When combined with the lack of kill sites, this demonstrates that the overkill model does not work in Australia. Archaeological investigations at Cuddie Springs, one of the best studied sites with extinct fauna, confirm this interpretation.

Cuddie Springs and the extinction of overkill hypotheses

For more than 15 years Judith Field excavated and studied bones from Cuddie Springs, a site that illustrates the nature of archaeological evidence for the extinction of megafauna. Cuddie Springs is significant because Field found evidence of long coexistence of megafauna and humans, and nothing to indicate that megafauna was destroyed by hunting overkill.

Cuddie Springs is located on a riverine plain, where it is currently a small claypan which sometimes fills to create a small swamp for short periods (Figure 4.4). This is now a semi-arid landscape, receiving highly variable rainfall and supporting woodland of scattered eucalypts, saltbush and grasses. However, pollen evidence reveals that when people first used the area 40,000 years ago or more, the environment was very different. At that time a large, full lake surrounded by open shrublands provided excellent conditions for large animals such as Diprotodon (Dodson et al. 1993). In this landscape many species of marsupial megafauna and humans lived together for a long period.

Stone artefacts, providing evidence for early human occupation at Cuddie Springs, were found in stratum 6, a series of silt and clay lenses about 33,000–40,000 years old and 1–2 metres below the modern ground surface (Field and Dodson 1999; Field et al. 2001; Field et al. 2002). In this layer Field and her team recovered bones of many large species including Diprotodon, Genyornis (Figure 4.5), Sthenurus, and the kangaroo Macropus giganteus titan. Some scientists contend that bones at this site had been stratigraphically jumbled (Roberts et al. 2001; Gillespie and Brook 2006), but it seems these concerns were unwarranted (Field and Fullagar

Figure 4.4 Cuddie Springs claypan. (Courtesy of J. Field.)

Figure 4.5 Excavations at Cuddie Springs revealing a dense concentration of limb bones from extinct *Genyornis* in a lower archaeological layer (SU6B/AL1). (Courtesy of J. Field.)

2001; Trueman et al. 2005). Stone artefacts and bones of megafauna were not spread through a homogenized deposit but rather were sealed together by well-defined ancient land surfaces rich in rocks, through which post-depositional movement of objects would be rare. Pollen, charcoal and even rare elements within the sediments all indicate that the broad stratigraphic sequence, although imprecisely dated, is real. Stratum 6 contains both human artefacts and megafauna bones deposited over a period of perhaps 7,000 years, evidence interpreted as showing creatures such as Diprotodon and Genyornis coexisted with humans for hundreds of generations (Field and Dodson 1999; Trueman et al. 2005).

When the lake partially dried out during droughts it became marshy, trapping animals which drank there. As a result large animals such as Diprotodon and Genyornis may have been stranded and died naturally at this location without any human hunting. Field and Dodson (1999) suggest it is unlikely that all large animal remains could be explained in this way, but there is no evidence they were killed by humans. On the contrary, partially articulated skeletons and carnivore tooth marks in bones indicate that humans were minimally involved in the deaths of many of the animals. Archaeological evidence in the form of small numbers of artefacts is consistent with early human occupation being at a low intensity; foragers visited the site infrequently and many animals may have died in the marshy spring between human visits. Researchers working on the site suggested that humans surely scavenged meat from these huge carcasses, even if they did not actually hunt the animals. Certainly stone artefacts used to cut meat have been found scattered among the bones of megafaunal species, but no Diprotodon or Genyornis bones were cut by a stone tool. Perhaps the absence of cut marks reflects infrequent human visitation, or that meat was so abundant on carcasses that people rarely cut them deeply. In any case, existing information from Cuddie Springs suggests that human hunting or scavenging of these large animals was not intensive. Cuddie Springs contains evidence of prolonged coexistence of people and megafauna but it is not a 'kill site' documenting over-hunting. To understand the context of extinctions, if they were not caused by humans, Field and her colleagues studied the environment in which humans lived and megafauna died at the site.

The most remarkable evidence from Cuddie Springs concerns the circumstances in which species of megafauna became extinct. The deep bone deposit at the site preserved a record of animals that died there before and after the arrival of people (Figure 4.6). When humans arrived at Cuddie Springs many species of megafauna were already extinct in the local region. For example, bones of the giant reptile Megalania, the cow-sized marsupial Zygomaturus, and the browser Palorchestes have been recovered from the pre-human strata of the site, but these animals are not represented in the very large collections of bone found in the archaeological levels. This illustrates a trend found throughout Australia over the last million years, particularly in the past 200,000 years, of ongoing extinctions of large animals (Wroe et al. 2004; Wroe and Field 2006). Those extinctions resulted from environmental changes, since humans were not present for much of that time.

Furthermore, after humans arrived at Cuddie Springs extinctions of megafauna did not occur at a single time but instead took place over thousands of years. Field

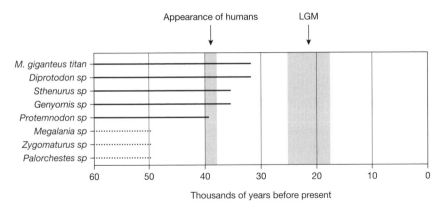

Figure 4.6 Approximate time spans of selected extinct species at Cuddie Springs (data from Field and Dodson 1999; Field pers. com. 2006). Broken lines indicate less precise chronology. Appearance of humans at the site based on the stratigraphically lowest artefacts.

recovered some species such as *Protemnodon* only in the lowest archaeological level, while *Genyornis*, *Diprotodon*, *Procoptodon*, *Sthenurus* and *Macropus giganteus titan* were present in higher, later stratigraphic levels, documenting the progressive extinction of megafauna species during a period of ongoing climatic change.

Long before the LGM there were significant alterations to the vegetation around Cuddie Springs. From 40,000 to 35,000 years ago Chenopodiacae pollen, indicating shrubland, was gradually replaced with pollen from grass, herbs and aquatic plants. Field interpreted this as evidence for the progressive transformation of local environments from dry shrublands to moister grasslands (Field et al. 2002). This change favoured grazers such as red kangaroos (*Macropus rufus*) and flexible feeders such as Emus (*Dromaius novaehollandiae*), both of which persisted in the region. However, species of large marsupials such as *Diprotodon* and *Genyornis* were poorly equipped for a grassland environment that increasingly dominated the area, and they became locally extinct.

The Cuddie Springs evidence demonstrates that extinctions of megafauna such as *Diprotodon* did not occur either at the moment humans arrived in the area or during the extreme aridity of the glacial maximum. Instead the phase of large marsupial extinctions continued throughout the intervening period (30,000–40,000 years bp) as habitats were reconfigured to form grasslands. It was not the extraordinary and rapid events, such as the arrival of humans or the LGM, that drove species to the brink; instead it was more subtle and gradual dynamics of habitat transformations which created conditions that gave an advantage to some species and disadvantaged others. This lesson helps us consider the role of environmental change in the extinction of Australian megafauna.

Environmental change and animal extinctions?

Although the extinctions that occurred before humans arrived indicate that environmental factors were often responsible it is not always easy to identify which specific ecological changes were important in the demise of extinct animals. The combination of many, subtle environmental changes, perhaps different for each species, inhibits scientists from making simple statements about the causes of ancient extinctions; although it appears that human hunting was not involved as the principal agent. For this reason researchers have sought to understand which environmental processes contributed to late-Pleistocene extinctions.

Although long-term climatic trends probably triggered a series of extinctions, immediate causes for the extinction of each species may have been different. Some species were inherently at higher risk of extinction than others; larger extinct marsupials probably had low reproduction rates (C. N. Johnson 2002), a characteristic that could be significant during periods of extreme climatic fluctuations, such as drought events. Different physiological responses of animals to environmental stresses also affect the way species cope, or fail to cope, with changes in their surroundings. For example, lower water needs and earlier maturation or reproduction of smaller-bodied macropods gave smaller individuals an evolutionary advantage during successive droughts, resulting not only in the survival of a species but also in greater reproductive success of small and rapidly maturing individuals, leading to a reduction of its size (Main 1978). Decreased size of individuals in any species may also reflect a well-known biological pattern, called Bergmann's Rule, which describes a relationship between temperature and animal size in response to their heat retention or heat loss needs. As climate became warmer following the LGM smaller body mass would have been advantageous, and so reductions of animal size would be predicted. In conjunction these kinds of factors created chronological and regional variations in the response of each species. This explains the discovery that, at Cuddie Springs and other sites, extinctions were a prolonged process, not a single event.

Another lesson from Cuddie Springs is that the nature of environmental change was as important for the survival or extinction of species as the extremity of climatic shifts. Archaeologists often surrendered to the notion that only the extraordinarily severe conditions of the glacial maximum could have caused so many kinds of animals to die out (Flannery 1990, 1994; C. N. Johnson 2005; see also Barnovsky et al. 2004). The LGM may have been the driest of all glacial cycles and was undoubtedly a stressful period, but there is no reason that the frequency of animal extinctions should have been proportional to the magnitude of changes in temperature or effective precipitation. Small climatic changes might have created conditions that produced catastrophic extinctions, while larger climatic shifts might have intensified but not otherwise altered existing circumstances, resulting in low extinction rates. As Jim Bowler (1998) explained, it is useful to distinguish between past climatic conditions and the landscape response to those conditions. This idea represents Bowler's answer to archaeologists who asked why, if environmental change was responsible for extinctions, those extinctions did not happen during earlier climatic cycles. His answer is that previous climatic periods did not always create landscape responses of the kind or magnitude seen in the past 60,000 years.

The gradual disappearance of species reflects a climatic trend towards drier and cooler conditions that began long before the initiation of the LGM; in fact deterioration in ancient climate began about the time humans reached Australia. This is shown in Figure 4.7, which displays a line through the lowest points in the oxygen isotope curve, a gross indicator of long-term trends in temperature, to reveal progressive declines from 50,000–17,000 years ago. Climatic deterioration prior to about 30,000 years bp was not as rapid or extreme as in later millennia, but nonetheless there were noticeable changes in climatic conditions throughout a long period in which large animal species became extinct.

This trend towards drier and cooler conditions triggered changes in vegetation, gradually expanding the arid and semi-arid zones of Australia, and altering the distribution of surface water and the availability of grasslands and shrublands that provided foods for herbivores (e.g. Gröcke 1997; Wroe and Field 2006). Substantial restructuring of vegetation communities across dry, interior Australia occurred approximately 40,000–50,000 years ago, recorded in pollen sequences (e.g. Kershaw and Nanson 1993), carbon isotope ratios in marsupial bones (Gröcke 1997) and eggshells (Miller et al. 1999). These changes benefited some kinds of animals but reduced the populations and survival prospects of others. Many extinct megafauna species were browsers; those with less diverse or flexible diets were so

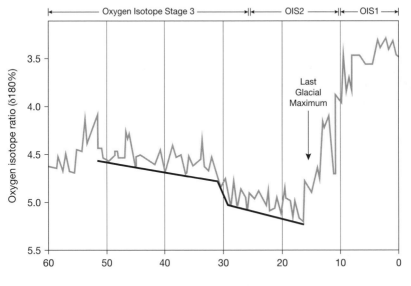

Figure 4.7 Oxygen isotope curve for Stages 1–3, showing the variable but directional trend in climate from before 50,000 until the LGM. Smoothed oxygen isotope data from Shackleton and Pisias (1985). Black unbroken line indicates the trend in minimum values of oxygen isotope ratios.

disadvantaged they could not survive. This was Field's conclusion at Cuddie Springs and the same process has been identified elsewhere.

In the Lake Eyre region there are well-documented sequences of environmental change during this period of cooling. From 100,000–45,000 years ago the climate was similar to, but cooler than, the present day (Nanson et al. 1991). Lake Eyre often contained water until about 60,000 years ago when it began to dry out. By 35,000 years ago Lake Eyre had become almost permanently dry (Magee and Miller 1998). About 45,000 years ago the Australian monsoon, bringing rains to the lake catchment, became less effective and vegetation changed (B. J. Johnson et al. 1999). Those changes were echoed in the isotopic composition of emu eggshells (Figure 4.8). Emus declined sharply in number about 55,000–60,000 years bp as the drying trend was initiated, and they adapted to a substantial change in food about 45,000 years ago, switching from a broad-based diet of arid grasses and shrubs to a more narrow exploitation of desert scrub. Emus survived because they were less specialized, opportunistic feeders, able to cope with the loss of grassland habitat and instead exploit the scrubs that became the dominant vegetation. But the giant flightless bird *Genyornis* had a more limited diet than the emus, requiring some access to grassland (C_4 plants) foods. When arid grasslands disappeared from the region 45,000 years ago *Genyornis* became locally extinct. The most likely cause for the extinction of *Genyornis* was therefore the loss of suitable food supply, as the region was transformed from one with abundant surface water and scattered grasslands to dry, less diverse shrublands.

Habitat loss at Cuddie Springs and at Lake Eyre was the primary culprit for Pleistocene faunal extinctions. The different chronology of extinction, in

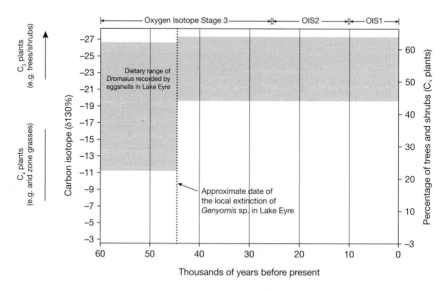

Figure 4.8 A graph showing the timing of a major change in the diet of emus (*Dromaius novaehollandiae*) living in the Lake Eyre region of central Australia during the past 60,000 years (data from Miller et al. 2005).

each species and each region, probably reflects variable local manifestations of continental-wide climatic trends. A sequence of extinctions can be predicted: species with specific habitat and dietary requirements would have become extinct before species with more habitat flexibility, and extinctions in more fragile ecosystems such as Lake Eyre probably occurred before those in other environments. Tests of these predictions already show that habitat loss rather than human hunting led to many changes in Australia's fauna.

Extinction of non-megafaunal animals on the Darling Downs

Gilbert Price discovered fossil deposits in the banks of Kings Creek, eastern Australia. He found the remains of megafauna species such as *Diprotodon*, *Protemnodon* and *Macropus giganteus titan*. In the lower of two layers, called 'horizon D', fossils were estimated to be 48,000 (46,500–50,000) years old (Price 2005a; Price and Sobbe 2005; Price et al. 2005). This estimate is near the limit of reliable radiocarbon analyses and Price considers that it underestimates the age of the sediments. Higher in the bank another fossil-rich layer, 'horizon B', is estimated to be 44,000 years old (Price 2005a). Animals present in the lower layer are absent from the higher one, indicating that extinctions gradually occurred between 44,000 and 48,000 years bp (Price 2005b; Price and Sobbe 2005).

Extinctions at Kings Creek resulted from habitat change rather than human hunting, a conclusion Price (2002, 2005a) reached because small animals such as bandicoot species and ground-dwelling and burrowing frogs went extinct at the same time as large animals. The species of small animals that became extinct were sensitive to ecological change but were not targets of intensive human hunting, revealing that it was habitat change that caused the extinctions. The diversity of frog and bandicoot fossils indicates that a mosaic of savanna, scrubby vine thickets, closed forest, open woodland, watercourses and lagoons were destroyed by growing aridity, creating more uniform grassland environments without suitable habitats for many species (Price and Sobbe 2005; Price et al. 2005). This pattern was as disadvantageous to specialized small animals as it was to large megafauna browsers. Species unable to exist in the transformed habitats became extinct, irrespective of whether they were giants or tiny marsupials.

A role for humans in environmental change?

The demise of the overkill theory does not mean that humans played no role in the extinction of some species. During prolonged deterioration of climate the arrival of humans added a predator to a landscape already becoming marginal for some kinds of animal. Occasional human hunting of those species, or even human activities that disrupted their foraging or breeding patterns, may have added to the factors working against their survival. It is therefore possible that even low levels of human hunting contributed to the extinction of some species.

Several scientists suggested that it was humanly induced habitat change which added to the difficulties of animal species struggling with environmental conditions.

In particular, some researchers attributed late-Pleistocene extinctions to the frequent and systematic burning of vegetation by people. The popularity of this idea owes much to Rhys Jones' (1969, 1979) conviction that human colonists of Australia employed fire to create vegetation regimes, in ways similar to Aboriginal use of fire in the historical period.

Miller and Magee hypothesized that systematic human burning around Lake Eyre was a primary cause of vegetation change (Miller et al. 1999, 2005a, 2005b). They argued that human burning prior to 45,000 years bp led to the collapse of previously stable ecosystems and extinctions; at Lake Eyre they thought burning reduced mosaic grasslands and shrublands, resulting in the extinction of Genyornis. The key problem with their suggestion was that archaeologists have no evidence of human fires at Lake Eyre at that time period, nor even that humans were in the region (Hughes and Hiscock 2005). Furthermore, Miller and Magee argued that no climatic change explained the vegetation shifts, yet their own evidence demonstrates that 45,000 years ago fundamental alterations in the pattern of monsoon rain occurred, creating the environmental transformations. Similar environmental changes in other regions indicate that long-term drying, not human activities, was the main cause of habitat modifications (Longmore and Heijnis 1999). Natural climatic trends explain habitat alterations and there is little reason to think that humans were responsible for the local Genyornis extinction.

The idea that human burning triggered megafauna extinctions was reversed by Tim Flannery (1994), who proposed that human hunting caused near instantaneous extinctions of very large herbivores, which left vast amounts of uneaten vegetation in the landscape. He suggested that unused vegetation fuelled large natural fires and ancient hunters developed 'fire stick farming' to reduce the devastation of uncontrolled natural fires. However, Flannery's theory is not supported: there is no evidence for rapid human overkill of megafauna; instead they disappeared gradually from the Australian continent and their extinction has not been shown to precede changes to human fire regimes.

Attempts to explain Pleistocene extinctions as a result of the use of fire by early foragers assumed they acted in much the same way as historic Aborigines, a proposition that is not consistent with our knowledge of both environmental and archaeological changes (C. N. Johnson and Wroe 2003). Human activities probably altered Australian landscapes during the Pleistocene, but it is unwise to assume that they did so in the same ways and to the same extent observed in the historic period. Our failure to identify dramatic human impacts on Australian megafauna and vegetation is one more indication that human life ways in the Pleistocene were unlike those observed in the historic period.

The last large animal?

By the end of the Pleistocene the largest terrestrial animal (substantially above 50 kg as an adult) still existing in Australia was Homo sapiens. If climatically induced habitat change was the main cause of most Pleistocene faunal extinctions then those environmental alterations might also have affected human foraging. Evidence of landscape abandonments and territorial contractions, discussed in Chapter 3, is the most obvious reflection of human responses to the trend towards drying as the LGM approached. It has been suggested that some human groups struggled during the LGM, and some even went extinct (Hiscock 1988a), but the diversity of landscapes settled by people helped them survive.

Persistence of humans throughout OIS3 and OIS2, when many species of large animal disappeared, reveals the resilience of humans to environmental fluctuations and harsh conditions. Pleistocene people were able to exploit many different foods, and it is likely that by at least 30,000–35,000 years ago many foraging groups had obtained a detailed knowledge of the resources available to them. Human adjustments to resource changes were facilitated by the ability not only to learn about their environment but also to effectively transmit that information using language. Furthermore, by hunting, people did not always need to find ways to procure and digest changing plant foods; by eating meat they could exploit the abilities of other animals to convert plant matter into human food (Hiscock 1994). However, before the end of the LGM foragers were also accessing plant foods by using elaborate preparation and storage techniques (Chapter 6). One technique that was employed by some foragers during the period of climatic deterioration was the use of grinding stones as an aide to processing seeds and other low return but reliable plant foods. Grindstones have been recovered in Pleistocene archaeological sites and may have assisted humans to survive in conditions that were devastating for other species. At Cuddie Springs (Fullagar and Field 1997) and the Willandra Lakes (H. Allen 1998) there were greater numbers of grindstones, and by implication plant processing, at periods of local environmental change. This indicates that diversification of diet and greater emphasis on seeds was a common response to drier and more variable climates. Some archaeologists argue that a trend towards economies incorporating seed processing was initiated during the past 35,000 years in response to greater stresses associated with increased aridity and the expansion of grasslands across the interior. These kinds of cultural and technological activities acted as buffers against deteriorating conditions and were the uniquely human response to habitat change. Technological, economic and social patterns of Pleistocene life are explored further in Chapter 6.

5   Who were the first Australians?

Following the announcement of Darwin's theory of evolution, researchers tried to understand ancient humans by examining supposedly 'primitive' features in the biology and culture of indigenous peoples around the world. Thomas Huxley (1864) and others began looking at crania of recent Aborigines, thinking they preserved characteristics that would also be found in the ancestors of Europeans. When the first fossil human was found in Australia, the encrusted skull from Talgai on the Darling Downs (Figure 5.1), anatomists Grafton Elliot Smith and Arthur Keith used it to argue that early Australians resembled the fossils of Europe, most infamously the Piltdown skull. Since that time more ancient human remains have been unearthed, but questions about the biological ancestry of Australian Aboriginal people proved difficult to answer.

Figure 5.1 Photograph of a cast of the Talgai skull.

Interpretations of archaeological skeletons were complicated by the observation that some ancient individuals had different cranial features from others. Two distinct explanations for cranial variation were offered. One proposal was that fossil skeletons came from individuals descended from separate populations who had originated in different places in East Asia, and arrived in Australia at different times. An alternative proposal claimed that variations in human crania during Australian pre-history reflected adaptive changes made by descendants of a single founding population in the large, environmentally diverse continent. Archaeological evidence, in the form of ancient human skeletons, and genetic signatures of recent Aborigines, are two important sources of information with which these competing interpretations can be evaluated.

Studying fossil skeletons

Archaeologists face many technical difficulties in studying fossil skeletons, and these difficulties should be reflected in reconstructions of ancient human biology. For example, despite the increased number of fossil human skeletons found, they are a miniscule sample of the humans who lived over the past 50,000 years. Each of the two hundred or so known skeletons older than 10,000 years bp could be the only representative of about ten generations of people living across the entire continent! This sample of Pleistocene-aged skeletons is concentrated in the southeast of the landmass (Figure 5.2), partly because dunes and lunettes with good bone preservation are abundant there. This geographical bias reminds archaeologists that they have a limited vista of pre-historic biological variation.

The rarity of fossil skeletons is further complicated because they are often only partially preserved and cannot contribute reliable information about the questions posed by archaeologists. For example, Talgai was a juvenile male whose cranium had been crushed and encrusted with carbonate. While the original location and approximate age of 13,420 (13,380–13,640) years bp of the skull was established (Macintosh 1952; Oakley et al. 1975), it is difficult to interpret and few archaeological studies utilized the specimen. For similar reasons many of the more than 130 skeletons found near Lake Mungo have not been used; fewer than 15 have enough of the skull preserved to employ them in analyses (S. G. Webb 1989a). As a result of poor preservation, only a small number of skeletons have been central to investigations of the biological characteristics of early humans in Australia.

Small samples of preserved bodies are only one difficulty for archaeologists. Few Pleistocene skeletons have been precisely dated, making it hard to trace ancestry through time (Pardoe 1993). Synthetic statements of chronological change in human anatomy have been based on stratigraphic estimates of age, sometimes even on assumptions that skeletons in the same region were of the same age. These inferences created potentially unreliable statements about the chronology of human evolution. Even when radiometric age-estimates were obtained they were not always trustworthy; the antiquity of some skeletons has been re-evaluated in recent years (Bowler et al. 2003; Stone and Cupper 2003), and further changes to their estimated age can be expected.

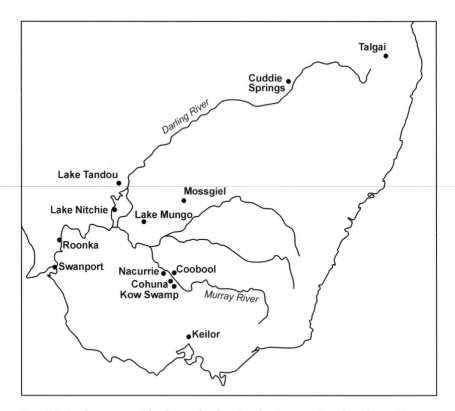

Figure 5.2 Southeastern mainland Australia showing the sites mentioned in Chapter 5.

A different problem confronting researchers is the lack of accurate and repeatable measurements of ancient skeletons. It has rarely been possible for scientists to reinspect and remeasure ancient skeletons found in Australia. Modern politics of control over those bones has meant they have sometimes been reburied or hidden, so only one or two researchers might have studied each skeleton. If doubts about a measurement arise it cannot be checked for error, and disputes about what skeletons look like result (Sim and Thorne 1990, 1994, 1995; Brown 1994a, 1995, 2000a, 2000b; Thorne and Curnoe 2000). Disputes about skeletons can be critical. For instance, very different models of Australia's past have been based on whether WLH3 was male or female, yet researchers do not agree on the evidence.

Fossil Australian skeletons

Despite the many technical problems the biology of ancient humans in Australia is revealed by the many skeletons studied in detail. Two skeletons from Lake Mungo have been fundamental in debates about human pre-history. Called WLH1 and WLH3 these individuals are the oldest human remains in Australia, dating to about 40,000 years bp (Bowler et al. 2003). WLH1 was described by Alan Thorne as the

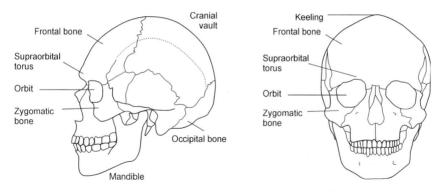

Figure 5.3 Guide to the terminology of some features on the human skull.

remains of a young female, short and slightly built (Bowler et al. 1970). Her cranium was repeatedly broken and charred in one of the earliest cremations known. Bone shrinks and distorts when burned, making it hard to reconstruct the original size and shape of the skull, and some statistical analyses that have used WLH1 are in error because the bone shrinkage was not adequately considered (Brown 2006). The woman's skull was delicate, her teeth were small, her brow ridges (called supraorbital torus) small, and her forehead rounded (Figure 5.3).

A second important burial, WLH3, was found a short distance from WLH1. As discussed in Chapter 2, this body was placed in a grave dug into the sands of the Lake Mungo lunette about 43,000 years ago. When discovered the left side of the skull was exposed by erosion (Figure 5.4), but the face and right side of the skull was poorly preserved. Since the mandible and post-cranial skeleton is nearly complete, a great deal can be said about the individual. WLH3 was an older adult with osteoarthritis in the vertebrae and right arm, and teeth worn down so much that the pulp cavities were exposed (S. G. Webb 1989a; Brown 2006). The head was spherically shaped, with a high forehead and moderately thin cranial bones, rather like WLH1. The face was relatively flat and above the eye sockets there was only a slight thickening of bone along the supraorbital ridge, giving it a modern appearance (Cameron and Groves 2004).

Was WLH3 male or female? It is theoretically possible to estimate the sex of individuals because our species has differences in the size and sturdiness of male and female skeletons; a pattern called 'sexual dimorphism'. The nature of differences between crania and mandibles of recent Aboriginal men and women in particular regions of Australia has long been established (Larnach and Freedman 1964; Larnach and Macintosh 1971). Alan Thorne and Darren Curnoe used skeletal differences of recent Aboriginal people to conclude WLH3 was male (Bowler and Thorne 1976; Thorne et al. 1999; Thorne and Curnoe 2000). However, such comparisons with modern Aboriginal people assumed that no biological changes had occurred, and it is known that Pleistocene skeletons which can be sexed by examination of the pelvis were larger and more robust than recent Aborigines. Peter Brown (1989, 2000a) observed that features of the skull such as its lightly built brow and cheek

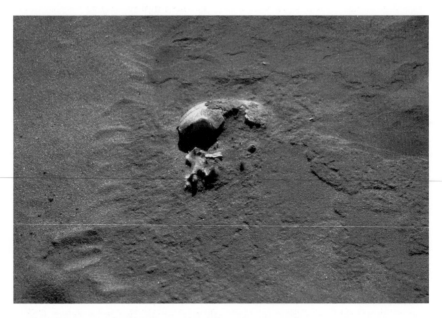

Figure 5.4 Cranium of WLH3 exposed on the Lake Mungo lunette, prior to excavation. (Courtesy of W. Shawcross.)

areas are consistent with WLH3 being a female. The person may have been a male with a feminine cranial shape or a large, heavily built female; archaeologists cannot currently determine which is correct. The uncertainty of this individual's sex is important in interpretations of Australian pre-history discussed below.

Many interpretations have considered only WLH1 and WLH3, but more than 130 skeletons have been recovered from the Lake Mungo area. Fragmented skeletons with portions of crania and/or mandible, such as WLH19, WLH22, WLH24, WLH45, WLH67, WLH68, WLH73, WLH100 and WLH130 are poorly preserved; some have been cremated, but each has yielded a few measurements that help describe the size and shape of Pleistocene humans in the region.

One skull, WLH50, stimulated much discussion. A variety of age-estimates have been offered for this cranium, but it is unlikely this person lived more than 25,000 years ago and they may be much younger (Flood 2001; Cameron and Groves 2004; Brown 2006). Stephen Webb (1989a) has shown that this skull is anatomically modern but has extraordinarily thick cranial bones, half as thick again as any other pre-historic individual known from the Mungo region. When discovered, the skull was fragmented but it has been reconstructed by Alan Thorne to show the individual as a male who had a large, long head with a flat frontal bone (forehead) and distinct supraorbital torus. WLH50 has since been studied in the hope it will provide information about the origins of Aboriginal people (Stringer 1998; Hawks et al. 2000; Wolpoff et al. 2001). However, the skull is abnormal in thickness and structure compared to other fossil skulls and those of recent Aboriginal people. Much of

WLH50's cranial thickness was created by expanded diploë, sponge-like bone that would normally be much thinner. Peter Brown (1989) and Stephen Webb (1989a, 1990) concluded that this feature is clearly a pathology. Nowadays similar pathologies occur in people with diseases and genetic disorders, and although his particular problem has not been diagnosed, it is likely that WLH50 also suffered an illness that changed his crania. It seems reckless, as Brown (2006) and Cameron and Groves (2004) have argued, to base any interpretation of human evolution on this unusual, pathological individual.

Remarkably, ancient skeletons from the Lake Mungo region may have had fragments of their genetic code extracted. Gregory Adcock and his colleagues claim they extracted mtDNA from bones of four individuals: WLH4, a female thought by Webb (1989a) to be recent; WLH15, a possible female with fresh-looking bones; WLH55, bleached bones of undetermined sex and unknown antiquity; and most significantly from WLH3, the oldest body yet discovered in Australia (Adcock et al. 2001a). As discussed in Chapter 2, mtDNA can measure genetic similarities of individuals, and claims for its recovery from these skeletons are significant. The mtDNA sequence reconstructed for WLH3 was thought to be different from sequences found in living Aboriginal people and sequences identified in the other skeletons, leading Adcock et al. (2001a, 2001b) to conclude that WLH3 was from a distinct ancient lineage. However, ancient DNA is difficult to extract and is rarely preserved in hot, dry environments such as Lake Mungo. Many specialists questioned whether the pattern from WLH3 is actually a result of contamination (Cooper et al. 2001; Nolch 2001; Cameron and Groves 2004) and/or postmortem damage to the mtDNA (Thomas et al. 2003). Until doubts about the reality of mtDNA claimed from WLH3 are resolved, no confidence can be attached to the inferred genetic patterns. Future testing of the skeleton may be necessary to resolve these doubts.

Away from Lake Mungo the next largest collection of skeletons comes from Kow Swamp, a small palaeo-lake on the Murray River floodplain. In the 1960s and 1970s excavations in a lunette on the lake margin uncovered more than 40 bodies (Thorne 1971; Thorne and Macumber 1972; Wright 1975). Many were poorly preserved and only 12 were measured in detail (Pardoe 1993). A single skeleton was female, giving a male-oriented image of the physical characteristics of people at that locality.

Radiocarbon analyses of bone from two Kow Swamp skeletons gave age-estimates of 11,070 (10,705–11,185) years bp and 9,550 (9,440–9,930) years bp, and associated charcoal yielded similar estimates. Shell found in another grave produced an estimate of 15,340 (15,020–15,740) years bp. Other undated skeletons at Kow Swamp have been assumed to have the same antiquity, and discussed as a population living in the region 10,000–16,000 years ago. However, the radiocarbon estimates reveal there were infrequent burials at Kow Swamp, over at least 4,000–5,000 years, that skeletons may represent people separated by many generations, and should not be imagined as having been contemporaries of each other (Thorne 1976).

Tim Stone and Matthew Cupper (2003) suggested that radiocarbon analyses of charcoal, bone and shell samples were contaminated by younger carbon, and therefore underestimate the antiquity of the skeletons. Luminescence estimates indicate that the sediments into which the bodies were buried were older, approximately 19,000– 22,000 years bp, but it is likely that the burials were dug from higher, more recent levels and are substantially younger than the sediments. Peter Brown (2006) therefore prefers the terminal Pleistocene age-estimate provided by radiocarbon analyses. Since the land surface into which graves were dug has not been established the Kow Swamp skeletons date to between the LGM and early-Holocene, probably the terminal Pleistocene, and represent people who lived over several thousand years.

Kow Swamp skulls share several features, including thick bones, prominent supraorbital ridges over each orbit (eye socket), a slight 'post-orbital constriction' (narrowing of the skull behind the eyes), flat and receding foreheads, and the middle of the face is 'prognathic' or protruding (Thorne 1976; Brown 1981a; Cameron and Groves 2004). The cranial vault is typically rounded, but KS9 displays some 'keeling' (pointedness). Their jaws and teeth were typically large (Brown 1981a). These were people with large heads, extreme facial features and thick bones, but in many ways their skulls are within the range seen in historical Aboriginal people.

Adcock et al. (2001a) claim to have extracted mtDNA from six Kow Swamp skeletons (KS1, KS7, KS8, KS9, KS13 and KS16), and they suggest that KS8 might be distinct from the genetic pattern known from living Aborigines, although statistical analyses indicated that this is unlikely. Methodological concerns have been raised about the claims for accurate mtDNA extraction at Kow Swamp.

Near the northern edge of Kow Swamp the Cohuna cranium was found during digging of an irrigation ditch in 1925. It is undated but mineralized, suggesting the person had not lived recently (Macumber and Thorne 1975). The skull is similar to those from Kow Swamp, and has been treated as though it were contemporary with and part of that population (Thorne 1976, 1977; Thorne and Wilson 1977). It is large, with relatively thick bones in a high cranial vault and a flattened frontal bone, prominent supraorbital ridge, and prognathic face (Figure 5.5). This individual had a broad face with heavy bone development around the cheeks and eyes, rectangular eye sockets, and a large palate (Figure 5.6). No post-cranial remains were recovered for this individual but it is usually thought to be a large, heavily built male.

A third large collection of Pleistocene skeletons in Australia comes from Coobool Creek. Peter Brown (1989) studied mineralized and carbonate encrusted crania that had been collected in the middle of the twentieth century about 70 km northwest of Kow Swamp. He reconstructed the skulls of 24 males and 9 females, most with associated mandibles. Unfortunately preservative chemicals applied to the skulls in 1950 prevent radiocarbon methods from being applied to them, but Brown attempted to date a pelvic bone, receiving a radiocarbon estimate of 8,010 (7,960–8,035) years bp and uranium-thorium estimates of 13,300–15,300 years bp. These analyses may also be affected by contamination and the exact antiquity of Coobool Creek skeletons is unknown, but they are probably terminal Pleistocene or early-Holocene in age (Brown 1989, 2006). Coobool Creek individuals may have lived many generations apart and need not be contemporaries.

Figure 5.5 Side view of the Cohuna skull (photographed from a cast).

Figure 5.6 Frontal view of the Cohuna skull (photographed from a cast).

Coobool Creek people were tall and heavily built, taller than humans who lived in the same region during the mid- and late-Holocene (Brown 1989, 1992a, 1992b). Their skulls were large, often with thick bones on the cranial vault, wide faces, broad noses and enormous 'zygomatic' (cheek) bones combined with prognathic, protruding mouths containing large teeth. Skulls were distinctive shapes, typically with high, long cranial vaults and flattened frontal bones, although variation existed in these features and some individuals had rounded foreheads. Mandibles were also large and thickened, with big, heavily worn teeth. These individuals were undoubtedly modern humans, clearly related to Aboriginal people of later periods, but their size and extremely robust looks gave them a distinctive appearance which Peter Brown captured in his drawing of a Coobool Creek man (Figure 5.7). Brown (1989) emphasized that Coobool Creek individuals physically resembled the people found at Kow Swamp and Cohuna, and they may have had a general resemblance to Pleistocene people across the broader Australian and southwest Pacific region (Bulbeck et al. 2006).

Figure 5.7 Artistic depiction of a man from the terminal Pleistocene period, based on Coobool Creek skeletons. (Courtesy of P. Brown.)

Mineralized and apparently old skeletons were also found at Nacurrie during the middle of the twentieth century. The most complete skeleton has a radiocarbon age-estimate of 13,290 (13,180–13,440) years bp (Brown 2006). This individual was a tall, elderly male with extremely worn teeth (Brown 1994b, 2006), similar to the Cohuna individual (Macintosh and Larnach 1976).

A somewhat different skull was found at Keilor. Its sex is unknown and its age is uncertain: radiocarbon estimates have ranged from 7,000–8,000 years bp to nearly 14,000 years bp. Most commentators think that it is terminal Pleistocene in age (Brown 1989, 2006). The Keilor skull is large and heavily built but has a rounded rather than flattened forehead, a flat rather than protruding mouth, and teeth that are moderate in size rather than extremely large (Brown 1987, 1989, 2006). These features have been cited by Brown (2006) as showing that a diverse regional pattern in human skull morphology existed during the Pleistocene.

Another Pleistocene skeleton was found at Lake Tandou lunette, northwest of Lake Mungo. A nearby shell midden, about 18,600 years old, has been used to suggest the age of the skeleton (Freedman and Lofgren 1983), but this association has been questioned and it is possible only to say that this individual lived between the LGM and the end of the Pleistocene (Pardoe 1993). The Tandou skull displays a mixture of traits: a steep, rounded forehead, weak supraorbital ridges but very thick bones on the cranial vault, reinforcing Brown's point about the diversity of Pleistocene humans (Freedman and Lofgren 1983).

Pleistocene skeletons from Kow Swamp, Coobool Creek, Keilor and near Lake Mungo have been interpreted through two kinds of comparisons. The first is with older skeletons found in southeast Asia, such as those from Wadjak, Ngandong and Sangiran in Indonesia. This comparison has been used to evaluate whether ancient Australian foragers descended from earlier southeast Asia hominids or whether they were descended from humans who had migrated from more distant places. A second comparison was between Pleistocene-aged skeletons and more recent Holocene ones from southeast Australia. The Holocene sample includes specimens from Lake Nitchie (Macintosh 1971), Mossgiel (Freedman 1985), Swanport (Pardoe 1988) and Roonka (Pretty 1977; Prokopec 1979), as well as one hundred sexed but undated skeletons from the Murray River Valley assumed to be less than 5,000 years old (Pietrusewsky 1979; Brown 1989). These comparisons allowed researchers to make statements about the way humans in the late-Pleistocene evolved the physical form of Aboriginal people living in southeastern Australia during recent centuries.

Approaches to explaining physical variation in humans

The fossil skeletons demonstrate that there were physical differences between Pleistocene and more recent humans. It is this variation that scientists have sought to explain, often by thinking in terms of ancient populations: reproductively connected people who shared a genetic 'lineage'. This is a biological not a cultural notion. There is no necessary relationship between ancient populations and their cultural characteristics: a genetically uniform population may contain groups with different social practices while people from two different populations may share a common set of social practices. Attempts to explain biological differences in ancient skeletons in population terms have taken two directions.

One approach focused on the origins of humans in Australia, and hypothesized that the migration of two or more genetically distinct populations explained the diversity of Pleistocene skeletons. Since, in the historical period, there was a geographical continuum in human biological variation across Australia, the model of multiple origins also incorporated the idea that multiple founding populations merged, producing a single 'homogenized' Aboriginal population by the end of the pre-historic period (Pardoe 2006).

A second approach focused on biological transformations of people within Australia, and hypothesized that processes of evolution and adaptation after the continent was settled explained the diversity of human physical forms. This perspective encouraged views of genetic continuity rather than of migration and population replacement. Biological variation was seen to result from a single founding population which diversified or homogenized at different times in pre-history (Pardoe 2006).

These approaches have been viewed as alternatives, but in fact they are not contradictory. It is conceivable that the merger of distinct founding populations and the production of biological diversity through evolutionary processes both occurred during Australian pre-history. Consequently when archaeologists advocated only one mechanism they may have created models that oversimplified past evolutionary processes. Furthermore, some variation in ancient skeletal characteristics may have been created by other factors such as differences in lifestyle and cultural practices. The possibility that illness caused unusual features on the WLH50 skull, or that cremation altered the dimensions of the skull of WLH1, has already been mentioned. Investigations of biological variation of ancient Australians are therefore complex and multifaceted debates about the interpretation of fossil skeletons have occurred.

Migration and models of multiple populations

There is a long tradition within Australian archaeology of invoking successive migrations to the continent as the explanation for changes in the archaeological record. An early, influential model of multiple migrations proposed by Joseph Birdsell (1967) suggested that geographical variation in body size and morphology of Aboriginal people observed in the 1930s was a result of three distinctive populations migrating into Australia during pre-history. He thought the first migration was by short, dark-skinned people who survived in southern and eastern regions, followed by migrations of people with greater stature and lighter skin colour who lived along the Murray River in historic times, and finally by tall, slender people who moved into northern Australia. This model is not supported; genetic and biological studies indicate one population of Aboriginal people, not three, and geographical differences in their physical characteristics point to adaptation to different environments over a long period of time (Lindsell 2001; Presser et al. 2002).

A different model of multiple migrations was advocated by Alan Thorne, who proposed a 'dihybrid' process in which two very different populations arrived and intermixed to create the diversity of Aboriginal people (Thorne 1971, 1976, 1977; Thorne and Wilson 1977; Thorne and Wolpoff 1981, 1992; Thorne and Curnoe 2000). Arguing that Pleistocene fossil skeletons in Australia had one of two distinctive sets of characteristics, and few or no individuals had intermediate or mixed features, he assigned each skeleton to membership of either 'gracile' or 'robust' populations. Gracile individuals were those with smooth, round cranial vaults of thin or medium thickness, slight supraorbital ridges, slight postorbital constriction, little prognathism, and relatively small jaws and teeth. Skeletons typifying this gracile type are WLH1, WLH3 and Keilor (Thorne 1977; Adcock et al. 2001a). Robust individuals had long cranial vaults of medium or thick bones, receding foreheads, pronounced supraorbital ridges, developed postorbital constrictions, pronounced prognathism below the nose, and relatively large jaws and teeth. Skeletons classified as robust are those from Kow Swamp, Coobool Creek, Cohuna and Mossgiel (Thorne 1977; Adcock et al. 2001a). Thorne argued that gracile and robust people were so different they must have belonged to separate populations.

Because he classified the two oldest skeletons as gracile, Thorne argued that gracile people arrived in Australia first, tens of thousands of years before the migration of robust people to the continent (Thorne and Curnoe 2000; Adcock et al. 2001a; Curnoe and Thorne 2006a, 2006b; but see Thorne 1977 for a different chronology). Thorne thought gracile people reached Australia more than 50,000 years ago but the robust population arrived only 20,000–30,000 years ago, bringing ground stone axes with them. This is a curious argument, because Pleistocene axes are found only in the north and robust skulls have been found only in the south of the continent, but the inconsistency is of little consequence since precise timing of purported migrations is not central to Thorne's dihybrid model.

Thorne's reasoning that gracile and robust skulls are so dissimilar that they could not belong to the same population has been challenged. Colin Pardoe (1991a, 1993, 2006) argues that the dihybrid argument was founded on an embarrassing mistake: the distinction between gracile and robust is little more than a separation of large, heavily built males from smaller, more slightly boned females. As evidence the categories really described sexual dimorphism, Pardoe (1991a) revealed that most skeletons in the Lake Mungo region classified as gracile were female but most of the robust skeletons were male (Figure 5.8). He concluded that they belonged to one population with substantial sexual dimorphism; it was not necessary to hypothesize two migrant populations, only to acknowledge that there were two sexes. Identification of an early gracile population relies almost entirely on the slightly built WLH3 being male, yet the sex of that individual is ambiguous. The gracility of the earliest skeletons, WLH1 and WLH3, may merely indicate that they are both female (Brown 2000a).

Pardoe's critique struck at the heart of Thorne's dihybrid model by declaring that there were no differences between gracile and robust individuals other than those related to sex. Changes in male and female crania over time, discussed below,

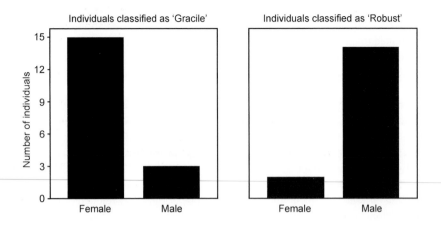

Figure 5.8 Illustration of Pardoe's (1991a) analysis of the Willandra hominids relationship between the sex and the robustness of individual skeletons ($\chi^2=14.29$, d.f.$=1$, p<0.001).

complicate sexing of skulls, but Pardoe's warning that differences between gracile and robust individuals is linked to their sex cannot be ignored. However, not all researchers are convinced that sexual dimorphism is the key distinction between Pleistocene skeletons; David Bulbeck reportedly identified robust-looking females and gracile males, concluding that there may indeed have been two populations (Flood 2001).

The origin of two genetically distinct populations predicted by Thorne's dihybrid model has also been contentious. Thorne linked his model to another, called the 'multi-regional model' of human evolution, which hypothesized that modern humans evolved from earlier hominids in a number of regions, each with specific genetic traits but unified as a single, global species by inter-regional gene flow (Thorne and Wolpoff 1981, 1992; Wolpoff et al. 1994, 2001). He used this model to suggest that gracile people in Australia were descended from hominids who lived in east Asia. Thorne (1976) argued that the receding frontal bone, pronounced postorbital constriction, and supraorbital torus were features of robust crania indicating that those individuals were descended from *Homo erectus*, a kind of hominid who lived in peninsular southeast Asia.

This idea seems improbable because no evidence of a direct genetic connection of ancient Australians with *Homo erectus* in Asia has been found; robust skulls are more convincingly explained in other ways. In *Homo sapiens* prominent supraorbital ridges on large males with narrow skulls, such as many Australian Aborigines, result from crania size and the morphology of the base of the skull; they are not a reflection of descent from *Homo erectus* (Lahr and Wright 1996; Cameron and Groves 2004). This explains why, when David Cameron and Michael Westaway analysed non-facial features of Kow Swamp skulls, they found them similar to other fossil *Homo sapiens* around the world but distinctly different from *Homo erectus*, a result that was not consistent with the multiregional model (Cameron and Groves 2004). Arthur Durband (2004) reached the same conclusion in his study of crania bases, arguing that none of the fossil skulls discovered in Asia was a link between Homo erectus and the human remains in Australia. These studies support the generally accepted idea that pre-historic people in Australia were descended from Homo sapiens who spread from Africa.

Cultural processes rather than descent from two different populations explain the flattened, receding foreheads of some Pleistocene Australians and rounded, upright foreheads of others. Don Brothwell (1975) challenged interpretations of Kow Swamp crania, suggesting that their heads had been deformed. 'Cranial deformation' is a practice that involves binding or repeatedly pushing the skull of an infant. Unable to expand in one direction, brain tissue grows in a different direction and skull growth is modified to accommodate. The brain grows to its normal size but is contained in a skull of radically different shape. During recent centuries cranial deformation was performed in many parts of the world, such as France, South America and the Pacific islands, but it was not used by Australian Aborigines.

The existence of cranial deformation in Pleistocene Australia was demonstrated by Peter Brown (1981b, 1989), who showed that skulls from Coobool Creek, Kow Swamp and Cohuna had been distorted during childhood. As adults those individuals had heads with flattened and receding frontal and occipital bones, great cranial height, increased postorbital constriction, and more prominent supraorbital ridges; all features typical of the 'robust' group of Australian fossils (Cameron and Groves 2004). Brown's findings have since been confirmed, particularly by Susan Antón and Karen Weinstein (1999), who concluded that artificial deformation of children's skulls had been common in southeastern Australia during the terminal Pleistocene, and the frontal bones of people buried at Kow Swamp were extremely deformed. Cranial deformation made Pleistocene people who would otherwise have had rounder skulls appear superficially like Homo erectus. With deformed skulls they looked very different from undeformed people of the time (Figure 5.9). These differences prompted archaeologists to distinguish between individuals with 'gracile' and 'robust' characteristics.

The effects of cranial deformation have not been fully determined but it is possible that the robustness of Pleistocene individuals was a consequence of factors in addition to their cultural treatment of children. Across the globe late-Pleistocene humans tended to be larger and more robust than recent people (La Blanc and Black 1974; P. Smith et al. 1986; Kidder et al. 1992). Human form in Australia follows this broader trend, and this is reason to suspect that evolutionary processes rather than the merger of multiple founding populations were responsible for the robustness of some terminal Pleistocene people.

Of course it is possible that several genetically distinct groups entered Australia prior to the terminal Pleistocene, perhaps merging well before the LGM and leaving few preserved remains. Alternatively, given the small, geographically restricted sample of skeletons, several early populations could conceivably have existed elsewhere in the continent, away from the southeast. However, the skeletal evidence discovered thus far gives little support to the proposition that they represent two very different founding populations. A similar conclusion emerges from genetic studies.

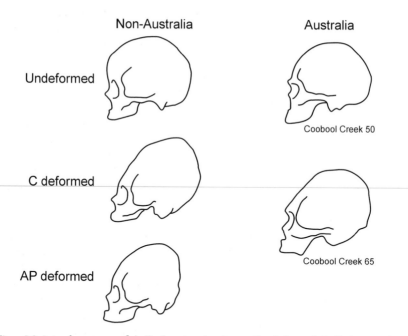

Figure 5.9 Lateral contours of skulls showing the shape of undeformed skulls (top row) and of skulls deformed by wrapping with soft materials (C deformed) or constricted at the front and back with hard objects (AP deformed). While some Pleistocene individuals, such as Coobool Creek 50, were probably not deformed, others, such as Coobool Creek 65, were affected by one or both forms of deformation (based on Antón and Weinstein 1999: Figure 1).

Genetic evidence for single or multiple origins

Genetic studies are an obvious way to evaluate whether recent Aborigines descended from two or more genetically distinct populations. Investigation of modern Aboriginal genetics is just beginning; samples are available from only a few regions and mtDNA rather than the full DNA sequence is typically reported. Consequently, it has been possible to develop many interpretations of existing genetic evidence. For example, mtDNA diversity was used by Alan Redd and Mark Stoneking (1999) to suggest multiple migrations to Greater Australia, with Aboriginal and New Guinea highlanders descended from different populations. There is little doubt that New Guinea highlands mtDNA is substantially different from Australian Aborigines, but the nature of their dissimilar genetic histories is debated (Redd and Stoneking 1999; Tommaseo-Ponzetta et al. 2002; Friedlaender et al. 2005; Merriwether et al. 2005). Their differences might reflect different founder populations (Ingman and Gyllensten 2003; Merriwether et al. 2005), or alternatively it might reflect mtDNA divergence since Australia and New Guinea were separated by rising sea levels (Huoponen et al. 2001; Kayser et al. 2001). Whatever the explanation, it does not help to explain variation between Aboriginal skeletons in southern Australia.

It initially appeared that differences in Pleistocene skeletons reflected a genetic link between desert and Murray Valley Aborigines and people from India (van Holst Pellekaan et al. 1997, 1998; Redd et al. 2002; Tommaseo-Ponzetta et al. 2002). However, further research found no evidence for substantial gene flow from the Indian subcontinent (Ingman and Gyllensten 2003; van Holst Pellekaan and Harding 2006; van Holst Pellekaan et al. 2006), and this proposition can be discounted in discussions about Pleistocene Australians.

A diversity of mtDNA lineages are found in living Aborigines. Although this diversity might result from multiple migration events, it is more likely to be a consequence of the complex histories of survival and extinction of populations living in Australia (Huoponen et al. 2001; Macaulay et al. 2005; van Holst Pellekaan et al. 2006). This is the strongest interpretation of the mtDNA from fossil skeletons in southeastern Australia. Initially it seemed that mtDNA reconstructed for WLH3 was different from lineages found in more recent fossils and living Aboriginal people, and might reveal a founding population replaced by subsequent migrations of people with the modern range of mtDNA sequences (Adcock et al. 2001a; Forster et al. 2001). In fact WLH3 mtDNA sequences have now been located among living people, showing that those lineages still exist, and so there is no unambiguous evidence of migration events replacing earlier populations (Cooper et al. 2001; Gutiérrez et al. 2002). Furthermore, the mtDNA lineages extracted from terminal Pleistocene skeletons classified as gracile and robust are not systematically different; they share a common origin, not descent from two populations (Adcock et al. 2001a). This finding alone indicates that Thorne's gracile/robust distinction provides no evidence for two founding populations.

Studies in Aboriginal genetics indicate that Australia was colonized by a single large and diverse population and has remained minimally affected by outside gene pools (Huoponen et al. 2001; Merriwether et al. 2005). Most of Australia had been settled by 40,000–45,000 years ago (Chapter 3), and after that time the arrival of small groups of people would not have had much impact on the genetic patterns of the people occupying the continent (Pardoe 1991b, 2006). The distinctive genetic character of Australian Aborigines, and the diversity of their mtDNA lineages is evidence of a lengthy occupation and a long period of genetic isolation (Huoponen et al. 2001). Differentiation occurred between Aboriginal groups as evolutionary processes were played out.

Evolutionary processes

Migration and merging of distinct populations is only one process that can change the way people appear. In the century and a half since Charles Darwin announced his discovery of natural selection, scientists have developed detailed understandings of mechanisms by which evolutionary change takes place. Adaptation is the process by which populations evolve in response to environmental constraints, via the mechanism of natural selection, as some humans are more reproductively successful than others, having more and/or healthier children. The evidence of physical adaptation of pre-historic humans to Australian landscapes is undeniable.

In the historical period Aboriginal people in each part of the continent had different body shapes, a pattern created in pre-historic times as natural selection altered the genetics of each group to suit the warmness of their environment (Pardoe 1994, 2006). That process operated continuously over time and in a non-directional way: when climates warmed human bodies tended to evolve smaller masses and longer limbs; when climates become colder the opposite trend occurred. This process, expressed in Bergmann's Rule (Chapter 4), could have contributed to the decreased size and robustness of humans living in the higher temperatures of the Holocene. In that way natural selection helps explain changes in human biological variation over time, without requiring the merger of different populations.

Another process creating biological differences is gene flow. The pattern of reproduction between individuals belonging to different groups regulates the frequency of genetic transmission; it may create reduced diversity in human appearance, even reproductive isolation which can promote differentiation between groups. Gene flow reflects geographical factors such as distance and physical barriers between groups, but it is also affected by the number of people in each group and by aspects of their social and political organization such as the frequency of marriage within and between groups. Consequently the demography and social practices of past forager groups, and the landscapes in which they lived, contributed to the differences recorded in ancient human skeletons across southeastern Australia.

The capacity of these, and other, processes to explain fossil skulls found in Australia has persuaded many researchers that it is not necessary to propose more than one founding population; that plus adaptation and gene flow would be sufficient to have created the archaeological evidence. This argument is significant because it has encouraged researchers to look at past social and environmental circumstances affecting ancient people in Australia.

One founding population and evolution

Advocates of the idea that Aboriginal people were descended from a single founding population have explored how features found on fossil and recent skulls evolved. Rather than dividing Pleistocene skeletons into robust and gracile populations these researchers acknowledged the complex nature of differences in crania and mandibles; they concluded there was continuous variation in features. For example, round-headed individuals such as WLH3 and Tandou have cranial vaults thicker than individuals from Kow Swamp or Coobool Creek, demonstrating that Pleistocene people did not simply have either gracile or robust features but often had a mix of characteristics. Peter Brown (1987) concluded that in the terminal Pleistocene and at the start of the Holocene, people typically had large, broad faces containing shallow orbits, facial prognathism, and long, high cranial vaults with thickened bones, with areas of massive muscle insertion related to the large powerful jaws. Biologically these Pleistocene people belonged to one population, but their features varied across space and through time, reflecting processes of adaptation and gene flow. Those processes also created differences between the people who lived in southeastern Australia during the Pleistocene and the people who lived there later in the Holocene.

Human bodies reduced by approximately 10–20 per cent at the end of the Pleistocene. Brown (1987) pointed out that vault thickness, cranial size and shape and tooth size all indicated that Pleistocene people were typically larger than humans living at later times. Brown found a way to measure the reduction of head and jaw sizes for humans who lived in the Murray River corridor (Brown 1987, 1989, 1992a, 1992b, 2000a). He did this by using skeletons from Coobool Creek to represent terminal Pleistocene populations and a sample of skeletons from the Murray Valley to represent later, Holocene periods. Neither sample is well dated, but the comparison describes broad change through time. For each sample Brown calculated an index which summarized the different dimensions on the crania and mandibles. The resulting 'discriminant function score' was larger when the dimensions of crania and mandibles were larger, and consequently higher values indicate bigger people. This analysis showed that both males and females tended to be larger in the Pleistocene, and that skeletal differences between the sexes were greater (Figure 5.10). Although these statistics have been criticized (Thorne and Curnoe 2000), they are merely a mathematically sophisticated way of compiling a number of different measurements of body dimension, and since each measurement shows a size reduction through time the composite calculation expressed a real trend. Reduction in robusticity necessarily accompanied reduced skull size because many bone structures in crania are strongly linked to cranial dimensions (Lahr and Wright 1996). Consequently as people became smaller, and differences between men and women decreased, they also became less robust in appearance.

Similar trends to smaller body mass and less robustness occurred elsewhere in the world at the same time (Brown 1987). The reason human bodies were smaller in the Holocene is multifactorial but related to well-known biological processes of adaptation such as Bergmann's Rule. Smaller individuals, with smaller faces and teeth, were at an advantage over the past 6,000–8,000 years, in the higher temperatures of the Holocene, and their body forms came to dominate (Brown 1987; Lindsell 2001; Pardoe 2006) – a process of adaptation.

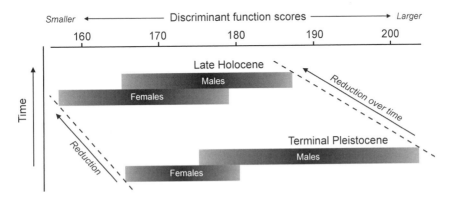

Figure 5.10 Diagram showing size reduction in cranial and mandible dimensions of humans living in the Murray River corridor during the terminal Pleistocene and late-Holocene (data from Brown 2000a; see also Brown 1987, 1989).

Differences between the Pleistocene skeletons, which initially prompted Thorne's idea of two populations inhabiting Australia, have also been reassessed in terms of adaptation. For example, Pardoe (1993, 2006) hypothesized that the diversity of Pleistocene skeletons reflected regional variations in body shape within the Pleistocene population. He noted that present-day desert-adapted Aboriginal people were more slightly built than Aboriginal people living in the Murray Valley. Pardoe hypothesized that this pattern also existed in the Pleistocene: early skeletons from Lake Mungo, WLH1 and WLH3, represent slightly built people living in an arid environment, while robust structures seen on Kow Swamp and Coobool Creek skeletons reflect their occupation of temperate and riverine environments. Such differences in skeletons indicate local adaptations rather than multiple origins.

Thorne had doubted that local evolutionary processes of this kind could not have produced the dramatic, robust kinds of crania found along the Murray River. He argued that there were no physical barriers, such as mountain chains, to isolate local groups from the larger gene pool while differentiation occurred. In fact there were mechanisms that regulated gene flow, but they were cultural and demographic situations rather than geographic ones. Pardoe (1990, 1994, 2006) offered a model of how demographic and social differences acted as a powerful mechanism controlling gene flow between ancient groups of people. He argued that groups who lived in more productive environments, such as the Murray River Valley, had smaller territories and hence higher population densities, whereas groups in the less productive hinterland had larger territories and hence lower densities. This idea is consistent with Birdsell's (1953) observation of a relationship between environmental productivity and territory area (Chapter 1). Those differences in population density would have determined the number of marriage partners able to move from one group to another. Figure 5.11 illustrates Pardoe's point, showing the configuration of marriage exchanges between groups if each had 100 people and 14 per cent married into neighbouring groups. Spatially extended hinterland groups would have had many neighbouring groups, whereas each group living in the river corridor would have had fewer neighbours. To maintain relationships with all its neighbours a hinterland group could arrange only a few marriages with each, whereas a riverine group would be obliged to have more marriages between neighbours along the river than with its hinterland neighbours because only in those groups would there be enough available partners. This configuration of people in the landscape directed gene flow along the river at a far higher rate than between the river and hinterland people; higher population density along riverine corridors acted as a barrier to gene flow with non-riverine groups. Marriage patterns were therefore a mechanism by which regional differences in physical form could have emerged. The higher the density of people living in riverine territories the more genetically secluded they would have been from other groups. For Pardoe (2006) this is the context in which we can understand skeletons from Kow Swamp and Coobool Creek, locations in the Murray River Valley where higher population densities presented barriers to gene flow and created conditions in which small biological distinctions arose in Pleistocene people.

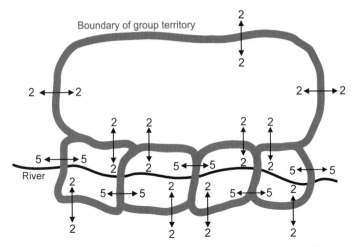

Figure 5.11 Gene flow model for regions with a rich riverine corridor and less resource-rich hinterland. Numbers represent the percentage of people married into a neighbouring group. The model assumes equal number of people available to be married in each group (N=100), but different sized territories. Marriage patterns are the same for all groups and involve an equal rate (14 per cent) of marriage between all neighbouring groups (based on model 2 presented by Pardoe 2006: Figure 3).

This vision of demographically regulated barriers to gene flow not only helps account for the features of Pleistocene skeletons, it is also consistent with behavioural differences between those people. Pleistocene people were not culturally homogeneous; their lifestyles, perceptions, identities and beliefs differed between regions and through time (Chapter 6). The practice of cranial deformation among Pleistocene occupants of the Murray Valley, represented by people buried at Kow Swamp and Coobool Creek, is evidence that people at that time were actively employing cultural signatures of their different ideologies in a way that helped construct distinctions between groups.

Models of evolutionary change describe some of the ways that ancient humans physically adapted to early environments and changed as climate altered through time. The central process creating the nature and diversity of ancient human physical features need not have been the arrival of new waves of people during pre-history, it was the adaptation of people to their social and material environment over long spans of time. Cultural as well as biological variation in humans throughout Australian pre-history can also be explained in terms of the dynamic adjustment of people descended from a single founding population to the changing contexts in which they lived rather than as a result of passively receiving genetic and social influences from outside Australia. Evidence of Pleistocene social diversity and change presented in Chapter 6 complements that viewpoint.

6   Life in Pleistocene Australia

In the 1960s, as a young environmental scientist, Jim Bowler inspected dry Lake Mungo in southeastern Australia (Figure 6.1). He obtained a radiocarbon age-estimate of 37,400 (36,200–38,700) years bp for shells eroded from lakeside sediments. Then, in July 1968, he found a small pile of burnt, carbonate-encrusted bones. Thinking this could be evidence of early human occupation Bowler invited archaeologists to excavate them. In those pioneering days the bones were packed in a suitcase for transport to the laboratory, where they were identified as the remains of a human labelled WLH1. Interpretations of this skeleton, and archaeological materials found nearby, initiated the search for a distinctive image of human life in the Pleistocene.

What can be called the 'progression' model of Australian Pleistocene life held that archaeological materials document a sequence of cultural and physical development throughout pre-history. Rebelling against earlier views of Aborigines as 'unchanging primitives' the archaeologists who travelled to Mungo to excavate WLH1, and many of their contemporaries, depicted the Aboriginal past as having changed, but concepts of nineteenth century biological and cultural evolutionists pervaded their views of Pleistocene life. Assuming cultural continuity across the entire time span of Australian pre-history, archaeologists imagined the economy and society of Pleistocene people at Lake Mungo as very similar to that of historical Aboriginal people (Chapter 1). They argued that distinctions between historical societies emerged within Australia from the slow differentiation of culturally simple founding groups, and they believed archaeological materials documented the evolution of increasingly sophisticated technologies, foraging practices and social organization. This view implied that prior to the emergence of regional distinctions ancestral Pleistocene social and economic systems were relatively uniform across the continent. Consequently they imagined Pleistocene life as plainer, simpler versions of nineteenth century Aboriginal life; as societies without the embellishments that accrued with time.

Simplicity, uniformity and conservatism as characteristics of Pleistocene life

This progression perspective is visible in the way archaeologists in the 1960s and 1970s thought about artefacts found at Lake Mungo and other Pleistocene sites.

Figure 6.1 Pleistocene Australia (grey) showing archaeological sites mentioned in Chapter 6.

Because stone artefacts preserved in every early archaeological deposit, long after wood and bone decayed, thinking about Pleistocene human life has been coloured by archaeological discussions of those tools. Building on ideas developed in Western Europe during the nineteenth century, Australian archaeologists focused on regularly shaped stone artefacts from which many flakes had been removed, believing these were tools made in accordance with a design for specific functions. Often stone tools were classified by reference to their shapes or the functions for which they were thought to have been designed. For example, in describing stone artefacts from Lake Mungo, Harry Allen and Rhys Jones used the terms 'core tools' or 'horse hoof cores' for large, heavy specimens they thought were suited to pounding and planing, 'steep edge scrapers' for thick ones with steep edges (70°–90°) which they believed were suited to scraping and planing, and 'flat scrapers' for thin ones with lower edge angles (45°–70°) which they thought were used to cut flesh or vegetables (Bowler et al. 1970). Figure 6.2 shows examples of these classifications. Functions assigned to each implement were based on the intuition of archaeologists;

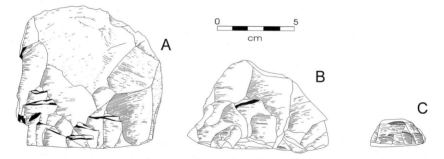

Figure 6.2 Examples of implement types recognized in Pleistocene deposits: A = 'Horse hoof' (redrawn from Mulvaney 1969: 145); B = 'Core scraper' (redrawn from Mulvaney 1969: 149); C = 'Flake scraper' (redrawn from Mulvaney 1969: 141).

microscope studies of damage to tools revealed that many tools were multifunctional or used for tasks other than those predicted in the classifications of the 1970s.

Archaeologists classified stone tools recovered from Pleistocene sites, concluding that they were similar across the continent. There were dissenting voices, particularly Johan Kamminga (1978, 1982), but even critical commentators concluded that Pleistocene stone tools everywhere had three characteristics (Howells 1973; Mulvaney 1975; Bowdler 1977; Jones 1979; White and O'Connell 1982; Flood 1983). First, instruments were large, relatively thick, robust, and capable of being employed in rugged tasks, but they were often roughly crafted. A second characteristic was that Pleistocene stone implements were seen as relatively simple, lacking in variation. The third characteristic was that tools were uniform and unvarying across Greater Australia. Such ideas were reflected in the proposal by Allen and Jones that Pleistocene stone artefacts at Lake Mungo were representative of a pancontinental technological practice they named the 'Core Tool and Scraper Tradition' (Bowler et al. 1970). They suggested this tradition existed on the mainland from the arrival of humans until the Holocene, while in Tasmania it persisted until European contact. Perceived uniformity in stone tools implied technological stasis or conservativism, with no substantial alteration to foraging toolkits throughout the Pleistocene. Comparable negative assessments of the uniformity and simplicity of Pleistocene stone artefacts have continued (e.g. Brumm and Moore 2005).

Images of unchanging technologies were paralleled by reconstructions of Pleistocene people as economically and culturally uniform and conservative. For example, Sandra Bowdler (1977) proposed her idea that early settlement was restricted to the continental margins by the inflexible coastal economy of 'marine-oriented' foragers, implying that people did not adapt their economic activities to new environments but instead maintained a single economic strategy throughout the Pleistocene (Chapter 3). Bowdler even suggested that the conservative economic strategy explained technological conservatism, since unchanging foraging patterns required only one set of tools. The vision of economically uninventive foragers occupying only coastal landscapes, unable or unwilling to develop strategies with which to settle the rest of the continent, was another expression of the idea of changeless Aboriginal people.

A similar image of cultural conservativism and homogeneity in Pleistocene artistic traditions was also suggested. Lesley Maynard (1976, 1977, 1979) hypothesized that Australian rock art could be divided into three stages. She argued that in the earliest stage, called 'Panaramitee', motifs were created by breaking through weathered rock surfaces to form pits and grooves that showed the different colour of unweathered rock (Figure 6.3). Ancient artists abraded the rock with hard objects or dislodged small pieces through battering, a process called 'pecking'. Most motifs made in these ways look like footprints of animals such as kangaroo, emu or humans. Non-figurative patterns such as circles or spirals were also common. Human faces were sometimes made. Maynard hypothesized that 'Panaramitee' art was old, noting that abraded and pecked images in Tasmania demonstrated that the tradition existed before sea-level rise isolated that region; while on mainland Australia 'Panaramitee' images had been smoothed and weathered since the art was made. Because 'Panaramitee' art was similar in many different regions, irrespective of how weathered it was, Maynard concluded that artistic activities in the Pleistocene were homogeneous and little changing.

Conservatism in early artistic practices was considered obvious because Maynard argued that later rock art in mainland Australia had paintings as well as engravings and displayed regional differences in style, making it more 'complex' and varied

Figure 6.3 Example of the pecked and heavily weathered art panels assigned to the 'Panaramitee' stage of Australian art.

than the 'Panaramitee'. Comparisons of archaeological evidence for Pleistocene and Holocene social and economic life were often at that generalized level: the perceived similarity and simplicity of cultural material preserved from the Pleistocene contrasted against more diverse and seemingly richer archaeological records for Holocene times. Inferred conservatism and uniformity of Pleistocene technologies, economies and art were emphasized through comparisons with Holocene cultural change, often thought to be faster and more regionalized (Mulvaney and Joyce 1965; Mulvaney 1969, 1975; Jones 1977a; Lampert 1981). During the 1990s this perspective became embedded in models of a 'late intensification' which stated that social life was more homogeneous and social change slower in the Pleistocene than in the Holocene, that later societies were more 'complex' than Pleistocene ones (Lourandos 1997).

Archaeologists interpreted the Pleistocene as a period in which ancient Australians maintained similar social, economic and technological systems over tens of thousands of years. This purported cultural stability was puzzling because people settled many different landscapes and existed through prolonged climatic changes. Implications of cultural stability were rarely considered: if foragers did not respond to different environments by altering their social and economic activities, their 'generalized' cultural systems would not have suited the lands in which they lived! Archaeologists offered few reasons for why early people would have maintained the same life ways when significant advantages existed for any group who developed specialized social, economic or technological approaches fitted to their situation. Initial settlement was claimed to have been carried out rapidly by foragers retaining a generalized adaptation (Jones 1979), but the value to subsequent generations of retaining the same approach rather than developing environment-specific activities was not explored. As further archaeological fieldwork was carried out, the proposition that humans inhabiting diverse environments maintained an unchanging technology, economy and social pattern throughout the Pleistocene found no support; evidence for different technologies, economies and artistic practices gradually emerged. However, many interpretations of archaeological evidence for diversity were coloured by the same idea of homogeneity and conservatism that had provided the foundations for images of changeless Pleistocene life ways.

Images of ancient Australian foragers as culturally and technologically simple, with generalized economic and social practices which altered little over long periods of time, owed more to nineteenth century stereotypes of Australian Aborigines as representatives of 'primitive' humanity than to the archaeological material being discovered at that time. When evidence for change was found some archaeologists interpreted it with a viewpoint similar to that offered by nineteenth century cultural evolutionists who had advocated stadial evolution of cultural complexity and modernity from a very simple ancestral culture. Parallels with cultural evolutionism, and the seductiveness of unilinear models of progress, are visible in the views archaeologists developed about cultural change during the Pleistocene.

As the idea of changeless Pleistocene foragers became untenable, archaeologists instead developed a detailed 'progression' model which hypothesized increases in the diversity, efficiency and elaborateness of human life during the Pleistocene. The model suggested that within Australia there was a sequence of gradual cultural development. Researchers typically acknowledged either gradual chronological changes or regional diversity but rarely both, thereby maintaining an element of 'primitiveness' in their image of ice-age foragers. More recent versions of this proposition have also been offered (Brumm and Moore 2005).

An example of this progression model was Rhys Jones' discussion of Pleistocene tools as displaying directional 'evolution' (Jones 1979; Lorblanchet and Jones 1979). He argued that contemporary toolkits were the same across the continent; regional differences between assemblages of stone implements existed simply because they were of different ages. Jones thought the size of stone tools decreased through time but artisans kept tool edges approximately the same length, resulting in tools that were more efficient because the same tool edge was produced on smaller items. He argued that 'typological evolution' of more efficient tools occurred because earlier artisans emphasized core tools and thick, steep-edged scrapers while later Pleistocene people made few core tools and increasingly manufactured refined scrapers on thin flakes. Jones hypothesized a directional trend, claiming that large tools dominated what he thought were older assemblages such as Lake Mungo, Kangaroo Island and Burrill Lake, but small implement types were more common in the terminal Pleistocene or Holocene (Figure 6.4). Subsequent research by Ron Lampert (1981) for the south-central region of Australia and Jim Kohen and Eugene Stockton for the east coast (Kohen et al. 1984) also argued for directional change in the character of stone tools. By reconstructing directional change through time

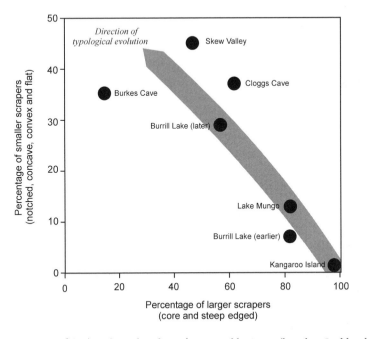

Figure 6.4 Image of the 'typological evolution' proposed by Jones (based on Lorblanchet and Jones 1979).

these arguments enabled archaeologists to retain perceptions of pan-continental uniformity and conservatism in Pleistocene technology. Hypothesizing that later tools were more efficient maintained an image of simplicity within Pleistocene cultures.

Claims for progressive improvement of Pleistocene tools have been exposed as unreliable. Jones' model was based on evidence from only a few carefully selected sites, and the arguments of Kohen and Stockton worked only for the sample of sites they used (Hiscock 1988a). When all assemblages were examined great variation, through both time and space, and no simple progression, was identified in the frequency of implement types. Terminal Pleistocene sites sometimes contain many large stone cores and implements (Stockton 1981); some of the oldest sites such as Devil's Lair and Upper Swan in western Australia contain only very small specimens (Dortch 1979a, 1979b, 1984; Pearce and Barbetti 1981; Dortch and Dortch 1996). Large horse hoof cores were made only in some regions (Kamminga 1978, 1982), which had large implements at many time periods. The belief that heavy 'core tools' from Kangaroo Island dated to the earliest periods of human occupation were falsified when radiocarbon estimates for such assemblages showed they were less than 9,000 years old (8,175–8,380), and similar assemblages on the mainland were older but still terminal Pleistocene in age (17,500–18,530) (Lampert 1985; Draper 1987). This evidence showed that the model of a continentally uniform toolkit gradually changing through time was incorrect.

Judgements about the crudeness and homogeneity of early stone tools proved unnecessary as new ways of understanding artefact variation emerged (White 1977). For example, Hiscock argued that implement sizes and shapes in Pleistocene assemblages did not relate to their position on a ladder of sophistication, or even the uses to which they were put, but rather to factors such as the intensity with which tools were transported, used, maintained and recycled (Hiscock and Allen 2000; Hiscock and Attenbrow 2003, 2005; Hiscock 2006). Specimens used for longer were intensively resharpened and reshaped, giving them more retouch and making them look different from specimens used quickly and discarded (Figure 6.5). Some tools might have been intensively resharpened for several reasons, such as high costs of obtaining the material or inconvenience of rescheduling activities to replace a tool when it became blunt. Resharpening larger artefacts is not an unsophisticated activity; it is a strategy that can offer flexibility and readiness to a toolkit.

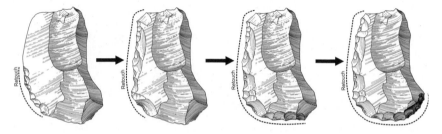

Figure 6.5 Maintenance and reworking creating morphological variation in stone artefacts (redrawn from Hiscock and Attenbrow 2005: 97).

Thick, steep-edged stone tools found on the Lake Mungo lunette resulted from transporting large specimens from a distant raw material source to the lunette where they were intensively maintained to provide long-lived tools. What had initially been seen as large, unsophisticated early tools are now interpreted as the result of a network of material procurement and tool repair.

Field research also demonstrated that the 'Panaramitee' was actually a series of regionally distinct styles that shared conventions rather than a single artistic tradition. Andre Rosenfeld's (1981) studies of rock engravings led her to identify the 'Early Man Complex' on Cape York. She concluded that 'Panaramitee' sites in northeast Australia differed from central Australian ones in the frequency with which different kinds of motif were created. In a separate study Natalie Franklin (1992, 1996) demonstrated that engraving sites near Mount Isa shared features with each other, emphasizing complex patterns of circles and crescents, but were different from early art sites in other regions (Figure 6.6). She interpreted this as evidence for a regional Mount Isa rock art style.

Even further from Mount Isa, across the Western Desert, engravings depict distinctive heads called 'Archaic faces' (Figure 6.7). They have pecked eyes and mouths, often in a stylized heart-shaped frame, sometimes with ears, noses and other body parts. Josephine McDonald (2005) demonstrated that across huge areas of central and western Australia, archaic faces display the same constellation of features. Their distribution in a single area of the interior suggests a cultural bloc existed in the desert. Within that bloc there were local variants of this distinctive motif type, further evidence that Pleistocene inhabitants of Australia did not possess

Figure 6.6 Engravings from the Mount Isa region showing elaborate curved lines.

Figure 6.7 Examples of pecked 'archaic faces' recorded from a variety of sites in central Australia (redrawn from McDonald 2005).

a single artistic practice. Archaeologists now have evidence of the distinctive character and history of human life in a number of regions across Australia. Examples reveal the unique economic, social and symbolic characteristics of ancient life in each region, as well as something of those lives.

A different story from the north

Claims that Pleistocene technologies were the same everywhere had ignored the discovery of the world's oldest stone axes only in northern Australia. These were made by grinding both sides of the stone with abrasives until the smoothed axe bevel was formed (Figure 6.8). Axes are thought to have been hafted on a wooden shaft, implying more engineering considerations than just the production of the axes themselves. Hafted axes allow forceful chopping and pounding actions to be performed; in some circumstances they allow people without great strength and skill to carry out percussive activities. More than 25,000–30,000 years ago in Arnhem Land, the Kimberley and on Cape York, people created axes similar to those made in the last millennium (White 1967; Morwood and Trezise 1989; O'Connor 1996). No evidence of this technology has been found in southern Australia prior to the last few thousand years. This is a compelling reason to conclude that there were long-standing regional distinctions in stone toolkits, and that Pleistocene technologies should not be burdened with labels such as simple or uniform.

Archaeologists viewed Pleistocene technology as simple and uniform partly because, although many kinds of tools were used by early foragers, only stone artefacts were commonly preserved. However, axe heads more than 25,000 years old imply that people hafted stone artefacts onto wooden handles and shafts, creating elaborate tools. Pleistocene axes provide an insight into rarely preserved organic components of ancient technologies. In Arnhem Land another, even more powerful, way to reconstruct ancient organic tools is by viewing remarkably preserved rock paintings.

In many parts of Australia weathered engravings have been thought of as the characteristic Pleistocene art, but paintings and other art works were probably also made. Early paintings may not have been preserved in many situations; the longevity of paint on rock varies significantly with the type of rock, nature of paint and the micro-environment of the painted surface (Bednarik 1994). Only in unusual situations, such as the formation of stabilizing silica skins over the rock

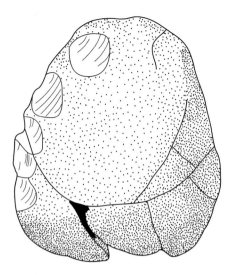

Figure 6.8 Axe recovered from Pleistocene levels of Malangangerr, Arnhem Land, estimated to be approximately 25,000–30,000 years old. The specimen was weathered and broken, and has been pieced together (redrawn from Schrire 1982: 107).

surface, are paintings likely to remain for tens of thousands of years. Outstanding preservation exists in some northern Australian regions, where rich records of paintings indicate that elaborate painted images were not only a recent phenomenon in Australia (Chaloupka 1984, 1985; Watchman 1993; Roberts et al. 1997, 2003; Chippindale and Taçon 1998; O'Connor and Fankhauser 2001).

One such region is western Arnhem Land where excavations in sandstone rock shelters, including Nauwalabila and Malakunanja, recovered Pleistocene-age fragments of ochre. Pieces of ochre came from the lowest levels of those sites and some have abraded facets showing they were used (Jones and Johnson 1985; Taçon and Brockwell 1995). While these ochre pellets may have had many uses, the existence of ochre throughout archaeological sequences probably indicates that paintings as well as engravings were part of the repertoire of Pleistocene artists, even in the earliest period of human settlement (Chippindale and Taçon 1998). Furthermore, ochre was not found in the same quantities throughout the deposits but as 'pulses' of abundant fragments that have been interpreted as indicating pulses of artistic activity, each perhaps associated with different kinds of paintings (Taçon and Brockwell 1995). A sequence of different painted styles and subjects is preserved on the walls of cliffs and rock shelters in Arnhem Land, where archaeologists have used them as an insight into changing economy, social life and ideology.

Rock art is difficult to date but studies of the layers of paint, subject matter, and even radiocarbon and OSL analyses have been used to build an understanding of the chronology of paintings in the vicinity of Jim Jim Creek and other areas on the Arnhem Land Plateau (Chippindale and Taçon 1998; Roberts et al. 2003). George Chaloupka (1984, 1985, 1993) described a sequence of changes in the plants and animals which artists had painted. He noted that earlier phases of painting contained images of grass, and large, naturalistically portrayed animals, including extinct species, such as thylacine, Tasmanian devil and perhaps megafauna (Murray and Chaloupka 1984). This art was followed by the 'Dynamic' phase, in which distinctively painted humans carry weapons, wear clothing and are often shown running or leaping (Figure 6.9). Later still was a phase dominated by anthropomorphic figures with characteristics of yams. Although the precise antiquity of those early paintings has not been established a terminal Pleistocene age has been estimated, perhaps 10,000–20,000 years ago (Chaloupka 1984, 1985, 1993; Lewis 1988; Chippindale and Taçon 1998). Large naturalistic, Dynamic and Yam phases are considered by Chaloupka to date from a period prior to Holocene sea-level rise and environmental change (Chapter 9). Only later did ancient artists paint the marine and swamp animals of the modern Arnhem Land environment, such as saltwater crocodiles and freshwater fish. Chaloupka argued that paintings of large naturalistic animals and Dynamic figures were technically sophisticated artistic representations by artists who lived in ice-age environments.

Pleistocene paintings of Arnhem Land provide us with a rare view of ancient life. Darrell Lewis (1988) observed that the art sequence depicted changes in the weapons and clothing used in different periods. In the Dynamic phase humans are frequently shown carrying spears with barbs, boomerangs, and sometimes axes and bags (Figure 6.9). Dynamic figures also commonly have clothing and ornamentation, perhaps belts or shirts, arm bands and elaborate headdresses. Although these images are difficult to interpret, we do not know if they are representations of humans or human-like supernatural beings, these paintings probably display images of weapons and dress that were used during the Pleistocene but have not survived in the archaeological record. This confirms the danger of using stone artefacts alone to construct an understanding of life in the Australian Pleistocene. Dynamic paintings reveal that ancient people had material possessions as diverse and elaborate as those of Aboriginal people observed historically. Paintings show differences between organic artefacts employed in the Pleistocene and in the historical period, revealing changes through time in the use of tools and symbols.

Figure 6.9 Dynamic figures from western Arnhem Land (redrawn from Chippindale et al. 2000). Figures not shown at the same scale.

For example, boomerangs are frequently depicted in the Dynamic phase but were not used as weapons or hunting tools in the region during recent centuries, while spear throwers were painted only in later art styles indicating that for part of the Pleistocene people of western Arnhem Land did not use them. This pattern is also seen in early paintings from the Kimberley region, where images estimated to be more than 20,000 years old show hunters carrying and using boomerangs and plain or multi-barbed hand-thrown spears, but not spear throwers (Walsh and Morwood 1999). However, artistic conventions used by Pleistocene artists in the Kimberley differed from those of the Dynamic figure artists of Arnhem Land, again demonstrating regional differentiation.

Dynamic phase paintings of Arnhem Land yield two further insights into Pleistocene human life in that area. One revelation comes from evocative images of humans hunting and interacting with each other. Artists painting Dynamic figures presented scenes of people running, alone and in groups, standing, sitting or falling, holding branches or branch-like artefacts, having sex, killing animals and killing each other (Chippindale et al. 2000). Of these activities the scenes of conflict have attracted most attention. Figures were shown throwing boomerangs and spears at each other, bending to avoid spears, and helping or finishing off speared individuals on the ground (Chaloupka 1984). Dynamic fighting scenes depict a small number of combatants, while later art sometimes showed more humans fighting, leading Taçon and Chippindale (1994) to conclude that larger, more organized warfare occurred in the Holocene. This literal interpretation of violent scenes may be misleading; the different representations could have arisen simply from early artistic conventions depicting battles as personal conflict between individuals. Without more direct evidence of the dimensions of conflict the structure of ancient artistic conventions remains unclear. Indeed archaeologists cannot be sure whether scenes of combat depict real or imagined events, or whether they were viewed as history or metaphor, but it seems that the Pleistocene artists of the north could at the very least conceive of conflict and war.

Dynamic paintings also give us an insight, albeit cryptic, into the ideology, cosmology and social life of Pleistocene people of the north. Elements of clothing and particularly headdresses are often displayed as large and elaborate; sometimes they are standardized for all figures in a scene. One explanation of these paintings is that people were shown wearing ceremonial paraphernalia, perhaps engaged in rituals of some kind. An alternative interpretation is that the paintings themselves were ritual performances and the dream-like quality of many scenes hints at one of the social functions of Dynamic art. Headdresses, for example, are not only ornate but sometimes impossibly large, and they replace the head of a human in some figures. Although these elements may be an expression of artistic licence in some paintings, non-existent entities are also depicted. For instance, Dynamic phase art panels often contain depictions of imaginary beings, part-human and part-animal, such as creatures with human bodies but animal heads, called 'therianthropes' by archaeologists (Chippindale et al. 2000). Therianthropes are depicted watching humans, running with people, and sometimes attacking and killing people (Figure 6.10). After perhaps 20,000 years it is hard to know what these disconcerting therianthrope

Figure 6.10 Painting of therianthrope and human from the Dynamic period of western Arnhem Land (from Chippindale et al. 2000). The therianthrope appears to be striking the human with a weapon similar to a boomerang or fighting-pick. Figures were about 35 cm high.

figures represented for Pleistocene people. An important creative theme in historical Aboriginal cosmology, the Rainbow Serpent, was a more recent invention (Chapter 13), and in the Pleistocene it is conceivable that creative beings and forces might have been represented in entities such as these. Christopher Chippindale and his colleagues proposed that therianthropes and other images painted in Dynamic art were depictions of hallucinatory visions experienced by people in altered states of consciousness (Chippindale et al. 2000). He suggests that during the Dynamic phase individuals emerged who were acknowledged by their social group as having capacities to engage with the supernatural, possibly by invoking familiars during altered states. Chippindale argued that individuals recognized as having this skill were known in some recent Aboriginal societies and this role may have a long time depth, although the function of such people in society may have been different in the past. Whether this or other cosmological beliefs and symbolic rules explains the visionary and incongruous character of Dynamic paintings is unclear, but there is no doubt that the art preserved from this remote period reveals the existence of elaborate ideologies and technologies in Pleistocene Australia.

In glimpsing the lives and attitudes of ancient people in Arnhem Land, we should be aware of the distance between them and Aboriginal people of the historic period. Different phases of artistic activity are distinguished from each other by the conventions of painters, the subject matter and the environment being depicted (Chaloupka 1984, 1985, 1993; Lewis 1988, 1997; Taçon and Brockwell 1995; Chippindale et al. 1998, 2000). These distinctions indicate cultural transformations and discontinuities between the major artistic phases, as people repeatedly reorganized their economies and ideologies, as well as altered cultural rules for painting. The existence of battle scenes throughout the artistic sequence prompted some researchers to suggest that replacement of groups, or culture contact between groups, had caused social and artistic changes (Lewis 1988). This proposition is consistent with the observation that there are limited similarities in subject matter and painting style between phases, a pattern that has been interpreted as revealing that the different phases were not part of a continuous social and artistic tradition (Chippindale and Taçon 1998). Additionally, hiatuses between some of the early artistic phases in Arnhem Land, in which little or no art was created in the rock shelters, might correspond with abandonment of the local region. Archaeological evidence that economic and social systems in the Pleistocene were not continuous, slowly evolving phenomena but were repeatedly adjusted, and perhaps extinguished, exists for this and other regions in northern Australia, but it is a case study from the opposite side of the continent that reinforces how widespread cultural reorganization was during that early period of human life in Australia.

A different story from the south

From the southern edge of Greater Australia the life ways of Pleistocene foragers inhabiting a sub-arctic environment again demonstrates the diversity of social and technological systems employed by early human groups. The deep river valleys of cold, mountainous southwestern Tasmania were occupied by humans more than 37,000–39,000 years ago but abandoned before the end of the Pleistocene (Cosgrove 1999). During this period the trend towards colder and drier conditions as the LGM approached is recorded in pollen records and lake levels (Cosgrove et al. 1990). Evidence for human occupation is preserved in limestone caves containing densely packed deposits of bone fragments and stone artefacts. A number of these sites, including Bone Cave, Nunamira Cave (Figure 6.11), Warreen Rockshelter, Mackintosh Cave, Pallawa Trounta and Kutikina have been excavated. Each cave had a different history of occupation, partly because climatic cooling had dissimilar effects on caves at different altitudes within the mountains (Porch and Allen 1995). As individual sites recorded human responses to the particular environments surrounding each cave, the total economic system of the southwestern plateau cannot be illustrated from any single cave deposit (Holdaway and Porch 1995; Cosgrove 1999).

The economy inferred from analysis of archaeological materials found in these caves is highly focused. Pleistocene hunters targeted two species of marsupial: Bennett's Wallaby (*Macropus rufogriseus*) and the wombat (*Vombatus ursinus*). Richard

Figure 6.11 Nunamira Cave during excavation. Richard Cosgrove is seen carrying buckets of sediment out of the cave to be sieved. (Courtesy of R. Cosgrove.)

Cosgrove (1999) has shown that bones from many other small animals, such as mice, were natural accumulations and that wallabies, supplemented by wombat, provided at least four-fifths of the meat consumed by humans living in the region.

Few traces of the technology used by these ancient wallaby hunters have been preserved. Bone points recovered from excavations at a number of caves were made by grinding wallaby limb bones. While these points may have been tools with which clothing was manufactured (Cosgrove 1999), some have use-damage consistent with their having been used as spear tips (C. Webb and Allen 1990). Hence these hunters may have used not only single piece wooden spears but also composite, bone-pointed spears; certainly there were organic artefacts which have not been preserved.

The most distinctive element in the stone technology was small disc-shaped retouched flakes, called 'thumbnail scrapers' (Figure 6.12). These stout tools were used for butchering, and bone and wood working, and they may have been hafted to create the working edges in multipurpose composite tools. Their role in highland Tasmanian hunting is still debated, but Cosgrove (1999) demonstrated that they were used for at least 15,000 years and argued that they do not indicate that people were highly mobile, as had initially been suggested (McNiven 1994; Jones 1995). The existence of these small, carefully shaped stone artefacts, manufactured for many millennia in Pleistocene Tasmania, once again documents regional and chronological diversity in tool production that had not been recognized by an earlier generation of researchers (McNiven 2000). These stone tools were part of

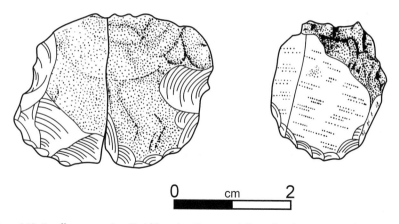

Figure 6.12 Small stone tools called 'thumbnail scrapers' from the Pleistocene rock shelters of southern Tasmania (redrawn from Cosgrove 1999: 374).

a systematic, focused economy specializing in wallaby hunting that allowed foragers to exploit an unusual ecosystem.

Pleistocene vegetation on the central plateau was largely resource-poor shrub and heath, but small patches of grassland were situated on fertile soils. This patchy ecological pattern existed, Cosgrove (1999) argued, because of moisture levels in past climatic conditions. Grassed patches were crucial because they supported the wallabies targeted by the hunters. Bennett's Wallaby are solitary feeders, tethered to patches of grassland; they grazed in almost the same spot every year, providing Pleistocene hunters with a predictable meat resource. Hunters travelled to grassland patches, located and killed wallabies which they butchered or transported whole back to the limestone caves that have preserved archaeological traces of their activities (Cosgrove et al. 1990; Cosgrove 1999; Cosgrove and Allen 2000). Anne Pike-Tay and Richard Cosgrove observed that it was young and older, larger walla-bies who were usually hunted, thereby efficiently obtaining meat but having a minimal impact on the ability of wallabies of breeding age to reproduce (Pike-Tay and Cosgrove 2002; Cosgrove and Pike-Tay 2004). Foragers most likely exploited patches until the wallaby harvest in each patch diminished, at which point they searched a new patch and perhaps moved their base camp to a different cave (Cosgrove and Allen 2000). In this sub-arctic environment plant foods were limited and humans relied on intense wallaby harvesting; the extraction of marrow from long bones resulted in archaeological deposits densely packed with macropod bone fragments. Reliance on wallaby harvesting would have been particularly important during lean seasons, as the bones of killed animals indicate that most of the cave use took place during autumn and late spring when few other resources were available (Cosgrove and Pike-Tay 2004). Cosgrove's reconstruction describes these hunting activities at a short, ethnographic time-scale, and while it explains how wallabies were exploited as a dietary staple it is not an economic strategy that could be applied at all time periods.

Pleistocene economy of the Tasmanian central plateau changed through time. By analysing information from multiple archaeological sites Simon Holdaway and Nick Porch identified alterations in the intensity of human occupation of the region. Changes in the abundance of artefacts mirror changes in the number of radiocarbon samples (and hence occupation/hearth levels). Holdaway and Porch (1995, 1996) argued the intensity of human occupation in the southwest was higher during periods with greater moisture and lower during the colder and drier climatic periods which occurred about every 3,000 years (Figure 6.13). There were three climatically moist periods, each several thousand years long, in which human occupation of this region was intense. Cosgrove's model of specialized wallaby hunting is applicable to each of these periods. During drier periods a different economic strategy was required. In eastern Tasmania, where drier conditions meant that food resources were more dispersed and less predictable, foragers were more mobile and hunters would have had to attack animals as they encountered them. This pattern appeared on the southwestern plateau with the onset of drier conditions. Reduction of game abundance and an increase in their dispersion meant that hunters were no longer able to anticipate the location of animals and could not base their settlement system around the intensive harvesting of animals concentrated in particular microhabitats. Irregular, short-term hunting visits to upland sites were typical of the economy during those conditions (Cosgrove and Pike-Tay 2004). Increased mobility and dispersion of people and/or, in some localities, reduction or cessation of occupation resulted.

Oscillation between dry and moist periods in southwestern Tasmania, each with a different economic system, created a cyclical pattern of occupation. The implications of economic cycles are challenging. On a number of occasions, when moister and more stable climatic conditions were renewed about 29,000 years ago, then again 22,000 years ago, local people reinvented or reconfigured economic systems based on the same ecological opportunity of habitat-tethered wallabies. These reconstituted wallaby-focused economic systems had much in common but archaeological evidence indicates they were variants on a theme, not identical. Some sites began to be occupied while others ceased to be used, revealing changing patterns of landscape usage; 'thumbnail scrapers' were emphasized more in the final period of intensive occupation (Cosgrove 1999), indicating alterations in the toolkit and the way technology was used to mediate growing environmental risks (McNiven 1994; Cosgrove 1999); hunting selectivity changed in the final period, becoming less focused on older wallabies (Pike-Tay and Cosgrove 2002); and the intensity of occupation may have been greater between 20,000 and 17,000 years ago than in earlier times, possibly as Cosgrove (1999) suggests because of reduced climatic stability in eastern Tasmania at that time. Each economic system persisted for a few thousand years before being reorganized in response to climate change. The repetition of economic cycles indicates that rather than long-term continuity in life ways there were similar adaptive strategies constructed on multiple occasions.

In Tasmania archaeologists observe cycles of economic activity rather than directional and gradual progression towards historical life ways. Disjunction between Pleistocene foraging systems and more recent ones is emphasized in this instance

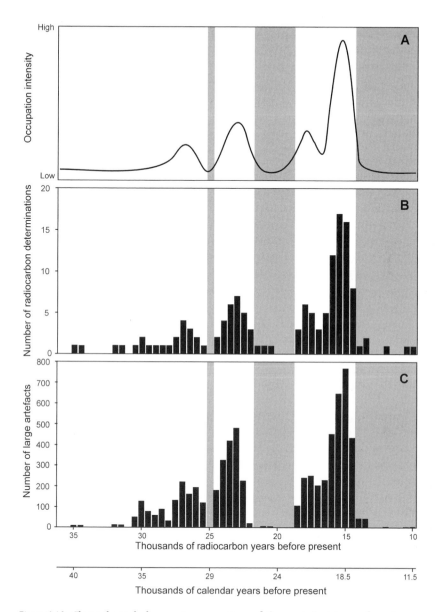

Figure 6.13 Chronological changes in occupation of the central plateau of southwestern Tasmania (from Holdaway and Porch 1995); A = estimates of occupational intensity, based on B and C; B = number of radiocarbon determinations in Bone Cave, Warreen, Mackintosh and Pallawa Trounta; C = number of large artefacts in spits with a radiocarbon determination. Grey strips denote periods of reduced occupation levels.

by archaeological evidence that before 15,000 years ago humans had abandoned the entire southwestern highland region of Tasmania as climate change led to an increase in rainforest and the consequent removal of the animal resources on which early foragers had relied, ending a prolonged and dynamic period of human occupation of that landscape.

Sophistication, diversity and change as characteristics of Pleistocene life

These two case studies illustrate some of the archaeological evidence that early humans in Australia had diverse, changing and often elaborate ways of life. We need not think of cultural change in Australian pre-history as a gradual and directional progression towards more complex cultural systems. Instead, there is evidence of transformations in economic and social elements of Pleistocene cultural systems in response to many factors, including reorganized land use, altered environments, modified social relationships with neighbouring groups, and demographic fluctuations. Long-term trends in cultural characteristics may have occurred in some regions but archaeological residues do not indicate that unidirectional change or simplicity was characteristic of early human life in Australia. On the contrary, evidence supports an adaptive model of Pleistocene occupation, in which people arriving in Australia came with efficient and diverse economic, technological and social practices. Preserved debris from Pleistocene deposits does not document the growth of cognitive capacities or cultural sophistication; it records the adaptation of social and economic practices to different circumstances encountered by ancient foragers. This is an evolutionary perspective that owes nothing to nineteenth century cultural evolution and its notion of cultural progression; this idea of adaptation owes more to the Darwinian mechanisms of evolution discussed in Chapter 5, although human adaptation is not principally biological but involves the modification and transmission of ideas and practices between generations of people. An adaptive model makes it possible to understand many of the patterns seen in the Arnhem Land and Tasmanian cases, such as cycles of change, multiple transformations of symbolic and ideological systems, geographical variation in life ways, elaborate early technologies, and even the cessation of land use and social systems. From an adaptive viewpoint these practices emerged, and changed, as ways to manipulate and comprehend the natural and social environments confronting people in each time and place.

It is hard to appreciate how much material debris of Pleistocene human life has been destroyed, but depictions in the Arnhem Land paintings begin to reveal how many kinds of artefacts and activities existed but are not preserved, and the cycles of Pleistocene economy in Tasmania reveal how complex, non-directional changes in life ways existed but are rarely visible. Archaeological residues of human occupation during the Pleistocene are highly patterned: with increasing antiquity there are fewer known sites, typically less material within each of those sites, and lower chronological resolution in radiometric dating (O'Connor and Veth 2006). Archaeologists often interpreted the sparseness of material evidence for the earliest occupation of Australia as an indication that there had been very few people in the landscape and that they lived within relatively simple social, economic and ideological frameworks (Chapters 12 and 13). A stronger, alternative interpretation is that perceived poverty and homogeneity of early archaeological sites, and the apparent subsequent growth in the abundance and diversity of cultural materials, mainly reflects the failure of early cultural expressions to be preserved and discovered. A number of discoveries indicate that poor preservation and small samples have played a key role in making Pleistocene life seem less varied and changing than life in more recent millennia.

For example, Michael Hanckel (1985) discovered that more than 20,000 years ago artisans at Burrill Lake rock shelter in southeastern Australia had carefully modified the properties of rocks from which they shaped artefacts. Called 'heat treating', this modification involved controlled heating of rocks, perhaps in specially constructed ovens, for many hours (Flenniken and White 1983). The result was rock that fractured more smoothly (Figure 6.14), giving artisans greater control over the shaping of tools, increasing success rates in tool manufacture and creating tool edges that were sharper than could be produced with natural, unmodified rock. Heat treatment at Burrill Lake is one expression of complex processes in the production of Pleistocene tools and also of technical knowledge possessed by those artisans.

A more significant discovery was the existence, in Pleistocene archaeological deposits, of stone-working technologies once thought to be restricted to the Holocene. Early axes in northern Australia, used more than 25,000 years ago, were described above. Another kind of artefact recovered from Pleistocene contexts is abraded stones (Figure 2.4B), used to grind materials, including distinctive ones that were probably used to process grass seeds. At lake systems in southeastern Australia, mortars and amorphously shaped blocks of rock with ground surfaces have been found in many archaeological sites. It is likely that they were employed to grind and pound many kinds of plants, ochre and animals; perhaps as multi-purpose tools (Balme 1991; H. Allen 1998). At Cuddie Springs extensive excavations also recovered similar grinding stones, complete with residues of plant use, from levels more than 35,000 years old (Dodson et al. 1993; Fullagar and Field 1997; Fullagar et al. 2007). These kinds of grinding stones have not been found in all

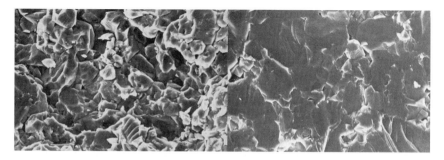

Figure 6.14 Fracture through the same rock, before (left) and after (right) heat treatment.

regions and appear be linked to the exploitation of inland environments, although in some regions grinding was also carried out using other objects such as non-portable boulders and rock outcrops (Gorecki et al. 1997).

During the 1980s discussions of Pleistocene grinding technologies focused on the apparent absence of specialized grinding stones called 'millstones'; dish-like ground slabs thought to have ground grass seeds (M. A. Smith 1986b; Balme 1991). Some researchers concluded that the invention of millstones and/or the broadening of diet to incorporate grass seeds must have been a much later phenomenon. Mike Smith (1986a, 1988) argued that intensive exploitation of grass seeds with mill-stones happened only within the last few thousand years. However, grinding stones were rarely discarded in archaeological sites, and dedicated millstones were even rarer, and hence the chance of finding them in Pleistocene deposits might be low even though they had been in use (Gorecki et al. 1997). Pleistocene-age fragments of broken millstones were finally discovered by Fullagar and Field (1997) at Cuddie Springs, in levels estimated to be 35,000–40,000 years old. The age of those millstones has been challenged (David 2002), but it is likely that Pleistocene foragers would have used grass seeds (Edwards and O'Connell 1995) and there is no compelling reason to dismiss the Cuddie Springs evidence as a product of distur-bance (Chapter 4). Many kinds of grinding stones, including millstones, were used during the Pleistocene, but in very low numbers, and they have been recovered from only some periods and places. Early foragers were equipped with the same range of grinding techniques and tools as later foragers, but appear to have used those techniques less frequently. If there was a greater emphasis on grinding tech-nologies, and seed-grinding tools in particular, later in Australian pre-history, that does not reflect a different technological capacity, but instead indicates shifts in the circumstances of Australian foragers.

Poor preservation and low chronological resolution often shroud interpretations of Pleistocene economies and technologies with uncertainty (Balme 1995), but there is a range of evidence that reveals a diversity of practices. Organic tools have also occasionally been recovered from archaeological deposits. Bones shaped into points or spatulas have been found in several Pleistocene deposits (Flood 1974; Dortch 1984; C. Webb and Allen 1990; Cosgrove 1999). Even wooden artefacts such as spears and boomerangs have been found in water-logged deposits dating to the end of the Pleistocene (Luebbers 1975). For the period before 20,000 years bp there is indirect evidence of the diversity of organic technology in the Pleistocene, such as the details of clothing, basketry and ornaments presented in preserved rock paintings. Additionally, Jane Balme (1983, 1995) has argued that fibre nets had been used to catch the fish whose remains she excavated at the Major Swale site on Lake Tandou. Estimated to be at least 27,000 years old the site contained three clusters of material, a dense pile of freshwater shells, bones from more than 250 Golden Perch fish, and a concentration containing fragments from more than 500 freshwater crayfish. These separate piles were deposited rapidly; each represents a single foraging event, perhaps the work of a single day or a few days. Balme's analysis of the bones revealed that the fish were roughly the same size, and had probably been caught with a net whose mesh determined the size of those trapped.

This is another indication that Pleistocene people had a diverse set of organic artefacts which have not been preserved in the archaeological record.

Archaeologists have sometimes thought Pleistocene people were normally dispersed but came together to capture plentiful but impermanent resources. This pattern may not be applicable everywhere. For instance, at Cuddie Springs a variety of resources were harvested, plant foods as well as small and large game, a pattern that does not suggest exploitation of a temporary food supply; while in southeast Tasmania targeting sedentary wallabies permitted more stable and predictable aggregations of people for prolonged periods. Even in regions where evidence indicates that inland Pleistocene foragers were highly mobile, ranging across large territories, there is data consistent with large aggregation events and information networks that coordinated economic and social activities. For example, Balme (1995) concluded that 25,000–30,000 years ago large numbers of humans, perhaps a hundred or more, congregated at Lake Tandou. Her interpretation was based on the remarkably preserved food remains at the Major Swale site where fishing with nets, perhaps a cooperative exercise for several people, resulted in catches of hundreds of fish, enough to feed large numbers of people. These were only short-term gatherings, perhaps a few days, and people did not repeatedly camp on these locations. This pattern is unlike Holocene occupation in the area, revealing that the early lacustrine-based inland economies discussed in Chapter 3 were different from those documented in the historical period. Evidence of large groups living at Lake Tandou also indicate that either large group sizes were common and those groups moved across large territories, but stayed a short time at most camp sites, or alternatively that Pleistocene humans often lived in smaller, dispersed groups but occasionally came together for larger gatherings. It is unclear which interpretation should be preferred, but either scenario indicates that more than 25,000 years ago economic and social systems involved regular, large gatherings and dispels suggestions that organized, communal hunting strategies emerged only at later times. Furthermore, regular, large gatherings of people required the maintenance of social networks by which gatherings were arranged. Evidence collected by Harry Allen (1998) at Lake Mungo indicated to him that during the Pleistocene dispersed family groups coalesced on lake margins to harvest foods. However, the economic flexibility displayed at temporary gatherings in these lakeside settings must have been coordinated by an effective system of information exchange and the regular gatherings ordered through social rules proscribing behaviour. Perhaps, in the rich environments of inland lakes, dispersed residential groups were rarely far apart, creating opportunities for ongoing social interactions without maintaining ongoing large residential groups.

The frequency and scale of Pleistocene aggregation events cannot be stated at the moment, but it can be reasoned that they may have been larger and more common than archaeologists have sometimes considered. Balme's Major Swale site contained few stone artefacts and the aggregation of a large number of people is only demonstrated by the bone debris, which in many other inland areas has not been preserved. The material remains of large but short-term gatherings of people can be minimal and fragile, and given poor preservation in many localities it is surprising that archaeologists have been able to identify such events at all. While the frequency of such gatherings cannot be estimated there is other evidence for the existence of the networks in which they operated.

The circulation of ochre and rare materials, such as marine shell, over hundreds of kilometres in the arid zone indicates early the operation of extensive social networks involving exchange or congregations (M. A. Smith et al. 1998; O'Connor 1999b; Balme 2000; Balme and Morse 2006). Pardoe (1991b) argued that variation in ancient skeletons indicates wider networks of marriage patterns during the Pleistocene than in the Holocene, a pattern that also implies social networks covering large territories. The scale and organization of Pleistocene networks are difficult to specify but even if they involved the interaction of mobile groups over large territories, we can infer that regular communication, group identity and shared symbols were key elements. As a permanent, distinctive and highly visible physical trait, cranial deformation created by binding the heads of infants (Chapter 5) may have been one way in which Pleistocene people in the southeast distinguished groups (Pardoe 1993). Regional art styles, such as the Western Desert archaic faces, the Dynamic figures of Arnhem Land or the Bradshaw figures of the Kimberley, encoded symbolism shared between human groups, and they probably reflect the existence of regional cultural networks maintained through inter-group gatherings prior to the LGM, something predicted by Claire Smith (1992), Mike Smith (Smith et al. 1998) and Peter Thorley (2001).

Transportation of ochre across large distances in the Pleistocene, perhaps by exchange between groups, has been documented in several regions. The best example, described in Chapter 3, was the acquisition, by people living at Puritjarra, of ochre from Karrku 125 km to the northwest; an activity that occurred intermittently at least 39,000 years ago. It is likely that the procurement and transportation of ochre not only had an economic dimension but also reveal the existence of social and ideological dimensions to life in the Pleistocene. Use of ochre in sites such as Puritjarra was probably associated with artistic performances, particularly rock painting. Noting that in layers older than about 16,000 years bp, ochre fragments were recovered only from the centre of the shelter, away from the rock wall, Rosenfeld and Smith (2002) argued that prior to the LGM, ochre in this site had not been used to paint the walls, but had been applied to human bodies or portable items such as implements and ornaments. A stronger interpretation of this evidence is that at Puritjarra rock paintings were made by humans throughout 40,000 years of occupation, but away from the centre of the cave ochre fragments had once been present but have not been preserved (Thorley 2004). It is also likely that early rock art has not survived and paintings that remain on the shelter walls are not Pleistocene in age. Hence ochre fragments preserved in some parts of the shelter floor indicate that paintings were made throughout the entire history of human occupation at Puritjarra but we have no record of their nature. This pattern is known from other Pleistocene sites where ochre fragments provide evidence of artistic activities which are not preserved and therefore cannot be described in detail. For example, Mike Morwood (2002) used ochre preserved in archaeological deposits and in weathered crusts on rock faces to conclude that artists had been painting in shelters on southeastern Cape York since at least 30,000–40,000 years bp, but none of the paintings that have been preserved is older than about 3,000 years bp.

Decorative and symbolic use of ochre is not limited to a few sites or time periods but is documented throughout Australian pre-history from the start of human occupation. Painting at Puritjarra nearly 40,000 years ago is only one example of evidence for very early art. At Carpenter's Gap (O'Connor 1995; O'Connor and Fankhauser 2001) a rock slab covered in ochre was recovered from a layer more than 40,000 years old, a find interpreted by some researchers as a section of painted shelter wall (Morwood 2002) that had fallen off and been buried. In Arnhem Land, at Nauwalabila and Malakunanja, there are ochre fragments, some with ground facets showing they had been abraded, deposited in the lowest portion of the archaeological deposit (Taçon and Brockwell 1995). The existence of ochre, often transported from distant locations, in the earliest levels of these Pleistocene sites, reveals that artistic and ritual activities of some kind were always part of social life in ancient Australia.

The most striking example of the early social use of red ochre is its association with rituals and burial rituals in particular. During excavation of WLH3 individual a dark red stain was visible, created when red ochre was scattered over the body during its burial 40,000 (38,000–42,000) years ago (Figure 6.15). This ochre had been procured at a distant location, processed and carried to the Lake Mungo lunette, embedding its ritual use in a web of economic and social relations. Using ochre during the WLH3 burial ritual undoubtedly invoked different meanings for the mourners, 40 millennia ago, than similar rituals would have in more recent times, but the existence of a burial ritual at Lake Mungo reveals the existence of beliefs, cosmologies and social attitudes soon after the human colonization of Australia.

The use, by the earliest occupants of Australia, of ochre for painting and as a symbol expressing ideologies and social relationships is no surprise. Systematic use of red ochre as a colouring agent has been employed by humans in Africa for hundreds of thousands of years (McBreaty and Brooks 2000; Barham 2002), and is undoubtedly a symbolic behaviour that was brought to Australia with the first humans to arrive. These uses of ochre probably helped ancient settlers develop a relationship with the land. Pigments such as red ochre can be used to place unmistakable human marks on surfaces of all kinds, and may have functioned to 'socialize' the Australian landscape by creating cultural signs where none had existed (Taçon 1994). Widespread use of art during the Pleistocene was also a way of expressing and constructing ideology and managing social interactions, and it is evidence of the existence of a rich symbolic code. Interpretations of the paintings of western Arnhem Land hint at the ideology and symbolism that may have been represented in Pleistocene art.

The antiquity and diversity of symbolism and ideology is not only recorded in ochre from Pleistocene deposits, it is also signified by other kinds of archaeological residues. Goods placed into Pleistocene graves, such as the shells in some Kow Swamp burials, and differences in the treatment of individual bodies, such as the cremation of some but interment of others, are additional examples of the presence

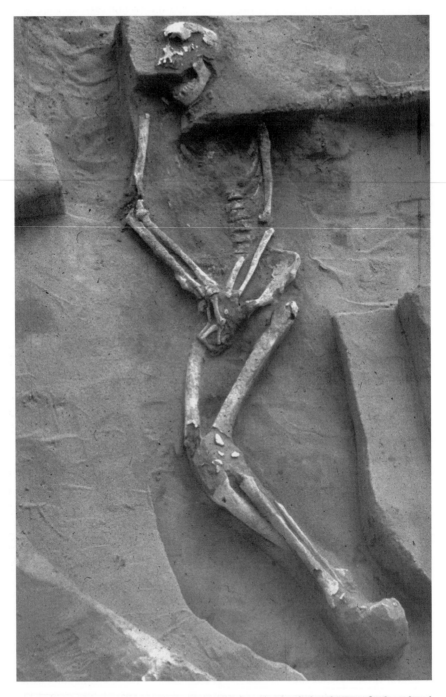

Figure 6.15 Excavation of WLH3 at Lake Mungo showing the dark red stain of ochre placed on and around the body in the grave. (Courtesy of W. Shawcross.)

and diversity of early ritual. Such residues are rare and do not offer archaeologists an extensive chronological framework; however, evidence for symbolic behaviour has survived from some of the earliest archaeological deposits in Australia, in the form of ornaments.

Ornaments made from shells and stones have been recovered from the early levels of rock shelter deposits. At the base of the Mandu Mandu Creek deposit, in a level with ochre fragments estimated to be more than 37,000 years old, Kate Morse found 22 cone shells that had been perforated and reshaped in such a way that they could be strung on a thread. In fact Morse found what might be abrasion from a thread on the inside surface of the perforations. These shells had been selected for their similar size and shapes, and Morse (1993a, 1993b) suggested they had formed the strand of shell beads shown in Figure 6.16. Her discovery is not unique. A perforated piece of stone found in the Devil's Lair rock shelter has also been interpreted as a Pleistocene ornament (Dortch 1979c; Bednarik 1997), and would perhaps have been used as a pendant on a fibre string. A third find was at the inland rock shelter of Riwi, where Jane Balme recovered ten beads made from fragments of tusk shell in a layer about 34,000 years old. These shells also appear to have been strung on fibre string, part of which has been preserved on the end of one of the beads (Balme and Morse 2006). Some of the beads still have an ochre residue on them, showing that the strand of shell beads had been artificially coloured. The Riwi

Figure 6.16 Morse's (1993a, 1993b) reconstruction of the shell beads from Mandu Mandu Creek as an ornament. (Courtesy of K. Morse.)

beads were not made from locally available shells and they had been transported at least 300 km, an observation again consistent with either individuals travelling across large territories or acquiring shells through exchange networks in existence at that time. Archaeologists cannot know what social meaning these ornaments contained, but they can be confident that the beads conveyed social information, such as signifying status or membership or wealth, as they do in all societies. These ornaments show that the early human occupants of Australia lived in contexts where population size and/or social interaction made visual communication of identity and relationships advantageous. This use of symbols was common among dispersing humans 40,000–60,000 years ago (Kuhn et al. 2001), and was probably a feature of foragers who colonized Australia.

This evidence is consistent with the idea that Australia was colonized by people able to exploit diverse and harsh landscapes, who used elaborate technologies, and possessed material expressions of ritual and symbolic practices. Following the dispersal of humans across the continent these cultural characteristics were possessed by human groups throughout Australian pre-history, although the patchy preservation of archaeological materials means they cannot always be recovered. Advocates of the 'progression' model misinterpreted poor preservation of early cultural residues as an indication that societies producing those residues had began as dispersed, socially simple groups of people who gradually acquired economic and social complexity through time. However, archaeological evidence now reveals that Pleistocene human societies in Australia were not uniform or unchanging; nor did they all progress directionally from simple technological and cultural beginnings. Instead it demonstrates regional and chronological diversity in economic systems, technologies, social and ritual practices, and their artistic and symbolic expression. Archaeologists are only beginning to understand the ways in which poor preservation and chronological ambiguity have cast an obscuring veil over the Pleistocene period, but their recognition of early settlement in many Australian landscapes, regionally diversified economic and technological practices, and changing social networks, symbolic and ideological systems now challenge depictions of Pleistocene people as merely simplified versions of historical Aboriginal people.

7 Tasmania isolated

Tasmania is the best example of a process of island formation that occurred at the end of the last ice-age. Rising seas created islands and archipelagos from what had once been landscapes of hills and plains. Bass Strait flooded nearly 14,000 years ago, separating Tasmania from mainland Australia and isolating Tasmanian Aborigines throughout the Holocene (Figure 7.1). The consequence for people in Tasmania has been vigorously debated. One view is that ancient Tasmanians struggled to cope with their isolation. This model interpreted archaeological change as revealing economic decline, social disarray and stagnation, with religious and intellectual dysfunction. Isolation of human groups is a powerful image in Western literature, often conveying hideous disadvantageous for anyone cut off from wider social interaction. Wrecked and wretched voyagers, lonely and desperate, surviving in a lowly state, were images in historical European thought that reflected perceived danger in nature and human reliance on society and technology as a buffer against nature. Some archaeologists argued that ancient Tasmanians were cultural castaways, stranded by sea-level rise, and their subsequent lifestyle changes resulted from their isolation.

Rocky Cape and the problem of the Tasmanians

In 1963 Rhys Jones began research on what he considered were the problems of explaining historical Tasmanian Aborigines. How had they travelled to the island, how successful and sophisticated were their lives, and why did these island dwellers not eat fish during historic times? These questions attracted him to caves located on a peninsula, called Rocky Cape, which protruded from the northern coastline of Tasmania into Bass Strait (Figure 7.1). These caves were large, horizontal crevices in cliffs; each was filled with sediment, creating deep deposits (Figure 7.2). Jones knew they contained archaeological materials and he correctly guessed they contained long records of human life that could help him answer his questions about ancient Tasmanians.

Jones (1971) excavated two caves: Rocky Cape North and Rock Cape South. The North Cave enclosed a deposit almost 3 metres deep, filled with bands of dumped shell, ash-rich layers marking the location of hearths, and black organic-rich sediment (Figure 7.3). Jones recognized four stratigraphic units. At the base of the

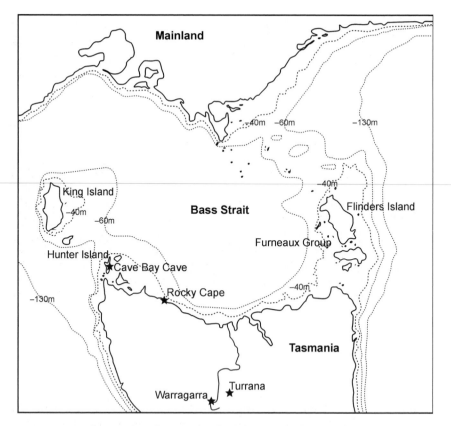

Figure 7.1 Map of Tasmania and Bass Strait Island showing localities mentioned in Chapter 7.

lowest level, an ash-rich shell midden called 'Unit 4', charcoal gave a radiocarbon estimate of 6,275 (6,170–6,315) years bp. Another charcoal sample with an estimated age of 3,690 (3,570–3,830) years bp came from the top of the overlaying midden level, called 'Unit 3'. After Unit 3 was created the deposit eroded, and then more human occupation built up the deposit further. The upper portion of the deposit contained evidence for the intensive use of small, hot hearths which left plentiful white ash and many burned shells. Near the surface Jones collected charcoal which gave a radiocarbon age-estimate of 510 (435–545) years bp. This is evidence that foragers intermittently lived in Rocky Cape North Cave during the past 6,000 years.

Human use of the neighbouring Rocky Cape South Cave was very different. There a 4-metre-deep deposit began to accumulate more than 8,000 years ago and a radiocarbon sample from the top of the deposit gave an age-estimate of nearly 4,000 years ago. Early in the twentieth century the surface deposits in this cave had been removed and the most recent archaeological material preserved in the site is 4,200 (3,900–4,500) years old.

Figure 7.2 The entrance to Rocky Cape North Cave in 1965. (Courtesy of H. Lourandos.)

Figure 7.3 Rhys Jones (left) and Harry Lourandos (right) drawing the complex stratigraphy at Rocky Cape North Cave in February 1965. (Courtesy of H. Lourandos.)

Jones realized that the archaeological deposit in Rocky Cape South overlapped in time with and extended the sequence of the human occupation that he had discovered at Rocky Cape North. He added the stratigraphic units at the South Cave to the upper three North Cave strata and constructed a composite archaeological sequence that stretched from more than 8,000 years ago up until the historic period (Figure 7.4).

Deposits in the Rocky Cape sites were rich in hearths, burnt and smashed bone which may have been food debris, mollusc shells, and artefacts made of stone and bone. Analysis of this debris tells us about the food procurement strategies that ancient people carried out in and near the sites.

Tasmanians probably always ate plant foods, as they did in the historic period, but evidence for this has not been extracted from the archaeological record. At Rocky Cape the debris demonstrated that foragers obtained much more than half of their meat from molluscs collected from the adjacent rocky shores. People gathered large numbers of molluscs, such as warrener or abalone, from rock platforms at low tide. They probably dived to shallow depths, levered them from rocks, and carried them back to the nearby caves, creating the dense shell middens. Diving for abalone was more common during the past 4,000 years (Dunnett 1993; Sim 1999). Molluscs were easily collected by any able-bodied person, without equipment other than a spatula to prise them off and a bag to carry them in. This was a profitable activity. A kilogram of meat could be retrieved from about 100 warrener or 10 abalone – a high return for the effort involved. Although mollusc collecting was potentially a reliable activity with a high chance of success and little danger, the number of creatures that could be harvested each year without damaging the resource must have been limited.

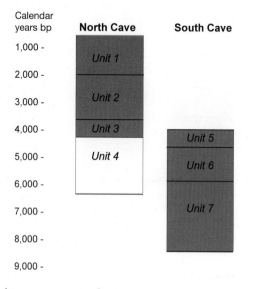

Figure 7.4 Stratigraphic sequences at Rocky Cape.

People living at Rocky Cape supplemented meat obtained from molluscs by hunting more mobile animals. Seals, the largest animal available in this landscape, were occasionally cooked and eaten within the cave. Bones from fur and elephant seals were found in most layers. Hunters killed some adult seals but they concentrated on easy-to-catch young animals who weighed 50–150 kilograms. These animals were probably attacked with spears and/or clubs while they were on land (Jones 1971, 1978), but it is not known how far hunters travelled to find vulnerable seals. Only some body parts of seals are present in the Rocky Cape sites, an indication that seals were caught and butchered elsewhere, and meat, stripped from large bones, was carried back to the sites. This strategy reduced the weight of transported material and allowed hunters to use the Rocky Cape caves as base camps for exploiting the local landscape. Jones (1978) calculated that the food represented by remains found in the caves would have supported a few families for only a week or so each year. However, since the seal bones in the cave are not an accurate indication of the amount of meat being consumed by its occupants, Jones' calculation is only a rough guide to the nature of occupation.

While seals and molluscs were the main sources of meat pre-historic foragers hunted a variety of other animals. Bones in the caves demonstrate that land animals were occasionally caught and consumed; red-necked wallabies, short-nosed bandicoots, wombats, brush-tail and ring-tail possums were sometimes caught. Bird bones in these sites were mostly cormorants that could have been caught locally while nesting.

Hundreds of fish bones were also recovered from the Caves, but it is not easy to interpret them in terms of pre-historic fishing. The fish bones are small and fragile; it is likely that many were not preserved or recovered in the sieves when Jones excavated. Furthermore, bones of some fish species, such as wrasse ('parrot fish'), were sturdier and preserved more readily, making it difficult for archaeologists to know which fish were caught frequently. Nevertheless, several conclusions have been reached. One is that fish were never economically important. They may have been appreciated by the foragers who caught them, but fish contributed only a minor proportion of meat to their diet. Jones (1978) estimated that fish made up 20 per cent of the animal meat consumed in Rocky Cape South, but his calculation assumed only small amounts of seal meat were brought into the site and he did not include any of the mollusc meat represented by tons of shell found in the deposit. When all the evidence is considered fish probably contributed less than 5–10 per cent by weight of the meat eaten by Rocky Cape foragers. Since each fish weighed only 0.5–1 kg, a single adult seal might have given more meat than all the fish brought to the site in a thousand years. Fish consumption was minimal. Robin Sim (1999) calculated that inhabitants of the caves ate on average only one fish every decade!

Initially archaeologists thought flexible nets were used to capture fish (Bowdler 1979; Bowdler and Lourandos 1982), but further studies point to a different technology. Sarah Colley carefully recorded bones of many fish species in the excavated sediments. Wrasse, leatherjacket, ling and conger eel were all being caught in the local rocky reefs (Colley and Jones 1987). The most effective way to catch these kinds of fish is with a baited box trap, a rigid structure with funnel-shaped entrances into which fish swim but cannot escape. Colley suggested that similar box traps were used in this locality during pre-history. Her conclusion is reinforced by the fact that fish which cannot be caught in box traps were not present in the archaeological bone material. Box traps placed near rocky platforms may have been used in conjunction with tidal traps such as rock walls constructed in the tidal zone. Fish such as Australian salmon, barracouta, mullet and black bream can be caught in tidal traps; their bones were also found in the archaeological deposit. Spears and nets might also have been used, but only tidal and box traps can explain the kinds of fish species that were caught. Hence Tasmanian fishing was centred on trapping rather than hooking, spearing or netting. The benefit gained from building traps depended on the amount of fish caught, the effort required to create traps, and alternative hunting opportunities that might exist. While a single box trap or rock wall may not have taken many hours to make, the construction and maintenance of a system of traps would involve an investment of labour that would have been worthwhile only in some circumstances. Laying traps for fish would have been effective if people were present in the area for long enough to place traps and harvest enough fish to give an adequate return on the labour invested.

Fish were never a major part of the pre-historic economy, but ironically questions about ancient fishing at Rocky Cape prompted decades of debate between archaeologists. Jones wondered why, in historic times, Tasmanian Aborigines did not catch fish. In his excavations at Rocky Cape, Jones discovered the date when people ceased to eat fish. Fish bones are numerous in the South Cave, even in the uppermost Unit 5, about 4,200 (3,900–4,500) years old. Fish bones also occur in Unit 4, the lowest stratum in the North Cave, but they are absent in Unit 3 and above. A single fish vertebra was found in Unit 1, but this has often been thought to have been brought into the site in the gut of a seal or bird. Fish were brought into the caves until 4,200 (3,900–4,500) years bp but not after 3,700 (3,500–3,900) years bp. This seems to be evidence that ancient Tasmanians at Rocky Cape ceased fishing approximately 3,700–4,200 years ago.

Finding an explanation for the abandonment of fishing was not the only puzzle confronting archaeologists. People occupying Rocky Cape also changed their technology at the same time, raising questions about whether cessation of fishing reflected a broader economic reorganization.

Bone points and spatulae were made by splitting and/or grinding the limb bones of wallabies. In the South Cave these tools were recovered, although they had rarely been made and discarded; about one specimen for every century of occupation. Bone tools were even rarer in the North Cave; only one was discarded in the past 3,700 years. This might reflect an activity difference between the two caves, but most archaeologists thought it showed there were fewer bone artefacts through time, and that bone tool manufacture ceased nearly 3,500 years ago. Jones (1971) argued that these bone tools were used to make clothing, so he interpreted the cessation of bone tool production as an indication that Tasmanian foragers had stopped sewing hides into elaborate clothing. Other archaeologists pointed out that bone tools could have had many functions such as spearing, cutting and scraping (C. Webb and Allen 1990). Sewing may never have been practised by ancient

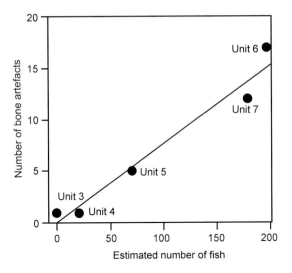

Figure 7.5 Relationship between abundance of fish remains and bone points in the Rocky Cape sequence (data from Jones 1971). The line drawn through the data points describes the linear regression ($r^2=0.962$).

Tasmanians. Sandra Bowdler and Harry Lourandos examined the functions of bone tools by describing archaeological objects with which they are commonly associated. They observed that within the Rocky Cape sequence bone artefacts and fish bones showed near identical chronological changes. When fish were numerous so were bone artefacts but when fish were rare so were bone artefacts (Figure 7.5). Bowdler and Lourandos suggested this meant that bone artefacts were used to catch fish rather than make clothing and that at Rocky Cape bone artefacts had been used to make fishing nets. It is now clear that box traps were the dominant technology being employed but the principle they proposed remains: perhaps bone artefacts were used to make or bait fish traps? If this was true, the end of bone artefact manufacture merely reflects the termination of fishing about 3,700 years ago and reveals that coastal foragers rationalized their toolkit at that time.

This cessation of fishing needs to be placed in the context of foraging life. Broader economic change about 3,700 years ago is indicated by other alterations in behaviour at Rocky Cape. At that time, more stone for artefacts was transported from distant inland locations, an indication that people visiting the cave exploited a broader inland region. Artefacts made of rock from the inland increased about twenty-fold! These stone artefacts were smaller and more extensively resharpened when they were discarded. The focus of occupation had shifted away from the Rocky Cape peninsula, towards the exploitation of inland locations. People transported and kept resharpening tools made in distant places, in preference to using poorer quality local rocks. This change was associated with alterations of cave use. Fewer stone artefacts and food remains were discarded at Rocky Cape during the last four millennia, perhaps reflecting reduced human use of the coast surrounding the caves. When foragers increased their use of inland parts of Tasmania, nearly

4,000 years ago, they spent less time at Rocky Cape than they had previously. Abandonment of fishing was part of a fundamental restructuring of Aboriginal life in northwest Tasmania. Archaeologists have debated why this happened.

A model of loss and dysfunction

Rhys Jones (1971, 1977a, 1978) initiated controversy when he proposed that the end of fishing at Rocky Cape could be explained as a cultural degeneration, a process in which all Tasmanian Aborigines became increasingly 'maladapted' (see Bowdler 1980). He based his proposition on three independent inferences: first, changes at Rocky Cape also occurred throughout the rest of Tasmania; second, cessation of fishing signals an arbitrary prohibition, not a response to circumstances in which people found themselves; and third, the prohibition on fish was significantly disadvantageous to Tasmanian Aborigines during the last four millennia. It is possible to accept one or more of these inferences while rejecting others, and each has been debated.

Jones (1978) argued that fishing and bone tool manufacture ceased throughout the island. He noted that other excavated sites in Tasmania, such as Sisters Creek, West Point midden, Cave Bay Cave and Little Swanport, had evidence comparable with that of Rocky Cape. These archaeological patterns are difficult to interpret. Sim (1999) argued that the bones of only one or two fish were recovered from some sites, and they could have been present in the stomach of a seal and might not represent human fishing at all. Nevertheless, evidence is consistent with human fishing and bone tool use only before 3,700–4,000 years ago, giving archaeologists reason to accept that these activities ceased across Tasmania. It seems true that although sea-level rise turned their land into an island Tasmanian foragers stopped exploiting some coastal resources that were available to them.

Jones (1977a) also claimed that Tasmanians lost many skills, but this assertion is less convincing. He speculated, with limited evidence, that behaviours in addition to fishing disappeared from the cultural repertoire. For example, Jones argued that historical Tasmanians had the simplest toolkit in the world but foragers had once made tools such as barbed spears, spear throwers, boomerangs, edge-ground axes and skin cloaks. However, there is little reason to believe Pleistocene people in Tasmania made boomerangs or spear throwers, or had sewn cloaks, although inland foragers may have had bone-tipped spears (C. Webb and Allen 1990). As explained in Chapter 6, axes were not used in southern Australia during the Pleistocene, and the distribution of boomerangs or spear throwers at that time is poorly known. Consequently there is no compelling evidence that those kinds of tools ceased to be used by Tasmanian foragers. Another idea, that historic Tasmanians were unable to start fires and had lost that skill, is also unlikely to be true (Gott 2002). Furthermore, it is now clear that the Tasmanian toolkit was not the simplest in historic times, and in any case simplicity is not a reliable measurement of the effectiveness of a toolkit (Golson 1977; Satterthwait 1980).

Jones (1978) additionally hypothesized that Tasmanians had ceased to hold large ceremonies, which he saw as another significant cultural loss. The evidence he cited for this was the accumulation of sediment on top of engravings at Mount Cameron West and over stone arrangements at the Bay of Fires, showing ritual activities had stopped at those sites. Rituals may have changed in nature or reduced in frequency but historical observations of Aboriginal people on the island are not unbiased enough to conclude that rituals were absent in the nineteenth century (e.g. Horton 1979; Breen 1992). Additionally, rock art and stone arrangements may not necessarily have ever been associated with large ceremonial gatherings or elaborate rituals. Furthermore, art sites and stone arrangements have rarely been dated; some may have been used during the last millennium. Claims that pre-historic Tasmanians lost the capacity for ritual interactions are insubstantial.

Some archaeologists continue to assert a loss of elaborate clothing, hafted tools such as axes, and barbed spears during Tasmanian pre-history (Henrich 2004), but there is no credible evidence that such tools were ever made in Tasmania. If we discount weak assertions about ritual, fire, and wooden technologies, the only clearly demonstrated and island-wide behaviours that ceased during the Holocene were fishing and bone tool use, and it is on these changes archaeologists have concentrated.

The explanation proposed by Jones for the cessation of fishing was that a cultural prohibition came into being. This idea of a prohibition caused consternation among some archaeologists, perhaps because they thought accepting it committed them to Jones' subsequent argument that foragers suffered from the prohibition. Consequently many alternatives were offered, arguing that it was economically beneficial to end fish consumption and a prohibition of fish as food made economic sense. Harry Allen (1979) went so far as to suggest that if a modern nutritionist had provided advice they would recommend pre-historic Tasmanians gave up fish in favour of foods with more fat! Several archaeologists proposed that fish were not as useful a food as other available animals, and that Tasmanians benefited by shifting the focus of their hunting away from fish and towards more valuable kinds of game (Allen 1979; Walters 1981). However, even if fish were unhealthy or a poor source of energy, those proposals rely on ecological theories that explain why some kinds of foods are emphasized; this does not explain the complete exclusion of a plentiful food resource when foragers could have occasionally consumed easily caught specimens (Bettinger 1991). It is hard to avoid the idea that prolonged abstinence reflected a formal or informal prohibition: avoiding fish for 4,000 years reflects a cultural view that fish was not a suitable food for humans.

Even if a prohibition against fish consumption emerged in Tasmanian society there may have been compelling ecological reasons to stop eating fish. For Jones the exclusion of fish from the diet was an arbitrary cultural rule, but he may have been wrong about which phenomenon caused the change. Dietary prohibitions might not have been responsible for causing economic change; on the contrary, new cultural rules about diet could have followed from new economic practices and functioned to reinforce, maintain or even amplify the new economy. This possibility was explored by Robin Sim (1999), who suggested that foragers chose to replace fish with abalone and crayfish, and their cultural views about fish emerged from and reflected that economic shift.

However, Rhys Jones did not see a prohibition as a result of economic restructuring; he saw it as a symptom of cultural degeneration and economic dysfunction. He thought the loss of fishing was an arbitrary cultural ban, embedded in ritual edicts, that was irrational and massively disadvantageous. Jones believed the cessation of fishing had imposed dietary hardship on Tasmanian foragers, especially during lean winter months when an additional food source would have been desirable. His view was that Tasmanians had forgotten how to make bone points and other useful items, that they had even lost artistic and ritual capacities, and he concluded that they increasingly made economically maladaptive choices, losing skills and failing to develop replacements. Inherent in this argument is an image of ancient Tasmanian society as lacking the capacity for innovation, so that when cultural elements were lost, they were unable to be replaced. Jones' model was based on an inference that the small population of Tasmania was insufficient to maintain communication systems between human groups and crucial knowledge disappeared when individuals died. A version of this idea was further developed by Joseph Henrich (2004), who has argued that the low population density of people in Tasmania meant that there were few inventers, and even if new techniques were developed by inventive individuals they had little chance of being passed on to others, thereby creating a situation in which knowledge and capacity would be progressively lost and never regained (but see Read 2006).

These depictions of maladapted Tasmanians, culturally degenerate and lacking innovative capacities, are almost certainly incorrect. The demographic models on which images of degeneration were based are unreliable and Tasmanian Aborigines probably had a viable population immediately prior to European colonization.

Theories built on the supposed small size of the Tasmanian population should be doubted because the population estimates are clearly untrustworthy. We don't know how many people lived in Tasmania prior to the arrival of Europeans, and images of only a small number reflect nineteenth century preconceptions about the Tasmanians. Discussions of demography often employ a synthesis by Jones (1974), who used eighteenth century records by British settlers and government employees, made during a period of rapid population decline following European colonization, to estimate a substantially lower population density in Tasmania than in the southern portion of mainland Australia. The value of these estimates is low; even Jones admitted that he doubled his calculated figure to arrive at a density that was believable. Following the arrival of Europeans, the economy, life and health of Tasmanians were severely disrupted; Tasmanian Aborigines often chose to go unobserved. Consequently the numbers of indigenous people seen by Europeans in the nineteenth century is a poor basis for estimating pre-contact population size.

Dubious historical reconstructions can be balanced against archaeological information, indicating that pre-historic populations might have been large and growing. For instance, Jim Stockton (1983) observed that there were many more middens during the past 3,000 years, and particularly the past 1,000 years, than were preserved from earlier time periods, and for him population increase was the most likely cause of a huge increase in archaeological sites during recent millennia. As discussed in Chapter 12, this pattern may result from the better preservation of recent sites, but an interpretation of population growth would be consistent with other evidence. At that time foragers expanded their territory, with people recolonizing long abandoned areas such as islands off the Tasmanian coast (Vanderwal 1978; Bowdler 1984, 1988; Vanderwal and Horton 1984), a pattern that indicates dynamic cultural and economic, perhaps population, change. Furthermore, Colin Pardoe (1991b) pointed out that biological similarities between Tasmanian and mainland Aborigines suggest a large population size inhibited genetic drift and that the pre-historic Tasmanian population may have been far larger than historical estimates.

This alternative view of a viable, dynamic, even growing population over the past four thousand years finds corroboration in the nature of Aboriginal activities during the eighteenth century. For instance, the flooding of Bass Strait prevented dingos from reaching Tasmania during pre-historic times and dogs were first introduced to Tasmanians by nineteenth century European settlers. Tasmanian Aborigines rapidly developed strategies to incorporate dogs in hunting, and embedded them into totemic or mythological beliefs (Jones 1972). These post-contact events potentially reveal a different cultural dynamic from the pre-historic period, but they demonstrate that Tasmanian aborigines were innovative. An image of adaptable people adjusting to new historical situations is consistent with the resistance and persistence of Tasmanian Aborigines in the face of European settlement (Plomley 1992; Ryan 1996). Indeed, beyond the European obsession that more material goods and permanent structures makes for a better adaptation and the bewilder-ment of European settlers, who themselves had various dietary prohibitions, that Tasmanian Aborigines did not eat fish, there is no evidence that Tasmanians had slipped into a spiral of dysfunction. If economic and social change, but not degen-eration, occurred in Tasmania 4,000 years ago, archaeologists are left with the question of why those changes happened and why did they occur when they did?

Mid-Holocene climatic change

Economic restructuring should be studied in the ecological context within which the economic activities took place. Because the magnitude of climatic and land-scape change in the Holocene was less than in the Pleistocene some researchers assumed climatic shifts could not have triggered substantial modifications to forager economies. Such arguments fail to recognize that the extent of cultural change need not be proportional to the magnitude of a triggering process, either social or environmental. In the case of climate change small alterations in effective pre-cipitation, and particularly its variability, could have had dire consequences for foragers living in marginal situations. Even in situations of relative abundance a small change in temperatures, length of growing season, and effective precipitation can cause alterations in the nature and patchiness of vegetation, and creating or constraining opportunities for foragers. Consequently it is imprudent to presume what magnitude of environmental change was required to stimulate changes in the economy of Tasmanian hunter-gatherers, and more profitable to ask whether there were climatic changes when Tasmanians stopped fishing and what economic consequences they might have had?

Climatic conditions in southern, eastern and northern Australia altered rapidly between 4,000 and 5,000 years ago, at or immediately before many economic alterations documented at Rocky Cape. At that time many regions in southern Australia began to suffer drier and more variable conditions. This reflects altered sea temperatures, reduced rainfall, and the onset of an El Niño-dominated period, from more than 4,000 years ago until approximately 2,000 years ago. El Niño is a term describing a climate with highly variable rainfall produced by a particular pattern in oceanic and atmospheric circulation across the tropical Pacific. During an El Niño event warm surface waters move eastward towards the central Pacific and ocean temperatures near Australia drop. Very little moisture is then picked up from colder ocean surfaces and the resulting cool, dry air produces little rain. The consequence is unpredictable rain and sometimes severe droughts across Indonesia, Papua New Guinea, and northern, central and eastern Australia.

Prior to 4,500–5,000 years ago, when modern sea circulation had not yet developed, El Niño events were not pronounced (Gagan et al. 2003). The early-Holocene was therefore a time of greater effective precipitation, creating more surface water and relatively stable, predictable resources. After about 5,000 years ago new atmospheric circulation and sea temperature systems were initiated, and El Niño events with related severe, prolonged droughts became common. Droughts were more intense than they are today, reducing water availability in northern, central and eastern Australia. One result of these shifts was greater climatic variability from before 4,000 years ago (Singh and Luly 1991; McGlone et al. 1992; Markgraf et al. 1992; Shulmeister and Lees 1995; Haberle et al. 2001; Gagan et al. 2003). The period between 5,000 and 2,000 years bp was dry, with fewer plant and animal foods. Resources were more costly to obtain and their distribution and availability often less easily predicted. Although the environment at that time was not as dry or harsh as it had been at the Last Glacial Maximum, this climatic shift represented a drastic deterioration in conditions that foragers had known for millennia. This climatic deterioration was at least as severe in Tasmania as elsewhere and was the ecological context of economic restructuring in Tasmania and Bass Strait.

Tasmanian economic change

Similarity in the timing of climatic change and economic restructuring led some archaeologists to suggest that people across Tasmania had responded to altered environmental conditions. Responses involved fundamental restructuring of foraging activities and in the case of fishing the economic strategy altered permanently.

Coastal foragers displayed several economic reactions to the new drier and more variable climate. In Bass Strait islands more than 10 km from Tasmania and the mainland were not inhabited at the start of the historic period (Jones 1977b). Sim (1994) found many shell middens more than 5,000 years old on Flinders Island, and other islands in the Furneaux group to the northeast of Tasmania, but no sites have been found after that time. This demonstrated that people lived on the islands after the sea-level rise isolated them but died out sometime soon after 4,500 years ago. Nowadays these islands do not have abundant, reliable water sources, and Sim (1994) concluded that drier conditions 4,000–5,000 years ago created extreme summer droughts, eliminated water from the landscape, and led to the deaths of the inhabitants. This is enough, by itself, to show that Jones' model of cultural degeneration is incorrect. Aboriginal foragers lived successfully on the Furneaux Islands for thousands of years, even with a small population. When they died out it was not from degeneration but from thirst and hunger brought about by climate change. Isolated from other Tasmanians, the Flinders Island people died out at approximately the same time that economic changes occurred across Tasmania; an indication that these events were all triggered by the onset of the drier El Niño conditions.

Archaeological evidence shows regional differences in human occupation because there were local differences in the nature of environmental change. For example, the other large island group in Bass Strait, the King Island group, was abandoned early in the Holocene but periodically visited in the last 3,000–4,000 years by voyagers travelling by watercraft from northeastern Tasmania (Sim 1994). Island use during recent millennia occurred along much of the Tasmanian coastline. The best example on the northeast coast is the sequence at Cave Bay Cave, Hunter Island, which was abandoned when the sea cut it off about 8,000 years ago but was visited by coastal foragers during the past 4,500 years (Bowdler 1977, 1984, 1988). Similar economic changes occurred off the coast of southwestern Tasmania, where islands show at least seasonal occupation by people during the past 3,500 years (Vanderwal 1978; Vanderwal and Horton 1984).

Seasonal occupation of islands during the past 4,500 years represents a territorial and ecological expansion in response to reduced biomass on Tasmania; foragers exploited seals, birds and molluscs that were abundant on the islands. Rafts have not been preserved but greater maritime activity encouraged archaeologists to reconstruct improved watercraft technology (Vanderwal 1978), a technological innovation that contrasts with the abandonment of some technologies such as bone tools at about the same time.

Economic restructuring and ecological expansion between 4,500 and 3,500 years ago is also indicated at Rocky Cape North. Greater exploitation of food from the lower literal zone, such as abalone and lobster, is one form of foraging expansion into a new environment. Birds and seals may also have been targeted intensively in the past 4,000 years, but at Rocky Cape the evidence is ambiguous. However, overall there was a decrease in the degree to which the economy was focused on the coast. About 3,700 years ago people began occupying Rocky Cape North less intensively and brought larger amounts of stone into the site from distant inland areas. As discussed above, this indicates that foragers not only altered their exploitation of coastal resources when the drier climate began 4,000–4,500 years ago, but also exploited this coastal locality less intensively. As ancient people reduced the amount of foraging carried out near Rocky Cape they began to exploit not only island but also inland landscapes more intensively. Archaeological research at inland sites such as Warragarra Rockshelter provides evidence of exactly this altered landscape use.

Warragarra Rockshelter and the story of Tasmanians

About 3,400–4,000 years bp thick forests in many parts of inland Tasmania were transformed into more mixed forest, woodland and grassland. Evidence of this is found in pollen recovered from sediments in lakes and bogs of the inland northern and central regions. Pollen cores from Lake Johnston, 875 metres above modern sea level, reveal that rainforest trees declined and *Eucalyptus*, conifers, grasses and heath increased about 3,600 (3850–3400) years bp (Anker et al. 2001). Similar shifts away from rainforest are recorded at other lakes in the region, such as Poets Hill (Colhoun 1992). Similarities in vegetation change in different lake catchments reflect the operation of broad climatic processes, particularly intensified El Niño-driven climatic variation. Local vegetation responses to reduced temperature and rainfall may have been exacerbated by human burning to parts of the landscape. However, John Dodson (2001) observed evidence of vegetation change associated with erosion of sediment in the catchment of Solomons Jewel Lake about 3,500 years ago, without a change in the production of charcoal fragments, which suggests prolonged drought rather than fire was the primary factor responsible for vegetation change. Between 4,000 and 3,400 years ago drier conditions in valleys and elevated areas of northwestern Tasmania had created a mixture of forests, woodlands, grassy plains and heathlands unlike the closed forests of the early-Holocene. These new open woodland and grassland environments were more easily traversed by humans and favoured small and medium-sized marsupials such as kangaroos, wallabies, pademelon, bettong and possums. Consequently, inland ridges and valleys became more attractive to hunters after 4,000 years bp.

Archaeological evidence of human exploitation of this transformed landscape was discovered at Warragarra Rockshelter, located in the upper Mersey River Valley (Figure 7.6). Situated at 700 metres above sea level, this large rockshelter protects archaeological deposits created over the past 10,000 years (Johnston 1982; Lourandos 1983b; Sutton 1985; Allen and Porch 1996). It is positioned at the base of a rainforest-covered slope and overlooks grassy plain which has probably been there for the past 4,000 years.

Excavations by Harry Lourandos demonstrated that the deposit had an older stratum, containing macropod and possum bones and artefacts made from locally available stone; evidence of hunting 4,000–11,000 years ago, possibly only for a brief period in the terminal Pleistocene or early-Holocene (Allen and Porch 1996). Later strata began to accumulate between 3,850 and 3,400 years bp and contain evidence of hunting, with many hearths, substantially more animal bones and stone artefacts, and artefacts made from stone carried from outside the local valley. Greater quantities of food and manufacturing debris in Warragarra at that time signal more intensive occupation: more frequent visits, more prolonged stays or perhaps larger groups visiting the site.

Other inland sites, such as Turrana Rockshelter, 1,000 metres above modern sea level, display trends similar to the one at Warragarra, a hint that there was a widespread pattern of exploitation. During the past 4,000 years, when climatic shifts opened up the central Tasmanian forests, foragers began exploiting inland

Figure 7.6 Excavations at Warragarra Shelter. (Courtesy of H. Lourandos.)

valleys more thoroughly and regularly than previously. This emphasis on inland hunting in the past four millennia had important implications for Aboriginal lifestyles.

Economic and ideological restructuring in Tasmania

Exploitation of coasts, inland valleys and islands were not independent; each was a component of an articulated economy operating in ancient Tasmania. All those landscapes were altered by the initiation of drier, more climatically variable conditions between 4,500 and 4,000 years ago. Some environments, such as Flinders Island, became unsuitable for humans. Other landscapes became richer and more accessible, and these were intensively exploited during the past four millennia. Archaeology records how ancient people reorganized their economic practices at that time, diversifying their foraging activities by giving greater emphasis to the exploitation of inland and island regions, becoming less focused on the coastline that previously sustained them.

When, in the past 4,000 years, people made brief visits to Rocky Cape they still hunted seal and collected molluscs, the mainstays of their diet, but they abandoned fishing and took up diving for abalone and crayfish in lower literal waters. This switch reflects the diversification of landscape use, and the chain of economic consequences initiated by more intensive and prolonged exploitation of island and inland portions of foraging territories. Some consequences involved the reconfiguration of foraging patterns and preferences in response to new schedules of land use, as economic exploitation of the inland, and of islands, reduced the time they spent exploiting marine resources on the coast of Tasmania.

Even when people had lived on the coast for prolonged periods of each year fish were one of their least valuable resources. Passive trapping of fish was profitable enough to justify the cost of building and maintaining trapping devices such as stone fish traps and box traps. But in the past four millennia, as foragers spent more time inland or on islands, their stays on the Tasmanian coast became shorter. Investing in the manufacture and maintenance of traps probably became too costly for the little return that could be gained during the short occupation of each coastal location. Switching to strategies which focused on killing and consuming mutton birds, seals, abalone and crayfish was advantageous because these animals required little investment in equipment and could be harvested in large numbers, even on a brief coastal visit. In this context abandoning fishing was a viable economic decision; it was one of a number of feasible foraging strategies suited to the new environment conditions.

Intriguingly it was ideological changes that cemented the new economic strategies in social practice and gave expression to altered social lives. The new emphasis on exploiting inland areas, and consequent reduction and reorganization of coastal living, probably contributed to reconceptualizations of the landscape. In this more diversified economy the emergence of new ideologies and social practices, incorporating a prohibition on fish, enforced and preserved the new ways in which foragers understood and engaged with their environment. Proscription against fish was maintained as foragers subsequently exploited some coastal and island landscapes intensively; even during the past two millennia when some Tasmanian Aborigines camped on the west coast for long periods each winter.

Economic changes in Holocene Tasmania were the product of interactions between environment, settlement, technology and ideology. Reorganization of economic and social practices was triggered by the shift to drier and more variable climates 4,000–5,000 years ago, revealed in economic changes on mainland Australia at the same time. Of course economic responses to altered environments on mainland Australia were not identical to those documented in Tasmania because the landscapes, economic history and social filters that shaped human responses differed between the regions. The nature of Holocene economic change on the mainland is examined in following chapters.

8 Technology in the Holocene

At the opening of the twentieth century Thomas Whitelegge was walking near Sydney's beaches when he discovered small, regularly shaped artefacts of stone in wind-blown erosion areas. These were flakes of stone with a long sharp edge opposite a blunted edge, creating objects like a penknife blade (Figure 8.1). Whitelegge went to Robert Etheridge, then Curator at the Australian Museum, who inspected the localities and identified ancient workshops for manufacturing the tiny, neatly shaped stone implements. In 1907 Etheridge and Whitelegge published a description of these artefacts and concluded they had been surgical knives, scalpels, because of their sharp edges and small size. Etheridge realized these artefacts had never been used by Aborigines during the historical period; they were evidence of a time when people used different tools and led a different lifestyle. Now called 'backed artefacts' by archaeologists, these tools are found on archaeological sites across much of the continent. Their discovery initiated a century-long debate about where they came from, when they appeared, why they were made, and when and why they stopped being used. These questions were the focus of many investigations into technological change during the Holocene.

Figure 8.1 An example of a backed artefact from the Sydney Basin (from Hiscock and Attenbrow 2005). Black bars are 1 cm long.

Diffusionist explanations

In 1901 Etheridge knew that similar instruments were found in Europe and India. At that time it was common to think that new technologies were usually invented only once. Distinctive tools were thought to spread from a single place of invention, either by migration of peoples with knowledge of the tool, or through diffusion of that knowledge from one culture to another. Migration and diffusion look similar in the archaeological record; both spread distinctive tools through time and space. For example, if backed artefacts had a greater antiquity overseas their later manufacture in Australia could have resulted from contact between Aboriginal people and outsiders, presumably from the north. Although Etheridge did not know where or when backed artefacts were found he nevertheless suggested they had been introduced into Australia in the past. This proposition was pursued by researchers throughout the twentieth century.

During the first half of the twentieth century archaeologists documented the distribution of ancient technologies in time and space. In southern and eastern Australia pioneering archaeologists Norman Tindale and Fred McCarthy excavated rock shelters. They discovered that distinctive stone implements were not evenly spread through deep archaeological deposits but were instead concentrated in only a few levels (Hale and Tindale 1930; McCarthy 1948, 1961, 1964). In sites such as Fromms Landing and Capertee they recognized strata with large numbers of backed artefacts, and lower levels with few or no specimens (Figure 8.2). This pattern was so clear in eastern Australia that McCarthy proposed three phases called the Eastern Regional Sequence. He labelled the earliest phase Capertian, the second phase Bondaian, and the last phase Eloueran. Only the Bondaian contained large numbers of backed artefacts; a pattern that could be interpreted as a period in which backed artefacts were invented or introduced, followed by a period in which they went out of fashion, precisely what might be expected if this kind of tool had arrived in Australia after diffusion from a foreign land.

Subsequent fieldwork in many areas of eastern, southern and central Australia appeared to validate the existence of a three-phase sequence, with backed artefacts abundant only in the middle phase. Mulvaney and Joyce (1965) reported this at Kenniff Cave, McBryde (1968, 1974) found it at Graman, Lampert (1971) found the sequence at Burrill Lake, Stockton, Holland (1974) reported it at Shaws Creek, and Gould (1969c, 1977) found similar phases at Puntutjarpa in the Western Desert. A three-phase industrial sequence seemed widespread across Australia, a parallel to Birdsell's tri-hybrid model of immigration into Australia, raising speculation that perhaps backed artefacts had been introduced into Australia by migrating people.

One piece of evidence that seemed to point directly to an external origin was the presence in Australia of the dingo: small, light-coloured, short-haired dogs similar to ones found across southeast Asia (Corbett 1995; Savolainen et al. 2004). Dingos did not evolve in Australia; they must have travelled across from mainland southeast Asia to reach Australia. This may have happened without the involvement of humans but it is likely that dingos were brought by people, raising questions of what else they may have carried to northern Australia.

Figure 8.2 Map of Australia showing the sites mentioned in Chapter 8.

By the late 1960s it was clear that neither dingos nor backed artefacts were found in Tasmania; an idea consistent with them being introduced into mainland Australia after the rise in sea level isolated Bass Strait (Golson 1972; Mulvaney 1975; White 1971). Shortly afterwards Klim Gollan (1984) analysed skeletons of dogs in Australia and in Asia, concluding that dingos closely resembled dogs found in India. Backed artefacts are found in large numbers in India and the biological similarity of dogs in both places was used to suggest that India was the source of both backed artefacts and dingos, perhaps with culture contact between the two regions or limited migration from India to Australia (Flood 2001). We can now be sure that this idea is wrong, because dingos did not come from India. Laurie Corbett (1995) demonstrated they are similar to dogs across southeast Asia, and the genetic analyses by Peter Savolainen and his colleagues confirm that dingos descended from East Asian not Indian dogs (Savolainen et al. 2004). Earlier generations of archaeologists, however, did not have this evidence and gave serious consideration to the idea that both dingos and backed artefacts came from India to Australia; they began to think that diffusion or migration from India might be real.

As radiocarbon chronologies for dingos and backed artefacts emerged in the 1970s it was possible they had come to Australia at the same time. Gollan (1984) argued that the earliest reliable date for a dingo skeleton was approximately 4,200 years bp, although carnivore damage found on bone fragments in archaeological sites now suggests dingos arrived more than 4,500 years ago (Walshe 1994). Similar estimates for the antiquity of backed artefacts were proposed. During the late 1970s and 1980s archaeologists pinpointed what they thought was the first appearance of backed artefacts to 4,500–5,000 years bp (I. Johnson 1979; Morwood 1981, 1984; Bowdler and O'Connor 1991). Similarity in ages of early backed artefacts and dingos was interpreted as evidence that they found their way into Australia by a common process, and Bowdler (1981) suggested they could be regarded as parts of a package introduced from overseas. Alan Redd and his colleagues raised this proposition again when they claimed to have found evidence for human gene flow, and by implication migration of populations, from India 4,000–5,000 years ago (Redd and Stoneking 1999; Redd et al. 2002). Genetic links with India have been refuted by Sheila van Holst Pellekaan and Rosalind Harding (2006; van Holst Pellekaan et al. 2006), and by Max Ingman and Ulf Gyllensten (2003), but ideas that backed artefacts and dingos were introduced from the north, particularly from India, found favour with Australian archaeologists over many decades (Flood 2001).

Evidence for the chronology of backed artefacts was actually complex and difficult to interpret. Across Australia charcoal stratigraphically associated with backed artefacts sometimes yielded radiocarbon estimates of more than 5,000 years bp. For example, backed artefacts were found at Capertee 3 associated with charcoal 5,400 (4,230–5,130) years old, Fromms Landing 2 with charcoal 5,400 (4,750–4,950) years old, Graman with a sample 6,000 (5,350–5,550) years old, and Bobadeen with charcoal 8,000 (7,630–7,870) years old. These age-estimates were incompatible with the hypothesis that backed artefacts appeared after the dingo arrived 4,000–5,000 years ago. Initially, archaeologists like Bob Pearce (1974) accepted these estimates and suggested that since all old specimens were located in the south of the continent backed artefacts had been invented within Australia. By the 1980s the opposite interpretation was offered. Ian Johnson (1979) argued that all samples more than 5,000 years old could be ignored as anomalies. Noting vertical movement of artefacts within some rock shelter deposits, he suggested that backed artefacts had sometimes moved downwards through the sediment to become falsely associated with much older charcoal samples. Asserting that all old specimens were disturbed Johnson argued that only specimens estimated to be younger than 5,000 years old should be included in analyses of backed artefact chronology. Consequently, he concluded that backed artefacts appeared only 4,000–5,000 years ago, at approximately the same time as the dingo.

Although these interpretations supported ideas that backed artefact manufacture began as a consequence of contact with people in the north, fieldwork across Australia produced evidence against such a theory. A diffusionist explanation of backed artefacts required a pathway connecting one or more source areas with regions in Australia where those artefacts were made. No pathway was obvious. Systematic surveys of remote localities and reviews of museum specimens revealed that backed artefacts were found across the southern two-thirds of mainland

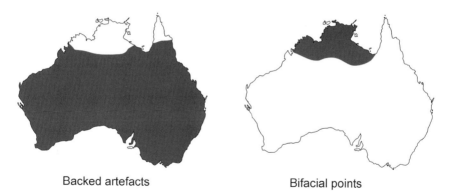

Backed artefacts   Bifacial points

Figure 8.3 Known geographical distribution of backed artefacts and bifacial points.

Australia, but were never made in northern portions of the continent (Figure 8.3; M. A. Smith and Cundy 1985). Furthermore, backed artefacts are unknown in many areas of southeast Asia, such as the Aru Islands or Timor, and in regions in which they have been discovered, such as southern Sulawesi, backed artefacts appear substantially younger than in Australia, making it plausible to suggest diffusion from Australia to Sulawesi rather than visa versa (O'Connor and Veth 2000). There is no obvious donor area in the landmass to the north of Australia, and no evidence that culture contact in northern Australia transmitted habits of tool manufacture into southern Australia.

Archaeologists advocating diffusion or migration of backed artefacts into Australia dealt with these difficulties in two ways. One suggestion was that it was not the process or concept of making backed artefacts that was introduced into Australia but an 'enabling technology' which created the capacity to make such tools. This proposition was contained in the notion that backed artefacts appeared in Australia because 'blade technology' was introduced. Archaeologists often refer to long, thin flakes of stone as 'blades' and describe a 'blade technology' as a set of knapping procedures which produce high frequencies of flakes classifiable as blades. In Europe archaeologists thought backed artefacts were manufactured from blades; if that association held in Australia it might imply that the appearance of backed artefacts resulted from the introduction of a specialized technology. This argument meant that backed artefacts might not exist in a donor region, although we should find evidence of distinctive blade technologies in both the donor area and in Australia after their introduction. This suggestion initially appeared to accommodate a diffusion model while still explaining the southerly distribution of backed artefacts, but further research showed that many backed artefacts were not made from blades, casting doubt on the notion that an enabling technology had appeared (Hiscock 2002).

Another suggestion, advocated by Josephine Flood (1995), was that the donor area was a more distant locality, and people moved directly to southern Australia without leaving obvious traces in peninsula and island southeast Asia or in northern

Australia. Flood (1995) nominated India as the most likely donor region, primarily because domesticated dogs and backed artefacts occurred there during the mid-Holocene. She hypothesized that by making long-distance ocean voyages, dog-owning and backed artefact-making people bypassed northern Australia and landed on the western Australian coast more than 4,500 years ago. While theoretically possible there is no evidence of this event, and it would be equally plausible to propose other distant regions such as Japan, northern Asia or Siberia, which had early dogs and backed artefacts, as remote donors (Bleed 2002; Elston and Brantingham 2002; Goebel 2002).

During the 1970s, 1980s and 1990s diffusionist theories helped to reconcile the distribution of different stone implements. Several kinds of distinctive, carefully and regularly flaked stone artefacts were made, but each has a different distribution across Australia. The most well studied of these are backed artefacts, bifacial and unifacial points, and tulas. In the 1960s it had been suggested that these different kinds of implement all belonged to a common historical tradition, which Richard Gould (1969c) named the 'Small Tool Tradition'. Researchers argued that backed artefacts and points appeared in Australia at approximately the same time, some 4,500–5,000 years ago, a proposal used to support the idea that they were part of a single tradition with a common origin (Bowdler and O'Connor 1991).

Points are found only on the mainland; their base is either flat or rounded but never concave, and the lateral margins are often straight and converging (Figure 8.4). Archaeologists distinguish between unifacial and bifacial points, based on whether margins converging to the point were worked on one or both faces. Points normally exhibit parallel percussion flake scars, but bifaces from the Kimberley and nearby regions have distinctive serrations created by pressure flaking (Akerman 1978; Tindale 1985). Unifacial points are found widely, but fully bifacial points are restricted to Arnhem Land and northwestern Australia (Figure 8.3), their distribution overlaps slightly with the southerly distribution of backed artefacts. (M. A. Smith and Cundy 1985; Hiscock 1994, 2002). By employing the concept of the Small Tool Tradition archaeologists treated points and backed artefacts as equal representatives of that tradition; implying that the northern distribution of bifacial points was evidence of the entry of the Tradition into the continent. However, backed artefacts and points are very different; the northern distribution of bifacial points does not constitute evidence for the diffusion of backed artefacts into southern Australia. Archaeologists therefore occasionally acknowledged that different geographical distribution of backed artefacts and points complicated any proposal of diffusion. For example, to maintain a diffusion model Josephine Flood (1995) hypothesized multiple migrations and culture contacts: at least one to Arnhem Land by people using points and separate ones to the western coast by people using backed artefacts. Why separate diffusions events might have occurred, along different paths but at the same time period, was not explained. Seafaring, Austronesian-speaking agriculturists spread throughout Melanesia, roughly between 4,200 and 3,700 years ago, a movement that could have resulted in culture contact along the northern coast. Called Lapita people by archaeologists, they transported animals such as dogs and it is conceivable that they introduced the dingo into

Figure 8.4 Two bifacial points from northern Australia.

Australia (Bellwood 1997; Savolainen et al. 2004; Bellwood and Hiscock 2005). However, the spread of these agricultural peoples outside Australia did not involve tools such as stone bifacial points or backed artefacts; hence the potential of that process to explain the pre-historic stone implements in Australia is minimal.

The inability to identify source areas and the direction of hypothesized diffusion and migration into Australia during the Holocene led some archaeologists to focus on questions of how introduced ideas spread across Australia and what impact they had on Aboriginal society. During the 1970s and 1980s it was fashionable for Australian archaeologists to argue that the distinctive backed artefacts and bifacial points were primarily symbols, claiming they were overly elaborate, with features that were not functionally necessary but which served as stylistic objects carrying social meaning (see Hiscock 1994). For example, effective spear barbs and points had previously been made from wood and it was claimed that adding stone points or barbs would serve little purpose (Peterson 1971; White and O'Connell 1982). Additionally it was assumed that backed artefacts should have a single specific function, and that they would therefore be found only in specific environments, whereas they were found in many landscapes. Researchers such as Ian Johnson (1979) and Sandra Bowdler (1981) thought that acceptance and manufacture of backed artefacts and points by ancient people could not be explained as an enthusiasm for useful tools. They viewed the objects as symbols of a new social or ideational system. They claimed that the introduction of new ideas and practices into Australia precipitated restructuring of social life, leading to large ceremonial gatherings and kinship patterns which had not existed previously, as well as the use of precisely made stone artefacts as emblems of identity or belief (Bowdler 1981).

Bowdler (1981) implied that new conceptual outlooks imported 4,000–5,000 years ago contained knowledge and economic strategies that created new opportunities for Australian foragers. She argued that dingos, backed artefacts and points were part of a larger package of behaviours transferred into the land at that time. Bowdler thought plant detoxifying techniques first appeared at the same time, a proposition developed by John Beaton and examined further in Chapter 10. She concluded that archaeologically 'invisible' technologies such as food preparation practices formed part of an imported 'cultural package', and more importantly so did fundamentally new social and ideological visions. This argument was based on the conviction that magnified and altered social and ritual relationships, of the kind observed in the historical period, emerged in the Holocene. For instance, Bowdler (1981) thought ritual-intensive occupation of southeastern upland lands recorded began 4,000–5,000 years bp, and Beaton (1977) argued that ceremonial gatherings in the region surrounding Kenniff Cave also began at that time. The advent of ritual involvement in large gatherings, seen ethnographically, has even been invoked as the mechanism by which backed artefacts and other less visible elements of the package spread far and so fast from the point of their introduction (Mulvaney 1976; Mulvaney and Kamminga 1999). Evidence for entirely new ceremonial activities only 4,000–5,000 years ago is now challenged (Chapters 10 and 13) and the idea that the Small Tool Tradition marked a thorough transformation of Aboriginal society wrought by the introduction of a cultural package into Australia has also been challenged.

The idea that ethnographic economic and social life began 4,000–5,000 years ago, with the Small Tool Tradition, gave little consideration to the decline or disappearance of the stone implements that were used to define that 'tradition'. During the 1970s and 1980s researchers often asserted that backed artefacts ceased being made at least 1,000 years ago, but the possible discontinuation of what were thought to be distinctive and important symbolic objects raised questions about whether historically recorded ideology and social practices continued unchanged or whether ethnographic practices may have arisen in the late pre-historic period, after backed artefact production had declined. One suggestion was that Aboriginal people became too busy with their social and religious activities to make these symbolically loaded artefacts (Walters 1989), a proposal that still raised the question of why material expressions of symbolic thought would have been abandoned as the focus on social/religious activities intensified. Claiming that the Small Tool Tradition was a symbolic and social revolution, perhaps introduced from overseas, seemed to offer an explanation for its emergence but merely created unresolved questions about its termination. Re-evaluations of archaeological evidence now reveal that technological changes 4,000–5,000 years ago were not introduced from overseas at that time and that other kinds of explanations are more fruitful.

Capertee 3

An archaeological site central to debates about changes in Holocene stone artefacts is Capertee 3, a small rock shelter overlooking the Capertee River, west of Sydney. Deposits within this shelter were excavated by Fred McCarthy between 1958 and 1961 (Figure 8.5). His team dug more than 2 metres down and recovered thousands of stone artefacts used and discarded during the past 10,000 years. McCarthy (1964) analysed the artefacts and concluded that the lower part of the deposit was dominated by what he thought were scrapers and knives but the upper part contained hundreds of backed artefacts. He decided that the upper artefacts were so distinctive they represented a new cultural phase, in which new traits were introduced at the one time. This image of a package of archaeological changes led McCarthy to speculate that it might signal the arrival of a new wave of people, an interpretation fundamental to the emerging diffusionist model.

Capertee 3 was excavated again in the 1970s by Ian Johnson (1979), who argued that abundant backed artefacts occurred only in the last 3,000 years. He thought that a few specimens lower in the deposit had been relocated by disturbance processes, and should not be trusted as indications of earlier manufacture and use. This interpretation led him to advocate that, across Australia, backed artefacts found

Figure 8.5 View of workers sieving and sorting sieve residues at Capertee 3 during McCarthy's 1960 excavation. (Courtesy of the Trustees of the Australian Museum.)

in layers more than 5,000 years old could be ignored and that backed artefacts appeared in Australia only 4,000–5,000 years ago, at the same time as the dingo.

These interpretations were overturned by Hiscock and Attenbrow (2004, 2005) in a detailed reanalysis of the Capertee 3 artefacts. They demonstrated that previously unrecognized backed artefacts existed in layers more than 6,000 years old, and were not falsely associated with early charcoal because they were highly weathered and had lain in the deposit for a long time (Hiscock and Attenbrow 2004). The production rate of backed artefacts increased substantially 3,500 years ago, several thousand years after those tools were first used at the site. Furthermore, in the period between 3,500 and 1,700 years bp all kinds of artefacts, not just backed ones, were worked more intensively, as people tried to extract more value from their tools. Technological change at Capertee 3 involved modifying the pre-existing toolkit, triggered by changes in the economy of foragers about 3,500 year ago. This represents a change in the adaptation of foragers in southeastern Australia, not a new technology introduced from overseas.

Models of Australian adaptation

Diffusionist explanations for backed artefacts were challenged by a number of archaeologists, led by Hiscock and Attenbrow (Hiscock 1994, 1999, 2001, 2002, 2003, 2006; Hiscock and Attenbrow 1998, 2002, 2003, 2004, 2005; McNiven 2000). The alternative they offered was a model of the adaptation of Aboriginal groups to changing conditions. This approach was less interested in whether or not social, economic, or technological practices came from outside the continent than why and how these things became popular and spread within Australia. Archaeologists proposing these 'adaptive models' typically used the nature and context of tool manufacture to work out the likely reasons for the intensive creation of particular artefacts. This perspective does not deny that migrations of people and diffusions of ideas sometimes occurred, but it posed questions of why people took up a behaviour rather than where it came from.

Initially an explanation offered for the widespread use of backed artefacts and points was that ancient Australians invented a hafting technique that allowed them to attach small pieces of stone to wooden handles/shafts to create tools such as stone-edged or barbed spears, saws, drills, knives or scrapers. Developed by John Mulvaney (1969), this 'hafting hypothesis' proposed that people adopted composite tools because they enabled small artefacts to be used more successfully: while it might be possible to use very small backed artefacts or points by themselves they were considered more effective when part of a hafted tool. The evidence for hafting is that many specimens have been found with residue or staining of a resin which might have 'glued' them into a shaft; for those specimens there is no doubt that they were hafted (Figure 8.6). In several sites Gail Robertson (2005) found microscopic evidence that backed artefacts were placed into wooden or bone hafts, fixed in place with resin, and decorated by attaching feathers to the resin and smearing ochre on the tool. Some backed artefacts were hafted as spear heads and barbs, as illustrated by the spectacular discovery, at Narrabeen in Sydney, of a man

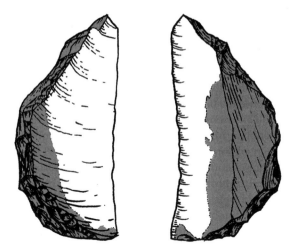

Figure 8.6 Backed artefact from Capertee 3 displaying resin staining, shown as the grey area (from Hiscock and Attenbrow 2005).

killed with a spear that had multiple backed artefacts hafted at its tip; his skeleton still has two backed artefacts embedded in its backbone (Jo McDonald, pers. com., 2006). The idea that many backed artefacts and points were hafted into composite tools is plausible given this evidence.

However, although backed artefacts were often hafted this does not mean hafting developed only when backed artefacts or points become common in archaeological sites. Hafting may have existed long before it was employed for those particular forms of stone artefact. As discussed in Chapter 6, ground-edge axes, which were presumably hafted, are known from Pleistocene deposits in northern Australia. Many archaeologists therefore concluded that hafting had been known throughout Australian pre-history and the large numbers of backed artefacts and bifacial points manufactured after 5,000 years bp cannot be explained by the invention of hafting at that time.

The situation is not straightforward. Pleistocene axes demonstrate that hafting was present in early times, but similar axes are not found in southern Australia before about 3,500 years ago. Furthermore, 11,000-year-old wooden spears pre-served in Wyrie Swamp have carved wooden barbs rather than inserted stone ones. Consequently there is little direct evidence for early hafting in southern Australia and Mulvaney's hafting hypothesis is still plausible for southern portions of mainland Australia. In any case, hafting can be accomplished in numerous ways and it is possible that new forms of hafting became available during the Holocene, facilitating innovations in composite tools. Nevertheless, while change of hafting techniques during the Holocene is interesting it is not the key to understanding the high rates of backed artefact and point production seen in archaeological sites; the question to be answered is why people would have been interested in hafting small stone artefacts and using them as tools.

A new adaptive model emerged in the 1990s as researchers revised their depiction of the archaeological evidence. One fundamental revision was the recognition that both backed artefacts and points were made long before 5,000 years bp. This was first demonstrated by Hiscock and Attenbrow (1998) at Mussel Shelter, where backed artefacts were recovered in levels between 6,200 (5,950–6,290) and 9,500 (9,100–9,700) years bp. These specimens had not moved downwards from younger levels; there is no doubt they were more than 6,000 years old. Backed artefacts the same age or older were identified at other sites in southeastern Australia: Loggers Shelter at about 9,400 (9,000–9,550) years bp (Hiscock and Attenbrow 1998), and Capertee 3 at more than 6,800 (6,500–7,200) years ago (Hiscock and Attenbrow 2004). In northeastern Australia backed artefacts appear even older: approximately 15,500 (14,400–15,900) years bp at Walkunder Arch on Cape York and 15,500 (14,450–16,000) years bp at OLH in the Gulf of Carpentaria (Slack et al. 2004). This evidence demonstrates backed artefacts were not brought into Australia in the last few millennia; they were made for at least 15,000 years. Whether the notion of making backed artefacts was invented within Pleistocene Australia or brought in from outside at that time is not known, but in either case the earliest use of this kind of tool is not an explanation for why it was made and used thousands of years later (Hiscock 2002).

Irrespective of the origin of Pleistocene backed artefacts, these sorts of artefacts were manufactured at very low rates for many millennia. The change that occurred about 4,000–4,500 years ago was not the appearance of backed artefacts in southeastern Australia, it was a dramatic increase in the rate at which they were made. At Mussel Shelter the production of backed artefacts increased by more than 200 times about 3,800 (3,500–4,100) years ago. In southeastern Australia high levels of backed artefact manufacture lasted for approximately 1,000–3,000 years, a phase called the 'backed artefact proliferation' by Hiscock (2002). Although the timing of this proliferation varied regionally it was similar in many inland areas of southeastern Australia, as illustrated in Figure 8.7 for three of the well-studied eastern rock shelters. In each site backed artefacts have been recovered in far greater numbers after about 3,500 years ago, and in each the production declined in the past 2,000 years. This phase of massively increased production rates, the backed artefact proliferation, is what an earlier generation of researchers had thought of as the 'Small Tool Tradition'. Adaptive models now seek to explain why pre-historic people emphasized this one kind of tool at that time.

One hypothesis, by Hiscock (1994), proposed the backed artefact proliferation was a widespread response to economic risk during the middle and later portions of the Holocene. This 'risk reduction model' recognizes that foragers might fail to obtain the resources they need, and in some conditions the probability of failure, or risk, might be high, threatening frequent failures and/or failures with severe consequences. In response to these risks foragers adopted behaviours that helped reduce the likelihood of failure and/or the severity of the consequences if they failed to obtain resources. Foragers can employ technology to help reduce risk, and Hiscock (1994) hypothesized that in Australia hunter-gatherers employed small, regularly shaped stone artefacts as standardized elements in hafted tools as an aid in

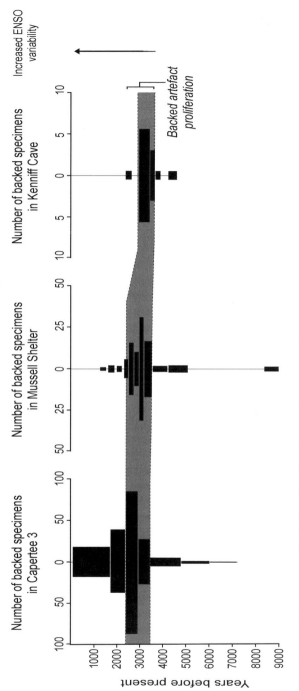

Figure 8.7 Battleship curves of backed artefact abundance in three excavated sites in eastern Australia.

dealing with foraging risks. This strategy provided them with a number of benefits. Large numbers of backed artefacts could have been manufactured from a small quantity of suitable rock, while at the same time their uniform shape and size increased the ease and speed with which composite tools could be built and repaired (Hiscock 2006). Such tools could reduce the chance of failure during foraging, by enhancing the 'readiness' of the toolkit, thereby giving people a better chance of capturing game when they encounter it. That could be an important way to deal with subsistence risk.

What environmental and economic context increased foraging risk to such an extent that a technological response emphasizing stone-hafted composite tools created the backed artefact proliferation? Hiscock (2002) suggested foraging risk increased with the onset of drier and more variable climatic conditions across southern Australia as the El Niño system intensified. This created environments in which resource distributions and availability were less reliably predicted, escalating foraging risk. In parts of eastern Australia Holocene precipitation was lowest and most variable 2,000–4,000 years ago, corresponding to the backed artefact proliferation in southeastern Australian shown in Figure 8.7 (Hiscock 2002). Correspondence of drier, more variable climates and increased backed artefact manufacture probably indicates that, in the southeast, toolkit changes were a reaction to greater foraging risk.

Reduced landscape productivity and increased climatic variation were not the only factors creating higher foraging risk. A number of factors, sometimes operating jointly, have been proposed as triggers of increased foraging risk, including landscape colonization, redefinition of social space, landscape change such as sea-level rise, reduction of resources, greater forager mobility, and greater climatic variability (Attenbrow 2004; Hiscock 2006). Population growth may have accentuated these risk factors but it has been hard to demonstrate (see Chapter 12). In all of these circumstances a toolkit that was always 'ready' might have been adopted because it would have improved the chance of capturing and processing vital resources. Hiscock's risk reduction model hypothesized that backed artefacts in the southeast could have been used as part of this kind of toolkit and the backed artefact proliferation represented an emphasis on specific technological strategies to help deal with foraging risk.

The widespread applicability of this adaptive explanation is suggested by the existence of a similar situation a thousand kilometres to the north, in western Arnhem Land. Here, at Nauwalabila, bifacial points were manufactured in low numbers between 8,000 and 5,500 years ago as well as in the past two millennia, but they were produced at high rates from 3,800 years bp until 2,000 years ago (Jones and Johnson 1985; Hiscock 1993, 1999). This pattern replicates the chronological trends in southeastern backed artefacts, with a 'bifacial point proliferation' 2,000–4,000 years bp, following the low-level use of bifacial points for a long period. Again this change is not the appearance of bifacial points; it is a substantial increase in the rate at which they were made. Because a bifacial point proliferation in Arnhem Land occurred at the same time as rapid environmental change creating patchy and unpredictable resources, and associated with an apparent increase in foraging mobility, it has been suggested that increased use of bifacial points in composite tools was a response to increased foraging risk (Cundy 1990; Hiscock 1999; Clarkson 2007; Clarkson and Wallis 2003).

Additional lines of evidence also lead to the same conclusion. If composite tools were to be ready for use in unreliable environments foragers may have needed them not only to be easily repaired but also able to be employed for many tasks, since it might have been difficult to predict which resource would be encountered. Microscopic investigations of backed artefacts and bifacial points suggest these kinds of artefacts were used for numerous tasks, including both subsistence ones in which animals and plants were captured and prepared, and also craft activities in which wooden, bone, skin and feather artefacts were manufactured and maintained (G. Robertson 2002, 2005; Slack et al. 2004; Hiscock 2006). Backed artefacts were used for many tasks: carving wood, working hides, cutting and scraping plants, stabbing animals, butchering meat; and many were used for more than one of these activities, demonstrating their multifunctional nature (G. Robertson 2005). Composite tools to which these stones were attached were often not used for a single purpose but worked to cut and scrape a variety of plants and animals, and occasionally to stab or spear animals. The functional evidence, as well as the absence of convincing data for greater violence in the last 4,000 years, is not consistent with Josephine Flood's (1995) suggestion that composite tools were primarily weapons of war and that the backed artefact and point proliferation events mark a phase of intensified warfare as sea-level rise ruined the territory of coastal foragers and forced them to invade the lands of their neighbours. Some specimens were undoubtedly used to stab or spear animals, including humans in the case of the Narrabeen individual. However, few specimens show evidence of having been used as projectile weapons (G. Robertson 2005). Additionally, the backed artefact proliferation in southeastern Australia occurred well after the main phase of the sea-level rise; the two phenomena were not directly linked. It is more likely that these tools were adequate for numerous functions, including attacking other humans, and were used as required for almost any task at hand. They may not have been highly efficient for every task; their value was in their readiness and multifunctionality rather than efficiency.

Functional evidence also has implications for symbolic interpretations of backed artefact and bifacial point proliferation events. Since many backed artefacts and bifacial points appear to have these sorts of functional residues, and many bifacial points are thought to have been resharpened and worn down (Hiscock 2006), the evidence is against them having a display-only symbolic purpose. A similar conclusion can be drawn for the tula, a stone artefact used in composite woodworking tools, discussed in Chapter 11. However it is likely that these technological reconfigurations were accompanied by ideological reconfigurations, as the new life ways involved in using altered toolkits found expression in socially defined views of the ancient world. What those ideologies were is difficult to state but it seems likely they were a component of, rather than the primary reason for, the technological shifts.

The connection of toolkit change with foraging risk is also indicated by evidence that all stone tools were treated in a different way during the proliferation event.

For instance, at Capertee 3 even tools that were not backed were reworked and resharpened more intensively during the period when backed artefacts were frequently made (Hiscock and Attenbrow 2005). This indicates that the proliferation of backed artefact manufacture and use was merely part of an economic trend towards greater cost reduction in stone tool production and use at that time, probably in response to increased raw material acquisition costs and greater foraging risk.

A further piece of evidence in favour of risk response explanations is the regional differences in technology and technological changes. Not all regions had a pronounced proliferation event, showing that foraging risk had not been high everywhere or perhaps that foragers in some regions employed other responses. In regions with a proliferation of backed artefacts or bifacial points those events occurred at different times. Massive increases in production rates for standardized tools appear to be associated with the onset of less stable and reduced resources. Since climatic changes creating these conditions differed between regions the proliferation event also varied in timing. For instance, in the Whitsunday Islands large backed artefacts were made most frequently between 8,000 and 6,000 years ago, at a time when the coastal landscape was being converted into islands through sea-level rise (Lamb 2005). These regional differences in the timing of risk might be expected; foraging risk was a phenomenon operating at a local scale, and the nature and timing of increased risks of any locale depended on the structure and richness of that area. Where several regions had backed artefact or point proliferation events beginning at approximately the same time this might indicate there was a triggering event, such as the onset of intensified El Niño conditions.

Regional variations in the timing of proliferation events would be expected if they reflect technological strategies for dealing with altered conditions of foraging risk; they cannot easily be explained in terms of diffusion because in each region these kinds of stone artefacts were known and used long before their manufacture and use was emphasized. It is possible that diffusion of a form of hafting or a conceptual framework for thinking about risk may have been involved, although this idea is hard to test in the archaeological evidence. What is clear is that the kind of implement emphasized in each region during proliferation events had previously been part of the technological repertoire employed by people living there, something that does not encourage construction of diffusionist models (Hiscock 2002). Intriguingly the same kind of situation appears to be found in other parts of the world, such as Africa (Hiscock and O'Connor 2005, 2006).

Risk-response models also make sense of what happened after each proliferation event. High levels of backed artefact or bifacial point production occurred for only a limited period, perhaps 1,000–1,500 years in some places and less than 300–400 years in others. These kinds of stone artefacts then either ceased being made or, in most localities, were made in much smaller numbers. The reduction of economic and social risk, or even change in the nature of risks, would decrease the benefit of these elaborate composite tools and foragers may have responded by switching to less costly and more efficient tools. That tendency would be archaeologically visible as a substantial reduction in the numbers of backed artefacts and bifacial points, creating the kind of archaeological pattern shown in Figure 8.7. Adaptive models of this kind therefore explain the beginning and end of proliferation events without needing to invoke radical social changes.

Implications of the adaptive models

Adaptive models of technology can incorporate processes such as migration, diffusion and symbolism, but in debates about changes in stone artefacts during the Holocene archaeologists have been polarized between two models. One sought to explain the sequences of backed artefacts and bifacial points as a result of a package of new ideological, social, technological and economic behaviours introduced into Australia 4,000–5,000 years ago, without considering why the package would have been attractive to recipient groups. The second model proposed that people in Holocene Australia responded to changes in the abundance and predictability of resources by emphasizing existing tools that gave them a 'ready' toolkit and assisted them in harvesting resources whenever they were encountered. While this technological response may have been transferred between regions within Australia the evidence indicates that new toolkits were not introduced in many regions at the time of the proliferation event; instead, foragers began accentuating existing tools in response to new situations. This second, adaptive, model comes closest to offering a sound explanation for changes in pre-historic production and use of points and backed artefacts.

Technological responses to risk were not a single, homogeneous process. There were probably multiple causes of increased risk for foragers, producing regional variations in the nature, timing and magnitude of foraging risk and costs. As a consequence, the timing, duration and magnitude of technological response varied between regions, and in each the toolkit was based on elements that were already present, creating geographical differences in toolkits emphasized during a proliferation event. Additional regional differences emerged because these technological strategies were not the only ones foragers could have made to uncertain economic contexts confronting them. Changes in technology were accompanied and supplemented by alterations to the resources hunted and collected, group composition and residential mobility, foraging territory, and intra- and inter-groups' political dynamics. Technology was not the only way Holocene foragers adjusted to new situations. This has already been illustrated for Tasmania, where many responses to El Niño climatic changes involved altered landscape use and prey selection, and incorporated new or revised ideologies, rather than modifications of technology alone. Geographical and chronological differences in economic and social changes are also apparent on mainland Australia during the Holocene. While some shifts may have been responses to more risky environmental contexts facing foragers there has been debate about how the archaeological evidence for economic activities can be interpreted and explained. These different interpretations are examined in subsequent chapters.

9 Coastal economies in the Holocene

The veil of pre-history often obscures less of the life ways of people living in the Holocene than it does of their Pleistocene ancestors. Higher chronological resolution and better preservation in Holocene sites allows archaeologists to document economic changes which cannot be identified for earlier periods. In comparison to the Pleistocene there is abundant evidence for economic practices in the Holocene, often finely dated or divided into three periods: early- (6,000–10,000 bp), mid- (3,000–6,000 bp) and late- (0–3,000 bp). As a result we know Australian forager economies were reconfigured during the Holocene, and that economic rearrangements varied between regions and through time. Archaeological materials demonstrate alterations in landscape use, modifications to the foods procured, reorganization of technologies, and adjustments to social interactions. These economic changes were adaptations to natural and social environments; they were not uniform across the continent but differed in response to the diversity of situations confronting foragers. This variation created debates among archaeologists about which factor was responsible for stimulating economic change. Some researchers argued that social processes were the cause; others argued that it was the natural environment which provoked responses from societies. These debates, founded on the idea that a single factor was responsible for changes in forager life ways in all parts of the continent, failed to recognize that diversity of economic strategies is a characteristic of the large and environmentally varied continent.

Similarly, perceptions that economic reconfigurations everywhere followed a single upward trajectory, in which economic practices became more efficient and 'complex', often failed to recognize not only the diversity of pre-historic adaptations but also that variation in preservation affected the archaeological record. Archaeologists have therefore debated whether their discoveries reveal increasingly complex economies during the Holocene or whether some patterns of change are a consequence of increasingly better preservation of evidence through time. These concerns were embedded in many archaeological investigations of the coastal economies operating on mainland Australia during the Holocene. Greater numbers of sites, increased amounts of debris within some sites, amplified use of islands, altered use of marine foods and alterations in technologies used to capture those foods; these patterns have been interpreted by some researchers as revealing a progressive amplification of human coastal economies during the late-Holocene.

This view is contained in the idea that humans developed specifically coastal economies only in the recent millennia.

Did coastal adaptations emerge in the late-Holocene?

In the late 1970s John Beaton examined archaeological sites at Princess Charlotte Bay, on the eastern side of the Cape York Peninsula (Figure 9.1). This bay formed around a crescent-shaped sandstone plateau overlooking silt and mud flats, with islands clustered at the eastern end. The earliest evidence of human occupation came from Walaemini Shelter, where radiocarbon methods gave an estimate of 5,480 (5,450–5,595) years bp for a midden of marine shell. Human use of the islands was based on evidence from Endaen, a rock shelter on Stanley Island, which indicated cultural activities there 2,350 (2,330–2,495) years ago but no earlier. In those and other rock shelters Beaton (1985) found evidence for mid- and late-Holocene consumption of molluscs, supplemented by meat from kangaroos and marine turtle. A similar economic focus was observed in shell middens on the mud flats. Beaton reported on only one of the middens, the 2.4-metre-deep South Mound, estimated to be between 1,700 and 1,000 years old from a large series of radiocarbon analyses. Although the mud flats themselves started to build up approximately 4,000 years ago, the shell mounds began to be deposited only after 2,000 years bp.

For Beaton (1985) human occupation in the region displayed a surprising chronology. He pointed to two occasions when he thought foragers did not use newly created landscapes. The first was when seas rose to nearly present-day level, about 7,000 years bp, bringing the ocean to the foot of the plateau; yet the earliest archaeological evidence of people in the area came 1,500 years later. Beaton reasoned that if groups of foragers had lived on the coast 7,000 years ago they would have been displaced by rising seas and appeared in Princess Charlotte Bay, but since he found no evidence of this he concluded that Pleistocene and early-Holocene foragers had not focused on marine resources. A second failure to immediately use marine resources was recognized by Beaton, who said that marine resources were not fully used when people moved into the area 5,500 years ago but instead developed gradually over a long period. His evidence was the absence of archaeological evidence for island use before 2,350 years bp and the absence of shell mounds indicating intensive exploitation of mollusc beds until even later.

Beaton thought these delays in settlement and resource use were a consequence of reduced marine productivity and low species diversity in near coastal waters created by rapid sea-level rise. He claimed that marine ecosystems were unstable and foods scarce after sea-level rise – extremely difficult conditions for foragers. Indeed, Beaton speculated that sea-level rise was so disruptive that large human populations could rarely be sustained on the coast until much later, when marine environments had stabilized. He hypothesized that on the coast there was a significant 'lag time' between the arrival of the seas at their current position and development of marine resources capable of feeding large human populations. One consequence of the late emergence of rich marine landscapes, he said, was substantial population increases late in Australia pre-history, a proposition examined further in Chapter 12.

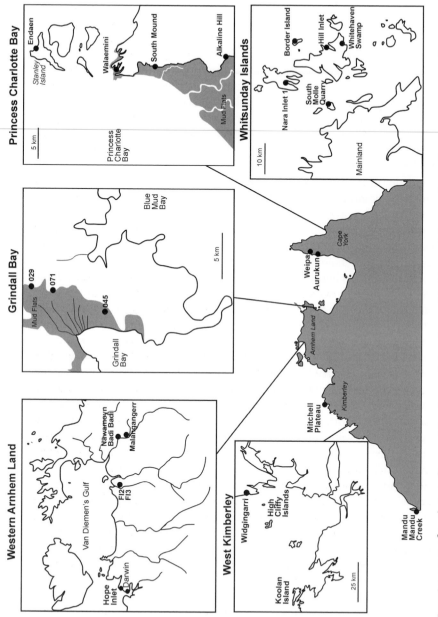

Figure 9.1 Maps of north Australian coastal regions and sites discussed in Chapter 9 (maps redrawn from Beaton 1985; Barker 1999; Hiscock 1999; Faulkner and Clarke 2004).

In a review of other coastal areas Beaton (1985) argued that the coastal time lag he inferred for Princess Charlotte Bay also occurred elsewhere. Early middens, he concluded, were only 5,000–6,000 years old, made long after the sea arrived at its present level. To Beaton this was evidence that ecological disruption wrought by sea-level rise often prevented concentrated coastal occupation until marine ecosystems stabilized. This 'coastal lag' model potentially denied that coastal economies had been the earliest, most fundamental strategy of Pleistocene foragers; hypothesizing instead that specialized use of coasts was everywhere only a late phenomenon that emerged after a long period in which marine resources had not been intensively exploited.

In several ways Beaton's coastal lag model reproduced elements of the 'progression' model of Pleistocene life discussed in Chapter 6. It is an image of coastal exploitation that became more sophisticated and intense through time, a process that occurred uniformly across the continent. Ecological disruption followed sea-level rise in a number of regions, and in some localities there is evidence that intense coastal exploitation of the kind seen historically developed only in the late-Holocene (Walters 1989, 1992). Reorganization of marine ecosystems during and after changes in ocean levels is inevitable, but the reality of major changes in coastal ecology in the mid- and late-Holocene, as a consequence of altered ocean levels, does not mean that Beaton's image of coastal life is correct.

At Princess Charlotte Bay Pleistocene and early-Holocene coastal occupation is not easily assessed. Beaton thought the absence of occupation debris between 7,000 and 5,500 years bp indicated that humans were absent, but this may not be a sound conclusion. Walaemini Shelter has evidence that people were present in the area 5,500 years ago, yet no other traces of human activity were found from that period, not even at Alkaline Hill shelter a few kilometres away. Furthermore, the oldest cultural deposit in Walaemini Shelter is a dense midden of marine shell, revealing that 5,500 years ago foragers in Princess Charlotte Bay collected marine molluscs, had fished and caught birds. Even though no open-air middens of this age are known they would have existed, as part of the same system of coastal resource use, but they have not been preserved. Little evidence for human use of the landscape between 5,500 and 4,000 years ago has been preserved, and the absence of older archaeological sites may simply reveal the extent to which material has been destroyed. Destruction of early middens at Princess Charlotte Bay is not surprising; cyclones can rapidly obliterate traces of coastal middens (M. K. Bird 1992) and special conditions, such as the build-up of chenier ridges during storm surges and cyclones (O'Connor and Sullivan 1994), help preserve mid- and late-Holocene shell middens. The image of more sites and more intensive coastal occupation in the late-Holocene may reflect better preservation of materials in recent millennia, rather than a change of resource use.

In any case the history of resource use at Princess Charlotte Bay is not an indication of early coastal economies elsewhere. Pleistocene archaeological sites have now been found at locations close to the ancient coastline, in places from where people could have exploited coastal resources (Neal and Stock 1986). In a few of them, such as Mandu Mandu Creek and Koolan Island Shelter, the remains of marine animals have been preserved, making it clear that some Pleistocene people captured and consumed sea foods (Morse 1988; O'Connor 1989a, 1999b; Bowdler 1990, 1999). Furthermore, there is evidence of the exploitation of marine foods during the early-Holocene in Tasmanian rock shelters (Chapter 7), the West Kimberley region (O'Connor 1994) and the Whitsunday Islands (Barker 2004), demonstrating that coastal foraging occurred long before the mid- or late-Holocene.

Beaton argued that environmental disruptions associated with sea-level rise prevented foragers from intensively exploiting marine resources until the mid- or late-Holocene when renewed stability in marine ecosystems enabled focused exploitation of marine resources. This is unlikely to have been true for all coastal areas since they had very different environmental and social histories during the Holocene. In fact, archaeological investigations demonstrate that people persisted in coastal landscapes during periods of dramatic environmental change by adjusting their economic activities. Coastal dwelling humans had a long history of adapting to environmental shifts created by sea-level rise. Oceans began rising at the end of the LGM, not just at the start of the Holocene. Increased sea levels during the early- and mid-Holocene merely continued existing processes of coastline transformation rather than creating new problems for foragers. An outstanding example of long-term economic change in coastal foraging comes from the tropical coastline, south of Princess Charlotte Bay, in the Whitsunday Islands region (Figure 9.1).

Forager resilience in the Whitsunday Islands

Economic practices in the Whitsunday area have been reconstructed from evidence found on several islands by Bryce Barker (1991, 1996, 1999, 2004; Lamb and Barker 2001). In a large rock shelter on Hook Island, called Nara Inlet 1, humans became archaeologically visible 10,000 years ago, when rising seas, still several metres below their current level, brought the coast to within a short walk of the site. The rock shelter was then part of mainland Australia, being in a narrow valley at the northern end of a long peninsula. It was not until 8,900 years ago that continuing sea-level rise cut through the peninsula, creating a chain of islands. Seas continued to rise, and about 7,500 years ago the valley below the shelter was flooded to create the inlet on Hook Island. During the period of sea-level rise foragers used the shelter and they continued to visit the island, now 20 km from the mainland, throughout the mid- and late-Holocene. Repeated occupation of the shelter over ten millennia demonstrates that people lived on the coast and exploited marine resources during the entire period of sea-level rise and island creation; transformation of their landscape was not a barrier to successful foraging. Barker concluded that human coastal foraging throughout the Holocene was economically diverse, enabling foragers to shift emphasis between resources as they varied in abundance and location.

Some economic shifts in the millennia of environmental change have been identified by Barker in his excavations of Nara Inlet 1 (Figure 9.2). At the base of the archaeological sequence there are large quantities of stone artefacts made from distinctive grey, fine-grained rocks which can be obtained only from a hilltop on

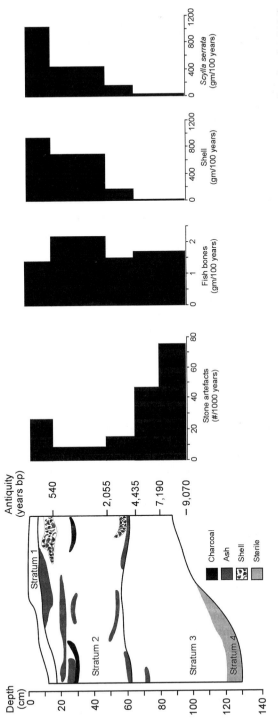

Figure 9.2 Stratigraphy and changing abundance of materials in squares H50 and G50 in Nara Inlet 1 (redrawn from Barker 1991; Lamb and Barker 2001).

what is now South Molle Island (Barker and Schon 1994; Lamb and Barker 2001; Lamb 2005; Figure 9.3). The deep valleys surrounding this hill were flooded by rising seas at an early date, creating the island of South Molle nearly 10,000 years ago. Stone artefacts used at Nara Inlet 1 during the early-Holocene had been obtained by people who had crossed more than 2 km of ocean to reach the quarry at South Molle (Lamb 2005). Transportation of stone from South Molle is evidence that people had watercraft more than 9,000 years ago (Barker 1991, 1999, 2004), but use of the quarry, and transportation of stone artefacts made there, was most intense during the final period of sea-level rise, between 9,000 and 6,500 years ago. Lara Lamb (2005) suggested that during that period of rapid environmental change foragers carried and used standardized stone tools; a technological device to help them explore and exploit the region at a time of high foraging risk (Chapter 8). She hypothesized that early-Holocene hunters relied on stone tools to butcher large marine mammals, such as turtle and dugong, and perhaps to manufacture essential fishing and boating gear. Archaeological evidence from Nara Inlet reveals that in the period prior to 6,000–7,000 years bp, before sea levels stabilized, foragers captured many kinds of marine animals, including fish, marine mammals, molluscs and crabs (Figure 9.2), demonstrating that with technological aides such as watercraft and stone artefacts foragers exploited the rising ocean. People even expanded their territory, colonizing newly formed islands, and Lamb suggested that exploration of the islands depended on watercraft and reliable tools. Large

Figure 9.3 Left: view from the quarry on South Molle Island to Whitsunday Island, showing the marine environments created by sea-level rise including the reefs and open water passages. Right: debris from artefact manufacture on the South Molle Island quarry.

numbers of such tools are found in early-Holocene levels of the remote Border Island.

What happened during the late-Holocene is more contentious. We know that the coastal economy, including the way resources were harvested, was not constant. In Nara Inlet 1 fish bones were regularly deposited, but during the past 2,000–4,000 years much greater amounts of mollusc shell and of mud crab (*Scylla serrata*) fragments were discarded (Figure 9.2). Bones from sea turtles and a small pilot whale were recovered only from upper portions of the deposit, but these specimens need not indicate a regional change in hunting patterns since turtle had been caught at Border Island more than 6,000 years ago (Lamb 2005). However, over the past 4,000 years transportation of stone artefacts was less frequent, and points, hooks and scrapers were made from organic material such as bone, shell and wood, indicating that foragers began to replace costly-to-obtain stone with materials that were readily available on each island.

Barker argued that late-Holocene diversification of subsistence activities, with greater emphasis on marine foods such as molluscs and crabs, indicates the emergence of a society and economy specialized in island use. Pointing to the existence in the Whitsunday Islands, during the early historic period, of an Aboriginal group who hunted and collected marine animals with the use of canoes and shell or bone fish hooks, Barker hypothesized that local foragers had initially been coastal generalists exploiting shore-based foods, then became marine specialists with a greater emphasis on hunting and fishing in the open seas. This change in subsistence and technology, he suggested, occurred 2,000–4,000 years bp. Barker thought the maritime society seen in the historic period began less than 3,000 years ago, and that its economic and social configuration evolved recently.

Explaining late-Holocene economic change in the Whitsunday Islands is an interpretative challenge for archaeologists, and Barker's model of a recent emphasis on open sea foraging is only one possible interpretation. Noting the abundance of turtle bones in the lowest levels of Border Island rock shelter, Lamb (2005) hypothesized that open sea foraging began more than 6,000–7,000 years ago. Although inferring open-sea turtle hunting from archaeological turtle bones is complicated by the possibility that some turtles were caught as they came ashore to nest, the undoubted use of watercraft to transport stone artefacts from South Molle Island during the early-Holocene makes Lamb's theory plausible.

Barker's model of increasing maritime specialization can be inverted to provide another, stronger interpretation of economic change. While Nara Inlet 1 has little fish or marine turtle bone preserved from the early-Holocene levels the other long archaeological sequence, at Border Island Rock shelter, gives evidence that consumption of marine food, including turtle meat, was far greater in the early-Holocene than later in time. Furthermore, at both Nara Inlet and Border Island, greater use of foods such as mollusc and crab meat since 4,000 years bp indicates an increased, not decreased, concentration on shore-based foraging in the late-Holocene. A trend away from specialized deep-water foraging towards the use of shore-based animals is demonstrated by Barker's evidence that local mollusc populations were intensively harvested in the past 1,000–2,000 years. Mangrove forests were present in the islands throughout the Holocene but they could have become more widespread and productive in the late-Holocene. Consequently, increasing shore-based foraging through time may reflect the greater availability of shores with muddy sediments and mangroves in the islands; foraging in these habitats was probably less costly and more reliable than hunting on the open seas. Greater exploitation of island shores is evidence for an expansion of diet breadth during the late-Holocene, rather than a narrowing of foraging focus. In these islands the economy altered from foraging focused on deep water fishing and hunting in the early- and mid-Holocene to a more generalist economy in the late-Holocene, when a large range of island and open sea resources were used.

The cause of these economic adjustments, whether they were initiated by cultural decisions or alterations in local ecology, is unclear. Barker claimed that social dynamics rather than environmental circumstances were the primary cause for economic changes but evidence for this is not compelling. Citing an investigation of pollen at Whitehaven Swamp he concluded that the main local environmental change occurred 4,500 years ago, too early to trigger the altered forager behaviour he thought occurred 3,000 years ago (Genever et al. 2003). However, changes in the Whitehaven pollen sequence are not dated, only estimated with unknown accuracy, and it reflects modifications to terrestrial vegetation on Whitsunday Island; it is not a record of change to the shorelines from which the ancient people collected molluscs, crabs and other foods. Dramatic climatic change, of the kind that might be visible in terrestrial pollen, was not required to trigger a minor expansion of mangroves, creating more varied shore ecologies and new foraging opportunities; localized sediment accumulations or minor changes in sea level could have produced altered conditions. The timing, nature and cause of changes in shore resources at these islands must still be investigated.

Archaeological evidence from the Whitsunday Islands is unambiguous in one aspect: it reveals continued exploitation of the tropical east coast throughout sea-level rises. The trend recorded in archaeological sites, from relatively focused open-sea hunters in the early- to mid-Holocene to diversified coastal foragers with a greater balance of open-sea and shore-based resource use, reveals the transformation of coastal economy as island ecologies evolved and social life altered. Repeated change in procurement of materials, manufacture of tools, foraging methods and diet demonstrate the remarkable capacity of local people to reconstruct their economy to deal with shifting environmental and social circumstances. This illustrates Bryce Barker's point that coastal economies have been flexible and resilient; it simultaneously reveals how the particular environmental and social histories of each region shaped the economic responses of the foragers who occupied them. The consequence of long-term adaptation was not a common continental-wide economic response but a diversity of responses, as foragers adjusted to the opportunities and risks confronting them. Furthermore, specialized or intensive exploitation of marine resources was not restricted to the late-Holocene, as Beaton had predicted. These patterns are clearly seen in the economic histories of other coastal regions of northern Australia.

Island use in the western Kimberley

On the opposite side of Australia, Sue O'Connor's work on islands off the Kimberley coast also demonstrates that coastal foragers exploited tropical marine landscapes throughout the Holocene; yet foraging techniques there differed from the Whitsunday region (O'Connor 1987, 1989a, 1989b, 1992, 1994, 1999a, 1999b; O'Connor and Sullivan 1994). Early use of marine resources is preserved in a rock shelter on Koolan Island where people deposited shells of mangrove molluscs more than 30,000 years ago. When sea-level rise following the LGM brought the ocean close to Koolan shelter again, nearly 13,000 years ago, midden material reveals that humans living at the site also exploited marine resources, and there was no measurable time lag between the arrival of the seas and human occupation.

Humans visited Koolan Island during the Holocene, perhaps irregularly, with radiocarbon analysis of one midden sample at Koolan shelter showing that people were present on the island about 3,620 (3,480–3,700) years bp. Elsewhere in the region middens also record Holocene use of the coast, despite poor preservation. At Widgingarri Shelter 2, on the mainland, a midden horizon was deposited by foragers about 8,300 years ago, and shortly after there is evidence of human occupation at High Cliffy island, about 10 kilometres from the mainland. Small, flat-topped and surrounded by large areas of productive reefs, High Cliffy had been cut off by rising seas perhaps 9,000 years ago. Foragers visited the island before 7,575 (7,315–7,835) years bp, and at least periodically after that time. O'Connor argued that the non-seasonal and mobile animals whose bones are found in archaeological deposits, such as fish and turtle, required regular monitoring and ancient foragers would have moved regularly between islands to track them. Consequently, forager activities in this area were flexible and changing throughout the Holocene.

What is challenging about pre-historic use of this west Kimberley coast is that there was early and continued use of coastal areas, even of small isolated islands, but there is no evidence that people developed specialized marine technologies. Islands in northeastern Australia, including the Whitsunday group, were exploited by people using complex fishing gear, such as shell or bone fish hooks and bone harpoons (Rowland 1987; Barker 1991, 2004); in the nineteenth century outrigger canoes were used, although their antiquity is unknown. However, such tools have not been found in the archaeological deposits of the west Kimberley, and historically simple wooden spears and basic rafts were all that coastal foragers needed to exploit the region. Specialized boats and hunting equipment may not have been responsible for the success of island occupation in some regions.

Stereotypes of early-Holocene foragers struggling to cope with changing coastal environments but becoming more capable and sophisticated in the late-Holocene, as implied by the lag model, are not borne out in O'Connor's work in the Kimberley, or studies of foraging in other northern regions. Even though the northeastern and northwestern coasts provide evidence of long and persistent human use of changing coastal landscapes, both with early-Holocene island use, archaeological evidence reveals differences in the ways people lived; in the use of technological aids and in the pattern and intensity of human use of those landscapes through time (O'Connor 1992; see also Bourke 2004). Strategies for exploiting coastal regions also changed chronologically, visible in the way ecological transformations of the Arnhem Land coast were accompanied by transformations in the economic activities of the people who lived there.

Transformation of the Arnhem Land coast

Between Princess Charlotte Bay in the east and the Kimberley in the west another long sequence of economic activity has been reconstructed from archaeological evidence in western Arnhem Land. There rock shelters and open middens demonstrate human occupation and use of coastal resources throughout the Holocene, and significant alterations to foraging through time (Hiscock 1999).

A succession of environmental changes was initiated by sea-level rise on the northern coast. Detailed palaeo-environmental reconstructions are available for the South Alligator River, a river flowing to the north coast (Woodroffe et al. 1986, 1988; Clark et al. 1992a, 1992b). Broadly similar processes operated in other valleys and embayments, although the speed and character of change varied in response to local conditions (Hiscock and Kershaw 1992; Woodroffe 2000). Archaeological studies of human economies near the South Alligator River therefore identify adaptations to environmental changes that are paralleled along the north coast. The South Alligator River valley has been described as passing through a number of phases (Figure 9.4).

In the terminal Pleistocene the South Alligator River lay within a broad river valley containing eucalypt woodlands. Rising seas flooded the valley about 9,000 years ago, creating a broad, shallow marine embayment fringed with mangroves. For the next 1,200 years, a period named the 'Transgressive phase', the embayment contained unvegetated intertidal flats and channels. About 7,800 years ago mangroves began to colonize the edges, and within a few hundred years they were established across most of the embayment, creating a mangrove forest 5–12 km across and more than 100 km long. At the edges of this huge mangrove swamp there was a variety of environments, including small freshwater lagoons (H. Allen 1989), but for several thousand years the mangrove swamp dominated the river valley. Called the 'Big Swamp phase' this mangrove environment persisted during continued sea-level rise, as sedimentation built up the estuary bottom at approximately the same rate as the ocean rose, maintaining shallow tidal conditions that allowed mangroves to flourish.

A radiocarbon analysis of marine shells in the Nawamoyn rock shelter gave an estimate of 7,950 (8025–7830) years ago (Schrire 1982), signalling that humans were exploiting marine foods at the very start of the Big Swamp phase. This midden, and others at nearby Malangangerr and Badi Badi, was dominated by shells from the large mangrove bivalve *Geloina coaxans*, and the mangrove gastropods *Telescopium telescopium* and *Cerithidea anticipate*. These animals were available on the swamp margins and their presence in middens has been interpreted as evidence that foragers exploited the mangrove margins (Hiscock 1999). People bringing shells to

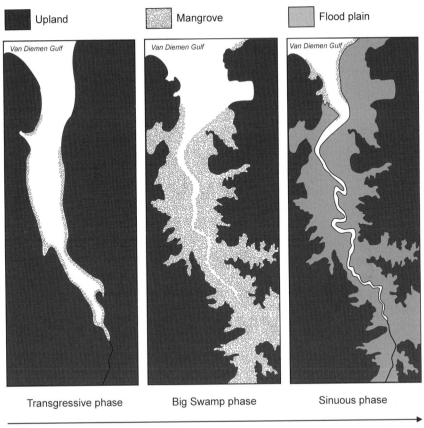

Figure 9.4 Three-phase model of landscape evolution proposed for the South Alligator River Valley (simplified and redrawn from Woodroffe et al. 1988).

Nawamoyn continued to hunt mammals in nearby woodlands and rainforests; their subsistence activities diversified as exploitation of the mangroves was added to pre-existing foraging activities targeting woodland flora and fauna.

Sedimentation continued but tidal inundation reduced and the mangrove forest changed. The big swamp was initially dominated by *Rhizophora*, but the mangrove community gradually altered until it was dominated by *Avicennia*. By 6,000 years ago pollen sequences record that plains covered by sedges and grasses were expanding at the expense of tidal mangroves, and by 4,500 years bp the Big Swamp had disappeared.

Human foraging along swamp edges yielded foods in proportions that roughly mirrored the abundance of species within the landscape; changes in the Big Swamp were reflected in archaeological middens (Hiscock 1999). At three rock shelters excavated by Carmel Schrire – Malangangerr, Nawamoyn and Badi Badi

– changes in the composition of shell middens record foragers using gradually changing mangrove forests. Lower middens in these sites were dominated by shells of *Geloina* or *Telescopium*, animals that live in moist Rhizophora-dominated forests (Figure 9.5). Upper middens in each site have a few shells from *Geloina* and *Telescopium* but are dominated by shells of *Cerithidea*, a creature that prefers drier mangroves dominated by Avicennia and Bruguiera plants. Hiscock (1999) argued that this demonstrated continued human use of the Big Swamp as it changed character, began to shrink and become smaller patches of mangrove.

Increasing sedimentation eventually resulted in mangroves being replaced with grassy plains that filled the river valleys, in what is called the sinuous phase of this landscape evolution (Figure 9.4). Disappearance of mangrove habitats and creation of terrestrial ecosystems on the floodplain caused mollusc exploitation within the valley to cease. However, shell middens in some rock shelters, dating to the period after the Big Swamp disappeared, is evidence that mosaic environments developed, containing patches of mangroves (Hiscock 1999). As mangrove forests vanished from the landscape, about 3,000–4,000 years ago, rock shelters were abandoned, indicating that the loss of molluscs greatly reduced the economic value of those patches of land.

About this time archaeological evidence demonstrates what may have been intensive use of the coast, near the mouths of the West and South Alligator Rivers, prompting Hiscock (1999) to hypothesize that near and after the end of the Big Swamp phase the focus of human activity shifted from the estuarine embayment to the coastal floodplains and shores. Between approximately 6,000 and 4,000 years ago the coast had sandy-silty beaches, backed by sand-ridges, and as the Big Swamp phase ended more sediment reached the coast, causing it to build up, or 'prograde', rapidly. This was a productive landscape; in it large shell middens, sometimes hundreds of metres in length and between 5,750 and 4,500 years old, were created by foragers. Fiona Mowat, who studied the sites, concluded that shells of *Anadara*,

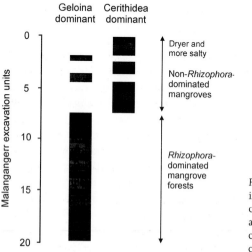

Figure 9.5 Hiscock's (1999) interpretation of the chronological changes in molluscs at Malangangerr as a reflection of change in the composition of mangrove communities.

Marcia and *Circe* show humans foraged along the bare mud-sand beaches that existed at that time (Hiscock and Mowat 1993; Mowat 1995).

Archaeological evidence for early- and mid-Holocene economic changes in western Arnhem Land again demonstrates that coastal people were resilient during environmental transformations that resulted from sea-level rise; they continued to exploit a changing suite of marine animals. The archaeology of Arnhem Land also reveals some of the diversity of economic responses made by coastal foragers during those millennia of environmental change. People not only altered the plants and animals that they frequently obtained and consumed, but also reorganized coastal settlement systems to take advantage of resources available in each period. Shifts in the location of ancient foraging within a region provide an alternative explanation for the absence of sites in one small area of Princess Charlotte Bay immediately after sea-level rise; at that time local people concentrated their economic activities in a different part of the landscape.

Western Arnhem Land also illustrates the variety of environmental changes and human responses to them following sea-level rise. Rising seas flooded valleys and led to increases in both the productivity and environmental diversity, adding huge mangrove reserves and open beaches to the existing terrestrial ecosystems. Near the South Alligator River environmental transformations in the early- and mid-Holocene enhanced opportunities for coastal foragers. Stabilization of the once flooded river valley created less productive, more homogeneous sedge and grass plains, reducing resources. Associated with those resource declines was local abandonment of areas that had been occupied for many centuries. In this landscape rapid environmental transformations created economic opportunities for coastal foragers, but the arrival of stable ecosystems brought a decline in exploitable resources. It was not environmental change itself that created a problem for ancient foragers but the nature of the changes. Since environmental transformations differed around the Australian coast it is no surprise that archaeological investigations document varied economic and social histories.

The puzzling period of *Anadara* mound building

Another example of economic change on the coast is the construction of mounds of marine shell for a limited period in the late-Holocene. Large shell mounds are found along more than 3,000 kilometres of northern, tropical coastline, from the Kimberley region to Cape York Peninsula. These are conical piles or steep ridges of shell that often also contain sediment, artefacts, animal bones and ash in small amounts (Figure 9.6). Tim Stone (1989) proposed that shell mounds were built by generations of nesting scrub-fowl and not by people, but archaeologists have now established criteria that distinguish mounds made by humans, and archaeological discussions deal only with mounds created by people (Bailey 1991, 1994; Mitchell 1993; Burns 1994). Shell mounds range from less than a cubic metre in volume to several hundred cubic metres; the largest are nearly 100 metres long or more than 10 metres high. Big mounds are estimated to contain more than 10,000 tons of shell, from more than 10 million molluscs (Bailey 1994, 1999). Mounds often

Figure 9.6 A 7 metre-high shell mound, located on a laterite ridge approximately 1,000 metres from the current coast at Hope Inlet near Darwin in western Arnhem Land.

occur in clusters, demonstrating that huge quantities of shell were discarded on a single location. Several different species of mollusc shells are found in each mound, but shells of the bivalve *Anadara granosa* usually dominate, often making up more than 90 per cent of shells recovered in excavations. Archaeologists refer to them simply as '*Anadara* mounds'.

Anadara mounds formed in the past, when environmental conditions were different from the present day. They are usually located away from the modern coast, sometimes hundreds of metres, sometimes many kilometres. Often mounds are positioned on ancient landforms such as cheniers or laterite slopes or benches, and the coast has since prograded, leaving them inland (Bailey 1977, 1994, 1999; Woodroffe et al. 1988; Hiscock and Mowat 1993; Bailey et al. 1994; Burns 1999; Faulkner and Clarke 2004; Hiscock and Faulkner 2006). Radiocarbon analyses of shell and charcoal samples from many sites indicate *Anadara* mounds were made for more than 2,000 years; beginning between 3,000 and 2,500 years ago in Arnhem Land and on Cape York, and earlier in the Kimberley. *Anadara* mounds stopped being built 800–600 years ago in most places; the only exception is one more recent mound on Cape York Peninsula (Bailey 1994). This information has been interpreted as indicating a period, between about 3,000 and 600 years bp, in which coastal foragers harvested *Anadara* in large numbers and piled up the shells into mounds (Hiscock and Faulkner 2006). Large beds of *Anadara* required open silty beaches, conditions which no longer exist in the regions where shell mounds are known, evidence that mound building ceased because the environment supporting that economy disappeared.

Archaeologists try to understand the economic and social system that built mounds. Some researchers thought humans piled up shells because of benefits they gained when mounds reached a large size. For example, camping on the top of high mounds would place people above flood waters and biting insects, and larger mounds provide suitable habitats for fruit-bearing plants which could be harvested by people visiting them (Cribb 1996). These benefits help us understand why foragers valued and used large mounds but they are not powerful reasons for building them. Mounds were constructed over several hundred years, a very long time to wait before having a good campsite or food source, and many mounds never reached the size at which those benefits were manifested. These benefits were fortuitous results of mound construction rather than the central reason for piling up shells. Mounds were not constructed in a single visit to the site; they resulted from a series of occupations. Geoff Bailey (1999) advanced what he called a 'self-selecting' model to explain why mounds developed, suggesting that people preferred to camp and discard shells on slightly raised areas already containing shells and so they were repeatedly attracted back to the same localities, increasing the size of mounds there. While this model explains many aspects of archaeological shell mounds, it implies that cultural rules encouraged people to reoccupy and discard shells not just in the vicinity of earlier middens but on exactly the same locations (Bailey 1999). These rules might have been ideological; several researchers suggested that mounds had symbolic significance for people (Morrison 2003; Bourke 2005), although the nature of those ideologies is hard to establish (see Chapters 13 and 14).

Large numbers of *Anadara* mounds raise the question of what role mollusc harvesting and consumption had in tropical coastal economies. The initial hypothesis offered by Bailey (1975, 1983, 1994, 1999) was that the mounds were constructed by small groups of foragers collecting sea foods in one season each year, and over long periods of time mounds grew larger. This image of regular, low-intensity, small group collecting reproduces the structure of foraging recorded in the twentieth century, but the fact that recent Aboriginal people did not build mounds with their shells is evidence that the behaviour of coastal foragers changed since the end of the mound building phase. Furthermore, radiocarbon chronologies of these mounds often hint at an irregular occupation, perhaps 'pulses' of occupation, rather than a low level of seasonal site use every year (Morrison 2003). This has been used as evidence that mounds accumulated through rare or unusual activities rather than through everyday behaviour.

The idea that mounds mark exceptional events forms the basis of a different hypothesis, in which they were constructed by irregular, high-intensity foraging events carried out by large groups of people who took advantage of locally abundant shell beds to support 'social gatherings'. This was proposed by Michael Morrison (2003) for mounds near Weipa on Cape York Peninsula, and adopted by researchers working in other parts of the northern coast (Bourke 2005). This hypothesis can explain the intermittent build-up of some mounds, as well as variation in the location and size of sites, but it still draws on life ways recorded in the early twentieth century and implies that no economic or social change occurred when mound building ceased. Economic activities on the northern coast a millennium ago were different from those observed historically. By drawing on details of historic land use Morrison's model of mounds, as a consequence of rare ceremonial gatherings, encouraged archaeologists to think that the economy and social life of people throughout late-Holocene was the same as in historic times. Archaeological data do not support such a notion.

A third hypothesis proposed that coastal foragers building *Anadara* mounds had different economic patterns from those seen in the twentieth century, with medium-sized groups regularly and intensively exploiting shell beds. The shells excavated from mounds are not consistent with interpretations of continuous low-level harvesting or very rare high-intensity harvesting of *Anadara*. Instead evidence indicates more constant, intensive harvesting of *Anadara* beds, supporting larger and more sedentary groups than observed in the recent past.

A study of mollusc harvesting during the mound building phase was presented by Patrick Faulkner (2006), who excavated *Anadara* mounds at Grindall Bay in eastern Arnhem Land, built between 3,000 and 600 years ago. No mounds are known in the centuries after 1,000 years bp, and the area may have been abandoned for several hundred years before a brief, final period of mound building 600 years bp. Over a prolonged period, until 1,000 years ago, there was consistent reduction in the size of *Anadara* shells (Figure 9.7). Molluscs grow larger as they grow older and the decline in average shell length indicates that over time people were obtaining younger animals.

If humans collected the biggest molluscs available, Faulkner argued that this trend showed that the age-structure of the *Anadara* population changed over time; by 1,500 years ago older individuals were rarely found in the shell beds. He hypothesized that large numbers of juvenile individuals in the later middens, as well as the reduced age of adults, is evidence that between 2,500 years bp and 1,000 years bp exploitation of the *Anadara* beds was so intensive it often matched or exceeded the reproductive capacity of the molluscs living in Grindall Bay. Human harvesting of

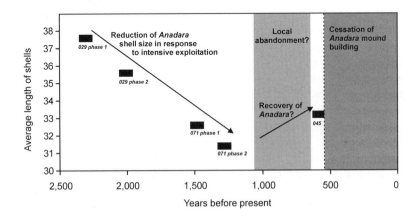

Figure 9.7 Illustration of Faulkner's (2006) observations of chronological change in *Anadara sp.* shell size and his economic interpretation of mollusc gathering at Grindall Bay in eastern Arnhem Land.

molluscs removed so many adults and older juveniles that very few individuals grew to be old and large. Large numbers of people probably harvested shells every year to have this effect on the mollusc population.

Human predation need not have been the only factor involved in the temporary cessation of *Anadara* consumption about 1,000 years ago, but intensive harvesting may have contributed to the local collapse of mollusc beds after excessive removal of adults prevented maintenance of the population. A short-lived phase of *Anadara* mound building about 600 years ago reflects partial recovery of the resource after a period of no or minimal human exploitation. Faulkner's interpretation of shell mound building in the Grindall Bay area implies that foraging for molluscs was focused, more intense and differently structured than it was in the historic period. It is unclear whether mound building economic systems were identical in all regions, but Faulkner suggests the Grindall Bay pattern was widespread. Economies of *Anadara* mound builders illustrate an adjustment of coastal foragers to changing conditions during the Holocene.

Cessation of *Anadara* mound building marked another restructuring of coastal economies on the north coast of Australia. This was discussed by Bruce Veitch (1999), who suggested *Anadara granosa* exploitation provided coastal foragers with large amounts of food, and reduced variations in food availability, enabling them to have higher population densities. The end of large-scale, intensive *Anadara* harvesting 600 years ago involved diversification of diet and alterations in the dispersion and mobility of foragers in coastal territories.

Environmental conditions creating a large biomass of easily harvested *Anadara* lasted for only a limited time. In the last millennium *Anadara* has disappeared entirely from much of the northern coastline, and now exists only in rare beds of very low densities. Landscape evolution, from shallow embayments and open beaches with large expanses of mud flats containing massive *Anadara* beds to mangrove-rich coasts and mud flats without abundant *Anadara*, occurred in many regions between 800 and 600 years ago. Reorganization of economy and land use resulted: economies focused on molluscan resources were transformed into ones exploiting diverse sets of terrestrial and aquatic resources available in the wetland areas as well as seashores. Social and ideological changes were associated with these economic shifts (Chapter 14), and economic and social adjustments varied regionally in response to differences in the rate at which *Anadara* diminished and the availability of alternative foraging opportunities.

Regional diversity in coastal economies

These examples of northern, coastal economies illustrate the regional diversity of economic responses to changing landscapes during the Holocene. They also demonstrate that economies often evolved in ways that enabled people to successfully exploit shifting environments, showing that the lag model formulated by Beaton (1985) is not generally applicable. There was not a single pathway for economic change, nor even a single direction of economic change (Bourke 2004). While human use of some coastal areas was greatest in the late-Holocene this was not so in all regions. Marine foods did not always increase through time, and so there was regional and chronological diversity in the use of coastal landscapes. It is likely, as O'Connor (1992) concluded, that there were many causes for economic modifications on Australia's coasts; the diversity of economic changes recorded archaeologically reflects the variety of stimuli for change.

Of course people living on the coast not only exploited marine resources, but also used nearby terrestrial ones, as Sylvia Hallam (1987) has noted. Consequently it is difficult to describe economic strategies of coast-dwelling groups only in terms of their use of sea foods. This represents another dimension in which coastal economies varied. In southwestern Australia, where Hallam worked, shell middens are rare and the abundance of archaeological sites on coastal plains indicates foragers focused on terrestrial plants and animals. There fish rather than molluscs were significant in nineteenth century Aboriginal economy and fish may have been caught in stone traps built across tidal waterways as long ago as the late-Pleistocene (Dortch 1997).

Coastal economies in southern Australia display different patterns to the tropical economies, reinforcing the proposition that foraging histories, like ecological histories, were local rather than continental. In some regions of northern Australia island use began in the terminal Pleistocene or early-Holocene, but in the southeast many islands have evidence of occupation only during the past 3,000 years, perhaps indicating that island use was often late in the Holocene. Marjorie Sullivan (1982) pointed out that along the southeast coast, sites on islands often had more bird and seal bones than in sites on the adjacent mainland, a pattern that probably indicates the primary use of islands for capturing and consuming those seasonally available animals. However, this pattern is not found in other southern coastal regions. For instance, Dortch and Morse (1984) concluded that islands in the southwest were never used since rising sea levels cut them off from the mainland, and during historical times watercraft were not known in that region.

In some regions catching and consumption of large quantities of fish is a relatively recent aspect of life on the coast. The most impressive example of the late emergence of a large-scale fishery comes from Moreton Bay, where Ian Walters, Jay Hall and their colleagues demonstrated massive increases in fish bone found in coastal middens, and increased use of local islands, during the past 1,200 years. Increased capture of fish in Moreton Bay reflects changes to the marine ecosystem, resulting in a greater fish biomass in the last millennium (Walters 1989, 1992). This evidence indicates that creation of highly productive marine landscapes was a prolonged and complex process, but it does not support Beaton's idea of a time lag in coastal exploitations because foragers exploited marine and terrestrial foods along this coastline long before the fishery emerged in Moreton Bay, and fishing was part of the foraging repertoire in this region for thousands of years (Bowen 1998). Further to the south fishing also changed during the last millennium, at about the same time that fish hooks made from shell began to be used, and some archaeologists suggested that the introduction or invention of line fishing triggered greater economic emphasis on fishing, possibly with women specializing in line fishing (Bowdler 1976; Sullivan 1989). Again the recent emphasis on fishing seen in the southeast is not evident in all regions. For example, fishing was carried out throughout the Holocene in the Whitsunday area.

On a continental scale archaeological evidence demonstrates continuous, ongoing economic and social adjustments to changing coastal environments throughout the Holocene. Some archaeologists have been concerned to discover whether the nature and complexity of pre-historic economies changed during the Holocene or whether an image of change is a consequence of increasingly better preservation of evidence through time, issues examined further in Chapters 12 and 13. This chapter reveals that for many coastal areas there is no clear evidence for increasing intense or complex economic patterns over time. Instead of a single economic trajectory the archaeological evidence documents diverse economic patterns during the Holocene, as people adapted to changing local conditions by modifying their economic and social life. While many economic activities have a long time depth they were frequently reconfigured in the Holocene, and the archaeological sequence in almost every region shows that the configuration of Aboriginal economies recorded historically was very recent, perhaps emerging only a few hundred years before the start of historical records.

10 Inland economies in the Holocene

In examining the economies of inland foragers, the question troubling archaeologists is, again, whether Holocene changes were unusual in the pre-history or part of a long series of economic adaptations. Regional differences in economic activities existed but archaeologists debate whether there was a unidirectional economic change in all parts of the continent. A number of archaeologists recast the 'progression' image of Pleistocene life; creating a model of Holocene 'intensification' which hypothesizes that foraging economies became more specialized, productive and efficient. Other researchers questioned the reality of economic 'intensification' in the late-Holocene, suggesting economic activities have a long time-depth or that recent economic transformations were not more efficient and sophisticated than earlier systems of production. This debate about how to best depict Holocene economic variation provides a framework for exploring evidence of ancient economic practices, and a way to illustrate interpretative difficulties confronting archaeologists. Discussion of inland economies has often floundered in confusion arising from entwining economic reconstructions with the hypotheses offered to explain them. In practice there is value in differentiating arguments about the nature of ancient economies from arguments about how to explain their emergence. Debates about Holocene 'intensification' often concentrated on what social and environmental circumstances might have given rise to directional economic changes, but such debates can be resolved only after the existence, nature and directionality of any economic reorganization has been established.

The nature of inland economies has sometimes been obscured when archaeologists focused on the amount of human activity in the landscape rather than the kinds of activities that ancient foragers undertook. To separate these aspects of ancient life the following discussion is restricted to evidence of the resources targeted and the ways people obtained and processed them; consideration of the amount of activities in Holocene sites, including estimates of the amount of occupation and residential mobility represented by debris, is reserved until Chapter 12. Influential analyses of foragers living in forests and uplands of eastern Australia and the southeast plains (Figure 10.1) illustrate the debates about whether there was late-Holocene 'intensification' of inland economies.

Many reconstructions of ancient inland forager economy have drawn on presumed connections between Holocene economic systems and the activities of Aborigines in

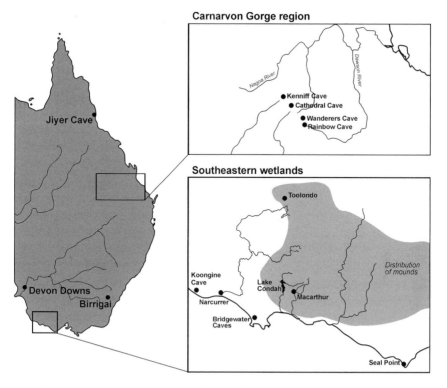

Figure 10.1 Location of sites discussed in Chapter 10 (drawn from information in Lourandos 1983a; Williams 1987; Bird and Frankel 1991a, 1991b; Asmussen 2005).

the historical period. As mentioned in Chapter 1, anthropological and historical research has replaced naive images of Aboriginal economy as uniform and simple with an understanding of geographical differences in foraging. Archaeological discoveries also document differences in pre-historic economic systems between regions, and chronological changes in them during the Holocene. Curiously, well-known interpretations about inland economies have drawn inspiration from nineteenth century observations of Aboriginal social and economic practices rather than from the materials recovered by excavations (e.g. Lourandos 1976, 1980a, 1980b). For example, late-Holocene occupation of the mountain chains of eastern Australia were said to have involved intensive exploitation of particular plants and insects as foods that were more productive than those used previously, and that surplus foods were consumed at large-scale, inter-group ceremonies (e.g. Beaton 1977, 1982; Jones 1977; Flood 1980, 2001; Bowdler 1981). Intangible phenomena such as productivity, ceremonial congregations and alliance networks are not easily reconstructed from the stone and bones that are archaeologically preserved (C. F. M. Bird and Frankel 1991a). These annual- or seasonal-scale reconstructions of the social dimensions of economies were developed using historical details about activities that existed after European exploration of Australia, with the goal of charting the pre-historic evolution of those historical systems. The danger that this approach contains, of veiling ancient economies with descriptions of historical life, was discussed in Chapter 1. That research agenda emerged strongly in archaeological research carried out in the 1970s and 1980s.

Identifying directional and synchronous change

Archaeological evidence demonstrates that Holocene foraging exploited the resources found locally and that economic change in each region is different from that known elsewhere. Archaeologists suggested this diversity was unified by a shared pattern of economic change: an elaboration of physical and social infrastructure used to obtain and redistribute resources (e.g. Beaton 1977; Bowdler 1981; Lourandos 1983a; Flood et al. 1987; Williams 1987, 1988). In particular resource harvesting strategies were thought to have changed in many regions, as a single species of plant or animal was intensively targeted. It was argued that resource focusing was made possible by detailed knowledge of management and preparation techniques and/or the creation of physical structures, called 'facilities', that aided in the control and harvesting of those resources. This manipulation and capture of plants and animals has been described as enhancing production and productivity, implying that they created food surpluses. Archaeologists who concluded that these altered foraging strategies created more food often linked creation of surpluses to large gatherings of people who were carrying out ceremonial activities. Large inter-group ceremonies were said to have stimulated not only increased ritual activity but also extension of political alliances and exchange networks, ultimately reshaping the social landscape of inland foragers. This reconstructed chain of social and economic changes was suggested to have had consequences for settlement patterns, tethering some foraging groups to the location of their resources and facilities while enabling other groups to occupy 'marginal' environments. These inferences represent a model in which the economy and society of inland foragers was radically transformed.

The perception that these economic reorganizations occurred in widely separated and different inland environments led some archaeologists to conclude they were not local adaptations but general trends that transcended environmental stimuli and revealed continent-wide cultural processes had been the cause for change. This idea, examined in later chapters, was connected with the proposition that intensified political and ceremonial networks accompanied, perhaps motivated, the economic changes (Jones 1977a; Lourandos 1983a; Lourandos and Ross 1994).

In the 1970s and 1980s, when archaeologists first discussed broad-scale economic change during the Holocene, prevailing diffusionist interpretations shaped economic explanations. At that time the popular explanation for technological changes invoked the arrival of overseas social and ideological systems which employed styles of tools for symbolic purposes (Chapter 8). Researchers such as Bowdler (1981) grafted this idea on to economic evidence by arguing that imported knowledge and ideology provided the ability to increase food production while simultaneously reconfiguring ritual and political systems so that food surpluses were used in supporting ceremonial and trading activities. That diffusionist theory had two consequences for archaeological thought; it encouraged the idea that all changes happened at the same time, as a consequence of the introduced cultural traits, and it compelled archaeologists to view whatever had been introduced as fundamentally new to the continent and without precursors within Australia. As a result researchers discussed economic change in all regions as beginning at the same time, in the mid-Holocene. They also suggested that late-Holocene economies were very different from previous ones, even though early-Holocene economies were poorly known. The rationale for an external origin of technological and economic changes has vanished; the notion that all inland regions simultaneously underwent significant and similar economic transformations, and that these were not variants or extensions of earlier economic strategies, has remained.

With this approach archaeologists implied that the economic and social practices of historical Aborigines originated with mid-Holocene economic restructuring, and whatever processes caused that restructuring were responsible for the operation of recent Aboriginal societies. This argument is seen in many examples: claims for the emergence of semi-sedentary eeling- and fishing-focused foragers in southeastern wetlands (Lourandos 1980b, 1983a), moth harvesting economies in southeastern uplands (Flood 1980, 1988; Flood et al. 1987), cycad seed using in the eastern highlands (Beaton 1977; Bowdler 1981), and seed using in the northeastern rainforest societies (Horsfall 1987). In each region the beginning of historical economies is not dated, nor has the magnitude of post-contact change been assessed. More importantly, the economy of early-Holocene people has not been reconstructed and it is unclear in what ways it differed from the economy of late-Holocene or historical foragers.

The most influential discussion of continental scale mid- and late- Holocene economic changes was by Harry Lourandos (1980a, 1980b, 1983a, 1985a, 1997), who argued that there was not a single diffusion event but a process of social evolution he termed 'intensification'. He argued that this process increased the productivity of foragers and was a response to desires for more complex social interactions. Lourandos hypothesized the following chain of changes: inter-group competition at ceremonial gatherings required economic support, driving greater efficiencies in food production through the adoption of specialized targeting and management of species with large biomass and the construction of facilities. He argued that this model was supported by archaeological evidence in many regions, and was a plausible mechanism by which dynamic historical societies emerged from less dynamic earlier ones (Lourandos and Ross 1994; Lourandos 1997).

Although Lourandos used his theory to deny that Aborigines had been unchanging he chose to combat static views of forager life with a 'progression'-based notion that there was a phase of intense change only after a long period of relatively uniform and unvarying life ways. This image of pre-history was little different from earlier ones. Although it hypothesized that change was caused by new energy extraction techniques and more intensive social interactions, replacing claims for cultural diffusion with a mechanism of internal social evolution, Lourandos' construction of 'intensification' retained the notion that accelerated change was continental in scope and everywhere mid-Holocene in age. In the following pages case studies from three regions show that the economic change in the Holocene did not necessarily involve the appearance of new and fundamentally more efficient foraging strategies, nor was change concentrated only in the past 3,000–4,000 years.

It is important to clarify that evidence showing economic restructuring was regionally different, not restricted to the past 3,000–4,000 years, and sometimes built upon pre-existing foraging patterns rather than being novel, does not test Lourandos' model about the evolutionary processes shaping economic change during the Holocene. Instead the evidence challenges only depictions of economic reconfiguration as late, synchrononous and unlike anything that existed before. For this reason the following discussions are focused on the nature, timing and context of economic changes rather than their causes.

Managing wetland resources and economic 'intensification'

Perceptions of intensifying economic systems during the Holocene emerged from discoveries in wetlands environments of the mainland southeast (Figure 10.1). Here archaeologists found evidence that foragers enhanced their meat acquisition by building facilities to catch fish or eels. One kind of facility, low stone walls that could direct or prevent the movement of riverine animals, is still visible at many localities but is exemplified by arranged basalt stones at Lake Condah. There, walls are found at the level of the present lake floor and up to heights of nearly 6 metres above it, and have been interpreted as traps for fish and eels as flood waters rose or subsided (Coutts et al. 1978). These structures are difficult to date but Leslie Head (1989) concluded that while lower walls might have functioned as traps more than 9,000 years ago the highest structures in the landscape were only functional during major floods in the past 2,000 years. She concluded that fish and eel traps at the lake were made only in the late-Holocene, even though walls could have been built, demolished, rebuilt or expanded at different times. Head's advocacy of a recent age for Lake Condah stone constructions prompted less cautious conclusions, that 'hydraulic engineering' at the lake were carried out only in the late-Holocene by people living in villages who used the eel meat as a food for ceremonial gatherings (Chapter 13). Existing dating of these facilities does not show that trapping of fish and eel in this lake occurred only in the late-Holocene.

An impressive example of facility construction is known from Toolondo, where, in an outstanding piece of archaeological detective work, Lourandos (1976, 1980a, 1980b) traced historical records to locate artificial drainage channels observed in the early period of European settlement. The main channels are visible as linear depressions connecting Clear Swamp with Budgeongutte Swamp. These were substantial structures, extending for more than 3 km, at some points being 2.5 metres wide and more than 1 metre deep. Lourandos argued that these channels drained surface runoff into both swamps and caused them to overflow, thereby flushing migratory eels and fish into a network of artificial channels where traps were laid. Redistribution of water altered local micro-environments and assisted the growth of food plants (Gott 1983). However, for Lourandos, the central economic outcome was the regulation of environments in which eels could be managed and caught. More than any other single piece of evidence these channels refute the popular image of inland foragers as having a limited economic capacity, while revealing details of one regionally distinct system of food procurement.

Where surface depressions indicated that channels were present, Lourandos excavated and discovered stratigraphic evidence for two adjacent channels (Figure 10.2). Dual channels might have permitted a high-volume water flow, but it is also possible that they were not contemporary and that one represented a redigging of the drainage system. Redigging channels to maintain them, after partially filling with sediment, perhaps during a period of abandonment, is seen in stratigraphic sections like the one in Figure 10.3 which shows a single, wide channel containing layers of different coloured sediment. Charcoal from sediment filling the base of the main channel gave a radiocarbon estimate of 285 (320–0) years bp, which Lourandos thought indicated the time when the drain ceased to operate, possibly as it was falling out of use after European settlement. The antiquity of Toolondo drainage systems is not known, but given the good condition of these fragile structures, they appear to be relatively recent.

Lourandos argued that these ditches were pre-historic attempts to stabilize the availability of local resources; a different kind of risk-minimizing technology to that discussed in Chapter 8. He suggested that artificial waterways increased the quantity

Figure 10.2 A trench excavated at Toolondo by Harry Lourandos, showing two adjacent channels dug into light-coloured sediments, then filled by darker sediments. (Courtesy of H. Lourandos.)

Figure 10.3 A trench excavated at Toolondo by Harry Lourandos, showing an early channel dug into dark brown sediments, then filled by lighter coloured sediments, redug and filled with light grey sediments. (Courtesy of H. Lourandos.)

of food, triggering local population increases, thereby creating the workforce necessary to dig and maintain the trenches. Using descriptions of nineteenth century Aboriginal people Lourandos (1980b, 1983a) hypothesized that facilities of the Toolondo kind supported seasonally occupied clusters of houses, 'villages', as well as people gathering for ceremonial activities.

Although these water regulation systems are of unknown antiquity, Lourandos argued that intensive resource management, and the 'villages' and gatherings they supported, were only a few thousand years old. This view was based principally on two pieces of evidence. One was the distribution of ground axes across southeastern Australia, which reflected their exchange between groups, a process consistent with inter-group gatherings supported by production of food surpluses (Lourandos 1983a; McBryde 1984, 1986). Production and exchange of axes in the region can be no older than about 4,000 years bp, since there is no reliable evidence that axes were made in southern Australia in earlier times. This has sometimes been construed as evidence for the late-Holocene development of trading and associated social networks, but it is also consistent with the axes merely being added to pre-existing exchange systems when they began to be made.

Another kind of archaeological evidence offers stronger indications that exploitation of wetlands resources altered within the past 3,000 years. Artificial earth mounds, visible as slightly raised, roughly oval and often dark-coloured areas of soil, are found across the southeastern volcanic plains on the margins of swamps and rivers. Some archaeologists concluded that mounds were the foundations of huts, and that clusters of mounds are remnants of ruined 'villages' reported in the nineteenth century (Williams 1987, 1988). A few mounds supported small wooden structures, but mounds were used for many different activities. Elizabeth Williams (1988) excavated mounds containing numerous hearths and cooking pits, others that had huts built on them, and some which had no evidence for extensive cooking or huts but instead contained scatters of artefacts that suggested occasional foraging or camping. Earth mounds served many purposes and within one cluster mounds were sometimes used in different ways and occupied at different times (Williams 1988; C. F. M. Bird and Frankel 1991a). Furthermore, the only mound with compelling evidence of a collapsed hut, at McCarthur Creek, had evidence that the structure was nineteenth century (Williams 1987, 1988). Perhaps building houses on earth mounds was something that happened only at the time of European exploration of the area?

Earth mounds may also have served as 'garden' areas. Jane Balme and Wendy Beck (1996) noted that being raised, well drained, often softer and richer in phosphate than surrounding soils, earth mounds provided ideal conditions for growing and harvesting tuberous plants. They hypothesized that mounds were built to facilitate the growth of the daisy yam (*Microseris lanceolata*), which was gathered by Aboriginal people in the nineteenth century and shows the same geographical distribution as earth mounds across inland southeast mainland (Gott 1983). Earth mounds probably increased the foods available in some wetlands, improving the reliability of returns from foraging.

Earth mounds had many functions, perhaps changing through time; their spatial and temporal distribution in the southeast is evidence that they were associated with exploitation of wetlands (Williams 1988; C. F. M. Bird and Frankel 1991a; Balme and Beck 1996). Earth mounds are absent from well-drained limestone areas to the west, and in the wetlands they are less than 2,500 years old, coinciding with local wet conditions at places such as Lake Keilambete (Figure 10.4). This evidence indicates that earth mounds are an expression of economic adaptation to foraging in the southeastern wetlands, but if mound building was a response to high water levels and expanding wetlands ecosystems in the last millennia, why do we not find mounds from previous wet periods such as the early-Holocene, more than 5,000 years ago? One possibility is that mounds were built by early-Holocene wetland foragers but have not survived. The alternative proposition, advocated by Lourandos (1983a), is that mound construction was new to the late-Holocene, part of an adaptive strategy that allowed foragers to exploit wetlands. Climatic variability was greater in the late-Holocene than early-Holocene and mound building probably assisted people to deal with conditions unlike any they had encountered previously. In that sense mound construction could be understood as a response to altered climatic conditions. However, Lourandos did not see changes in the way foragers exploited the southern wetlands as a local adaptation to the prevailing environment, but as one regional example of continent-wide social evolution he termed 'intensification'.

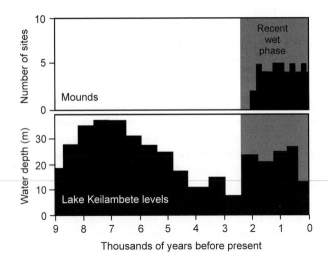

Figure 10.4 Chronology of dated earth mounds compared to changes in water availability in the landscape as indicated by water levels in Lake Keilambete. Grey area denotes the wetter and variable late-Holocene phase. (Mound dates from Bird and Frankel 1991a; lake level data from Lourandos and Ross 1994.)

Peering through the veil to measure directional change?

Claims of improving economic productivity linked to enhanced ceremonial activity are hard to demonstrate and have been contested. The most resolute critique was by Caroline Bird and David Frankel (1991a, 1991b), who pointed out that archaeologists have no evidence that stone structures and trap-like facilities were built only in the last few thousand years or were responsible for greater production. Facilities could have been made for many millennia, they argued, but evidence is hidden from us because the structures have not been preserved or dated. The wisdom of this cautious approach was shown by the research of Heather Builth (2002), who discovered dry stone walls that may have been constructed before the late-Holocene. It is possible that fixed capture devices were not purely a late development in this region, and late-Holocene economic configurations emerged piecemeal from a combination of long-term and more recent strategies.

Reconstructions in which intensive economies existed only in the late-Holocene have also been built on perceptions that number of sites and objects within sites were more abundant towards the end of the pre-historic period, and that this indicates more people, larger residential groups, and by implication heightened economic productivity (Lourandos and Ross 1994; Lourandos 1997). However, Bird and Frankel (1991a, 1991b) offered counterexamples in the southeast: while some sites near the coast such as Bridgewater Cave and the Seal Point midden (Lourandos 1983a) have abundant cultural materials of late-Holocene age, other sites such as Koongine Cave (Frankel 1986) show regular use in the early-Holocene but little or no use at later times. Furthermore, in locations with unusual preservation open sites of terminal Pleistocene and early-Holocene age as well as late-Holocene age are known (Godfrey 1989), a reminder to archaeologists that preservation is a significant factor creating chronological differences in the abundance of archaeological objects (see Chapter 12). In addition to the effects of preservation the small numbers of sites with reliable dates have made statements about change in economic productivity unreliable. Bird and Frankel (1991a) concluded that current evidence does not allow archaeologists to judge whether economic systems of southeastern Australia were more productive in the late-Holocene than at earlier times. They used that critique to contest socially oriented mechanisms of cultural change proposed by Lourandos but (as discussed above) this was not really a test of Lourandos' model; the main value of their reanalysis was to show that directional change is not unambiguously demonstrated.

In the southeast archaeological evidence indicates economic restructuring during the Holocene, and the foraging system observed historically emerged only within the past few millennia. New forms of activity occurred in the past 3,000 years, most notably the mound building involved in exploitation of wetland areas and production of stone axes which would have changed the pattern of wood working and construction. More ancient economic strategies, such as facility building, may have received greater emphasis in recent millennia, although the magnitude of change cannot be defined at the moment. However, it is not clear that late-Holocene economies were more efficient or productive than ever before, and the antiquity of trade and ceremonial networks has not been independently established and may have existed throughout the Holocene. Consequently there is no reason to identify progressive improvements in economic output.

This conclusion reflects the ambiguity of existing archaeological evidence and again reveals the difficulty of peering through the veil of pre-history. Site destruction and loss of information about chronology make it hard for archaeologists to identify what humans did and when they did it. Additionally, imposition of ethnographic images on the past, to imply that all components of historical Aboriginal life were in place when axe trade began or when mounds were first constructed, encouraged researchers to see the past in terms of the creation of the known ethnographic system rather than the transformation of one economic system to another. These situations produced a picture of progressive cultural development, and the important question archaeologists have debated is whether there was indeed a progression to more efficient and complex socio-economic systems in the late-Holocene or whether multiple economic adjustments without 'progress' have been misinterpreted.

This question has been examined across the continent. In the 1980s and 1990s some researchers suggested that economic intensification, supplying ceremonial activities, could be seen in many parts of Australia. The case study often used to support this proposition is the inferences of cycad consumption and ceremonies at Cathedral Cave in northeastern Australia.

Cathedral Cave, cycad consumption and ceremonial congregations

In the region of Carnarvon Gorge, a sandstone upland dissected by vertical gorges, John Beaton excavated several rock shelters, including Rainbow Cave and Wanderers Cave, but his work centred on the excavation of deep deposits found in Cathedral Cave (Figure 10.1). Located on the bank of Carnarvon Creek the huge Cathedral Cave contained a sandy floor into which Beaton (1977, 1991b) dug more than 4 metres. He obtained radiocarbon estimates of 3,850 (3,930–3,720) years bp for a sample towards the base of the excavation and 2,340 (2,355–2,305) years bp near the surface. The deposit accumulated as a succession of massive floods dumped sediments in this narrow part of the gorge, and Beaton concluded that there were several occupation horizons separated by flood deposits, dating between 4,000 and 2,300 years ago. There was little or no occupation debris from the last two millennia.

Excavations recovered the kinds of objects often deposited by inland foragers, such as stone artefacts and bone fragments. Archaeologists discussed the possible meaning of changes to the kinds of stone artefacts found in each level of the deposit (Beaton 1977, 1991b; Clegg 1977), but it is likely that those differences are merely a consequence of changes in the number of artefacts deposited (Hiscock 2001). Bones and shells indicate that humans hunted in diverse micro-environments close to the cave (Beaton 1991b). Interpretation of bones in terms of foraging strategies is difficult because they are poorly preserved and not all were caught by humans. For instance, nearly half of all macropod bones were gnawed and digested by dogs; this might have resulted when dingos scavenged the bones of animals hunted by humans but it could alternatively have been produced when dingos hunted animals and consumed their carcasses. Similar problems of knowing whether or not small, often badly burned and eroded, bone fragments indicate that human hunting was common. Predators such as dogs or owls brought bones into many rock shelters, making it hard to isolate what animals were being caught by humans. Brit Asmussen (2005) examined this possibility and concluded that the pattern of bone damage at Cathedral Cave was produced because many of the rock wallabies had been caught and eaten by dogs. Both the destruction and addition of bones by dingos in Cathedral Cave makes it difficult for archaeologists to infer ancient human hunting in the region.

Excavations in Cathedral, Rainbow and Wanderers Caves recovered seed shell fragments from *Macrozamia moreii*, plants commonly called cycads (Figure 10.5), from most occupation horizons. Although Beaton (1977) found it difficult to calculate the abundance of seeds from the small fragments found archaeologically, he estimated that there were about 400–600 seeds per cubic metre in each cave. Fragments seemed so abundant that he described them as cycad middens. Beaton (1977, 1991b) reported that most seed shells were burned and fragmented, and he concluded that ancient foragers had collected seeds in large numbers and transported them to the caves, where they prepared them for consumption by roasting them before breaking the shells open to access the seed.

Figure 10.5 *Macrozamia moreii* plants. (Courtesy of B. Asmussen.)

Beaton concluded that pre-historic people manipulated cycad production to enhance their occupation of the region. Portraying Carnarvon Gorge as a marginal, relatively food-poor environment he reasoned that by eating the seeds of M. *moreii*, a starch-rich food, foragers would have had a reliable additional food supply. Under normal conditions M. *moreii* produced seeds throughout the year; even in a single grove not all plants would yield seeds simultaneously, making it unlikely that many seeds would be available at one time. Since large quantities of seed shells were recovered from the sites, Beaton (1977, 1982, 1991a, 1991b) hypothesized that M. *moreii* plants had been altered, perhaps when pre-historic people set fire to a grove, and that this stimulated and synchronized fruiting, producing massive crops to support large groups. Because the maximum age of M. *moreii* seeds in these caves was 4,000–4,500 years bp, Beaton suggested that this was the time when manipulating and intensively using M. *moreii* began. He also concluded that there were other innovations at the same time.

When fresh the seeds from M. *moreii* are poisonous to humans; if consumed they can kill rapidly. Beaton reasoned that ancient foragers must have developed a solution to the deadly problem of seed toxicity. Drawing on historic observations of Aboriginal people elsewhere in Australia, who detoxified seeds by leaching them in water for long periods, Beaton hypothesized that pre-historic people had made M. *moreii* seeds safe to eat by similarly leaching them or by roasting them in fires, thereby burning their shells, before discarding them in Cathedral Cave. Because he argued that seed consumption had begun at Cathedral, Rainbow and Wanderers Caves between 4,500 and 4,000 years bp he thought that knowledge of how to detoxify plants arrived in the region at that time. Furthermore Beaton hypothesized that plant detoxifying procedures could not have been invented by local experimentation, simply because fresh seeds were so toxic people would have died before discovering the correct process. He conjectured that the knowledge of detoxification had been imported from elsewhere.

This conclusion reinforced models of diffusion advocated in the early 1980s, particularly as explanations for changes in stone artefacts (Chapter 8). At that time Bowdler (1981) cited the introduction of knowledge about treating toxic plants as a central prop for her claim that archaeologically 'invisible' phenomena, such as food preparation practices, formed a 'cultural package' introduced into Australia during the mid-Holocene. She also asserted that archaeological evidence, such as that found at Cathedral Cave, demonstrated the importation of fundamentally new social and ideological systems involving large gatherings of people associated with, perhaps driven by, ritual activities. This focus on social and ritual aspects of provisioning for large gatherings was stimulated by another conclusion that John Beaton drew about Cathedral Cave.

The existence of many *Macrozamia* seeds in the cave deposits encouraged Beaton to think that a large number of people were involved in their collection, detoxification, cooking and consumption. He concluded that the discarded seeds had resulted from gatherings of several hundred people for a week or two, bringing together different groups of foragers. He thought *Macrozamia* seeds were communion food for people attending ceremonies near Cathedral Cave during the past four millennia, somewhat like Arnhem Land in the historic period when Aboriginal people used slightly similar plants, *Cycas media*, to provide food for congregations during ceremonies. Beaton argued that ritual elements were also present in the production of food at Cathedral Cave and nearby sites.

Beaton's inference of ritually mediated gatherings was an influential statement about connections between inferred changes in Holocene economy and the idea that ceremonial and social practices were elaborated. His synthesis stated that during the mid-Holocene people arriving from overseas introduced technological and ideological changes to Aboriginal societies, resulting in greater interaction between groups, coordinated and maintained through new and augmented ceremonial processes and events, supported by economic and technological innovations that provided a greater economic production. This idea was widely cited by researchers favouring the idea that a strong, distinctive association between ceremonial congregations and reorganized forager economies emerged in the mid-Holocene. However, interpreting archaeological evidence in this way has proved hazardous.

The dangerous harvest of inferring ceremonial cycad use

The idea that complex food production techniques supported large gatherings associated with ceremonies, but only in the past four millennia, is now known to be a misreading of the archaeological evidence from Carnarvon Gorge. The chronology of cycad use proposed by Beaton was always dubious. Since his sites began to accumulate only in the mid-Holocene archaeologists have no record of earlier occupation there to tell them whether or not cycads had been used in the Pleistocene or early-Holocene. Nor have other sites in the region yielded well-preserved organic assemblages of mid-Holocene age (e.g. Mulvaney and Joyce 1965; Morwood 1984; Ulm 2004). In fact, conditions which would preserve much older *Macrozamia* seeds are very rare in Australian rock shelters, making it difficult to find evidence for human use of plants in the early-Holocene or before. However, sometimes archaeologists discover examples of remarkable preservation. One such discovery was made at Cheetup Cave in western Australia by Moya Smith (1982, 1996), who uncovered an ancient pit lined with *Xanthorrhoea* leaves and containing ten *Macrozamia* seeds. Smith interpreted this as evidence that pre-historic people had tried to detoxify the seeds. Charcoal from a layer of charred wood and ash stratigraphically above the pit gave a radiocarbon estimate of 15,680 (16,120–15,240) years bp; the pit must be older than that. Although Cheetup is on the other side of the continent to Carnarvon Gorge, Smith's research demonstrates that *Macrozamia* detoxification was not introduced into Australia in the Holocene; it was practised by foragers during the Pleistocene.

Even though Lourandos (1997) accepted the Cheetup evidence demonstrated Pleistocene antiquity of cycad processing and consumption he still proposed that there had been economic intensification. Emphasizing the small quantities of shells at Cheetup and the much larger quantity that Beaton reported from Cathedral Cave, Lourandos thought that intensive cycad use occurred only in recent millennia. This interpretation still suffered from the low probability that plant remains would have survived from the early-Holocene or Pleistocene age, even if cycads had been used at those times. Nevertheless, this seemed a plausible interpretation of the evidence until reassessment of the Cathedral Cave materials created a new understanding of cycad usage there.

It has been revealed that Beaton's inferences about the detoxification of M. *moreii* were flawed. While fresh seeds are highly toxic and require treatment such as prolonged leaching, old naturally weathered ones need little or no handling to make them safe to consume (Beck et al. 1988; Beck 1992). Consequently the discovery of M. *moreii* seed shells in archaeological deposits need not signal elaborate detoxifying treatments by ancient foragers. Specific examinations of the shell fragments recovered from Carnarvon Gorge have been carried out and the resulting information about the nature of processing shows that large congregations of people never occurred at those sites.

To understand how M. *moreii* shell came to be in Cathedral Cave, Asmussen (2005) examined each fragment in detail. By studying cracks on the shells she confirmed Beaton's idea that most seeds had been opened by human force. However, employing new, sophisticated calculations of seed abundance Asmussen estimated that only 400–450 seeds were represented by all the fragments in Beaton's excavation of the Cathedral Cave deposit. Over the thousands of years during which humans visited the site they discarded only an average of less than one seed per year in the excavated areas. Even if this calculation underestimates the number of seeds originally present, it is clear there were never enough seeds to feed a large group of people! Furthermore, non-seed parts of *Macrozamia* plants are found in the deposit and some shells were weathered and unburned when they were broken, showing that a few *Macrozamia* plants probably grew in the site. Humans merely collected and broke open a few weathered seeds that had naturally lost their poisons, or detoxified small numbers of fresh seeds, when they occasionally visited the site (Asmussen 2005). Occupation was by small groups of people, not large gatherings, and was not dependent on the acquisition of abundant M. *moreii* seeds.

This revised interpretation of Holocene economy in Carnarvon Gorge illustrates how difficult it is to create accurate images of inland foraging, and that historical economic and ceremonial activities cannot be superimposed on to ancient situations with safety. Furthermore, sites such as Cathedral Cave do not contain evidence for increases through time in economic productivity or the complexity of social networks, a conclusion that challenges the proposal that economic and social intensification took place in all regions.

Change in rainforest economies

Claims for economic and social change involving improvements in foraging productivity in the mid- or late-Holocene have also been reassessed in regions other than Carnarvon Gorge. For instance, human occupation of the tropical Australian rainforests has been investigated by researchers exploring the area around Jiyer Cave in northeastern Australia (Figure 10.1). Excavations at the cave, a concavity in volcanic rock, yielded the oldest archaeological evidence for human activity in Australian tropical rainforests. At this site the oldest stone artefacts were recovered by Nicky Horsfall (1983, 1987, 1996) from a layer with a radiocarbon estimate of 5,910 (5,920–5,895) years bp; in more recent levels ochre fragments and nut shells were found.

Ideas of increased economic productivity and social interactions were applied to Jiyer Cave by researchers who argued that a distinctive rainforest economy and society was supported by the intensive processing of nuts (Horsfall 1987, 1996; Cosgrove 1996). Beaton (1982) thought the mid-Holocene antiquity for occupation at the cave was a consequence of the arrival of plant detoxifying technology, which enhanced the capacity of humans to exploit the rainforest. However, Horsfall (1987) and Lourandos (1997) considered the presence of a few seed shells in levels less than 4,000 years old, but at higher densities in levels less than 1,000 years old, as evidence that human use of rainforests had increased, representing the local manifestation of continent-wide economic intensification.

Identifying the initiation of intensive and distinctive rainforest economies is not straightforward: the timing and nature of economic change is unclear even at Jiyer

Cave. Asmussen (2003) even argued that there had never been specialized and exclusively rainforest societies. Other researchers accept the existence of specialized societies in the historical period but hypothesized it to be a result of culture contact with Europeans. For example, substantially more cultural material in the past 200–300 years might indicate that greater rainforest occupation was a response to nineteenth century European encroachment into the area and that at earlier times only rainforest margins were the focus of human use (Horsfall 1983; Hiscock and Kershaw 1992). However, abundant plant material in recent levels of the cave might merely reflect the failure of older organic debris to be preserved and a greater time depth to rainforest use can be contemplated. Richard Cosgrove interpreted the 5,000-year-old history of human use of Jiyer Cave as an indication that specialized rainforest economies operated in the terminal Pleistocene and early-Holocene (Cosgrove 1996; Cosgrove and Raymont 2002). Pleistocene rainforest use has additionally been inferred from disturbance to rainforest vegetation (Kershaw 1985, 1986; Hiscock and Kershaw 1992). Reconstructions of change in rainforest economy currently rely on a single archaeological site that can be interpreted in these multiple ways; the chronology of rainforest exploitation has not been established. Existing evidence from rainforests does not unambiguously document mid- or late-Holocene economic intensification of the kind Lourandos hypothesized in the southeast.

Change and diversity without directionality?

Claims that economic changes throughout inland Australia follow a single trend are difficult to test with the available evidence. Even for the past few millennia preservation of archaeological materials is patchy; for earlier periods material is rarely preserved at all. In many regions there is little evidence for the character of early-Holocene economic activity, making it difficult to define the nature of economic change through the Holocene. Furthermore, plant and animal remains were not always brought into sites by humans, making statements about past foraging strategies uncertain. Destruction of older sites, and of plant and animal residues in the older levels of sites, veils the past by making it hard to distinguish changed economic activities and altered levels of preservation from increases in population size and economic productivity.

Existing studies document regional diversity in economic practices and, in some regions, changes in the diet, capture strategies and land use patterns during the Holocene; increased production within Holocene economies is not indicated in all regions. This conclusion implies nothing about the causes of change or stability in Holocene economic systems. Although social dynamics have been invoked as a central mechanism creating economic restructuring it is possible that they could also have contributed to the lack of change in some regional economies. We cannot identify a continent-wide trend to 'intensification', but this does not mean that directional trends did not occur in specific areas or that economic transformations in the Holocene were not connected to social competition and altered territorial patterns. Nevertheless, initial research which concluded that the same kind of economic and ceremonial changes occurred across all inland plains and uplands has been overturned. In particular, the idea that in all regions resources were obtained more efficiently through managing and preparing specific plant and animal species, and large ceremonial gatherings held for the first time in the mid- or late-Holocene, is not consistent with the available evidence. The antiquity of economic and social changes is often ill defined, and in several regions there is now no reason to think that radical economic and social changes occurred at all during the Holocene.

Where late-Holocene economic changes occurred they appear to have been adjustments to local conditions and therefore they differed between regions. For example, game hunting in some eastern Australian woodlands was reorientated over the past three millennia, as foragers altered the emphasis between capturing mobile kangaroos and less mobile arboreal animals such as possums (e.g. David 1991; Attenbrow 2004). At Devon Downs, a rock shelter on the lower Murray River, the amount of mammal meat brought to the site reduced about 3,200 (3,335–3,000) years ago, but there was an increase in the use of freshwater molluscs from the river (M. A. Smith 1982). These examples reveal diverse patterns of restructuring in foraging and occupation; they present a mosaic of subtlty different foraging strategies that can be understood as the exploitation of local opportunities rather than as a single narrative of directional economic change. There is no necessity to conceive of social and economic change during the Holocene as being continent-wide, unidirectional in nature or initiated only in the mid-Holocene. Questions of whether late-Holocene economic activities were different from those in earlier periods of Australian pre-history, and therefore represent unique cultural changes, or were part of a long series of somewhat similar economic and social adaptations has preoccupied archaeologists in Australia. Some researchers turned to inferences of population growth (Chapter 12) and social reorganization (Chapter 13) to bolster their idea that there had been a substantial transformation of foraging economies and societies late in pre-history. Other researchers focused on the archaeological evidence from Australia's deserts as a way to evaluate models of continuity and change. Like interpretations of inland economies, all of these investigations have been complicated by the poor preservation of older archaeological materials and by the temptation to use ethnographic life as an analogy for ancient life.

11 Arid zone economies in the Holocene

Tension between images of conservative pre-historic economies and past societies that underwent rapid economic changes during later times is epitomized by debates about life in the Australian deserts. Both images have been interwoven into the progression model of Pleistocene life, and similarities in caricatures of Pleistocene people and historical desert dwellers, as conservative, low-density mobile hunters, is no coincidence. Beginning in the 1960s, some archaeologists advocated that desert societies or economies were conservative, reflecting the harsh conditions in which they existed, and as a consequence of the delicate balance between economic activities and the environmental opportunities there had been little change in the life of desert foragers during the Holocene. This notion of unchanging desert dwellers not only influenced interpretations of life in Pleistocene Australia as being unchanging, but also reinforced the idea that the historical economy seen in the nineteenth century had existed throughout the Holocene. The result was a model of desert adaptation in which the society and economy of desert foragers was uniform and had been the same since at least the terminal Pleistocene. This was an influential description of desert pre-history but is increasingly challenged by claims that desert economies were regionally varied and changing.

Debate about conservatism and uniformity in desert life has centred on research carried out in the Western Desert, an extensive amalgam of deserts in the western portion of the modern-day arid zone (Figure 11.1). That region is the focus of case studies in this chapter.

Gould's 'desert culture' and Puntutjarpa

During the 1960s Richard Gould's study of twentieth century Ngatatjara Aboriginal people foraging provided him with information that he used to reconstruct the historic desert economy (Gould 1967, 1968b, 1969a, 1969b, 1971). He listed features that were central to the diet of foragers at that time, such as reliance on plant foods collected by women, infrequent acquisition of meat by hunters, a daily regime of foraging with little storage of food, and variation in foods as rainfall altered available resources. Gould argued that many characteristics of Ngatatjara settlement and society were necessary if foragers were to exploit the unreliable and low productivity of desert environment. He cited their low population density, high

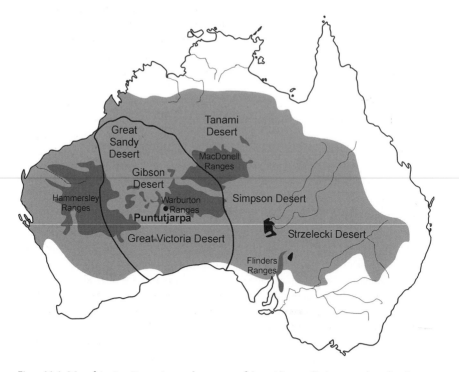

Figure 11.1 Map showing Puntutjarpa, the extent of the arid zone (lighter grey), upland areas above 500 metres (darker grey) and major deserts (based on Veth et al. 2001). Boundary of the Western Desert is shown.

mobility as they moved frequently between food-poor patches, a portable material culture, flexible systems of group aggregation and fissioning which allowed them to fragment during periods of drought, and elaborate marriage and kinship systems that created a web of social obligations with neighbouring groups.

In the historical period, Gould argued, these economic and social practices formed an adaptive mechanism that minimized risks inherent to desert landscapes. Low population densities and flexible settlement strategy permitted foragers to disperse and move to water, a necessity when the location and timing of water sources were hard to predict. Portable equipment and minimal food storage were consequences of highly mobile searches for temporary resources. Vegetable staples were reliable foods, providing a buffer against the variable results of hunting. Political relationships established in marriage and kinship were seen by Gould to enhance food sharing within groups and could enable people to exploit resources on the territories of their neighbours.

Gould (1971, 1977, 1978, 1980) hypothesized that this risk-minimizing desert economic system could be identified in the archaeological record, because it left a characteristic record of stone artefacts. Distinctive stone scrapers called tulas by archaeologists, sometimes used to adze hardwoods, were, he said, a signature of the wooden toolkit known in the historical period. Gould emphasized grindstones as highly visible tools used to process the plant foods which were so important in the diet. He also suggested that crushing bones to extract marrow indicated the meat scarcity suffered by desert foragers (Gould 1996; but see P. Smith 2000). Most significantly Gould (1977) argued that the existence in archaeological deposits of stone artefacts carried from distant areas, which he called 'exotic lithic raw material', was evidence for the existence of long-distance social networks and the resource sharing they facilitated.

Gould claimed that the widespread discovery of tulas, grindstones and transported rock revealed that the historical desert adaptation had occurred across much of the arid zone. The antiquity of that historical desert adaptation, Gould reasoned, could be established by dating the oldest archaeological examples of these phenomena. The desert culture had existed for as long as these materials had been discarded in roughly the same frequency!

In the late 1960s Gould excavated Puntutjarpa Rockshelter, a deep archaeological site near the Warburton Range, and reported no noteworthy change in archaeological materials throughout the deposit. He concluded that the desert culture has existed for about 10,000 years, and that in that time life in the Australian deserts changed little. Gould declared that economic and social continuity existed over long tracts of time because desert dwellers had maintained the same basic adaptive strategy, which he termed the 'Australian desert culture'.

Claims for the same economic strategy in all parts of the arid zone, and over a long time span, can be assessed separately. The idea of a uniform economic adaptation across the arid interior during the late-Holocene fails to account for the environmental diversity within and between deserts. When differences in arid landscapes were considered it became clear to archaeologists that there had been different economic systems employed in different places.

Desert diversity in present-day Australia

Australian deserts are extremely diverse. Covering approximately three million square kilometres of land desert environments are located in tropical and non-tropical climates, coastal and inland situations, and low-lying and upland topography reflecting regional differences in geological regimes (Figure 11.1). Some of that variation was expressed in Veth's 'refuge, corridor and barrier' model, where he distinguished sand-ridge landscapes, rocky uplands, stony and scrub plains. Those broad categories of desert also contain much variation. For example, sand-ridge deserts, characterized by elongated bodies of sand (Figure 11.2), display local differences in sand masses and the frequency of water sources, such as the density of claypans in which water might sit after rain. Each sandy desert currently has different vegetation and moisture regimes (M. A. Smith 1993). Those distinctions affect the way foragers could have moved across each region, the abundance and distribution of resources available, and the distribution and nature of water sources; ultimately leading to differences in the mobility of people living in each desert. Veth also suggested that in areas with temporarily abundant water and plant foods people

Figure 11.2 Aerial view of a sand-ridge desert.

Figure 11.3 View of archaeological excavations in desert uplands.

aggregated to maintain necessary social networks (Veth 2000, 2006; McDonald and Veth 2006).

Variation within desert uplands would have been important for ancient foragers (Figure 11.3). Riverine and gorge systems and localities with coordinated drainage provided networks of relatively reliable water sources which may have been critical as refuge areas during drought conditions (e.g. M. A. Smith 1989c). Such areas are relatively insensitive to climatic change, and their position within desert landscapes would have been a factor in the pattern of life for the broader region in which they were located. Small upland areas also contain rock shelters that preserve a signal of human activity in the surrounding landscape.

Although all deserts have potential evaporation rates far in excess of rainfall they receive, they differ markedly in the way they receive their rain. Winter rain is typical on the southern desert fringes, northern deserts have a pronounced pattern of seasonal summer rainfall, but across a central band of arid lands rainfall is weakly seasonal or non-seasonal (Figure 11.4). Since the rhythm of life in deserts is attuned to patterns of water availability and drought, climatic and topographic differences between deserts would often be matched by differences in the economic and social systems of people living there.

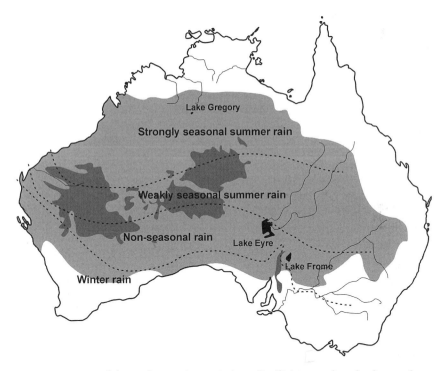

Figure 11.4 Extent of the modern arid zone in Australia (lighter grey), upland areas above 500 metres (darker grey) and rainfall seasonality across that area (based on Veth et al. 2001; Hesse et al. 2004). Place names are locations at which palaeo-environmental information has been obtained.

Desert settlement in the late-Holocene

Richard Gould initially implied that the characteristics of desert life he reconstructed for the region around Puntutjarpa had existed throughout the arid zone. It is now clear that the location of Puntutjarpa in the almost non-seasonal southern portion of the Western Desert explains the historic and late pre-historic economy that existed there. Donald Pate (1986) concluded that plant use there was a response to the unpredictable rainfall of the region, and Gould (1996) himself proposed that humans living in Puntutjarpa's non-seasonal environment had more dietary stress than desert-dwellers in more seasonal environments to the north.

In reconsidering his original view Gould (1991) argued that flexibility required by foragers living in arid environments probably implied that a diversity of economic and settlement strategies had existed. To illustrate this point he contrasted two strategies by which Western Desert people sought to cope with hardships imposed by prolonged drought. He termed these strategies drought escape and drought evasion. Drought escape involved abandoning areas for the duration of the drought, a sound strategy when no reliable supplies of drinkable water were present in the local landscape. Drought evasion involved retreating to places within the drought-affected area where there were reliable water sources. The dominant strategy in any region reflected several factors, including the distribution and reliability of water and the severity of droughts. Near Puntutjarpa both strategies were employed in the historical period, although drought escape may have been dominant.

The effect of water sources on settlement has been investigated in other non-seasonal deserts, with different resources to those available near Puntutjarpa. Archaeological evidence in these deserts demonstrates strategies of pre-historic occupation. One example is the mounded springs located between the southern end of Lake Eyre and the Flinders Ranges. These mound springs were the only permanent sources of drinkable water in the region, and were a focus of occupation, shown by the millions of stone artefacts surrounding them (Florek 1986). These springs were a refuge from drought, enabling people to continue using the area during severe droughts rather than abandoning the entire region (Hughes and Hiscock 2005). Stan Florek (1993) proposed that depletion of food and water during dry periods forced foragers to stay close to the springs, but this rapidly led to the exhaustion of food in the vicinity of each, forcing them to move frequently between the springs. In droughts the people of this region fragmented into smaller groups and moved from spring to spring to exploit dwindling food supplies. When droughts ended people dispersed far from the springs, not only because surface water and food was more widely available but also to allow food resources in the localities surrounding springs to regenerate. The refuge provided by permanently flowing mound springs near Lake Eyre South was a reason foragers in that region employed drought evasion as the dominant response to drought (Hughes and Hiscock 2005).

Not surprisingly research from the northern deserts, which have distinctly seasonal rainfall patterns, have found them to contain a seasonal cycle of land use. In the Little and Great Sandy Deserts, Peter Veth (1987, 1993, 1996) combined historical observations of Aboriginal life ways with the distribution of archae-ological materials in the landscape to reconstruct the pre-historic settlement pattern. He hypothesized that there had been a strongly seasonal pattern of land use. After summer rains, people dispersed into small groups and were highly mobile, moving opportunistically between scattered ephemeral water sources to exploit food resources in more risky and resource-poor parts of their environment. During winter, foragers focused on locations with more reliable water supplies and established longer term base camps, sending subgroups to exploit resources not available in the local area. The result was a seasonal cycle of dispersal and coalescence of people as they moved to use the seasonally fluctuating food resources.

Veth's inference of seasonal desert land use in the Little and Great Sandy Deserts contrasts with settlement patterns reconstructed by Gould for the less seasonal south of the Western Desert. In both regions, as in all parts of the arid zone, foragers shared characteristics of low population densities and high mobility, but the struc-ture of landscape use differed. The existence of different settlement strategies within the Western Desert during the late-Holocene demonstrates that there was not a homogeneous desert adaptation. There is also growing evidence of change over time in desert environments and human economies.

Desert change

Characteristics of deserts not only varied geographically, but also changed over time in response to climatic shifts. Palaeo-environmental sequences from different deserts vary (Ross et al. 1992), although they shared broad trends. Approximately 14,000 years ago climate became warmer and moister than at present (Kershaw 1995; Wyrwoll and Miller 2001). This wetter phase is visible in the centre and north as high water levels at lakes such as Lake Gregory, and as flood deposits along central Australian rivers (Patton et al. 1993; Hesse et al. 2004). On the southern edge of the arid zone animal middens and dune fields indicate that from about 6,000–10,000 years ago conditions were warmer and wetter, supporting open woodlands with a grass under storey in the Flinders Ranges (Ross et al. 1992; McCarthy et al. 1996; McCarthy and Head 2001). These conditions persisted until 6,000 years ago.

Starting 5,000–6,000 years ago the climate became drier and more variable. In the Flinders Ranges drier, cooler conditions after 5,000 years bp caused a shift from woodlands to shrublands, and near Lake Frome dune building commenced (McCarthy et al. 1996; McCarthy and Head 2001). This drier period coincided with the onset of intensified El Niño conditions and lasted until about 2,000 years ago. Across arid Australia greater variability in effective precipitation and unpredictable patterns of prolonged, severe droughts at this time represented a climatic regime that was far more arid and difficult for foragers than the one existing in the historical period. Mid-Holocene drying was not as harsh as the LGM but it was a severe deterioration from the early-Holocene situation and may have encouraged adaptive strategies unlike those of more recent times.

Climate ameliorated in the past 2,000 years when slightly wetter conditions may have been more common (Singh 1981; Patton et al. 1993; Pearson and Dodson

1993). Evidence from Puritjarra suggests desert grasslands stabilized about 1,500 years bp after millennia of instability (Bowdery 1998; M. A. Smith 2005). However, the climate was still drier and more variable than in the early-Holocene, and at some sites flash flooding may have disturbed or destroyed earlier deposits (Veth et al. 2001).

The climatic cycle from more reliable water availability in the early-Holocene to drier, less predictable surface water in the mid-Holocene and a return to slightly more reliable water availability in the past 1,000–2,000 years was superimposed on shorter term and localized variations. For instance, during the dry mid-Holocene there were brief lacustral events between 4,000 and 3,000 years ago at Lake Frome and Lake Eyre (Magee and Miller 1998; Luly 2001; Hesse et al. 2004). Hence the pattern of Holocene climatic change is complex and regional, but it has still been used by archaeologists to understand temporal variation in desert use.

Linguistic and population change?

In the Western Desert there were two cultural mechanisms with the potential to create significant culture change. Some researchers consider that these mechanisms caused substantial economic and social change in the Holocene, thereby challenging Gould's view of cultural continuity and stability in the deserts (McConvell 1996).

One mechanism of culture change is the migration of people eastward from the Hamersely Ranges into the Western Desert during the Holocene, displacing previous inhabitants. Evidence from linguistics and biology has suggested this migration. Patrick McConvell (1996) hypothesized that similarity in Western Desert languages indicated that most had diverged and spread relatively recently. He suggested language spread occurred mainly through movements of people and that languages of the region moved into place through a series of migrations. Geographical similarities in Aboriginal physical appearance and language distributions during the historical period were used by him as evidence that languages had moved with people. McConvell reconstructed a sequence of language and social changes and attempted to estimate the age of each by reference to archaeological evidence; a valuable but technically difficult task (M. A. Smith 2005). People spread into the Western Desert 2,000–3,000 years ago, he argued, and then continued to move eastwards. McConvell focused on pre-historic social transformations, proposing that subsections, an important nineteenth century practice in which people were classified into eight social divisions with defined relationships, spread across the desert in less than a millennium. Similarities in Western Desert life ways can be explained by recent dispersals of people carrying a common language and culture, and need not reflect long-term cultural stability (M. A. Smith 2005).

Implications of McConvell's model for forager use of deserts were discussed by Veth (2000, 2006), who suggested that archaeological and linguistic changes could be correlated to provide an image of economic and social transformations in Western Desert life. Veth noted that more sites and artefacts are known from the past 1,500 years than from earlier periods; he suggested this showed that the spread of Western Desert languages was accompanied by expanded trade networks and more ritual or ceremonial activities. Ramified social networks in the historical period, which Gould had thought characterized desert adaptations, therefore emerged, Veth said, 1,000–1,500 years ago. He and McDonald infer greater production of rock art in the last two millennia, as local territories were defined and alliance networks between groups developed (McDonald and Veth 2006), although Veth (2006) suggests this was initiated prior to the spread of the Western Desert language. The connection of language change with the reorganization of desert economy and society was questioned by Mike Smith (1993, 2005), who suggested recolonization of deserts after the LGM, population increase, and development of new inter-group economic and social networks explained changes in site numbers and art production, without needing to interpret the language spread as a process of population replacement (also Veth 1987). He noted that age-estimates for language spread are imprecise and it may have occurred substantially earlier or later than 1,500 years bp (M. A. Smith 2005). Furthermore, while evidence of abundant rock art dating to the past 1,500 years may signal increased territoriality and group identity it can alternatively be explained by the non-preservation of earlier art (Thorley 2004). Since in many parts of Australia recent rock art is better preserved it is unclear whether this indicates a fundamental social change (Chapter 13).

A second mechanism sometimes thought to have triggered economic change in the Western Desert is population growth. Archaeologists have reported large numbers of sites and stone artefacts in contexts that are probably mid- or late-Holocene in age and less archaeological material from earlier times (M. A. Smith 1993, 2005; Veth 1996, 2006). Many factors, such as forager mobility and the preservation or identification of sites of different ages may create such variations, but these patterns have usually been interpreted as evidence of population growth within the past 1,500 years (Chapter 12). Demographic interpretations have been reinforced by excavations in rock shelters which yielded far greater numbers of artefacts in the last millennium that in levels dating to earlier times (Figure 11.5). Veth (1987, 1993, 1996) reported this from sites such as Karlamilyl on the margin of the Great Sandy Desert, and Mike Smith (2005, 2006) found this pattern at Puritjarra near the MacDonell Ranges (also Law 2004).

Inferred population increase in the Western Desert has sometimes been linked to economic changes. This proposition was initiated by Mike Smith (1986a), who argued that greater exploitation of grass seeds was a response to a late-Holocene decline in easily obtained foods following population growth in the mid-Holocene. The low calorific benefit obtained from collecting and laboriously processing grass seed was, he argued, worthwhile because abundant grasses were a reliable food capable of supporting the population size that had developed (see D. W. Bird and R. B. Bird 2005). This proposition was based on the recovery of millstones suitable for wet milling of seeds (Figure 2.4B) in late-Holocene levels of rock shelters excavated in the Western Desert such as Puntutjarpa (Smith 1986a), Karlamilyl (Veth 1993) and Kaalpi (Veth et al. 2001; Veth 2006). Although desert sites are often outdoors and undated, archaeologists have employed excavated shelters with large artefact assemblages as a reliable indication that the millstone use increased during the last two millennia. Smith suggested that millstones were used to prepare

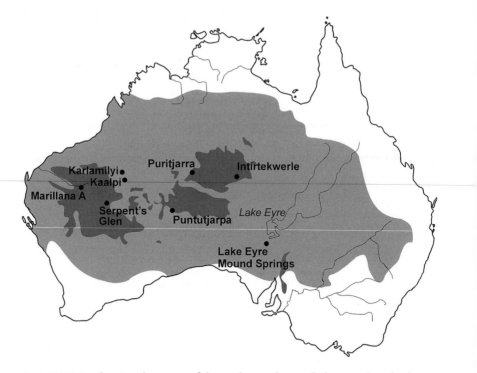

Figure 11.5 Map showing the extent of the modern arid zone (lighter grey), upland areas above 500 metres (darker grey) and archaeological sites mentioned in Chapter 11 (based on Veth et al. 2001).

seed and increased millstone fragments demonstrated an increase in the amount of grass seed processed by desert dwellers (M. A. Smith 1985, 1986a, 1988, 1989a, 1989b, 1996, 2005; David 2002; Veth 2006).

An alternative viewpoint provided by Veth and O'Connor (1996), Gorecki et al. (1997) and Balme et al. (2001) is that at earlier times Holoseed grinding may also have been economically important but carried out with tools such as fixed rock surfaces, 'amorphous' grindstones or wooden bowls which are not easily observed in rock shelter deposits. Consequently seed processing might have been part of desert economies since at least the terminal Pleistocene (Edwards and O'Connell 1995), an idea consistent with the discovery of Pleistocene grindstones outside the Western Desert (Fullagar and Field 1997). This possibility can be seriously considered because although Mike Smith (2005) has continued to associate the economic shift towards greater seed use with demographic growth, there is no evidence for the links he initially hypothesized. In fact the abundance of preserved sites and artefacts increased most about the same time or later than the late-Holocene increase in the abundance of millstone fragments, evidence not consistent with the idea that there had previously been a substantial population increase in deserts during the mid-Holocene. Furthermore, there appears to be greater rainfall rather than climatic deterioration in the last millennium, contrary to the mechanism Smith proposed. It seems that factors other than population increase were involved in the late-Holocene increase of grindstones.

Migration of new people into the region is one process already discussed that may have been associated with late-Holocene economic change, but other processes are also known. For instance, environmental changes took place 1,000–2,000 years ago, about the same time grindstone discard increased at a number of sites. The combination of slightly wetter climatic conditions and more stable grassland environments in some regions may have altered the economic benefits of intensive grass seed exploitation. Reduced mobility of desert foragers at this time has also been suggested, and perhaps the adoption of intensive seed processing would have broadened the diet and allowed more prolonged occupation of smaller territories (M. A. Smith 1986a; Veth 2000, 2006). Patterns of human aggregation are also suggested to have changed about the same time. According to McDonald and Veth (2006) expanded social networks of the kind seen historically, which Gould referred to as distributing stone artefacts over long distances, probably began 1,000–1,500 years ago. They suggest social networks were orchestrated during aggregations of people, that these were held at places and times when sufficient food was available, and that seed grinding was the principal economic practice that allowed those congregations to occur (also David 2002).

These are examples of the focus within recent archaeological studies on changes 1,000–2,000 years ago in Western Desert economies. The nature of economic and social changes is debated, but evidence consistently indicates that desert life was configured differently in the mid-Holocene than in the late-Holocene: fewer sites and artefacts are known (often interpreted as showing lower population densities and/or more mobile settlement), foraging either occurred without an emphasis on seed use or seeds were exploited with techniques unlike in the historical period, and there are differences in preserved rock art (often interpreted as showing that extended inter-group networks were less common or active). The identification of one process as the principal cause for these changes has been much discussed, but there is no obvious reason to single out demography, climate change, population replacement, or inter-group aggregation as a trigger for change in all deserts (Edwards and O'Connell 1995). Complicating attempts to understand late-Holocene transformations of desert economies is the lack of archaeological information about earlier economic changes. Focusing on evidence for economic, technological, and perhaps social, change in sand-ridge regions of the Western Desert some archaeologists suggested there had been economic and social intensification 1,000–2,000 years ago. Evidence for foraging throughout the Holocene provides a broader context for interpreting late-Holocene change in desert economies.

Human use of deserts in the early-Holocene

The view that historical desert economies emerged only in the past two millennia challenges archaeologists to reconstruct Western Desert life earlier in the Holocene.

However, information about desert life during the early-Holocene has been hard to find. Despite detailed excavations, many rock shelters such as Kaalpi (Veth et al. 2001), Karlamilyl (Veth 1996) and Intirtekwerle (M. A. Smith 1986b) only yielded cultural material less than 3,000–4,000 years old. It was initially thought this showed that a number of deserts, particularly sand-ridge ones, were not occupied prior to 4–5,000 years bp (Veth 1989), but this interpretation now appears unlikely.

On the eastern margin of the Western Desert the archaeological sequence identified by Mike Smith (1989c, 2006) at Puritjarra documents occupation of central Australia throughout the terminal Pleistocene and Holocene. On the western margin of the region sites have also revealed early occupation. At Serpents Glen occupation of the Western Desert began before the LGM but the site was then abandoned until about 5,500 years bp (O'Connor et al. 1998). The absence of archaeological evidence for early-Holocene occupation has been puzzling, since more abundant surface water at that time might have made it easier for people to use these landscapes. One proposed explanation is that slow demographic recovery from reduced population size during the LGM delayed desert use until after 5,000 years bp (Veth 2000). However, whether resettlement of vacated regions was gradual or rapid, and whether it was linked to expansions of people carrying particular languages, is unresolved (see Veth 1995; M. A. Smith 2005). Furthermore, some sites immediately outside the Western Desert appear to have had more human activity in the early-Holocene than in the late-Holocene. For instance, Ben Marwick (2005) concluded that near Marillana A in the Hamersley Range, forager mobility and site activities had changed little, but there had been more frequent human visits to the site between 9,000 and 3,000 years bp than earlier or later. This could reflect alterations in local landscape use rather than broad shifts in population. Alternatively it might hint at broader population processes: people may have also occupied adjacent sand-ridge deserts in the early-Holocene, or moved into lands to the east in the last three millennia.

Researchers advocating Holocene migration into the Western Desert, such as McConvell (1996) and Veth (1987), suggested foragers expanded from gorges in the Hamersley Range into sand-ridge and grassland landscapes during the early- and mid-Holocene, but the archaeological evidence is not easy to interpret. While many excavated rock shelters within the sand-ridge deserts have cultural evidence only from the past few thousand years people may already have been there during the early-Holocene. Veth (2000) observed that weathered rock art panels at Kaalpi appear substantially older than archaeological deposits in the shelter, indicating that early occupation of desert areas may have occurred without leaving many preserved traces. Doubts about whether terminal Pleistocene and early-Holocene human use of deserts is always visible in the archaeological record mean site numbers may not be as reliable for interpreting early- and mid-Holocene economic patterns as the contents of long archaeological sequences. For that reason Mike Smith (1993) observed that the lack of sites with complete occupation sequences between 5,000 and 10,000 years ago limits the ability of archaeologists to test many models about economic and demographic change in the deserts.

Western Desert sites occupied throughout the Holocene, principally Puritjarra and Puntutjarpa, not only demonstrate that people lived there during all climatic phases following the LGM, but also provide evidence for changes in the way people exploited those arid landscapes (M. A. Smith 2005). Puntutjarpa is the critical site for understanding the occupation of Western Desert lowlands; it remains the only site within a huge region of sandy deserts with uncoordinated drainage in which a large archaeological assemblage documents economic activities throughout the Holocene (Veth 1995).

Puntutjarpa and change in desert adaptations

Economic and social change in the Western Desert can be assessed by returning to Puntutjarpa, the long and rich archaeological sequence that prompted visions of a stable desert adaptation. Only economic change in the local region, rather than the whole Western Desert, can be tested at this site; nevertheless it allows contrasting images of desert life to be evaluated. On the one hand Richard Gould, claiming the archaeological sequence displayed no significant change, hypothesized foragers had the same adaptive strategy from first occupation of Puntutjarpa until the historical period. A contrasting picture of desert life was given by other researchers, including Peter Veth and Mike Smith, who argued for a long sequence of economic and technological reorganization, in which historical long-distance social networks and seed exploitation emerged in the past 1,000–2,000 years. The value of these images can be examined for the archaeological evidence from Puntutjarpa.

Gould's (1977) main excavation of Puntutjarpa was during 1969–70, and across most of the trench he reached bedrock at a depth of about 130 cm. The sandy deposit was similar in colour and texture, and there were signs of recent disturbance by roots and burrowing animals. There was no simple sequence of layers; Gould discusses the accumulation of the deposit by reference to two rockfall events that had created slightly sloping rows of large rocks in the deposit (Figure 11.6). These rocks had fallen from the shelter roof and probably rest on what was the surface of the deposit at different times in the past. Gould called the higher row of rocks and boulders the 'Upper Rockfall', concluding from the position of jumbled rocks that they had not fallen all at once but in at least two or three different roof collapse events. Gould also recognized an earlier rockfall, near the base of the deposit, which he called the 'Lower Rockfall'.

When these rocks fell Puntutjarpa would have been dangerous, although they may have fallen between human visits to the site, and rocks protruding from the ground may have altered the ways that humans used the shelter at different times. However, these rockfalls provided Gould with a way to define three periods of deposit formation: sands above the Upper Rockfall were called stratigraphic Zone A; sands between the two rocky layers were called Zone B; sands below the Lower Rockfall were called Zone C.

There are eight radiocarbon age-estimates for the deposit and Gould employed these to describe the antiquity of the site. The oldest was from a sample of charcoal found only 8 cm above bedrock; it gave an estimate of 11,890 (12,360–11,315)

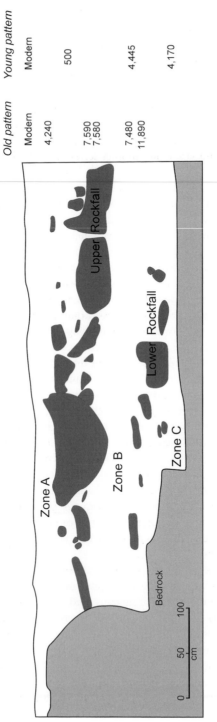

	Old pattern	Young pattern
Zone A	Modern	Modern
	4,240	
		500
Zone B	7,590	
	7,580	
Upper Rockfall		
Lower Rockfall	7,480	4,445
Zone C	11,890	
Bedrock		4,170

Figure 11.6 Simplified stratigraphic section from Trench 2 at Puntutjarpa, showing the approximate depths and approximate estimated ages of the radiocarbon samples (information from Gould 1977).

years bp. Gould (1977, 1980, 1996) accepted this estimate and concluded that foragers visited the site throughout the past 12,000 years, providing a record of human foraging in the desert during the Holocene.

Not all archaeologists are persuaded by Gould's conclusions about human antiquity at Puntutjarpa. For instance, Ian Johnson (1979) pointed out that the radiocarbon age-estimates did not form a well-ordered sequence, and two different interpretations of the chronology are possible. A number of estimates, the 'old pattern' in Figure 11.6, could be used to suggest that strata were old, indicating the deposit began forming more than 12,000 years ago and that Zone B and Upper Rockfall were about 7,000 years old. Another series of dates, the 'young pattern', could suggest the deposit started forming only 5,000 years ago. Gould (1977, 1996) preferred the older pattern in his interpretation of the base of the deposit and the younger pattern for his interpretation of the top, concluding that some charcoal samples were contaminated. These alternative estimates of antiquity indicate that the formation of the deposit was complex and the antiquity of each level is not certain.

Uncertainties about how to understand the chronology of this deposit complicate archaeological interpretations, and ultimately re-excavation of the sequence is required to determine its nature and antiquity. Until then it is sensible to cautiously employ Gould's three stratigraphic zones as the basis of a chronological framework. The following approach is employed here. At the top of the stratigraphic sequence Zone A is certainly less than about 6,000 years old, and much of it might be only 600 years old or less. The number of objects in this zone that are between 6,000 and 1,000 years old is unknown, but many probably date to the last millennium. Zone A is therefore discussed as being late-Holocene in age, mostly less than 600 years bp (Gould 1996; Balme et al. 2001). Central stratigraphic levels, Zone B and the Upper Rockfall, probably contain objects between 7,600 and 4,500 years old, and can be treated as being mid-Holocene in age. Below the Lower Rockfall, sediments Gould defined as Zone C contain early material, although the antiquity of the material is unclear. Zone C might be entirely mid-Holocene or alternatively it could incorporate material of early-Holocene and even terminal Pleistocene age. Here Zone C is discussed as early-Holocene, following Gould (1977, 1996; Balme et al. 2001), although dating uncertainties are acknowledged. This chronology is consistent with the one advocated by Gould and allows a consideration of his interpretations of the cultural evidence.

Using these estimates of antiquity it seems that humans occupied Puntutjarpa for only a few short periods during the Holocene. Zone C contains little cultural material representing low levels of human activity at some time in the early-Holocene. The highest density of stone artefacts and bone fragments came from Zone B (Gould 1977, 1996), indicating relatively intense occupation during the climatic optimum, between 8,000 and 5,000 years ago. The length of that phase is unknown; multiple radiocarbon estimates of about 7,500 years bp might indicate that most human activity occurred during only a few centuries but it is also possible that Zone B contains occupation over a 2,000–3,000-year period. Whatever the length of that mid-Holocene occupational period, it was probably followed by abandonment of the site for a prolonged period, from or before 4,500 years bp until less than 1,000 years ago, after which much of Zone A accumulated. While minimal occupation or abandonment may have been related to the multiple roof collapses in the shelter, represented by the Upper Rockfall layer, it occurred during the mid- and late-Holocene phase of drier and more variable climatic conditions. Prolonged abandonment of the site probably reflects reduced human use of the region as settlement strategies were reorganized to accommodate that Holocene period of intensified aridity.

Excavation recovered thousands of bone fragments which show that the occupants captured and ate kangaroos and wallabies, possums, bandicoots and lizards (Archer 1977). These animals may have been caught whenever they were encountered and poor bone preservation makes it hard to know whether there were changes through time in the animals captured. There are more animal species known in Zone A than in Zone B, but whether this reflects alterations to the environment, or to hunting patterns, or merely reflects preservation is not established. Interpretation of the animal remains is difficult because only one-tenth of the bone fragments recovered from Puntutjarpa could be identified; most bones were so fragmented that their features had been destroyed (Archer 1977). Bone fragmentation made it difficult to estimate the numbers of animals consumed during different periods of occupation. While Keryn Walshe (2000) has suggested that non-human scavengers and burning may be responsible for much of the bone fragmentation in the site, other archaeologists argued that humans were primarily responsible (Gould et al. 2002).

Gould (1996) hypothesized that extreme fragmentation of bone resulted from humans crushing and pulverizing whole carcasses and smashing bones to extract marrow, in an attempt to maximize their protein intake. He thought this was evidence that desert foragers visiting Puntutjarpa suffered from shortages of meat and extracted protein from bone (Gould 1996). The level of bone fragmentation did not change throughout the Puntutjarpa sequence, suggesting to Gould that chronic scarcity of meat had always been a part of the desert economy and bone pulverizing, as a response, had been in place throughout the Holocene. This conclusion conformed to his idea of economic continuity.

It is hard to generalize Gould's conclusion to all desert economies. Veth (2005) argued that similarly high levels of bone fragmentation at other archaeological sites show bone pulverizing was a long-term pattern and that bone breakage was most intense in the harshest lowland desert landscapes. While evidence from Intirtekwerle over the past 1,000 years (Gould 1996), Serpent's Glen over the past several hundred years (O'Connor et al. 1998) and Kaalpi from the past two centuries (Veth et al. 2001) shows that strategies of protein extraction were widespread in the last millennium, it hardly indicates long-term persistence of intensive bone processing. Because bone is rarely preserved in desert sites for more than a few hundred years, Puntutjarpa offers a unique insight into Western Desert animal consumption and bone processing throughout the Holocene. Consequently protein stress in deserts might have existed throughout the Holocene but the evidence does not yet demonstrate that it was always at the same level or that foragers everywhere responded to it in identical ways.

Gould's model of economic continuity therefore still rests on propositions about stone artefacts that he initially framed: tulas, grindstones and exotic stone being found in similar frequencies in all stratigraphic zones. The stratigraphic distribution of different kinds of artefacts is shown in Figure 11.7. Gould (1977, 1980) claimed that adzing tools like tulas were found throughout the deposit, even though tulas were not found in the lowest zone, because he said there were other adzing tools at the base of the sequence which showed that production of hardwood artefacts occurred throughout the Holocene. Tulas are identified not only by their initial shape but especially by their distinctive exhausted shape, attained after they were resharpened. In that exhausted state, called a 'slug', they are typically short and wide, with a steep edge of numerous small step scars (Figure 11.8). In a re-examination of artefacts from Puntutjarpa, Hiscock and Veth (1991) showed that these kinds of objects were present in Zones A and B but not in Zone C, and hence the characteristic desert wood-working tula had not been present during the early-Holocene.

Without preserved plant remains, the change or continuity in seed use has been assessed by the distribution within the deposit of plant-processing artefacts. In particular Gould (1977) argued that grinding stones which could have helped people prepare hard seeds for consumption were present in all stratigraphic zones, and this indicated the continued importance of plant foods in the desert economy. Mike Smith (1985, 1986a, 1988, 1989a) challenged this conclusion; he reanalysed stone artefacts with grinding marks and argued that millstones were found only in Zone A (Figure 11.7). Smith hypothesized that amorphous grindstones were found

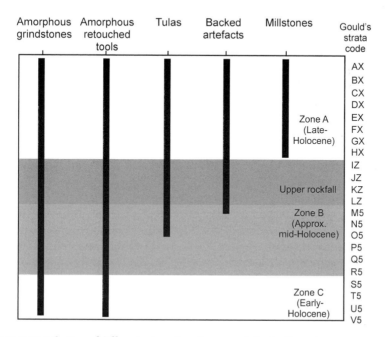

Figure 11.7 Distribution of different categories of stone tools in the Puntutjarpa sequence.

Figure 11.8 Views of a tula slug recovered by Gould in his excavations of the Puntutjarpa rock shelter. White bar is 1 cm.

in all levels of the deposit but the distinctive millstones so commonly observed in historical times were not present until the late-Holocene. According to Smith (1986a), amorphous grindstones were used to pulp fruit, pulverize parts of animals, and process bush tobacco; he thought seed processing was not part of the desert economy until the last millennium or two when millstones were used. However, Smith's association of millstones and seed processing is incorrect for Puntutjarpa. A study by Balme, Garbin and Gould of the residues on grindstones left by use demonstrated that while amorphous grindstones had often been used for multiple purposes almost every one had processed starchy siliceous plants such as seeds (Balme et al. 2001). This indicates that seed use and processing occurred throughout the entire Holocene at Puntutjarpa, and the shape of grindstones is not a reliable indication of whether or not they were used as seed grinders (see Veth and O'Connor 1996; Veth et al. 1997). This implies that inferences about the late emergence of seed processing elsewhere in the desert may also be dubious. However, the late-Holocene emphasis on millstones as a type of seed-processing tool is a real phenomenon that might indicate changed access to suitable stone slabs as trade networks altered, development of a more efficient technology, or some other as yet unspecified cultural change.

Gould's claim that there had been long-distance social networks throughout the Holocene was based on the presence of materials not originating locally. However, the scale of social networks is not easily inferred from the non-local stone materials. For example, long-distance exchange networks transporting only organic objects would not be visible in stone artefacts, and isolated social networks that rarely had contact with other networks might still receive a few pieces of exotic stone every few centuries. This last scenario suggests that it is relevant to look at how much non-local stone was received. When the frequency of non-local artefacts is calculated, as the percentage of all stone artefacts, it is apparent that rock was imported at varying rates during the Holocene (Figure 11.9). A cycle of material supply is visible: exotic materials were common during the early-Holocene, became rare during the mid-Holocene, and very common in the late-Holocene. If the transportation rate indicates the strength or scale of social networks, rather than some other factor such as the mobility of foragers, then the cycle could reveal the collapse or contraction of broad networks in the mid-Holocene dry climatic phase and their reinstigatation in the last millennium or so. This interpretation offers a more dynamic image of economic change than the one proposed by Gould but it is also less directional than the image of unique late-Holocene social reorganizations of territoriality and social interaction offered by researchers such as Veth and McDonald. Additionally alterations to territory or social affiliation may be signalled by the switch from chert as the dominant material in the early-Holocene to quartz at later times.

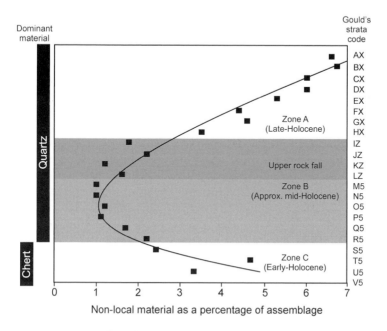

Figure 11.9 Distribution of artefacts made from non-local material in the Puntutjarpa sequence.

The presence at Puntutjarpa, in the early-Holocene, of foragers who processed seed and accessed resources through social networks, is evidence that some elements of desert life ways observed historically were present at the end of the Pleistocene. The suggestion that all elements of desert economy appeared in the recent past is therefore incorrect. However, the Puntutjarpa evidence indicates preserved archaeological materials do not always record the diversity and amount of human use of deserts during the terminal Pleistocene and early-Holocene; sites such as Puritjarra and Puntutjarpa reveal the presence of forager societies unlike those observed historically.

Gould's proposition that historical economic and social systems were in place for 10,000 years is not correct even for Puntutjarpa. Specialized millstones and woodworking tools appear only in mid- and late-Holocene parts of the site, and over time the transportation of artefacts to the site was reorganized. If the rate at which exotic materials were brought to Puntutjarpa reflects the connection of occupants to social activity in the Western Desert then the evidence may indicate a mid-Holocene period of reduced connection separating early and late phases of greater connectedness. Archaeological evidence such as this indicates that historically observed desert life did not exist unchanged throughout the Holocene but was the culmination of multiple reconfigurations of technological, economic and social practices. Archaeologists have discussed how those reconfigurations might be understood.

Stress cycles

Veth (2005) advocates that the history of desert occupation can be viewed as a series of cycles of human mobility and risk-reducing behaviour patterns reflecting cycles of greater and lesser aridity. These cycles were not merely repetitions of previous economic systems. Desert foragers could organize mobility in many ways and employ different strategies to limit the effects of foraging risk. During each cycle of aridity the nature and severity of environmental conditions were different, and the economic and social strategies of people also varied in response. This model provides a way of understanding the risk-minimizing nature of historical desert adaptations and the archaeological evidence for altered adaptations to different environmental conditions, while acknowledging long-term persistence in some economic practices, the development of new behaviours, and fluctuations in the presence and strength of other practices. In adapting to the environmental cycles that characterize desert pre-history foragers sometimes employed new strategies while on other occasions they repeated and adapted variants of strategies used before. The broader applicability of models describing oscillating patterns of cultural change rather than linear changes towards the historical configurations of Aboriginal life is discussed in the next chapter.

12 Population growth and mobility

Images of an increased number of people through time, implying ever-increasing 'control' over their environment, are embedded in many interpretations of pre-history. Such ideas have been presented as graphs of estimated total population, usually with a consistent non-linear increase that is interpreted as a relentless, ever faster growth of population size and density. Such visions of simple uninterrupted, unidirectional population rise have been invoked by researchers discussing the demographic pre-history of humans in Australia (Figure 12.1A).

Although ideas of pre-historic population change have been advanced since the 1950s, the 1980s saw deliberations on the subject become intense. Since then debate has often focused on two competing models. The most popular one proposed that the total population size of Australia was small throughout the Pleistocene and increased rapidly only during the last few thousand years. The fundamental question about this 'late growth' scenario was how to explain the lack of change it predicted for the first 45 millennium of human occupation. A number of ideas were offered. Beaton (1983) suggests a small total population size persisted for many millennia because there had been a small founding population, long generation times, and low survivorship. However, the meagre evidence does not support a model of early humans dying young or breeding late slowly. The rapid spread of people throughout Australia shortly after colonization is indicative of a successful, growing population (see Chapter 3), and genetic evidence discussed below is also consistent with Pleistocene population growth.

Another idea for why 'late growth' might have occurred was put forward by Lourandos (1983a), who suggested that altered social networks in the late-Holocene stimulated greater production and reduced resource fluctuations, a combination he believed enabled population growth (also David and Lourandos 1998, 1999). Evidence for such a proposition is equivocal for many environments. Since social systems changed throughout the Pleistocene (Chapter 6), this idea depends on claims of elaborations in late-Holocene social networks and their positive effect on food production. Such claims that are not well demonstrated (Chapters 9 and 10) and the chain of inference that social change caused increased productivity that facilitated population growth only late in pre-history have been challenged (O'Connor 1990; C. F. M. Bird and Frankel 1991b).

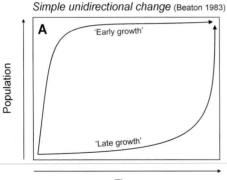

Simple unidirectional change (Beaton 1983)

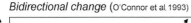
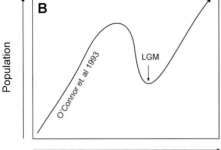

Bidirectional change (O'Connor et al. 1993)

Complex non-directional change

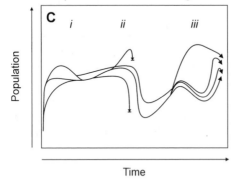

Figure 12.1 Illustrations of alternative models of population change, contrasting models of change: A = unidirectional; B = bidirectional; C = non-directional

A third mechanism was proposed by Philip Hughes and Ron Lampert, who argued that population growth was triggered by the loss of territory and environmental changes that occurred in the mid-Holocene as sea levels reached their current levels (Lampert and Hughes 1974; Hughes and Lampert 1982). However, archaeological changes often interpreted as signals of population growth did not occur at the time of sea-level stabilization; removing the rationale for seeing them as linked (Attenbrow 2003, 2004). In any case sea-level changes also occurred throughout the Pleistocene, and so there is a question of why similar periods of population growth had not been experienced at earlier times.

Each of these proposed explanations for late growth of human numbers fails to find support in the archaeological evidence, and they all share the presumption that substantial population growth occurred only during the past few thousand years. An important question is whether inferences of only late population growth are correct.

Beaton (1983) discussed the late growth model as an alternative to the 'early growth' model, which is how he characterized the settlement hypothesis made famous by Birdsell (1953, 1957). Birdsell emphasized the relationship between population densities and geographical differences in environmental characteristics across the continent during the historical period, predicting that population size reflected the availability of resources in each region. Rapid population growth in the few thousand years after colonization, he argued, had led to a similar situation, and total population size had remained in equilibrium with the resource base ever since. In the 1980s this notion was often misconstrued as implying that there had been no change in the population size after the initial dispersal of people to most environments. Hence, when Beaton reviewed Birdsell's ideas, he claimed they implied demographic stability during Australian pre-history and could be depicted as a simple growth curve which rapidly reached high population levels and remained there (Figure 12.1A). When constructed this way the early and late growth models of population change shared many features; both were thought to involve one unique period of rapid, non-reversable increase in total population size. The only difference in the growth curves was the antiquity of the increase.

In fact, Birdsell's proposition that population size was in equilibrium with environmental resources did not imply stable pre-historic demography; it predicted fluctuating population levels as resource levels fluctuated through time. Hence this was not a view of unidirectional population change but a model of bidirectional change in which population sizes both increased and decreased (Figure 12.1B). This was largely ignored as much archaeological debate focused on the idea that a single demographic expansion occurred in Australian pre-history and that it was either an early or a late change but not both.

These ideas about ancient population change have been tested using several kinds of evidence. An obvious source of information about the number of people who lived in the past comes from biological evidence; studies of genetics or the skeletons of ancient people.

Genetic evidence for demographic change

Genetic patterns in living people reflect the population history of their ancestors. Several kinds of analyses identify signatures of past population expansions in modern mtDNA variation, each analytic technique distinguishing the pattern created by a constant population size from those produced by rapidly growing populations (Relethford 1998, 2001). For example, a 'mismatch analysis' compares mtDNA sequences between all individuals in a sample; less diverse, more clustered patterns indicate that a population had expanded in the past (Rogers and Harpending 1992; Harpending 1994). Other techniques, such as 'star contraction' patterns, use diagrams and statistics to identify clusters of similar mtDNA sequences which may be diagnostic of ancient demographic expansions (Forster et al. 2001). Antiquity of past population expansions can be roughly estimated by making assumptions about mutation rates and generation lengths.

These techniques have been used to evaluate the possibility of demographic change in Australian pre-history. World-wide mtDNA analyses indicate large increases in African populations approximately 50,000–100,000 years ago, probably associated with the expansion of *Homo sapiens* out of Africa (Sherry et al. 1994; Relethford 2001). Subsequent population expansions occurred in each landmass colonized by modern humans, including Australia. For example, Ingman and Gyllensten (2003) measured mtDNA diversity consistent with rapid and substantial population growth shortly after colonization. Demographic increase as people settled the continent is an inference consistent with the archaeological evidence for settlement in many regions. Genetic evidence from Papua New Guinea and the Pacific has also been seen as consistent with ancient population increase (Friedlaender et al. 2005). However, mtDNA data from Australian Aborigines has not yielded evidence for population expansions in all analyses (e.g. van Holst Pellekaan et al. 2006). Interpretation of genetic patterns in terms of demography is complex; mtDNA patterns can be affected by events other than changes in total population size, such as isolation and genetic drift of groups spreading out across the continent following colonization (see Huoponen et al. 2001).

Little genetic evidence has been presented for terminal Pleistocene and late-Holocene population changes, but technical reasons rather than patterns of past demography may be responsible for this. Given the rates of mtDNA mutation, Manfred Kayser suggested that late-Holocene population expansions might not be detectable by mtDNA analyses, and that other forms of DNA, such as Y chromosomes that contain genetic sequences inherited through the male line, need to be examined for demographic information (Kayser et al. 2001). To illustrate this point his study of Y chromosomes from a small sample of individuals in northwestern Australia gave indications of a terminal Pleistocene or Holocene population increase, sometime between 16,000 and 2,000 years ago (Kayser et al. 2001). The imprecision of his time estimate reveals the uncertainties currently associated with genetic studies, and the nature of later pre-historic demographic change can only be clarified by additional work.

These results cannot be interpreted as indicating that population changes occurred only once, and so do not unambiguously support either early or late growth models. Future DNA studies may enhance understandings of demographic change but are unlikely to identify all modifications in past population size. While rapid growth or reduction of populations alters the genetic structure of foraging groups and creates signals that are readily detectable, slow, steady demographic changes of the kind that might have happened on multiple occasions are not so easy to diagnose.

Similar difficulties exist with the use of human skeletons to examine demographic change. Bodies and graves have formed the basis of interpretations of past population trends, and have been cited as evidence in favour of a 'late growth' model. However, the interpretation of skeletons in terms of the size of ancient populations is not straightforward.

Skeletons, health and population

Ambiguity of biological evidence can be seen in the interpretation of pathologies on skeletons as indicators of pre-historic demography. By studying features of ancient skeletons, archaeologists such as Stephen Webb (1982, 1984, 1987, 1989b, 1995) tried to characterize pre-historic health levels as a way to identify high population density and population growth. The skulls he examined often had features showing that ancient people suffered from illness or disease, and he interpreted regional differences in the frequencies of those features as evidence of different levels of stress and ill-health that were connected to population density.

One such pattern involves cribra orbitalia, a term which describes a large number of holes in the bone of the skull immediately above the eye (Figure 12.2). These are technically described as porotic lesions located on and adjacent to the orbital plate of the frontal bone (Wapler et al. 2004). Webb advocated a commonly held view that cribra orbitalia resulted from iron-deficiency anaemia. He argued that high frequencies of cribra orbitalia in pre-historic skeletons revealed high frequencies of chronic anaemia in ancient human groups.

The frequency of skeletons with cribra orbitalia varied across Australia (Figure 12.3). Webb concluded that during the late-Holocene iron-deficiency anaemia was more prevalent in lands surrounding the central portion of the Murray River than elsewhere. On the Murray River more than 30–40 per cent of skeletons have cribra orbitalia, whereas a lower incidence was recorded in southern and eastern coastal areas, and far lower frequencies in the desert and northern parts of Australia.

Webb (1989b, 1995) hypothesized that the high incidence of cribra orbitalia along the Murray River indicated that anaemia was common there because many

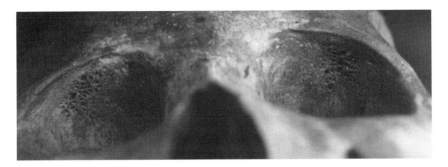

Figure 12.2 Photograph of a skull with cribra orbitalia: this individual is not an Aborigine. (Courtesy of M. Oxenham.)

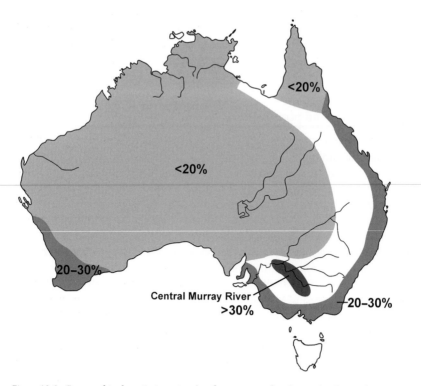

Figure 12.3 Geographical variations in the frequency of cribra orbitalia in human skulls (percentages are the relative frequency of lesions in each area for both sexes and all age groups combined) (data from Webb 1989b). No data available from unshaded areas.

people suffered badly from intestinal parasites and infectious diseases. The important role he attributed to parasitism in creating anaemia was puzzling in the cool, temperate environment of southeastern Australia where parasite numbers were suppressed by climatic conditions. The answer to this puzzle, Webb suggested, was that unusual conditions in human settlements along the Murray River had created circumstances in which parasite infestations thrived. He argued that relatively high levels of aggregation and sedentism resulted in locally high population densities, producing conditions that promoted greater parasite burdens, frequently resulting in chronic anaemia. Webb concluded that there had been population growth and a reduction of residential mobility. He believed this conclusion was consistent with the geographical differences in some other skeletal markers of stress, such as dental enamel hypoplasia, reduced areas of enamel thickness on teeth. Such an interpretation was used to support 'late growth' models of pre-historic demography (e.g. Lourandos and Ross 1994; Lourandos 1997; Mulvaney and Kamminga 1999).

Interpretations of cribra orbitalia lesions as evidence for recent population growth have now been revealed as weak and probably incorrect. Most of the skulls in Webb's analysis were undated and they represent several time periods, each with a different frequency of lesions. Furthermore, if skulls from the early historical period had been included, from people with different health levels, this may have affected the calculated abundance of cribra orbitalia (S. Robertson 2003; Littleton 2005; Littleton and Allen 2007). Even Webb's own data is inconsistent with his idea of population growth only in recent millennia. He observed cribra orbitalia lesions on more than half of the crania from Coobool Creek, the Cohuna skull, and most of the Kow Swamp skulls. Those observations reveal that some Pleistocene groups in the Murray River corridor had similar or even higher frequencies of lesions than in the late-Holocene, a pattern that does not provide evidence for a late growth demographic model.

Additionally, it is now known that cribra orbitalia lesions are not a reliable indicator of whether an individual was suffering from anaemia, since they can occur on individuals who did not have anaemia and suffered from other conditions such as chronic inflammation or osteoporosis (Wapler et al. 2004). Accurate diagnosis of these lesions can be made only through histological analysis (Schultz 2001), a technique which has not been applied to Australian skeletons. Furthermore, lesions need not accurately reveal the prevalence of ill-health and population stress in an ancient group of humans because of the 'osteological paradox' (Wood et al. 1992), which represents the veiling effect of differential death or survival on the frequency of traits in archaeological skeletons. For example, across Australia many skeletons with cribra orbitalia come from individuals who were young when they died; 60–70 per cent of people who died before the age of 11 display cribra orbitalia whereas only 10–20 per cent of adult skeletons show this feature, indicating that children with it faced greater risk of death (S. G. Webb 1982). However, some individuals survived childhood illness, dying as adults, and although their skeletons still display cribra orbitalia they were healthier than the children who died. Consequently cribra orbitalia does not necessarily signal poor health; survival of sufferers into adulthood reveals recovery and improved health. Sarah Robertson (2003) has pointed out that along the Murray River more cribra sufferers than elsewhere survived into adulthood, and if the risk of acquiring anaemia as a child had been the same in all regions this is evidence that people were healthier and had lower mortality rates on the Murray River – the opposite of Webb's view. Cribra orbitalia actually reflects a number of conditions and is not necessarily diagnostic of anaemia or population density. A different interpretation of the skeletal data is therefore required.

The frequencies of cribra orbitalia lesions, and other skeletal markers of health, probably tell us about variations in cultural practices rather than the size and growth of populations. The most robust hypothesis of this kind was presented by Robertson (2003), who argued that the specific location of cribra orbitalia, and its absence from frontal and parietal bones, shows that only children below the age of 5 were usually affected. This is not consistent with Webb's notion that parasite infection caused anaemia, since older children and adults would have suffered from a parasite burden as well. Instead Robertson hypothesized that juvenile anaemia, creating cribra orbitalia, resulted from cultural choices about weaning. Infants are normally born with enough stores of iron to last a few months; after that time the iron content of breast milk does not meet the demands of growing children. As a result children between the ages of 6 months and 5 years are at a high risk of becoming anaemic. Even solid food does not provide sufficient iron while children continue to breast-feed, and consequently the higher the age of weaning the more likely it is that a child might suffer from prolonged anaemia. However, weaning children early can also be dangerous since it exposes them to diarrhoeal infections because they eat new foods while the protective effect of breast milk is removed (e.g. Gordon 1963; Cutting and Elliott 1994).

Robertson (2003) argued that geographical and chronological differences in the frequency of cribra orbitalia lesions should be interpreted as evidence for dissimilar weaning practices during Australian pre-history. Lower weaning ages can create more intensive bouts of diarrhoea; higher weaning ages can lead to a greater long-term risk of anaemia. Different human groups across the continent had weaning strategies suited to their environments and ideologies. If people along the Murray River breast-fed their children for a longer period than in other regions while desert and tropical groups weaned children earlier, this could have produced the geographical pattern of cribra orbitalia seen in archaeological skeletons. Variations in childhood health therefore may reflect local conditions and cultural practices; they are a poor indicator of population size or population growth.

Another attempt to identify demographic change focused on the evidence from graves. Colin Pardoe (1988) noted that some of the skeletons found within the Murray River corridor, of both Holocene and terminal Pleistocene age, occurred as groups of associated graves which he called 'cemeteries'. For example, more than 40 individuals were recovered at Kow Swamp, more than 100 at Coobool Creek, more than 400 from graveyards near Robinvale, more than 150 at Snaggy Bend, more than 500 at Lake Victoria, 25 bodies at Katarapko, 142 at Roonka, and more than 90 at Swanport (Figure 12.4). One interpretation of the large number of buried humans is that these riverine environments had been densely populated in the pre-historic period. However, many skeletons are undated and 'cemeteries' for which antiquity is known typically built up over long time periods, making it hard to estimate the size of groups who interred their dead in these places. When the chronology of these cemeteries is known it seems that people were infrequently buried in them. For instance, if 40 individuals had been buried at Kow Swamp over 4,000–5,000 years that represents only one burial per century. Even the highest estimates of total burial numbers at Lake Victoria represent only one burial per generation on average (Littleton and Allen 2007). Numbers of buried people in these places is therefore not compelling evidence of a large population in this region.

Pardoe argued that six dated Murray River corridor cemeteries showed an increased density of bodies through time, beginning with as much as ten square metres per body in the Pleistocene but sometimes having less than one square metre per body in the late-Holocene (Figure 12.5). Some late-Holocene cemeteries were similar in density to Kow Swamp, indicating that the only chronological change may be the appearance of a few densely packed graveyards. However, since only one dated Pleistocene cemetery, Kow Swamp, is known, it may not express the full range of early graveyards. Pardoe (1988) also claimed that although graveyards have

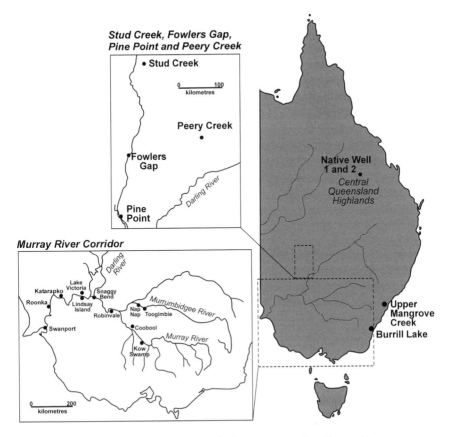

Figure 12.4 Map of eastern Australia, showing places mentioned in Chapter 12.

a long antiquity they were more numerous in the past 6,000 years. He argued that observations of increasing numbers of cemeteries and greater burial densities within some were consistent with population increase through time, perhaps supporting a late growth demographic model.

A number of factors make it difficult to be certain that population change was responsible for this pattern. The small number of Pleistocene or early-Holocene 'cemeteries' might merely reflect the greater erosion of older sediments and destruction of early material within them. Better preservation of younger material would create this archaeological pattern, even if the size of local groups had remained constant over time. Chronological change in cultural rules about where and when to bury people may also have helped create the pattern. People can return to particular localities to bury their dead or alternatively they can dispose of the dead in isolated graves. If densely packed 'cemeteries' are more common in the late-Holocene, this could result from a trend towards the use of recognized cemeteries, rather than population growth. Variations in 'cemetery' abundance and grave

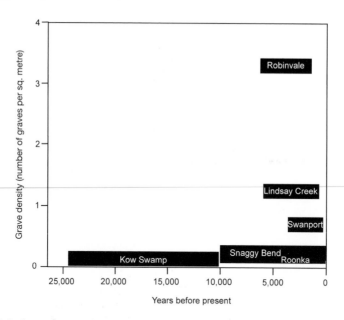

Figure 12.5 Grave density in Murray River corridor cemeteries through time. (Density estimates recalculated from data in Pardoe 1988.)

density may therefore reflect changing local cultural practices and life ways, and be a poor indicator of population size or population growth. Debates about the interpretation of burial behaviour in southeastern Australia are discussed further in Chapter 13. Other kinds of archaeological sites have proved similarly complex to interpret demographically.

Increased abundance of sites

Change in the abundance of archaeological sites has been interpreted as an indication of population increase. Although this notion was discussed during the 1960s it was Ronald Lampert and Philip Hughes who first explored this proposition in detail (Lampert and Hughes 1974; Hughes and Lampert 1982). They observed that on the southeast coast of Australia there was a substantial, unidirectional increase in the number of occupied rock shelters, in which people lived and discarded tools and food debris (Figure 12.6A). They argued that during the past 5,000 years the numbers of occupied sites had increased two- or threefold, and that this revealed population growth after the sea rose in response to greater environmental resources. Hughes (1977) also observed that in some rock shelters more artefacts had accumulated in the past 5,000 years than at any earlier period, indicating to him that the sites had been more intensively occupied in recent millennia. The conjunction of increased site numbers and increased artefacts in those sites was used by Hughes and Lampert (1982) as evidence that there had been population growth in the mid- to late-Holocene.

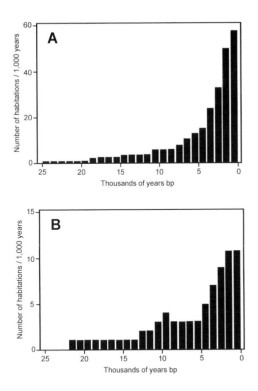

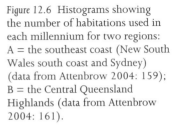

Figure 12.6 Histograms showing the number of habitations used in each millennium for two regions: A = the southeast coast (New South Wales south coast and Sydney) (data from Attenbrow 2004: 159); B = the Central Queensland Highlands (data from Attenbrow 2004: 161).

The idea that population growth is revealed by increased mid-Holocene site numbers was employed by researchers advocating a late growth demographic model (Lourandos and Ross 1994; David and Lourandos 1999; David 2002). A pattern of greater numbers of recent sites is observed in many parts of the continent. Attenbrow (2004) presented a detailed review of several regions of eastern Australia, and in each of these, site numbers increased during recent millennia. For example, Figure 12.6B shows that in the Central Queensland Highlands, a region in northeastern Australia, there are more sites from recent millennia than from the Pleistocene or early-Holocene. The regularity of this pattern convinced a number of researchers that there had been population growth, not only in a few localities but also over wide portions of the continent (Beaton 1983; Ross 1986). Although the complexities of reaching this conclusion have been discussed (Attenbrow 1982, 2003, 2004; Hiscock 1986; Rowland 1989, 1992; Lourandos 1997), broad-scale population increase in the late-Holocene is still advocated (e.g. Flood 2001; David 2002; C. N. Johnson and Wroe 2003; Turney and Hobbs 2006).

The magnitude of any population change is not easily inferred from variations in site numbers, and a substantial change in population size in recent millennia cannot be inferred from current evidence. It is unlikely that site abundance is proportional to ancient population size, and hence there is no reason to think that double or triple the number of sites indicates a doubling or tripling in the number of people. This point was emphasized by Alan Gray (1985), who observed that if the number of people tripled during the late-Holocene this would have represented a growth of only 0.1 per cent per annum, a low rate that is little different from a long-term balance between births and deaths. Archaeological evidence for two or three times more site numbers in recent millennia therefore does not indicate rapid population rises, as some archaeologists have suggested (e.g. David 2002). In fact, gradual increases in population of this kind would not have been noticeable to the ancient peoples living at the time, and could have occurred many times during the human occupation of the continent.

Advocates of a late population growth model attempt to translate the numbers of archaeological sites into statements about the number of people living in the landscape. The trouble with reading site numbers as demographic patterns has been clarified by studies of the complexity of archaeological evidence. Anne Ross (1986) observed that an increase in the number of sites was not, by itself, diagnostic of an increase in the size of Holocene populations. For example, if site numbers increased but the amount of occupation in each was reduced, this might represent a reorganized settlement pattern, such as when the same number of people used more places for a shorter length of time (see Rowland 1989). Consequently Ross expected population increase to be displayed by increased numbers of sites, each containing more occupational debris than previously. Initially it was thought that the archaeological record in multiple regions displayed such a pattern and population change could be identified (Ross 1986; David 2002), but further examination of the late-Holocene chronological trends showed that the situation was not so simple. In a few regions the numbers of both sites and artefacts within many of them became more abundant, but in most locations and time periods during the Holocene that was not the case (Attenbrow 1982, 2004). In the past thousand years the pattern observed in most regions is for the number of sites to be greater than in preceding few millennia, but for the numbers of artefacts discarded within each site to be less (Hiscock 1986; Attenbrow 2004). Evidence from Upper Mangrove Creek (discussed below) exemplifies this pattern.

The complexity and multiplicity of trends in site abundance and artefact numbers do not unambiguously support a model of continuous population growth during the mid- and late-Holocene. Indeed, those trends are not easily interpreted as the result of population at all. Changes in site abundance may have little to do with the size of ancient populations, or even of the behaviour of ancient humans. Archaeology cannot focus exclusively on studying past human behaviour; it must also consider preservation.

Patterns of preservation and discovery

Some researchers have suggested that the large number of sites dated to recent millennia and the small number of sites dated to earlier time periods can be interpreted as a growth curve, reflecting an increasing number of people living in more sites. This proposition assumes that an equal proportion of pre-historic sites have been preserved from all time periods. Such an assumption is almost certainly false, and it is likely that in most circumstances young sites will be better preserved than older ones, simply because they have been exposed to destructive processes for a shorter time. It is more realistic to interpret this archaeological pattern as a decay curve, revealing the greater destruction of older sites rather than the rapid addition of new ones. Typical decay curves display reduced abundance with greater age; like the archaeological evidence. If the larger numbers of sites dated to recent millennia are a consequence of the destruction of older sites, rather than of increases in the rate of site creation, the main evidence supporting a late growth model is eliminated. Greater abundance of Holocene, particularly late-Holocene, archaeological sites is a pattern that could be equally consistent with Birdsell's early growth model once the effects of site decay are taken into account (O'Connor 1990).

To illustrate the potential of non-preservation to create these archaeological patterns computer simulations created a constant number of sites and then randomly destroyed them at varying rates. The resulting numbers of sites depended on the amount of elapsed time and the pattern of site destruction. Figure 12.7 shows results when there was constant site destruction (simulation 1) or a cyclical pattern of destruction (simulation 2). The extended repetition of simulated site creation and destruction creates patterns with a curvilinear increase in the number of sites towards the present; a product of more extensive destruction of old sites rather than population change since the same numbers of sites were added in every phase. Different simulation rules produced subtle alterations in the patterns of site abundance. Simulation 1 (Figure 12.7B), destroying a constant proportion of sites, produced a roughly linear increase in sites in later phases, resembling the archaeological pattern known from the Central Queensland Highlands (Figure 12.6B). Simulation 2 (Figure 12.7D), with periods of more rapid site destruction, produced a curving increase in sites in later phases, resembling the archaeological pattern known from the southeast coast (Figure 12.6A). Computer simulations indicate that the abundance curves from different regions could reflect the conditions of preservation that prevailed in each. These simulations are not evidence that population growth never occurred in Australian pre-history; they indicate that the archaeological pattern found in every region, of larger numbers of more recent sites, can reflect the disappearance of archaeological sites over time.

The hypothesis that site destruction created chronological change in site abundance is consistent with the similar archaeological trends observed in many regions, despite their dissimilar environmental histories and resources. In particular it helps to explain why greater site numbers occur during the late-Holocene in both Tasmania (J. Stockton 1983) and the mainland (Attenbrow 2004), even though they were isolated from each other. Rather than indicating independent and parallel population growth trends, those patterns indicate the operation of similar trends in age-related site destruction.

Evidence of the impact of site destruction on the abundance of archaeological sites has been presented for only a few regions (Rowland 1989, 1992; M. K. Bird 1992), and some archaeologists have argued that preservation may not account for the archaeological patterns recorded in every region (David and Lourandos 1998, 1999). On the southeast coast Hughes and Lampert (1982) dismissed the idea that

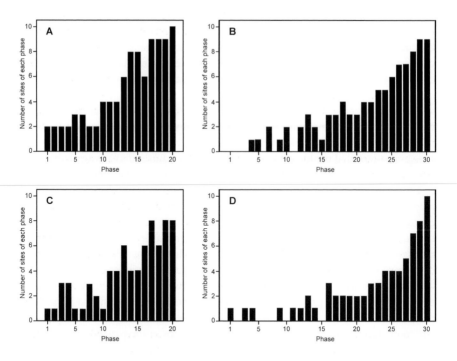

Figure 12.7 Computer simulations of site numbers after long periods of site destruction. Simulation 1 (10 new sites per phase, destruction of 10 per cent of sites each phase) produced the patterns shown in graph A after 20 phases and graph B after 30 phases. Simulation 2 (10 new sites per phase, destruction of 5 per cent of sites each phase and an additional 30 per cent of sites after every 5 phases) produced the patterns shown in graph C after 20 phases and graph D after 30 phases.

preservation caused temporal differences in site numbers, arguing that if there was site destruction many sites would have been extensively disturbed but not yet destroyed. They also claimed that studies of site abundance were often calculated using information from excavations in rock shelters, and that since these were often protected places the observed chronological trends are resilient to the effects of differential destruction. However, processes involved in site destruction vary geographically, and not even rock shelters are always protected. There are well-documented examples of the destruction of deposits within shelters (e.g. Mulvaney and Joyce 1965; Hall et al. 1989). An example comes from the work of Ingrid Ward (2004), who described, in one area of northern Australia, the survival of Pleistocene occupation debris in sands outside rock shelters while none of the excavated rock shelters contained material older than 5,000–6,000 years bp. This discovery indicates that archaeologists cannot presume that rock shelters always preserve an accurate record of local human occupation. Furthermore, conditions of preservation in cave and rock shelter deposits are not the only issues to be considered.

Few archaeological sites are securely dated, and reconstructions of past population change have often employed limited evidence. Analyses of large regions have been based on only 10–50 sites with radiometric age-estimates, and those sites are often atypical: large rock shelters, earth mounds or middens. Marine middens are not preserved from the Pleistocene or early-Holocene, and there is no record of earth mounds from those periods either. Hence for many areas, studies of changing site abundance concentrated almost entirely on information from rock shelters. It has been technically difficult to establish antiquity of other sites, such as the numerous open-air scatters of stone artefacts. Consequently, periods in which foragers emphasized the use of open-air sites might appear to have fewer occupation sites when measured by counts of occupied rock shelters; a pattern that would be exaggerated if rock shelters were preserved at a higher rate than open sites.

Physical destruction of sites is therefore not the only process to be considered. Low counts of sites could result from any process that prevented sites from being identified, such as being hidden by sediment, or inaccurately assigned a chronology, such as when material from different time periods is mixed together. Attenbrow (2004) also pointed to bias in the location of archaeological surveys and excavations as another mechanism causing differences in observed site numbers. Archaeologists prefer to excavate large rock shelters with deep deposits or shelters that have artefacts visible on the surface of the deposit. Other rock shelters have typically been left unexplored. These preferences can identify greater site numbers for some periods simply through the choices archaeologists have made.

The variety of preservation and recognition factors that impinge on measured changes in site abundance means that observed numbers of dated archaeological sites are often not an accurate record of the number and distribution of sites than existed in the past.

Bidirectional change and Pleistocene population sizes

Rejection of the idea that preserved site numbers indicate directional population growth led Sue O'Connor (1990, 1999b; O'Connor et al. 1993; O'Connor and Veth 2006) to consider the possibility that ancient populations had decreased as well as increased in size. Because so many Pleistocene deposits had been destroyed, she argued their frequency could not measure ancient population size or demographic change. Instead, she suggested, the rate at which artefacts were discarded in the few surviving sites could reveal demographic change. O'Connor pointed out that many Pleistocene sites contained high artefact discard rates in OIS2, particularly 22,000–32,000 years bp, before the LGM. Indeed the abundance of artefacts deposited at that time exceeded the numbers discarded later in the Pleistocene or during the early-Holocene. She argued that high levels of artefact discard in the late-Pleistocene mirrored high population levels at that time, and that subsequent reductions in artefact discard in many sites during the LGM reflected reductions in population size. O'Connor therefore proposed a bidirectional model of population change in which human numbers gradually grew to a high level in the Pleistocene, then crashed during the LGM, before gradually recovering and growing to even higher levels in the mid- to late-Holocene (Figure 12.1B). This model predicts that population size fluctuates with changing resource levels (O'Connor et al. 1993), and is therefore similar to Birdsell's hypothesis about population change in the past.

O'Connor's (1990) model, and a similar one by Iain Davidson (1990), hypothesized that there had been increases and decreases in total population size during Australian pre-history, and that late-Holocene population growth is the most recent of several phases of growth. While there may have been several periods in which total population size declined the model suggested the largest, most sustained reduction was associated with the climatic deterioration of the LGM, an idea consistent with evidence of abandonments and reduced site use at that time (Chapter 3). O'Connor's model of fluctuating population size also implied that any late-Holocene population growth built on low population levels that existed after the LGM, and populations in the late-Holocene were similar in size to those prior to the LGM. She termed the pre-LGM phase of high artefact discard rates a period of 'Pleistocene intensification' to emphasize that a late growth model was not unambiguously supported by the available evidence, and that the Pleistocene was also a time of demographic change.

However, O'Connor's model (Figure 12.1B) still hypothesized an overall direction of population growth, with the largest total population size at the end of the pre-historic period. High artefact discard rates in the mid- and late-Holocene levels of some sites might be evidence of population growth in the recent pre-historic period, in some regions, but in many sites much lower discard rates are found in the recent pre-historic period. In fact, Hiscock (1986) and Attenbrow (2004) observed that artefact densities often decreased substantially during the last millennium. If those trends are interpreted in demographic terms they might signal widespread population reductions in the late-Holocene. Such an interpretation would reinforce the perception of multiple bidirectional demographic changes in pre-history, but it is not consistent with the idea that population was largest immediately before Europeans arrived.

The difficulty for researchers using artefact discard as an indication of demography is that variation in the abundance of artefacts may reflect alterations to the nature of human activities rather than the number of people. Some archaeologists have argued that, as basic tools in pre-historic life, the number of artefacts indicates the number of people in the landscape (e.g. Ferguson 1985). However, the number of artefacts discarded in each time period was the cumulative result of many different factors, and does not accurately reveal trends in population size (Hiscock 1981, 1984; I. Davidson 1990; Dortch and Smith 2001; Attenbrow 2004). For instance, different kinds of tool manufacture can produce different numbers of artefacts, even when there is no difference in the size of human groups, and the choice to make artefacts from rocks or from organic materials such as bone or shell will affect the abundance of stone artefacts in archaeological deposits. Furthermore, people might occupy a small number of sites, discarding large numbers of artefacts in each, or a larger number of sites, discarding fewer artefacts in each. Foragers who were sedentary, had smaller territories, or lived in environments with patchy distributions of resources probably followed the former pattern, while those who were residentially mobile, with large territories, or who lived in more uniform environments probably followed the latter pattern. Change from one context to the other would increase or decrease the rate of artefact discard at any one site, even if the number of people using the area remained the same. Consequently alterations in artefact discard can result from restructuring of land use rather than changes to the number of people exploiting the landscape. One indication that this happened is when different trends in artefact discard rates are observed in the same area. This occurred in the Central Queensland Highlands of northeastern Australia where excavations at Native Well 1 showed that high numbers of artefacts were discarded between about 2,500 and 4,500 years bp, and far fewer were discarded after 2,500 year bp. In contrast, excavations at the adjacent Native Well 2 shelter showed that high artefact discard rates began about 2,500 years ago, at the same time that artefact discard reduced in the nearby Native Well 1 site. Differences in these archaeological sequences are likely to have resulted from changes in land use and the choice of activity locations, not from alterations in the size of human populations in the region.

A similar process may be involved in increased artefact discard rates in the period leading to the LGM. Contraction of foraging to smaller, more reliable portions of the landscape is a documented response to the altered environments of that time (Chapter 3). By more intensively exploiting portions of their territory people would have increased the rate of artefact discard in some sites. Reorganized landscape use and increased population can both result in more discarded artefacts, and it is difficult to diagnose the mechanism causing the change in particular sites or regions. This complicates interpretations of past population size but does not prevent archaeologists from making cautious statements about demographic change. For example, the multi-site study of Pleistocene occupation in Tasmania by Holdaway and Porch (described in Chapter 6) identified regional-scale cycles of more and less intensive occupation that probably implies fluctuations in population size as well as land use patterns and is inconsistent with suggestions of stable population levels during the Pleistocene. Although the Tasmanian evidence shows that there were multiple episodes of population expansion and contraction, rather than a single cycle of Pleistocene population growth and decline as O'Connor hypothesized, there is support for her idea of population changes throughout the Pleistocene.

These considerations combine to make it difficult to infer the size of the ancient population from either artefact densities or site numbers. Multiple processes involving site destruction, technological strategies and land use patterns can change the numbers of preserved sites and artefacts without any substantial change in the size of the pre-historic population. Furthermore, phases of demographic growth could have occurred without a commensurate increase in the number of sites or artefacts used, and as a result are hidden from view. The difficulty of distinguishing changes in population size from changes in the nature of human activities has been explored by research at Upper Mangrove Creek.

Controlled data at Upper Mangrove Creek

Over a number of years Val Attenbrow investigated the catchment of Upper Mangrove Creek, a roughly 100 square kilometre area near the south eastern coast of mainland Australia (Figure 12.4). Her goal was to record and excavate sites in a way that gave unbiased and representative evidence of the preserved archaeological record (Attenbrow 1982, 2004). She accomplished this by dividing the environment into a number of zones (such as ridge tops, ridge sides and valley bottoms) and intensively surveying 10 per cent of each. Surveyed areas were randomly selected and Attenbrow attempted to date all deposits, not merely the large or deep ones, thereby eliminating systematic bias that affects other regional studies. This is the only region in Australia where archaeologists have obtained a statistically unbiased sample of sites that avoid many problems arising from site selection.

Many sites that Attenbrow discovered and excavated were rock shelters (Figure 12.8). Organic preservation was often poor in the deposits, especially in their lower levels, and consequently stone artefacts are the main evidence of human habitation. Some shelters contained hundreds of thousands of artefacts while others had only a few hundred. Some had archaeological evidence dating back more than 10,000–12,000 years, while the oldest cultural materials in others were less than 500 years bp. Attenbrow (2004) studied chronological change by calculating how many sites were occupied in each millennium, and how many artefacts accumulated per millennium. Her results revealed a complex picture of human use of this landscape.

Figure 12.8 Drawing stratigraphy at Mussel Shelter in August 1981. (Courtesy of V. Attenbrow.)

Changes in the number of habitations occupied and artefacts discarded per millennium are shown in Figure 12.9. The number of dated sites in each millennium gradually increased towards the present (Figure 12.9A). While this pattern is consistent with either an increase in the number of people in the area or a decay curve Attenbrow has argued that alterations in economy and land use were also involved. One line of evidence for this conclusion was that the chronological changes in number of artefacts were different from changes of site numbers (Figure 12.9B). Combining all of the sites in the catchment Attenbrow observed two increases in the numbers of artefacts discarded, one in the early-Holocene and another in the late-Holocene, showing that changes in artefact discard were not restricted to the last few millennia. Furthermore, artefact accumulation was greatest in the past 3,000 years, but the rate of artefact accumulation decreased during the past 2,000 years. This is not necessarily consistent with population growth, and could represent restructuring of landscape use, with people using more sites but discarding fewer artefacts in some of them.

Attenbrow (2003) explored this possibility with several different analyses. For instance, seeking a way to study functional differences in site use she classified each site, for each millennium of its occupation, as either an 'activity location' or a 'base camp'. She defined activity locations, where there had been equipment

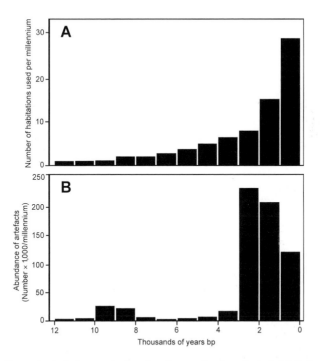

Figure 12.9 Chronological changes in the abundance of archaeological debris in the Upper Mangrove Creek catchment: A = number of habitation sites per millennium; B = number of artefacts per millennium (redrawn from Attenbrow 2004: Figure 9.1).

maintenance, butchering of large animals, or transit camps, as those with a small, low density assemblage of artefacts. She classified as base camps those residences where family groups carried out domestic tasks, creating large, higher density assemblages. Attenbrow found that base camps and activity locations did not exist in the same proportions at all time periods (Figure 12.10). During the mid-Holocene, approximately 4,000–6,000 years bp, and again in the last millennium, many more activity locations are known, whereas in other periods few activity locations appear to have been used. Although the small, fragile activity locations of Pleistocene and early-Holocene age may not have been well preserved, making the pattern partly a reflection of destruction, it seems that Attenbrow has discovered evidence of cyclical patterns in settlement structure over the past 12,000 years. While foragers in the Upper Mangrove Creek area had always been residentially mobile their use of the landscape was repeatedly reorganized; in some periods they regularly used activity stations away from base camps but in other periods they foraged more directly from base camps. In the last millennium this adjustment reflected changing access to food resources: climate change resulted in dense shrub-lands replacing open woodlands, which reduced the abundance of grazing animals and decreased the ease of human movement in pursuit of game (Attenbrow 2004). In that new environment foragers made a large number of activity locations away from their base camps, to facilitate hunting, gathering and processing of material. The absence of preserved animal remains prevents similar reconstructions of settlement reorganization for earlier periods.

At Mangrove Creek the restructuring of settlement and site use throughout the Holocene helped create chronological variations in site abundance. Attenbrow (2003, 2004) calculated that the large increase in observed numbers of sites in the past 2,000 years was due mainly to increases in the abundance of activity locations rather than any change in the number of base camps. This indicates reorganization

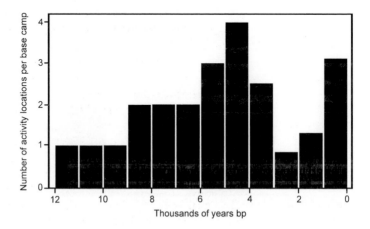

Figure 12.10 Chronological variation in the abundance of 'activity locations' relative to 'base camps' in the Upper Mangrove Creek catchment, using Attenbrow's (2003, 2004) classification (data from Attenbrow 2004: Table 10.2).

of land use and altered resource use strategies, and is not consistent with a substantial population increase in the late-Holocene.

Other processes also operated to create chronological changes in the numbers of artefacts discarded in the Upper Mangrove Creek sites (Figure 12.9B). At the same time that artefact numbers increased dramatically, about 2,500–3,500 years ago, the manufacture of backed artefacts was emphasized (Hiscock and Attenbrow 1998, 2004, 2005). Backed artefact production is an 'abundance strategy' (Hiscock 2006) that makes many small flakes and the preference for this technology contributed to the increased quantities of artefacts discarded about three millennia ago. Bipolar knapping, which can also create large numbers of small flakes, was increasingly emphasized in Upper Mangrove Creek and this also added to late-Holocene changes in artefact abundance (Attenbrow 2004). Additionally, there was a shift in raw material use, with foragers using more quartz in the last three millennia, and in conjunction with bipolar techniques this increased the number of artefacts created. Furthermore, declines in artefact discard over the last two millennia coincided with an increased emphasis on the manufacture and use of ground-edge axes. Axes can be repaired and used for extended periods, and using them reduced the numbers of other tools that need to be made. These are examples of many technological changes that affected the quantity of artefacts discarded in archaeological sites. Reorganization of technology alone does not explain changes in the numbers of artefacts per millennium, but it is another contributing factor.

Attenbrow's research at Upper Mangrove Creek illustrated how multiple factors combined to generate patterns of site numbers and artefact discard. Greater numbers of sites in recent times is explained largely by the failure of older sites to be preserved and identified at the same rate as younger sites, but in this region the effects of preservation were combined with regular modifications of how people lived. Economy, technology, mobility, dispersal of people across the landscape, population size and site preservation all changed through time and it is not reasonable to single out one aspect, such as demographic change, to explain the archaeological evidence. The implication of this discovery is that while population size need not have remained unchanged throughout the Holocene there is no compelling evidence of substantial population growth in the last few millennia.

What is noteworthy about Upper Mangrove Creek is the record of repeated reorganization of economy and land use throughout the terminal Pleistocene and the Holocene. These transformations were complex, displaying cyclical patterns of change as well as ones that may have been unique. Frequent restructuring of land use reveals that economic and social strategies of foragers in this area were not stable and regularly underwent adjustments. The millennial time-scale of evidence at Upper Mangrove Creek prevents an analysis of shorter term fluctuations in land use patterns or population size. The result is a smoothed record of human life in the area, and an image of continuous occupation that may not accurately express the extent of economic or demographic reorganization in such localities. The dynamic nature of shorter term settlement changes has been studied in another region of eastern Australia where high resolution evidence has been obtained.

Population pulses on the arid margins

Low chronological resolution in archaeological sites can obscure the nature of human occupation. What seems to be evidence of continuous, low intensity occupation at a site may in reality have been created by a series of visits separated in time but not easily distinguished by archaeologists (Frankel 1988, 1993). The question is whether change in archaeological materials represents growth of a continuously resident population or altered cycles of visitation by people occasionally using an area. High resolution age-estimation which might answer this question is technically difficult, perhaps impossible, in many rock shelters. However, detailed examinations of open sites have demonstrated that the use of some landscapes by foragers involved periods of repeated visitation interspersed with decades or centuries of abandonment.

One example of intermittent land use is provided by Simon Holdaway and Patricia Fanning, who worked along creeks in the margins of the arid zone of southeastern Australia (Figure 12.4). They studied four localities in which small streams drain shallow valleys in escarpments and ranges: Stud Creek, Fowlers Gap, Pine Point and Peery Creek (Holdaway et al. 2000; Fanning and Holdaway 2001a, 2001b; Holdaway et al. 2002, 2005). In these valleys they found evidence of ancient foraging in the form of stone artefacts near creeks where people had camped, quarries where the stone to make artefacts was obtained, and hearths where people had cooked their foods. Since the antiquity of hearths could sometimes be determined, they are the basis for assessing changes in occupation.

Nowadays the hearths that are preserved and easily recognizable are those that used rocks as heat retainers and these are found as small piles of heat-fractured rocks covering low pedestals of sediment (Figure 12.11). They were originally stone-lined cooking pits which have since been eroded down until the former heat-retaining stones remain above what had been the base of the oven. Excavations into these piles revealed discoloured sediments, altered by baking, and sometimes small, preserved fragments of charcoal from the wood burned in the fire. Where charcoal was recovered Holdaway and Fanning were able to employ radiocarbon analyses to estimate the antiquity of the hearths.

The oldest hearths on these creeks are approximately 6,000 years bp, demonstrating that humans probably occupied these valleys in the early- and mid- as well as the late-Holocene. However, hearths estimated to be more than 1,500 years old are infrequent. Figure 12.12 shows the number of hearths per 500-year period for the past two millennia. There are more recent hearths than earlier ones, but Holdaway and Fanning interpret this as a result of poor preservation rather than increasing numbers of people inhabiting the area. These are eroding landscapes and older sediments are rarely preserved, leaving thin sediments that have survived multiple erosion events (Fanning and Holdaway 2001b). At Stud Creek all excavated hearths were less than 1,500–2,000 years old because older land surfaces had been destroyed by erosion (Holdaway et al. 2000, 2002, 2005). Differences in the number of hearths from each time period reflect the destruction of sites through erosion; recent land surfaces tend to have survived in good condition while older

Figure 12.11 Hearth NPH1, before excavation (above) and with a quadrant excavated (below) showing oven-stones, charcoal and baked/stained sediment. (Courtesy of S. Holdaway.)

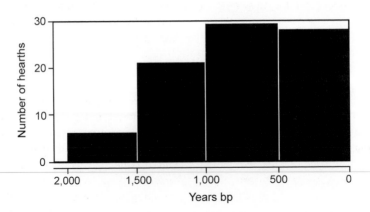

Figure 12.12 Number of hearths per 500-year period for the past two millennia at Stud Creek, Fowlers Gap, Pine Point and Peery Creek (data from Holdaway et al. 2005: Figure 9).

surfaces have been destroyed. In these circumstances it is unwise to use the number of datable hearths as an indication of the intensity of human occupation in each locality, and reconstructions of the presence or absence of people in these landscapes can currently be made for only the past 2,000 years.

Holdaway and Fanning examined radiocarbon estimates for hearth ages to assess whether occupation was constant or whether there were periods of occupation alternating with periods of abandonment (Holdaway et al. 2002, 2005). They used a statistical method, called Bayesian analysis, to test hypotheses about whether age-estimates were spread randomly through time or clustered. The evidence strongly supports a model in which there were periods of hearth construction separated by one or more periods without hearth building in which the local region may have been abandoned. It is likely that between 900 and 1,150 years bp no hearths were constructed at any of the four localities. This was an unusual climatic period, the Medieval Climatic Anomaly, and environmental changes at the time appear to have triggered changes in human settlement. Later in time, at Pine Point and Fowlers Gap but not at Stud Creek or Peery Creek, there was another period in which no hearths were built, suggesting abandonment of those localities. The reason that people abandoned small, local areas while continuing to live in the broader region is not obvious, but it need not reflect continental scale climatic changes.

Holdaway and Fanning revealed a cyclical pattern of landscape use on the desert margins, with foragers using valleys for 200–300 years and then not using them for almost as long before regularly visiting them again. The discontinuous character of land use by groups that spent much of their time elsewhere does not reveal a fixed and stable long-term adaptation to the environment, nor the emergence of markedly high population sizes in recent millennia (Holdaway et al. 2002).

Periodic abandonment of the landscape points to settlement in the form of a series of 'pulses' of occupation. This is not consistent with models of a uni-directional increase in population size or non-reversible economic 'intensification' in the late-Holocene (Holdaway et al. 2002: 360). For this reason archaeologists have begun to examine the possibility that changes through time in demography and land use might have been non-directional, even cyclical.

Fluctuations and cycles of change in Australian pre-history

The difficulties of inferring population size from archaeological residues make reconstructions of Australian population history uncertain. The abundance of archaeological materials is largely a reflection of conditions of preservation. Periods containing increased archaeological materials, prior to the LGM and again in the late-Holocene, also have evidence for restructured settlement patterns and land use; processes that create uncertainty for interpretations of population growth. Furthermore, for most time periods low chronological resolution means that shorter term fluctuations in population size and settlement organization cannot be distinguished. Additionally, few regions have been studied in ways that provide a representative sample. Finally, there are regional differences in population trends through time and it is difficult to construct a single curve describing the total size of the population across the continent.

Even though accurate estimates of past population size are hard to develop from archaeological evidence we can conclude that unidirectional models of inexorable population growth are unlikely to be correct. Research by Attenbrow, Holdaway, Fanning and others does not reveal major continent-wide population growth in the late-Holocene. Archaeological and genetic evidence indicates that there was substantial population growth shortly after colonization, combined with the likelihood that large numbers of sites of recent antiquity are a product of better preservation, does not support a late growth model. A simple early growth model, presented by Beaton (1983), with no change in population size during the Holocene and much of the Pleistocene, is hard to reconcile with the chronological and geographical diversity of the archaeological record. Unidirectional population growth, either early or late, can be rejected as too simplistic to account for the available evidence.

Cycles of population change, in which the number of people in a region or across the continent increased, decreased, increased again, and so on, are more appropriate depictions of Australia's pre-historic past. Case studies such as those provided by O'Connor (1990) in the north and by Holdaway and Porch (1995) in the south hypothesize fluctuations, or cycles, in regional population size and settlement patterns long after people had occupied the continent. Cycles of occupation and settlement restructuring have also been inferred through the Holocene in regions such as Upper Mangrove Creek and the Stud and Peery Creek regions.

Models of fluctuating population levels offer a more realistic image of the demographic pre-history of the continent. Cycles in population size and settlement patterns during the Pleistocene have been advocated by a number of archaeologists, including Richard Cosgrove (1995a, 1995b), Simon Holdaway (Holdaway and Porch 1995; Holdaway et al. 2005), Sue O'Connor (1990; O'Connor et al. 1993) and Peter Veth (2005). Available evidence suggests fluctuations were complex in character: regionally based, of varying magnitudes and at different scales.

However, the technical difficulties described in this chapter mean it is not yet possible to specify the frequency or magnitude of population growth or reduction during these cycles. Additionally, archaeological evidence cannot yet specify whether or not there was a long-term trend in the total population size of Australia underlying the regional variation and population fluctuations. O'Connor's bidirectional model of population change implied that although there had been large fluctuations in total population size the largest number of people had lived in the most recent period (Figure 12.1B). This is possible but not a compelling suggestion. Claims for far larger population sizes at the end of the pre-historic period have not been demonstrated and other, equally plausible, images of past population change can be offered.

An alternative model is that there was no single, directional, continent-wide trend in pre-historic population size, and following initial population growth and dispersal of people across the continent population size fluctuated but did not follow a clear trend. Periods of low or declining site numbers and artefacts are consistent with fluctuating population sizes that were nearly constant over the long term (Dortch and Smith 2001; Attenbrow 2004). In this model, population sizes comparable to the late-Holocene may have existed at earlier times. Figure 12.1C illustrates this model as a complex series of regional fluctuations through time, but it is notional and not intended to specify the timing of particular population changes during pre-history. It depicts fluctuations of population change that were regionally varied in magnitude, with different rates of population growth or reduction (Figure 12.1Ci). Local extinctions of some forager groups probably occurred but other groups suffered only population reductions (Figure 12.1Cii). Furthermore, it is likely that population size sometimes increased in one region at the same time it reduced in others (Figure 12.1Ciii). Evidence for regional variations and population fluctuations has been discussed in previous chapters.

Pre-historic cycles of settlement and demography observed by archaeologists operated on a long temporal scale and may reflect different processes than those recorded for nineteenth and twentieth century Aboriginal life. Indeed, the existence of fluctuating, even cyclical, demographic patterns represents a challenge to images of stable economic and social systems during pre-history. Cycles of change additionally imply that not all past human groups were demographically, economically or socially on a direct pathway to an ethnographic, historical cultural system. Applying historically observed processes as explanations for archaeologically recognized patterns of pre-historic occupation and demography is therefore potentially incongruous and dangerous. This is also a fundamental concern for reconstructions of changing social life in ancient Australia.

13 Social identity and interaction during the Holocene

Even though archaeologists have found evidence for alterations in ritual and artistic performance, and political and trading networks, during the Pleistocene some researchers believe that major changes in social practice occurred only in the Holocene, in recent millennia. The most influential depiction of this kind was offered by Harry Lourandos, who proposed a model of alliance formation in which forager groups grew in size and became sedentary in the late-Holocene. He argued that sedentary foragers developed restricted patterns of access to territory and resources, and expanded and formalized alliances and ceremonial networks. Lourandos refined and re-expressed this idea over several decades (Lourandos 1980a, 1980b, 1983a, 1985a, 1985b, 1997; David and Lourandos 1997, 1998, 1999). The alliance formation model of Lourandos, and its application as a holistic image of progression in the guise of 'intensification', explored altered group identity and reorganized alliance networks as a potent description of pre-historic social life. This idea has been employed by many researchers trying to understand changing social life in the Holocene. However, in applying this model the complexities of interpreting archaeological evidence, and the existence of other social processes that may have been involved, has often been ignored.

Archaeologists once thought that there was evidence of directional changes in Holocene economy, population size, settlement, or political life that led to a more dynamic, sophisticated and intensive social system than anything that had existed before in Australian pre-history. Such depictions of cultural life on mainland Australia, as a transformation of 'simple' social systems into 'complex' ones, are now revealed to have resulted from a series of over-interpretations of difficult to understand archaeological patterns, combined with an under-appreciation of how many traces of ancient life had been destroyed and the uncritical use of ethnographic images in reconstructing the past. Together these ways of interpreting the evidence veiled the richness of human life that existed prior to the late-Holocene while enriching an understanding of societies in recent millennia through the application of ethnographic analogies. The Holocene archaeological record, described in Chapters 7–12, indicates geographical and chronological diversity in economies, technologies, settlement and demography; it does not unambiguously demonstrate unidirectional trends to more sophisticated economic systems.

Re-examination of claims for alliance formation and 'intensification' in the late-Holocene not only exposes problems with inferences of progressive increases in social complexity, but also illuminates a debate about the cause of ancient social change. For decades debate about why pre-historic social life altered focused on whether change was driven by the formation of alliance networks or by social reconfigurations in response to demographic or environmental change; the idea being that one process would be responsible for all alterations to social practice. The limited nature of this debate is revealed by the recognition that multiple mechanisms, including many kinds of social process, may have been involved in the production of ancient social lives and archaeological materials. That realization implies that at different places and times the mechanisms involved in altered social practice could have been different; there is no reason to advocate that change always had the same cause – a claim that would invoke substantive uniformitarianism. The proposition that there were multiple pathways to altered social practice stands in contrast to the idea that the patterns of life observed in the historical period arose everywhere at the same time and through the single process of late-Holocene alliance formation.

Alliance formation and social change

The model of alliance formation initially proposed by Lourandos (1976, 1980a, 1980b, 1983a) focused on how the status of individuals, the organization of labour, and ceremonial and political activities of groups may have been connected. Drawing on historical descriptions of nineteenth century Aboriginal society he suggested that an individual's status and power was achieved in a number of ways: initiation and progression through the hierarchical ceremonial system, shamanism, economic achievement in the organization of mass hunts, and participation in trading. In particular, individuals and lineages enhanced their control through the development of larger networks of alliances. Alliances were constructed and maintained in many ways, such as through multiple marriages which acted to expand kinship connections, or through the acquisition of reciprocal exchange partners from other groups. Ceremonial gatherings provided a context for the negotiation of alliances and also gave opportunities for individuals and lineages to display economic achievement. Lourandos argued that people hosting inter-group congregations for ceremony and/or trade needed to provide food and other resources, and that this encouraged modifications of economic activities to produce local surplus.

Lourandos suggested that these interconnections between economy, inter-group relationships and social dynamics within groups resulted in a number of trends. One was increased production, achieved when pre-historic groups increasingly expended greater labour to obtain and process abundant but costly food resources. Eels, yams, cycads, moths, nuts, marine mammals and other plants and animals have been nominated as filling this economic role (see Chapters 9–11). Lourandos also expected an increased production of non-food items, such as the manufacture of axes or quarrying of ochre, to create a surplus with which to supply heightened demands of inter-group trade. Increased economic production was sometimes thought to have been associated with a less mobile lifestyle, as foragers became tethered to the resources they relied on, particularly when exploitation of those resources required the construction and maintenance of facilities (Chapter 10). Another inferred that social change, perhaps linked to decreased mobility, was the emergence of group identities and ideologies that encouraged greater control over resources by the conception of well-defined and restrictive territorial boundaries; creating political geographies in which formalized inter-group trade and ceremonial networks were key mechanisms for accessing resources located in the territory of other groups.

During the 1990s Lourandos (1997) emphasized political geography when he re-expressed his alliance formation model in terms of different kinds of inter-group social interactions. He contrasted what he called 'open' social systems with 'closed' ones. In open systems there were few distinctions between groups, and individuals could move relatively easily between groups and interact with people across large tracts of land in which there was homogeneous cultural life. Such open social structures were suited to situations with low population densities and high residential mobility.

Closed systems displayed greater differences in ideology and social practice between groups, giving each group a distinctive identity and constraining movement of individuals between groups. Inter-group relationships were regulated by formalized processes of ritual and kinship. Closed social systems, Lourandos argued, involved people in territorial marking by modifying their landscape, such as making rock art or constructing cemeteries and ritual precincts. These marks signal closed systems in the archaeological record. Closed social systems were suited to higher population densities, particularly where there was competition over patchy resources. Lourandos, and other archaeologists following him, argued that a transformation of open to closed systems occurred during the late-Holocene and this social reorganization was associated with heightened competition between groups and population growth (see Taçon 1993; David and Chant 1995; David and Lourandos 1998, 1999; Barker 2004).

A conundrum for this proposition is why such a transformation happened 2,000–4,000 years ago and not earlier or later. Reconstructions of more rigidly bounded territories, based on evidence such as differentiation of rock paintings, have been interpreted as revealing that late-Holocene people lived within smaller territories than they had previously. While some researchers suggested that increased environmental productivity in the mid- and late-Holocene facilitated reduced mobility and territory size (e.g. Taçon 1993), others argued that it was a time of lower environmental productivity and social rather than environmental factors were responsible for changes in territoriality (David and Chant 1995). David and Lourandos (1998, 1999) hypothesized that the transition to closed social systems was triggered by reduced and more variable rainfall associated with the amplification of El Niño at that time (see Chapters 7 and 8). They argued that when the El Niño-triggered drier climatic conditions began about 4,000 years ago, foragers in many environments adjusted their economic and social strategies to obtain enough food so that they could maintain or even increase their population sizes. In this context Lourandos and David interpret territorial protocols as a mechanism with which each group controlled access to resources on its land. Reconceived territoriality, with associated trade and ceremonial networks, was therefore a social risk-reduction response that complemented the technological ones described in Chapter 8.

The principal evidence for a late-Holocene development of closed social systems comes from rock art. Archaeologists working in widely separated places concluded that painted images became more diverse and regionally distinctive in the late-Holocene (Taçon 1993; David and Chant 1995; David and Lourandos 1999; Morwood 2002). This implies that in earlier periods artistic works were homogeneous across large tracts, and more varied paintings from the late-Holocene indicate localized marking of the landscape, symbolizing and helping to create geographic distinctions in culture (David and Lourandos 1998).

Those inferences about art were supplemented by claims that sedentary settlement patterns emerged in the late-Holocene, when 'monuments' that could have been territorial markers were built. David and Lourandos (1998) suggested that phenomena such as cemeteries and earth mounds may have fulfilled this social function. This proposition reflects the ideas of Pardoe (1988), who hypothesized that cemeteries in the Murray River corridor and dated to the mid- to late-Holocene were visible symbols of land ownership used by people to emphasize and legitimize their claim to territory. Pardoe (1988, 1990, 1994, 2006) suggested that distinct territorial identities and the exclusive nature of social groups along the riverine corridor restricted gene flow, leading to biological differentiation along the Murray River. The antiquity of those closed systems is unclear but he suggested that they had been in place during the terminal Pleistocene, as revealed by the cemetery at Kow Swamp (Figure 13.1), and need not be only late-Holocene in age.

Researchers also hypothesized that the emergence of small, closed social systems was facilitated by economic improvements. Intensified and more efficient economic systems have been suggested for most environments during the Holocene (see Chapters 9–11), and reconstructions of more productive economic practices have been cited as the means by which people lived not only in smaller foraging territories but also hosted enlarged inter-group congregations (e.g. Lourandos 1980a, 1983a, 1997; Flood et al. 1987; David and Lourandos 1998).

Using these arguments Lourandos, David and others offer a unified model for cultural change across the Australian mainland during the past few thousand years. They argue that population growth and a trend towards closed social systems was associated with more distinct regional identities (reflecting the closure of social life to outsiders), more artistic and symbolic activity (marking territories), more formalized ritual and exchange events (negotiating access across territory boundaries), more productive but labour-costly economies (extracting resources from smaller territories) and more sedentary settlement patterns (matching the more focused and demanding economy). All of these practices were claimed to have occurred together, across much of the mainland, and the process was hypothesized to primarily be one of social reorganization.

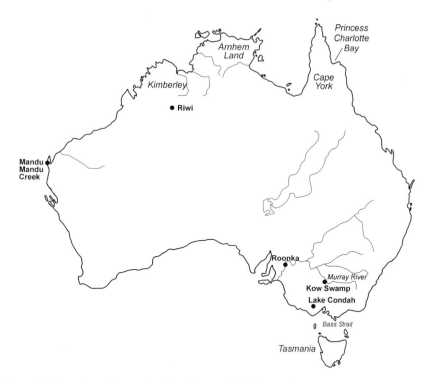

Figure 13.1 Location of sites and regions discussed in Chapter 13.

Evaluating intensification as a progression model

By wedding the alliance formation explanation for economic and social change to the proposition that political systems altered only in the late-Holocene, and imbuing that interpretation with notions of greater economic specialization and efficiency in recent millennia, some researchers presented a model of cultural progression called 'intensification'. This model entwined the alliance formation mechanism with interpretations of unidirectional trends in pre-history to create a sense of greater elaboration in the social lives of people during the final millennia of pre-history. This depiction was shaped by the way archaeologists labelled pre-historic economic and social systems as being either 'simple' or 'complex'. For example, Lourandos (1997) argued that late-Holocene social networks were more 'complex' than earlier ones. Such classifications were attempts to express perceived chronological differences in the social behaviours, but the idea that all ancient societies in Australia progressed only from 'simple' to 'complex' and display a single trend to social and economic intensification (David and Lourandos 1998) recalls elements of cultural evolutionary models that projected images of progress on the past. The imagined complexity of the late-Holocene, and cultural simplicity inferred for the Pleistocene, led some to believe the pace of development and innovation had quickened (Flood

2001), and that the past few thousand years was a time of heightened cultural dynamism (David 2002, 2006).

Progression from 'simple' to 'complex', and from stable to rapidly changing, social life has been disputed for several reasons. In reflecting on the diversity of Aboriginal societies Ian Keen (2004, 2006) argued that distinctions between 'simple' and 'complex' forager societies were an inadequate depiction of the geographically varied social lives of historical groups. In the historical period Aboriginal social practice was a consequence of multiple factors including environmental productivity, demography and social rules. Keen concluded that social systems with inequalities, which focused control in a few individuals and lineages through the practice of high levels of polygamy (men marrying large numbers of women) occurred in localities with abundant resources and higher population densities, but only when kinship systems were suited to the practice. If population growth had been limited to recent millennia then high polygamy, competition and alliance networks may have arisen only in the late pre-historic period. However, as archaeological evidence demonstrates that population growth was not restricted to the Holocene (Chapter 12), closed social systems with political inequality may have occurred much earlier in pre-history. Keen also argued that in Australia environmental variability and scarce resources inhibited the development of enduring political inequality in Aboriginal societies. His conclusions are consistent with the idea that short-term (in an archaeological sense of centuries or a few millennia) and regionally localized instances of high polygamy may have coincided with periods of population growth multiple times during Australian pre-history, and might not be a phenomenon of the late-Holocene alone.

Territorial social systems with specialized, labour-intensive economies, high population densities and social inequality might have emerged and disappeared multiple times during the 50 millennia of human occupation of Australia. A model of fluctuating regional population sizes can therefore be expanded to suggest that the nature of social and economic practice as well as demography oscillated through time rather than changing only once in pre-history. If social conditions fluctuated rather than progressed then many concepts used in the intensification model, such as 'elaboration' and 'increased complexity' through time, need to be replaced with less loaded descriptions, such as periodic restructuring or reconfiguration of social and economic systems.

How can we be sure whether patterns of social interaction and territorial closure changed radically only in the late-Holocene? It is difficult for archaeologists to offer an unconditional answer to such a question. At the moment we know so little of life in the Pleistocene that early patterns of settlement and social relationships are hard to specify. The intensification model asserts that there were changes in territory size and accessibility during the late-Holocene, and implied that broadly similar social and economic practices were absent at earlier times. Progression implied in the intensification model is therefore tested by investigations of the nature of social interaction prior to the mid-Holocene.

The lives of Pleistocene people now appear more diverse than was discussed in the 1980s when intensification was proposed. We now have evidence for large congregations of people, specialized foraging strategies and small territories in some times and places, regional differentiation in art and technology, and labour-intensive processing of plants such as grass seeds and Macrozamia. The circulation of ochre and ornaments over hundreds of kilometres may indicate exchange networks in the Pleistocene, although direct procurement may also be involved. Pardoe's (1988, 2006) interpretation of terminal Pleistocene skeletons, such as from Kow Swamp, as revealing restricted gene flow, suggested to him that closed territorial systems in resource-rich regions such as the Murray River had existed before the Holocene (see Chapter 5). These reconstructions of life in the Pleistocene could encourage archaeologists to apply the alliance formation model to times prior to the Holocene, but the low chronological resolution and rarity of sites constrain detailed interpretations of early social life.

Evidence on which claims for late-Holocene intensification have been based is poorly preserved for the Pleistocene. The difficulty this creates for reconstructions of Pleistocene social life and territoriality is illustrated by claims that increased regionalism in the symbolism of late-Holocene rock paintings represents a social fragmentation and differentiation of identity that was unknown at earlier times. The problem for archaeologists is to demonstrate that earlier symbolic activity did not also display small-scale variations, at least in some periods.

It seems likely that rock paintings were made in Australia for more than 40,000 years but little evidence of it has survived from the Pleistocene. Even in regions with outstanding preservation, such as Arnhem Land and the Kimberley, the earliest paintings with radiometric age-estimates date only from the terminal Pleistocene and fluctuations in the uniformity or local distinctiveness of Pleistocene paintings are largely invisible to archaeologists. The evidence of other forms of symbolism more than 30,000 years ago, in ornaments or burial rituals, is also unambiguous, but each archaeological example is separated by thousands of years and kilometres. In the circumstance it is hard to interpret these rare discoveries in terms of the uniformity or regional differentiation of cultural practices. Take the example of the strands of shell beads discovered at Mandu Mandu Creek and Riwi; they were made in different ways, from different species of shell, and would have been recognizable as different ornaments, but do those differences represent symbols of inter-group distinctions that indicate closed social systems or should they be considered as minor variants within a uniform symbolic code and indications of open social systems? The rarity of preserved ornaments, art and burials across thousands of kilometres of Pleistocene landscape means that archaeologists cannot be sure of the homogeneity of such objects, or develop reliable statements about their meaning as indicators of social differentiation.

Poor preservation of Pleistocene material is complicated further by the way archaeologists have selectively emphasized some phenomena as markers of group identity and social closure, while downplaying others. For instance, while rock art is often discussed as an indicator of closed social systems the existence of cranial deformation, also conceivably a symbol of group identity among some Pleistocene people, has not been used as evidence for an early phase of inter-group distinctions.

Even discovery of further art works or ornamentation preserved from the Pleistocene may not clarify the character of social relationships in the Pleistocene because social practice is not directly or unambiguously encoded in the material debris that forms the archaeological record. Claims for greater social closure in late-Holocene have been based primarily on three inferences: those that reconstructed high levels of sedentism and intensive economic practices, those that identified localized practices of rock art production thought to indicate small territory sizes, and those that interpreted places like burial grounds as markers of territorial attachment and ownership. A review of all three claims demonstrates that the archaeological evidence is equivocal, often representing overly enthusiastic interpretations of ambiguous archaeological records supplemented by an emphasis on historical observations and lacking consideration of interpretative difficulties associated with archaeological materials. One of the best examples is found in the claims for sedentary settlement systems in southeastern Australia.

Historical and archaeological evidence for late-Holocene sedentism

Archaeologists reconstructing late-Holocene economies often rely on analogies with nineteenth century observations of Aboriginal social and economic practices, creating elaborate images of later pre-historic life. Some researchers invoke historical depictions of Aborigines to reconstruct the past because they see it as a valuable and necessary interdisciplinary method for obtaining information of the late pre-historic period (Bowdler 2006; McNiven et al. 2006; Tamisari and Wallace 2006). Some archaeologists were also tempted to understand the detailed knowledge and processing of resources, multiple dimensions of social interactions, well-defined identity and ramified inter-group political networks of foragers recorded in the historical period as an indication that recent societies were 'complex', while interpreting the sparseness of archaeological information about such knowledge or social interactions in earlier times as indicating that those societies were relatively 'simple'. The trouble with this inference is that knowledge, identity and social interactions of pre-historic people are the phenomena least readily preserved in ancient debris and least susceptible to archaeological investigations. Comparing reconstructions based on textual records of detailed observations of social life with those built more on sparse archaeological materials creates an image of more sophisticated cultural life in the recent period, even if it had not been so. The view that human societies evolved from 'simple' to 'complex' was entrenched in the thinking of nineteenth century archaeologists and present-day researchers are justifiably concerned that depictions of pre-historic cultural change are not unnecessarily imbued with judgements about human progression.

An example of the influence of historical documents is seen in the idea that large, permanent communities who regulated access to their territory through networks of political alliances built upon trade and ritual obligations emerged only in the past 2,000–3,000 years. Drawing on historical accounts of huts several researchers argued that historical Aboriginal people in southeastern mainland Australia lived in houses as large sedentary communities of several hundred individuals, an almost medieval image of 'villages' in which elaborate social and political systems were needed to regulate the interactions of large numbers of people. Williams (1985, 1987, 1988) and Flood (1983, 1989, 2001) nominated earth mounds and arranged stones as the archaeological residues they believed had been left by these 'villages', and concluded that this lifestyle evolved only in the late-Holocene. However, the logic of interpreting those archaeological materials as the remnants of villages is not persuasive. Williams hypothesized that clusters of earth mounds were the remains of multiple huts but the chronology and content of earth mounds excavated in the southeast is not consistent with an interpretation of them as hut foundations or villages (Chapter 10). Flood's suggestion that circles or lines of rocks were the foundations of village huts is equally problematic. Anne Clarke (1994a) carried out fieldwork near Lake Condah and argued that many patterns of stones were caused by natural processes. It was difficult to distinguish cultural and natural patterns of rocks in that landscape, and even when patterns were human constructions they could represent short-term occupation by mobile foragers exploiting the region rather than permanent dwellings and villages. Furthermore, in that region there is no evidence that circles or lines of stone on ridges frequently date to the late-Holocene; most are probably nineteenth century in age, leading several researchers to suggest that they were constructed as refuges following European disruption to Aboriginal life ways (C. F. M. Bird and Frankel 1991a; Clarke 1994a; Mitchell 1994a). Clarke concluded that archaeologists had conceived a mythical cultural landscape of villages that was not supported by the archaeological evidence.

Overwrought claims of village life in the late-Holocene exemplify the way historical texts, rather than archaeological approaches, have been used to construct interpretations of 'complex' late-Holocene economic and social activities. Similar arguments were used to claim that, in eastern Australia, ceremonial and ritual activities visible in the historical period and associated settlement systems and economic patterns began or intensified in the last few thousand years (Beaton 1977; Lourandos 1980; Bowdler 1981; Flood 1989, 2001). Neither the economic shifts nor the antiquity of different forms of ceremonial activity have been demonstrated in many of the regions for which claims have been made (Chapter 10) and the hypothesized intensification of social life has proved difficult to measure. The difficulties of inferring change in social practices are seen in the attempts to distinguish 'open' from 'closed' social systems in pre-history.

Rock art and claims for the emergence of territorially closed social systems

Researchers such as Lourandos and David have inferred changes in the nature of political boundaries and social interactions from reconstructions of altered past population growth and artistic activity on Cape York during the late-Holocene. They interpreted greater site numbers in recent millennia as evidence of greater numbers of people, and argued that recent population growth had been regulated by altered social practices and not by biological processes alone (Lourandos 1997; David and

Lourandos 1998, 1999). Their reading of site and artefact abundance as a measure of the number of humans is troubled by the uncertainties discussed in Chapter 12, including the effects of sampling bias and preservation. For instance, David and Lourandos interpreted archaeological materials at Princess Charlotte Bay as indicating development of new forms of marine resource exploitation, settlement restructuring and population growth in the late-Holocene. However, evidence from that region indicates extensive destruction of early- and mid-Holocene archae-ological deposits (Chapter 9); it is not necessary to hypothesize that change was concentrated in the late-Holocene. Questions about the preservation of Pleistocene and early-Holocene materials also plague their interpretation of altered territorial access.

David and Lourandos (1999: 112–14) claimed there had been a major increase in painting during the past 2,000 years, describing it as an 'explosion' of painted art and explaining it as the development of more closed territorial systems which meant more restricted access to land, symbolized in the painting of rock faces. This reconstruction was based on the recovery of more ochre in late-Holocene levels of archaeological deposits, but the failure of older materials to be preserved may be responsible for the pattern. There are reasons to suspect that preservation was a factor creating this archaeological sequence. Ochre is occasionally found in Pleistocene levels of some Cape York sites but in general the preservation of bones, plant material, and even stone artefacts of that antiquity is poor. For instance, residues are well preserved on the edges of tools of late-Holocene age but are rarely preserved on artefacts of Pleistocene age (Fullagar and David 1997; David and Lourandos 1999). Ochre has probably not been well preserved in the lower levels of many sites in this region. This conclusion was reached by Mike Morwood; as explained in Chapter 6 he demonstrated that ochre paintings were made in southeastern Cape York more than 30,000 years ago, but none of the ones currently visible are older than about 3,000 years bp because earlier paintings were not preserved. Interpretations of chronological change in rock art are difficult in most regions because well-preserved paintings date only from the past few thousand years.

Claims for increased regionalism in rock art have also been made for a few regions, such as Arnhem Land, where exceptional conditions have preserved some painted surfaces throughout the Holocene. Paul Taçon (1993) investigated seven areas in Arnhem Land, located at increasing distance from the coast. X-ray paintings, which show skeletons and/or internal organs, and varied in the subjects shown between localities in a pattern resembling the ideology of historical Aboriginal groups. Arguing that X-ray paintings were less than 4,000 years old, Taçon concluded that local differences in artistic practice and group identity could be traced back millennia, but that those geographic differences were not present in earlier rock paintings, such as Dynamic figures, and hence regional art distinctions in Arnhem Land arose in the past few thousand years. Taçon suggested that people in the late-Holocene associated themselves with smaller territories than those who lived in the region in the early-Holocene, with each group developing a different way of performing its art.

While Taçon's study has the advantage that earlier paintings in Arnhem Land are better preserved than in many areas, allowing chronological comparisons to be made, the evidence of altered group identity and territoriality is still not straightforward. X-ray paintings documented by Taçon reflect the environmental variations of the late-Holocene landscape; fish were more frequently depicted in areas near the coast and kangaroos were painted more often in inland areas. If artists had drawn animals they encountered commonly local differences in paintings during the X-ray period might have arisen in response to diversification of the local environment during the Holocene. In western Arnhem Land the landscape was transformed following sea-level rise, from relatively uniform woodlands to a location with a large marine embayment and then to a complexly changing and patchy environment of sandy beaches, mangrove swamps, riverine plains, freshwater lagoons as well as woodlands (Hiscock and Kershaw 1992; Hiscock 1999). The diversity of animals portrayed in X-ray paintings reflects the greater environmental diversity during the past few millennia, while the lesser diversity in Dynamic paintings reflects the more uniform environment of the terminal Pleistocene.

Paintings were made in slightly different ways in each area and so environmental diversification alone may not completely explain the archaeological patterns. However, existence of local varieties of X-ray art does not unambiguously demonstrate that people had small territories or distinctive identities when the paintings were made. A single group moving through these areas might have performed their art slightly differently in each location, in reference to mythology attached to each place or even in response to art they already found there. Artistic practices reflect many religious or profane purposes, can be designed to facilitate and encourage interpretation or obscure meaning, and are dependent on the social context of performance. Reconfiguration of these factors can create alterations in rock art without signalling changing territory size. For instance, paintings and carvings of Aboriginal people in the historical period are mostly temporary – body paintings and sand sculptures that disappear shortly after they are produced (Morphy 1999). If ancient artists shifted their emphasis from the production of transitory art to rock painting this would be reflected in the amount and diversity of images found by archaeologists of rock surfaces. In western Arnhem Land and other regions the connection between diversity of rock paintings and the distinctiveness of group identity and size of territories remains subtle and difficult to establish.

The technical difficulties involved in inferring changed territory size or modified barriers to group membership are amply illustrated by these examples, but many archaeologists still suspect that regional distinctions in cultural practice became more pronounced during the late-Holocene (David 2002, 2006; Barker 2004; McDonald and Veth 2006; Veth 2006). Although claims for such a trend are based on the ambiguous evidence reviewed here it remains possible that in some regions restructuring of territorial organization occurred during the later millennia of the Holocene. Small territories, distinct group identities or social inequality could have emerged when conditions were appropriate; during the late-Holocene in some localities. However, other kinds of social process may also have been involved in the production of archaeological materials and this can be illustrated using the competing interpretations of places with multiple graves.

Cemeteries and territory: treatment of the dead at Roonka

Burial sites in southeastern Australia provide a record of changing mortuary practices, as well as economic and social activities, throughout the Holocene (Figure 13.1). For example, hundreds of skeletons were excavated on Roonka Flat, a sandy bank on the Murray River. The excavator, Graeme Pretty, identified four phases of human occupation (Figure 13.2). The earliest, a small shell midden called phase I, was Pleistocene in age; while near the surface objects of historical age were labelled phase IV. Pre-historic burials occurred in phases II and III. The oldest skeletons, from phase II, came from the base of a layer of red sand, about 7,000–10,000 years old, while stratigraphically higher burials assigned to phase III are estimated to be less than about 7,000 years old (Pretty 1977; Pretty and Kricun 1989; Pate et al. 1998). Classifying graves into phase II or III, although difficult, allowed archaeologists to describe the chronology of burials.

There were shallow oval graves in which bodies lay on their sides with arms and legs contracted towards the chest, long shallow graves in which bodies were laid out fully extended, and deep shaft graves in which bodies were placed vertically. Shaft pits were left open, allowing visitors to see the buried individual(s). Sometimes more than one person was buried in a grave, and on a number of occasions infants and small children were buried with an adult. Some skeletons also

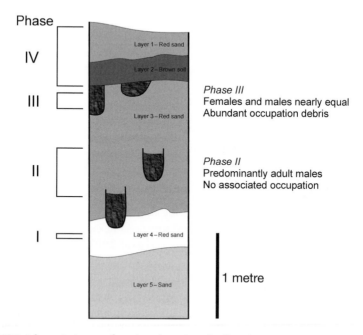

Figure 13.2 Schematic image of stratigraphy at Roonka (based on Pretty 1977).

show signs of being altered, even cut apart, after death; one adult male was found with the skeleton of an infant placed into his chest cavity (Pretty and Kricun 1989). Such burials were probably loaded with symbolism, but we do not know what that may have been. There is little evidence for trends in these mortuary practices; they were always varied.

People were buried at Roonka with stone artefacts, ornaments, fragments of ochre or scraps of food. The most spectacular grave goods were headbands of bone and teeth – the remains of clothing and ornaments. One skull had a headband of notched wallaby teeth sewn or plaited in a double strand (Figure 13.3). A series of bone pins on this man's chest indicate that he was buried wearing clothing or in a shroud. In the same grave an infant's skeleton had a bird skull on its chest, ochre staining near its feet, and reptile vertebrae that may have been ornaments by its side. These individuals are 6,000–7,000 years old (Pate et al. 1998), but the grave goods exemplify materials regularly interred with the dead throughout the Holocene. Pate (2006) suggested burial goods symbolized sex and age differences, with hunting equipment being placed with men more often than with women, and more elaborate goods were often found in the graves of older people, particularly older males.

Some archaeologists used this evidence to reconstruct ancient social life at Roonka. Pretty argued that there was social inequality in which individuals of high status were given elaborate funerals which included sacrificed children buried with them. He concluded that in the early-Holocene (phase II) graves were not associated with habitation debris and were frequently adult males rather than a balanced

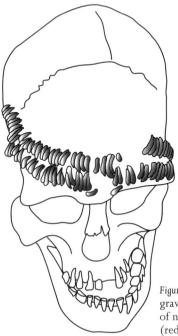

Figure 13.3 Sketch of the skull of an adult buried in grave 108 at Roonka, showing the double strand of notched marsupial teeth placed across the forehead (redrawn from Pretty 1977: 314).

cross-section of a population, whereas during the past few thousand years (phase III) there were large quantities of campsite debris in the fill of burial pits and males and females were almost evenly represented, showing that in recent millennia people lived on the flat and did not limit their use of it to a burial place. This, he said, indicated not only a change in site function but also a restructuring of social relationships and ideology in the past few thousand years.

A similar interpretation was offered by proponents of the alliance formation model. Lourandos (1997) suggested the Roonka sequence revealed greater social differentiation through time, while Pate (2006) concluded that Roonka demonstrated the emergence of more 'complex' social life in the late-Holocene as a consequence of increased sedentism, inter-group competition and more rigid territorial boundaries. Pardoe (1988) also used evidence from Roonka to suggest that territorially bounded corporate groups emerged in the Murray River Valley during the terminal Pleistocene. He interpreted places with multiple burials, such as Roonka, as socially recognized cemeteries which affirmed the group membership of those who buried their dead there and symbolized their ownership over land. The abundance of cemeteries in the late-Holocene led Pardoe to suggest an elaboration of social organization, as mechanisms were developed with which to regulate inter-group competition.

These interpretations of Roonka presented it as a formal cemetery belonging to a long-term residence group, perhaps a lineage or clan group, who lived in the surrounding landscape and buried their dead in it to define their ancestral connection to land. The group burying dead at Roonka is said to have become more socially differentiated, with closed territorial behaviour, and according to Pretty even hierarchical political structures. Such views were consistent with the notion of 'intensification' but alternative reconstructions of ancient life at Roonka have now been offered.

Claims for hierarchical political systems were based on Pretty's idea that infants buried with adults were sacrifices to accompany important people, but there are other possible explanations. One is that the infants had died long before the adult and their bodies were carried or stored until they could be interred with another body. Evidence that adult bodies decayed in open pits and were modified post-mortem demonstrates that viewing and altering the dead was a common cultural practice; retaining the skeleton of a infant for burial with an adult might have been another aspect of those practices. Furthermore, in hierarchical social systems individuals of higher rank would have had better access to food, something that can be determined by analyses of the chemical composition and pathologies of ancient skeletons. A study of Roonka skeletons by Pate (2006) led him to conclude that there was no difference between people in diet or lifestyle that would support reconstructions of a hereditary, stratified political structure. Instead grave goods suggest that older people attained status within their group through their achievements in life, but this status was not passed on.

Claims for increased social inequality over time are also unconvincing. Grave goods were similar throughout the Holocene and so do not indicate altered social conditions. In fact at Roonka burials in the mid- and late-Holocene were more representative of the composition of the group(s) using the area, compared to the early-Holocene burials which were dominated by older males; a change that could be interpreted as a reduction of inequality over time.

More significantly, Littleton and Allen (2007) argued that Roonka and similar burial places were not exclusively or continually used by a single sedentary group of people, and were not symbols of bounded territories or common group identity. The number of people buried at Roonka is very low; on average one person was buried every two or three generations, and there may have been hundreds of years between burials at the site. Littleton and Allen (2007) suggest that during the Holocene small groups of foragers were not tethered to specific territories; instead Roonka was used by several groups who did not have ideologies fixing them to specific places and who moved flexibly across the land. Some of the variation in burial practices at Roonka probably resulted from the use of the site by different groups, and it is not necessary to see chronological changes in terms of the intensification of a single resident group. Repeated burials at Roonka do not reflect continuous occupation of a local land owning group, according to Littleton and Allen; instead they reflect similar practices by many groups who judged Roonka to be a potential place for burying bodies; a judgement that may have been aided by observation of visible burials placed there in the past. The potential for ancient people to respond not only to their contemporary social and natural environments but also to the archaeological materials in their world is a powerful process that shaped patterns of change and repetition in the cultural practices.

Echoes of the past: influence of archaeology on ancient life

Archaeologists are not the first people to recognize the existence of archaeological materials, or to realize that they are residues preserved from the past. Although much cultural material decays rapidly, there are places in which exceptional preservation allowed objects to persist for hundreds, even thousands of years. During pre-history ancient Australians regularly encountered relics of earlier human occupation, and their responses to this debris may have been a stimulus for change or recurrence in ancient human activities. This can be termed the 'echo principle': archaeological materials, as echoes of the past, provoked later human activities and ideologies.

Bradley (2002) argued that archaeological residues represented a challenge for ancient people who required ways to understand relics they found in their landscape and to reconcile them with their own activities (also Thomas 1999). Different responses to this challenge were possible, and all probably occurred at some times and places. Ancient people destroyed or obscured archaeological materials on some occasions, signalling alterations of ideology and social practices. Examples of this include battering away of rock surfaces which once contained art and painting over rock art with different images. Another response was to copy older materials or duplicate the actions that produced relics. In this case there may not be continuity in the cultural meanings attributed to objects, as new perceptions or beliefs could be attached to copied objects or actions. Imitation of earlier events and items was not always faithful, and consequently details or associations could diverge through a series of reproductions. Acts of simulation occurred in many contexts, repainting earlier paintings or recreating old motifs in new paintings, adding material to earth or shell mounds, replicating scavenged artefacts, and burying people in places that already contained human remains. An additional way ancient humans could respond was by creating their own interpretations of the archaeological materials in their landscape. Later people, with ideologies and social practices different from the earlier humans who created the archaeological record, could reinterpret relics in ways that reflected their perceptions of the world. While archaeological materials were created to represent a particular view, subsequent generations may have developed other understandings of the objects they viewed.

The cumulative results of responses to echoes of the past helped create patterns archaeologists find in the archaeological record. This process is exemplified by human skeletons and painted art, evocative archaeological materials which may always have elicited responses from ancient people. In the case of skeletons, Littleton and Allen (2007) suggest the discovery of a burial sometimes provoked people to consider it a suitable location to inter further bodies, thereby creating a cluster of burials without conceiving of the place as a formal cemetery or a symbol of land ownership. Persistence of burials at places such as Roonka does not, therefore, compel archaeologists to interpret it in terms of either alliance formation or intensification. Indeed, the occupation debris at Roonka is consistent with the hypothesis that during the past 6,000–7,000 years the place was visited only periodically, and after each period of non-use (lasting generations or centuries) people revisiting the river flat chose to camp or to bury their dead, depending on what materials they saw.

The echo principle would also have been involved in the construction of rock art. In the same way that visible burials could encourage further bodies to be interred at one location the existence of rock art could influence artists to use or avoid particular places. Artists chose to cover or to avoid existing images. More significantly, rock paintings and engravings had the potential to influence many generations of artists who observed them. The continued visibility of rock art may sometimes have had a stabilizing influence on the way an image was presented, by preserving a record of the way it had been presented in the past. However, the meaning or interpretation of those images remained mutable and new understandings of the phenomenon being represented could emerge. This is difficult for archaeologists to discern, but we can identify when artistic performances were not accurate replicas of earlier versions, leading to transformation or diversification of particular motifs through time, as newer, modified images became new references for later generations. Consequently alterations in the way an image was created can sometimes reflect modifications to its meaning but sometimes it may occur haphazardly without a coherent shift in the interpretation of the art; while persistence of an image over time is no guarantee that its cultural meaning remained stable. Despite this mutable association between images and their cultural meanings it is still true that modifications in the performance of rock art is a change of cultural practice, and in that sense rock art informs archaeologists about alterations in ancient social life, even if the cultural practice was not directly related to changes in the system of inter-group interactions or alliance formation. An example of the modification and diversification of rock art images exists in western Arnhem Land, where preserved paintings provide insights into the emergence and subsequent transformation of what was an important religious concept in the historical period. This example also introduces another aspect of social life, namely its articulation with environmental and economic changes in ancient Australia. Cultural practices such as art were not only shaped by social interactions and observations of relics, but also created in the context of people's interpretation of the environments they experienced and used.

Emergence and transformation of Rainbow Serpent imagery

Rock art gives archaeologists the opportunity to trace the antiquity and transformation of motifs that carry social and religious meanings in the historic period, and to reflect on the emergence of symbols and beliefs in pre-history. An outstanding example is the evidence for the emergence of Rainbow Serpent images.

Nineteenth and twentieth century Aboriginal people living in northern Australia believed that a family of mythological beings called 'Rainbow Serpents', who created the landscape during past journeys, still live in waterholes and are manifested in rainbows, crystals and other phenomena (Radcliffe-Brown 1926). In the historical period images of these ancestral beings were composite in nature, signifying their generative and transformative capacity (Taylor 1990). Painted, sinuous, elongated, snake-like animal images with pointed tails are preserved on rock faces in western Arnhem Land (Taçon et al. 1996). These are often composite images with snake-like bodies but the heads, ears and tails of other animals, and associated with depictions of what seem to be plants such as yams, waterlilies and seaweed (Figure 13.4). Paintings with these attributes are recognized by historical Aborigines as representations of Rainbow Serpents, and so archaeologists have used these attributes to recognize ancient representations of these creatures on rock faces (Taçon et al. 1996).

The oldest depiction of a Rainbow Serpent recorded in Arnhem Land was probably made in the early-Holocene (Chippindale et al. 2000) and painted in a style called the 'Yam' phase by archaeologists because many images seem to depict or allude to yams. Earlier 'Dynamic Figure' paintings, generally accepted to be terminal Pleistocene in age, contain images of snakes but no recognizable Rainbow Serpents (Taçon et al. 1996). Consequently the invention of this motif, at least not with recognizable similarities to modern imagery, occurred in the early-Holocene.

Analyses of Rainbow Serpent rock paintings by Taçon, Wilson and Chippindale (1996) indicated that those made in the Yam phase were standardized, coherent representations and were probably examples of the first Serpent motifs made. Taçon and his colleagues hypothesized that elements of Rainbow Serpent mythology and imagery originated in the early- or mid-Holocene. That conclusion does not mean the historical cosmology of the Rainbow Serpent, or even involving ancestral beings, was in place more than 6,000 years ago. If these images had been created to represent an earlier ideology they could have been appropriated to depict

A Yam phase   **B Modern phase**

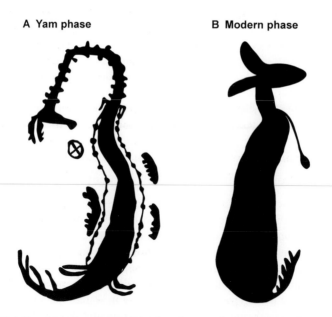

Figure 13.4 Two examples of painted Rainbow Serpents from western Arnhem Land: A = from the Yam phase; B = a 'Modern' phase painting (redrawn from Taçon et al. 1996).

Rainbow Serpents at a later time, a possibility raised by the chronological transformations discussed below. While recognizable Rainbow Serpent motifs were present in the early-Holocene we cannot claim that the historical mythologies attached to those motifs are necessarily that old.

Painted Rainbow Serpents in Arnhem Land show many variations in the elements used to construct the composite images. Some have a marine theme, such as Figure 13.4A which Taçon et al. (1996) interpreted as something like a seahorse surrounded by what could be sea urchins (spoked circles), sea cucumbers (comblike objects) and seaweed (trailing). Other paintings have terrestrial themes, such as Figure 13.4B which shows a Serpent with a rotund body, head and ears like a kangaroo and a bulging chest resembling an emu. The variety of painted Rainbow Serpents illustrates the rich and flexible symbolic code embedded in artistic activities, and still exists in historical painting, but it also reveals changes in the way these beings were depicted.

Archaeologists divided the Holocene rock art in western Arnhem Land into a number of phases (e.g. Brandl 1973; Chaloupka 1984, 1985, 1993; Lewis 1988; Chippindale and Taçon 1998). The earliest Rainbow Serpent paintings come from the Yam phase, painted at or immediately before the time of estuarine inundation, approximately 5,000–12,000 years bp. Yam phase paintings showed unusual activities, unfamiliar motifs, and superseded weapons. Historical Aborigines claimed this art had been made, not by their ancestors, but by Mimi people who they believed had lived in the land before them (Brandl 1973). Such statements about Mimi art measure the extent of Holocene cultural change, making Yam phase paintings seem culturally strange and distant to recent Aboriginal people. Later phases of rock art, often with elaborate multicoloured, cross-hatching infill and X-ray conventions, was analysed as a single group which Taçon, Wilson and Chippindale called 'Modern'. Rainbow Serpents painted in the manner of this Modern phase are probably of late-Holocene in age, no more than 3,500–4,000 years old.

Taçon et al. (1996) examined chronological change in Rainbow Serpent paintings by comparing those made in the early-Holocene Yam phase with later ones from the Modern phase. Figure 13.5 shows the result, and because the Modern images plot on the right of this figure and the Yam images on the left, they concluded that earlier paintings were on the left while later ones were those on the right. Paintings furthest to the left have a combination of distinctive features, including long, tubular noses, heads bent down towards their chest, an elongated and curving body, small spines protruding from the neck and body, a curving tail with spines, and small projecting ears, sometimes with long trailing appendages (e.g. Figure 13.4A). These features are all found on marine animals belonging to the family *Syngnathidae*, such as seahorses and pipefish. The earliest painted Rainbow Serpents therefore resemble seahorses, and Taçon et al. (1996) concluded that Rainbow Serpents were initially modelled on such creatures, perhaps with additional characteristics from water pythons. Images of seahorse-like Rainbow Serpents were first painted when rising seas inundated local lands, transforming the northern environment from inland woods and plains to coastal embayments and beaches. Taçon and his colleagues hypothesized that the concept of Rainbow Serpents was invented at that time of environmental change; as the bizarre and unfamiliar image of seahorse-like animals, representing the new seascape, was combined with more familiar images of snakes to produce a composite imaginary creature by people

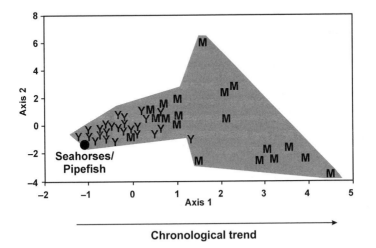

Figure 13.5 Simplified version of the correspondence analysis graph presented by Taçon et al. (1996: Figure 13), showing the distribution of Rainbow Serpent images from the Yam and Modern phases in relation to the position of seahorses/pipefish: Y = Yam figure; M = Modern figure.

seeking a metaphor for and symbol of the disruption and transformation of their world. Perhaps the generative power assigned to Rainbow Serpents and the associations of those beings with water bodies emerged in the context of the watery rebirth of the modern continental margins during the early-Holocene?

After Rainbow Serpent images were invented representations of this kind of composite creature were modified throughout the Holocene. Late-Holocene images of Rainbow Serpents no longer had the seahorse-like features (Figure 13.4A), but instead were painted with characteristics of kangaroos and crocodiles (Figure 13.4B), indicating that over time the features of different animals were substituted for the earlier conventions, creating more varied depictions of Rainbow Serpents in recent millennia (Taçon et al. 1996). While this could indicate a gradual drift away from the original conceptualization of these beings, for no particular reason except the well-documented plasticity of image transmission (Gombrich 1965), chronological change in representations may also reveal changes in ideology. Alterations and elaboration of Rainbow Serpent mythology over time might be implicated in the transfiguration of painted images. In the sub-coastal region of western Arnhem Land sediment accumulation in the large river valleys replaced open water and mangrove forests with unproductive sedge and grassland plains during the late-Holocene, and modifications to Rainbow Serpent imagery at that time might reflect reworking of symbolism in response to perceptions about the altered environment and associated social disruption. Even during the historical period representations of Rainbow serpents were modified, by the addition of water-buffalo horns for example, suggesting that changes in past physical and social environments may have been rapidly reflected in the iconography of Rainbow Serpents.

The development of Rainbow Serpent images in western Arnhem Land gives archaeologists an insight into social and ideological change. From their initial production in the early-Holocene there were regular transformations in the way these paintings were performed, perhaps signifying a series of changes in the nature or social uses of mythologies associated with them. In this region ideological change, along with economic change, does not appear to be limited to the late-Holocene, or to any single period, but would have been ongoing. More significantly, in this landscape there are observable articulations between all domains of cultural change and environmental reconfigurations: when artistic and ideological changes occurred there were also alterations in foraging, settlement and technology (see Chapter 9; Hiscock 1999). This raises the question of how environmental and economic factors are connected to social change.

Social change, economy and the environment

The fundamental tenets of the alliance model, that past cultural change was often mediated through processes of political interactions and reconceptualized through transformations of ideology, and that these social dynamics have implications for settlement and economy, cannot be dismissed. However, it is diversity rather than uniformity that characterizes processes of social change in Australian prehistory. The proposition that there was a single period of social reorganization, a single mechanism by which it happened, and a single cause for change seems unwarranted.

While ideology and social life is difficult to study from material residues, archaeological evidence indicates that dynamic social change occurred throughout Australian pre-history rather than everywhere being restricted to the late-Holocene. Better preservation of late-Holocene materials, as well as its temporal proximity to ethnographic observations, led some researchers to infer increased economic specialization and efficiency, enduring population growth, intensified ritual practices, the onset of social closure and greatly heightened sedentism in that period. The evidence for all of those conclusions is equivocal. Reviews of archaeological evidence in previous chapters have shown claims for a substantial reorganization of life ways only in the late-Holocene have little empirical support, although regional fluctuations in foraging strategies, settlement systems, technological emphasis and population size undoubtedly occurred. In this chapter the same conclusion has been reached for social change and the mechanisms for social change. Evidence for altered symbolism and belief, and modifications of social practice, are known from the Pleistocene and early-Holocene, and acknowledging the poor preservation of those early residues there is no reason to assert that change was limited to the last millennia.

There were multiple dimensions to cultural change, and territorial tethering and social permeability of territory boundaries are not the only processes that were involved. Furthermore, geographical and chronological differences in the nature and cause of social change are likely. Reconstructions of, and explanations for, ancient social activities may be sound for one region without necessarily being applicable to the continent as a whole. For instance, there is no reason why Taçon's (1993) inference of decreased territory size as a consequence of increased environmental productivity could not be correct for Arnhem Land while on Cape York David and Lourandos' (1998, 1999) suggestion that decreased territory size followed from reduced environmental productivity which stimulated changed social strategies might also be correct. This possibility was denied by archaeologists who argued that explanations of pre-historic life in Australia should consider all regions simultaneously and that a common process of change would be found in all regions (e.g. Lourandos and Ross 1994). While the purpose of this argument was to focus attention on the 'general patterns' it effectively denied multiple, divergent or asynchronous evolutionary trajectories by asserting that regional differences in pre-historic life were merely variants of a single process of change. This perspective encouraged researchers in the 1980s and 1990s to presume that only one process could have caused economic and social changes across the continent and to debate which process should be invoked. These debates polarized between archaeologists who saw the articulation of economic, environmental and social domains in different ways: those who advocated simple materialistic or Marxist-like models in which material conditions like environmental change or population growth were the primary reasons for the configuration of social life (e.g. Beaton 1983; Rowland 1989, 1999), and those who believed ecological relationships were less important in the formation of social life than the imperatives of social and political dimensions (e.g. Lourandos 1984; Lourandos and Ross 1994; David 2002). Advocates of each viewpoint asserted the priority of one domain as agent of change but none offered a compelling reason why the reorganization of cultural life in all places and times had been triggered in the same way. Since the economic strategies of historical Aborigines are embedded in social practices, and social interactions always have economic dimensions, the idea that archaeologists could simply disentangle a web of relationships to distinguish cause and effect is unrealistic, especially when ancient forager life is viewed through material debris with low chronological resolution.

Claims about the causal role of social processes or responses to environment that are embedded within debates of the intensification model centre on questions of whether events and trends in history, and pre-history before it, were caused by material forces or alternatively by ideas and social interactions. This is an unnecessary contrast because both phenomena were perpetually present in ancient foraging life and each shaped the other. As Anthony Giddens (1984) argued, social life and social structures reflect complicated interactions between behaviour and social forces; social structures are reproduced or changed as people repeat or alter their acts. As social and physical contexts alter, social life can be transformed, not merely in response to new economic activities, or despite them, but in articulation with them. It is valuable to understand altered social life as not being a direct and automatic consequence of changed social structure (say, open or closed territoriality in the alliance model), but as modified social practices that emerge from the interaction of multiple phenomena. The articulation of ideology with economy and settlement illustrates this point.

Archaeological evidence of the invention and evolution of Rainbow Serpent imagery, and by implication attached mythologies, illustrates the entanglement of environment, economy, social life and ideology, and how that offers archaeologists a way to understand ancient social change. Taçon, Wilson and Chippindale concluded that this imagery emerged at a time of substantial environmental change, suggesting that the initial choice of the representation in the early-Holocene symbolized the social and ideological transformations that were occurring. Subsequent transformations of painted Rainbow Serpent images were associated with the restoration of more terrestrial landscapes, and in the historical period with yet further economic and social changes. These connections between environmental and ideological transformations do not imply there was a simple causal relationship; instead they indicate the articulation of social worlds to the physical one. Such articulations are visible in historical Aboriginal societies, where myth is credited with a variety of roles in expressing and managing social/ideological tensions associated with ongoing political and economic change (e.g. Morphy 1990; Swain 1993). Comparable articulations between landscape, economy, and social practice in the past are indicated in the archaeological sequence of Arnhem Land in repeated, seemingly linked, transformations of both art and economy. The regularity with which the domains of economy, ecology and social practice appear to be articulated in the archaeological record points to them often being entangled in the past. Archaeologists need not single out one as the universal cause of change in the social lives of ancient people. Regular connections of transformed ideology and belief in pre-historic Australia with modified systems for exploiting the environment are described in the following chapter as a way to explore the dynamic and articulated character of culture change in the last millennium.

14 The ethnographic challenge

Change in the last millennium

From the initial movements of people into the already ancient Australian landscape until shortly before European settlement and the beginning of historical texts, archaeological evidence gives us reason to imagine that past societies changed regularly and were noticeably different from those in the historic period. At the start of this book rapid, far-reaching social and economic changes following the transmission of disease to Aboriginal people during the eighteenth and nineteenth centuries illustrated the magnitude of alterations that took place within a short time. The book now returns to a consideration of economic, technological and social transformations that had occurred within Aboriginal cultures in the centuries immediately before the arrival of Europeans.

Not only does the end of the pre-historic period complete the chronological journey upon which this book is structured, but also consideration of life in the last millennium allows issues already raised to be pursued further. One issue that can be clarified is the speed and interconnectedness of changes in Aboriginal life. For earlier time periods it is difficult to see details of rapid changes in Aboriginal society and economy because they are veiled by the effects of reduced preservation and imprecise dating. Chronological uncertainties and destruction of ancient materials are ever present, but they are often more mildly expressed for relatively recent sites, particularly those created in the past thousand years. In several regions extensive archaeological excavations combined with relatively high resolution radiocarbon dates or historic records make it possible to evaluate the speed and magnitude of transformations in the ways people exploited their environment and perceived their world.

Case studies from northern Australia are used to explore the timing, scale and process of culture change during the last millennium. These studies from northern Australia exemplify the variety and multiplicity of transformative events that took place in any single part of the landmass; they do not indicate that changes identical in nature or timing occurred across the continent since regional variations are known.

Insights into cultural change in the north emerge from the contrast between the lives of Aboriginal people recorded in the historical period and the archaeological evidence for the lives of people who lived in the same place a few hundred years earlier. Historical and archaeological data are different records of life but they can sometimes be used to shed light on the same aspect of human behaviour. Across tropical Australia archaeological studies which contrast landscape use in historic and pre-historic times indicate that changes in land use reflect not only economic shifts in Aboriginal foragers but also transformations in their cosmology and social life. This observation reinforces and extends the image of entangled social, economic and ideological practices.

Economy and settlement changes during the past thousand years provide information about the ongoing evolution of Aboriginal life ways, and potentially about processes of culture change earlier in pre-history. One proposition emerging from studies of this recent period is that economic alterations in foraging and land use were not isolated from other domains of cultural practice; they were associated with the ways Aboriginal people interacted socially and viewed their interactions. Connections between social, ideological and economic spheres would also have existed in earlier times, throughout Australian pre-history, as foraging activities supported and shaped social lives while cosmology and social interactions represented and reconciled people's understandings of their world with their landscape, economic lives, and social structures. The entanglement of economy with cosmology and social life meant that a change in one cultural domain would often have been accompanied by changes in the others. Ideology and social and political relationships may have been modified if there were substantial alterations to land use and settlement, just as economic and foraging activities might have been restructured to conform to modified social interactions between people and their perceptions of the world. These interconnections are visible in studies of the millennium prior to European contact. An example of the way land use changed was when Aboriginal people began to believe that Ngarrabullgan was a dangerous place.

When 'danger' emerged at Ngarrabullgan

Within the last millennium Aboriginal settlement on northeastern Cape York was restructured (Figure 14.1). Cosmology of the historical Aboriginal community focused on a singular landscape feature (David and Wilson 1999). Rising from a landscape of low rolling hills, open ironbark woods and seasonal streams is a stunning table-top mountain called Ngarrabullgan by the local Djungan people. Ngarrabullgan is a sandstone plateau, surrounded by difficult-to-climb cliffs more than 200 metres high, creating a visible landmark (Figure 14.2). The mountain is large, nearly 18 km long and 6 km wide, and the vegetation on top is different from that of the surrounding environment. Very few species of terrestrial animals now exist on top of the mountain and hunting on the plateau was probably unproductive throughout the Holocene. By contrast water was plentiful on the top of the mountain, where there were many permanent waterholes.

In the historic period it was these waterholes on Ngarrabullgan that were the focus of Djungan mythological stories. In the early years of the twentieth century Francis Richards (1926) recorded Aboriginal stories about supernatural

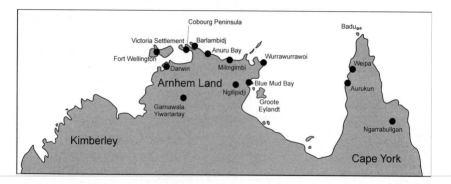

Figure 14.1 Localities discussed in Chapter 14.

beings living on the mountain. At the end of the twentieth century Bruno David was told similar stories about spirit-beings inhabiting waterholes on Ngarrabullgan (David and Wilson 1999). These stories, heard at either end of the twentieth century, reveal that Djungan people believed the mountain was a dangerous place because two malevolent spirits were believed to exist there. One was a water-being called Mooramully, who resided in waterholes on Ngarrabullgan and drowned or sickened people who swam there. This magically powerful creature was associated with the knowledge and abilities of local shamans. A second, even more dangerous, dreaming-being named Eekoo was associated with the transformation of Ngarrabullgan into the isolated plateau we see nowadays. An origin story described how, in the Dreaming, the mountain was created by wallabies, and inhabited by the swamp pheasant. Eekoo found the pheasant's nest and killed its young, but the pheasant retaliated by burning the bush in an attempt to kill Eekoo. The fire was so hot it melted the rock and created the mountain cliffs. To escape the blaze Eekoo made a lake on Ngarrabullgan and sheltered in the waters. Eekoo lives there still, but it is able to roam across the mountain top and can injure or sicken people who climb Ngarrabullgan. Modern Djungan people consider the mountain is a dangerous place and visit the top infrequently and cautiously, warning the spirits of their approach and intentions (David and Wilson 1999). Irregular use of Ngarrabullgan in historical times is a signature of the danger that modern Aboriginal people with Mooramully and Eekoo mythologies believed existed in that landscape.

Archaeologists have used this signature of land use to estimate the antiquity of the historical cosmology. In a cleverly designed investigation Bruno David sought evidence for the history of occupation on the mountain (David 1993, 1998, 2002, 2006; Fullagar and David 1997; David and Lourandos 1999; David and Wilson 1999). If Ngarrabullgan had always been regarded as the home of dangerous supernatural beings it would always have had only low levels of human visitation, but if the cosmology associating dangerous spirits with the mountain began at some time the archaeological record should reveal a period of more intensive exploitation followed by an abandonment or reduction of occupation when it began to be perceived as a hazardous area.

Figure 14.2 The table-top mountain called Ngarrabullgan. (Courtesy of B. David.)

To reconstruct a pre-history of land use at Ngarrabullgan, David excavated a number of rock shelters on the top of the plateau. All shelters revealed the same sequence of occupation. People had camped on the mountain, building fireplaces and earth ovens lined with paperbark or hearthstones. Microscopic studies of stone artefacts show that many different tasks were carried out in the largest site, Ngarrabullgan Cave, and archaeologists concluded that such sites were base camps at which people stayed for some time. However, concentrated occupational debris stopped near the top of each deposit, indicating that human visitation declined or ceased at the same time everywhere on the mountain. The last occupation at Ngarrabullgan Cave occurred 450–750 years ago, at Tunnel Shelter 600–800 years ago, at Bush Peg Shelter 450–600 years ago; at Grass Tree shelter, occupation ceased 600–800 years ago, and so on. David and Wilson (1999) concluded that about 600–700 years ago frequent occupation of the mountain top ceased and in the last 600 years Aboriginal visits were short and infrequent.

Abandonment of Ngarrabullgan marks the beginning of the modern land use pattern, and may signal the creation of the modern Djungan beliefs that an evil spirit inhabits the mountain top. This conclusion implies that current Djungan Dreaming mythology about Mooramully and Eekoo emerged only 600 years ago, and was part of a redefinition of Aboriginal world views associated with an altered pattern of regional land use.

What caused those changes at Ngarrabullgan is unknown. Local environmental changes 600–800 years ago are not known, and freshwater lakes and waterholes on the plateau were at that time more reliable than elsewhere in the area. Perhaps the abandonment of Ngarrabullgan arose solely from cultural redefinitions of the local world, a social process not stimulated by climatic alterations? Yet abandonment of the mountain may also have reflected economic factors. For instance, marsupial species whose bones are found within the archaeological deposits are now very rare or extinct on the mountain, indicating that reduced human use of the area followed a reduction in the availability of animals – perhaps through over-hunting. Furthermore, abandonment of Ngarrabullgan was accompanied by a similar reduction of human use in the surrounding region, and so these decreases in land use may have been articulated to change in a larger economic system. Whatever the causes for the abandonment of Ngarrabullgan may have been it seems that use and perceptions of the landscape were closely connected. David and Wilson (1999) state that irrespective of the cause, what we are seeing at Ngarrabullgan is the conjunction of altered settlement and the initiation of new cosmologies: transformed ideology mediated the reorganization of the cultural system.

Antiquity of remembered landscapes along the northern coast

Some researchers have argued that there were rapid, recent reconfigurations of cosmology not associated with changes in landscape or resource use. For instance, on Badu Island isolated arrangements of large trumpet shells were employed in rituals during the historical period, but radiocarbon analysis indicates that many of the still preserved trumpet shell structures were no more than 400–700 years bp. Since most trumpet shells were less than 400 years old perhaps associated rituals and ideologies developed only in the past few hundred years? Although earlier shell arrangements may have existed but not been preserved Bruno David argued they were a new phenomenon that began 400 years ago. He suggested these shell structures signified new rituals that emerged from reconceptualization of the world by island societies following the psychological trauma of the arrival of Spanish sailors in AD 1606 (David et al. 2005). He also proposed that these rituals began without associated alterations to resource use, but the collecting of hundreds of these meat-rich shells, which can be used to store water, was itself an economic activity that may have changed.

Not surprisingly, many studies, such as the research at Ngarrabullgan, demonstrate the connection of ideological and economic spheres in cultural change during the last millennium. In the historic period use and perceptions of landscape were articulated within Aboriginal cultural systems; archaeological evidence suggests these elements were often entangled in the lives of ancient Australian foragers. Cultural reorganization involving connected alterations of landscape use and landscape perceptions was repeated across the northern coastline within the last millennium (Hiscock and Faulkner 2006). Reformed resource use and reconceptualization of the environment is identified through comparisons of archaeological residues with modern Aboriginal knowledge and social interpretations of those places. The patterns found are intriguing.

Along the northern coastline historical Aboriginal people have detailed knowledge about landscapes that formed within the last millennium or so, reflected in the naming of and stories about locations. For example, near Milingimbi in Arnhem Land, Betty Meehan (1982) and Rhys Jones (1990) recorded elaborate layers of named places and stories describing the cosmology of historic An-barra people. Much of this coastal landscape was created little more than a thousand years ago and archaeological sites found on it indicate that the historically recorded economy started only about 800 years ago when freshwater foods such as turtle began being intensively harvested. Historical religious perceptions and social mapping cannot have a greater antiquity than the landscape; they are perhaps only 800–1,400 years old according to Sally Brockwell and colleagues (2005). An-barra people adapted to this new landscape not only by adjusting their foraging practices to accommodate altered resources forming within their territory but also by constructing under-standings of this landscape through the creation of place names and stories. Clearly it did not take long, in archaeological terms, for cultural systems to be reconfigured in ways which matched new environments and altered patterns of land use.

Frequent economic and ideological reorganization is seen in archaeological sequences at sites such as Garnawala and Yiwarlalay, located south of Arnhem Land (David et al. 1990, 1994, 1995; David 2002). Altered deposition of ochre frag-ments has been interpreted by Bruno David and Ian McNiven as an indication that painting styles and motifs changed on multiple occasions, about 800–900 years ago and then 100–400 years bp. They suggest changing art styles reveal modified social relationships and ideologies, and that paintings of ethnographic stories of mytho-logical beings acquired their ethnographic configuration only recently. David and McNiven argue that the latest artistic changes at Yiwarlalay reflect the emergence of new territorial markers as land use and group connections to land were reorganized following the arrival of Europeans (David et al. 1990). Chris Clarkson (2007) docu-mented alterations in stone artefact technology and landscape use at approximately the same periods (also Clarkson and David 1995). Repeatedly modified land use and ideology about the land in this region, during the last millennium, is another demonstration of the recentness of some social/cultural configurations observed historically (also Head and Fullagar 1997).

In some regions there is evidence that detailed knowledge and mythology about land was lost when land fell out of use. For example, on Groote Eylandt, the largest island in the Gulf of Carpentaria, Clarke (1994b, 2002) recorded and excavated middens known to Aboriginal people living on the island nowadays. These middens were located on the present coast, were less than 350 years old, and were considered by local Aborigines to be 'old people camps'. When Clarke surveyed away from the current coastline, in the hills towards the island centre, little used by contemporary indigenous people, she also found sites. Her excavation of two inland rock shelters showed Aboriginal people had lived there 1,000–2,000 years ago. Yet there were no oral traditions about these sites; they were not part of the remembered landscape. During the last millennium Aboriginal people who had lived in these shelters focused their activities on the coast and thereafter rarely visited inland areas. Clarke's findings indicate that the modern cultural landscape, represented by places with names and a history of occupation recalled by present-day Aborigines living on Groote Eylandt, dates to the last few hundred years.

Constructing knowledge about new physical or social environments, or losing knowledge about abandoned or altered landscapes, are aspects of the same process. Social descriptions of a landscape were required by, and facilitated, its economic exploitation. When exploitation of an environment altered, the social perceptions of foragers were reconfigured in ways that incorporated and made sense of new environmental features and resources, while knowledge about abandoned features or economic and social practices was sometimes lost or reinterpreted. Archaeological evidence from northern Australia indicates that this was not only a widespread process in the last millennium but also a rapid one, occurring in just a few generations. At Ngarrabullgan, Milingimbi and Groote Eylandt archaeologists are witnessing social mapping of territory and the construction of elaborate myth-ologies; ideological perceptions incorporated and conformed to new patterns of land and resource use and social interaction. This maintained an equilibrium between foraging practices employed at any time, the landscapes which people occupied and the ideology held by people living in a changing world.

Myths and mounds

The idea that economic activities and ideology were articulated was employed by Hiscock and Faulkner (2006) to explain how shell mounds on Australia's north coast acquired their modern mythological configurations and ritual roles. Shell mound-building economies ceased about 800 years ago as the environment altered and the *Anadara*-rich shorelines disappeared (Chapter 9). Aboriginal groups then reorganized their foraging and settlement patterns to exploit productive landscapes that remained, such as freshwater wetlands. With the disappearance of open shore-lines and the advent of freshwater habitats, foragers in many locations along the coast shifted to more diversified, less shoreline-focused foraging strategies, and perhaps to smaller residential group sizes operating within smaller and more bounded territories. Hiscock and Faulkner (2006) argue that people not only changed their exploitation of the landscape, but also altered their perceptions of it.

Indications that the environment was reconceptualized are found in historically recorded Aboriginal stories about the *Anadara* mounds. Many stories denied that shell mounds were built by people, and some stories described the mounds as being natural accumulations, resulting from either storms or animal activity. The idea that *Anadara* mounds had been built by generations of nesting scrub-fowl is one such story. More often Aboriginal creation stories explained huge piles of shell as having been made by ancestral beings. Near Aurukun, on the eastern side of Cape York, some mounds are said to mark the places where the two sisters who created Aboriginal people, camped as they journeyed across the landscape. Other mounds with elongated, sinuous shapes were described in stories as having been created by two gigantic Carpet Snakes who piled up shells with the power of their writhing. Stories explaining shell mounds in supernatural terms were also created during the twentieth century as Aboriginal people incorporated them into present beliefs, such as the creation of mounds during Noah's flood. All these stories about mounds were probably created since the termination of intensive *Anadara* harvesting and mound building.

According to Hiscock and Faulkner (2006), historical stories associated with mounds do not describe them as debris created by earlier people because those stories were constructed by foragers who did not make *Anadara* mounds and were puzzled by phenomena alien to the modern bush setting. In the past 600–800 years these mounds were anomalous features in barren salt flats or on the edges of open woodlands. At that time Aboriginal people, unfamiliar with the shell mound-building economy, encountered these curious features in unexpected environmental settings and invented explanations for them. The names and stories they attached to mounds do not directly inform us of the ideologies and activities of the mound builders; instead those origin stories reflect the concerns of newer, historically recorded social systems. The ethnographic ideational system, including many dream-time narratives about mounds, probably emerged in its current form within the past 600 years.

Recent production of mythologies about mounds is another example of the interconnectedness of altered economic practices and ideology and social perceptions, but it also illustrates again why historical social and economic systems do not give a direct insight into pre-historic life. Explaining residues of ancient life simply as a reflection of the behaviour and ideology of historically recorded societies would be anachronistic: imposing images of modern social life and cultural beliefs on ancestral societies that inhabited different physical and social environments. Instead of obscuring the past with a veil of ethnographic analogy the case studies discussed here contrast interpretations of pre-historic life ways based on archaeological evidence with historical records of Aboriginal economy and society to reveal the speed and enormity of change immediately preceding the historic period. A dramatic and detailed case study of entwined economic and ideological change during the last millennium is the response of Aboriginal people to the arrival of Macassans.

Macassan visits to Australia

British explorations on the northern coast found the signs of foreigners in many places. Matthew Flinders observed this at the dawn of the nineteenth century, as did the residents of British outposts at Fort Wellington and Victoria Settlement. Archaeologists and historians call these foreigners 'Macassans', trepang fishermen sailing from the region of Sulawesi to Australia. Our knowledge about the impact of Macassans on central and western Arnhem Land owes much to the work of Campbell Macknight (1976, 1986), who pioneered the study of Macassan sites in the 1960s, and Scott Mitchell (1994a, 1994b), whose fieldwork in the 1990s focused on the Aboriginal response to Macassan visits.

Historical records indicate that after 1720 AD fleets of Macassan boats visited Arnhem Land or the Kimberley coast (Figure 14.3). They sailed to Australia at the start of the wet season, when the monsoon winds favoured the voyage, and returned north at the end of the wet season. During their stay these fishermen camped on beaches, collecting and processing the marine creature known as 'trepang' or

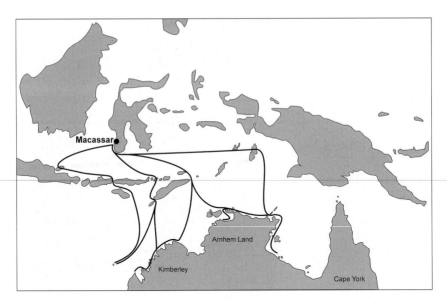

Figure 14.3 Shipping routes for trepang fishermen visiting the northern Australian coast (adapted from Morwood and Hobbs 1997). Macassar is now called Ujung Pandang.

'sea-slug'. Gutted and dried trepang were shipped back to Macassar to be sold as a delicacy to Chinese merchants.

While historians are now convinced that large-scale trepang fishing along the northern coast began in only about 1720 AD there was initially uncertainty about the antiquity of these events. Some researchers literally interpreted Aboriginal stories about a group called 'Baijini', said to have collected trepang and grown rice, as evidence that Asian fishermen had been on Australian shores for a very long time. Since 'Baijini' is a modified Macassarese word, and the historic records are unambiguous, it is more likely those stories were a transformation of recollections of Aboriginal people who saw, worked with, and sometimes even sailed with Macassans in the eighteenth century. There is no persuasive archaeological evidence for trepang encampments prior to the eighteenth century. Some radiocarbon analyses on mangrove wood charcoal found at Macassan sites gave estimates several hundred years older, but Mitchell (1994a, 1994b) argued that these values are suspect and result from technical problems with radiocarbon analysis of mangrove wood (also Morwood and Hobbs 1997). Archaeological debris from which the radiocarbon samples came are identical with Macassan material of eighteenth or nineteenth century age and it is clear that trepang fishing was initiated in the early 1700s, as the historic records indicate.

Industrial activities to preserve trepang prior to its transportation back to Macassar left an archaeological record. Ruins of processing sites are typically located on sheltered sandy beaches and headlands. The most impressive relics are stacked and arranged rocks, called *stonelines* by archaeologists, which created multiple, connected

Figure 14.4 Detail of a depiction of Macassan activities at Victoria, Port Essington, by H. S. Melville, 1845 (from *The Queen*, 8 February 1862).

fireplaces. On each fireplace gutted trepang were boiled in a large metal cauldron. Figure 14.4 reproduces a representation of Macassan industrial activities observed in 1845. In the foreground Macassans are shown placing trepang into cauldrons. The valuable cauldrons were usually carried away for further use, leaving behind only stonelines and charcoal from fires. An archaeological stoneline is shown in Figure 14.5.

Archaeological investigations also revealed the barely tangible remains of other stages in the preserving process. Trepang was dried after boiling, often placed in wooden sheds covering an artificial hollow in which a smokey fire burned. These *smokehouses* are shown in the background of Figure 14.4. At Anuru Bay, Macknight exposed the charcoal-stained depression, once surrounded by the walls of a make-shift smokehouse. This depression is visible in Figure 14.6, which shows the stained floor of Smokehouse F exposed by excavation; dark coloured sand of the floor sits on top of lighter coloured sand revealed in deeper pits towards the ocean.

Archaeological residues such as stonelines and smokehouse depressions record the intensive activities of Macassan fishermen. Scattered along large stretches of the Arnhem Land and Kimberley coasts these industrial sites were a focal point for Macassan interactions with Aboriginal people. Many kinds of contact have been documented or inferred. Both groups sometimes found trade profitable. European observers in the nineteenth century wrote of Aboriginal people giving turtle shells, pearl shells, pearls and mineral ores to Macassans in exchange for cloth, metal fish hooks, knives or axes. Aboriginal men also worked for Macassans in return for goods. Trading or working for exotic items such as metal meant an Aboriginal could

Figure 14.5 Part of one stoneline recorded at Barlambidj by Scott Mitchell. (Courtesy of S. Mitchell.)

Figure 14.6 Remains of Smokehouse F revealed by Campbell Macknight's excavations at Anuru Bay in central Arnhem Land, west of Milingimbi. (Courtesy of C. Macknight.)

acquire new tools, but additionally Mitchell suggests their social standing might be improved through their ability to give foreign artefacts to other Aboriginal people. Maintaining good relationships with Aboriginal groups was probably an advantage to Macassans who desired safety, trade and enhanced access to women or resources such as timber. However, disputes and occasionally violence between Macassans and Aborigines also occurred for a number of reasons, including access to Aboriginal women and tensions emerging from exchanges. In the nineteenth century, when written descriptions of this culture contact were made, Aboriginal societies had already been altered by a century of Macassan visits and the devastation of smallpox (Chapter 1). Archaeological and anthropological research has pieced together evidence of the magnitude of the transformation of Aboriginal societies in response to contact with Macassans.

Economic transformations at Barlambidj

A remarkable record of economic change was found by Scott Mitchell in his excavations on the Cobourg Peninsula, a tongue of land curling northwest from Arnhem Land. At Copeland Island he studied an archaeological site named Barlambidj by local Aboriginal people. Foragers had occasionally exploited this small island, even though it has no water sources, because the rock platforms, sandy beaches and nearby deep water and reefs meant abundant molluscs, fish and marine turtle were available. Aboriginal middens containing the shells of molluscs and the bones of fish and marine turtle are spread across a sandy flat on the southern edge of this island. Radiocarbon analyses of these middens indicate that Aboriginal people foraged on the island during the historical 'contact' period when Macassans visited the northern coast. At that time Barlambidj was also a Macassan processing site; six stonelines and three depressions are evidence of Macassan activities. Barlambidj was a place where Macassans and Aborigines met and lived in close proximity.

Excavating near a stoneline, hoping to obtain information about Macassan activities, Mitchell uncovered an earlier shell midden buried below the stonelines (Figure 14.7). Radiocarbon analyses indicated that the base of this buried, lower midden was 950–1,200 years old, and recorded the pre-historic foraging activities that occurred at this locality before Aborigines encountered Macassans. Evidence of food remains in the lower (pre-Macassan-contact) midden and the surface (post-Macassan-contact) midden indicates that patterns of hunting probably changed following the arrival of Macassans.

The most noticeable difference between the two middens was the increased amount of turtle caught and butchered in the historic period. In the pre-Macassan midden, turtle bone was rare; it made up only 9 per cent of all bone, whereas in the post-Macassan-contact midden turtle bone was much more common: 45 per cent of all bones came from turtles. More turtle was consumed in the historic period but there were other changes in Aboriginal diet as well. In the pre-historic period fish had been caught from many marine environments, but a more limited range of fish was recovered from the historical-age midden. We know that these dietary changes were not restricted to Aborigines living at Barlambidj because similar

Figure 14.7   Excavations at Barlambidj. (Courtesy of F. Mowat.)

evidence has been found along the Cobourg Peninsula. For example, only a tiny proportion (less than 4 per cent) of pre-Macassan-contact middens have turtle and/or dugong bones but many (53 per cent) of the later middens of the post-Macassan-contact have bones from those animals. Alterations in food consumption reflect changes in Aboriginal hunting during the last 1,000 years.

Economic change following Macassan contact

Some elements of economy show commonalities between many historical Aboriginal groups, suggesting economic practices such as the gendered division of labour are not recent, but other practices changed markedly following contact. In particular, Aboriginal coastal economies were transformed by the new technologies introduced by Macassans. Scott Mitchell argued that iron axes, fish hooks and harpoon heads obtained from Macassans altered multiple aspects of Aboriginal foraging. With metal axes it was possible to hollow out solid wooden canoes, something stone axes could not do. Because these solid canoes were seaworthy, Aborigines could row into deep, open seas and reefs in search of large marine mammals, such as sea turtles and dugong. With iron harpoon heads it became possible to efficiently kill these large animals, bigger than any available on land. With this new source of highly desired meat Aboriginal hunters became much more selective in their other hunting activities, and so fishing became less important and more focused on a few preferred species of fish. These changes in foraging and diet were connected to significant modifications to the settlement patterns of coastal Aboriginal foragers.

On the Cobourg Peninsula Mitchell found that Aboriginal camp sites from the contact period were on average almost three times the size of those created in the centuries before Macassans arrived. This probably indicates an increase in the size of residential groups and a decrease in residential mobility in the period of Macassan activity. Some large sites reflect the advantage of being near foreigners; at Macassan workshops and British towns and forts Aboriginal people could work or trade (Schrire 1972). However, other large camps are located away from places visited by foreigners, showing there was a fundamental reorganization of settlement which resulted from changes in technology, economy and political and social life.

Introduction of a new toolkit, particularly dugout canoes and metal harpoon heads, enabled Aboriginal hunters not only to increase their capture of large marine mammals but also to rapidly transport large amounts of meat from distant hunting grounds to their base camps. The foraging radius of each group was enlarged, allowing people to bring food to an encampment when they would previously have been obliged to move to a new residence in search of food. Foraging at much greater distances from each camp reduced the frequency with which people moved to new camping sites and allowed larger groups of people to camp together rather than dispersing to hunt (Hiscock 1999). Larger groups of people camped together for longer periods as an outcome of new technology, but social practices and political relationships also altered.

Social change following Macassan contact

Some social structures, such as modes of land tenure or systems of marriage and kin classification, displayed similarities across Arnhem Land in the historical period; indicating that they may have been little affected by Macassan contact. However, changes in other aspects of social life have been identified. The magnitude of social and ideological change triggered by Macassans was obvious to early anthropologists working in Arnhem Land (e.g. Thomson 1949; Berndt and Berndt 1954; Capell 1965). The production of material symbols acted as statements about Macassan contact and was involved in the mediation of social responses to it. For example, rock paintings of Macassan ships, images of vessels bringing foreigners to Aboriginal land, are a poignant symbol of this contact; painted ships obscured older motifs and expressed a new layer of cultural interaction. Painted ships have also articulated a connection between marine-oriented Aborigines and the intruders from across the sea (Clarke and Frederick 2006). Representations of ships were created using many mediums. Figure 14.8 shows one of the stone arrangements at Wurrawurrawoi, a site in eastern Arnhem Land (Macknight and Gray 1970). Made by collecting and placing stones on a flat land surface, the image is clearly a Macassan ship, and Aboriginal people labelled each of the cabins, represented by internal rows of rock, with names derived from Macassan words. This familiarity with the ships is not surprising; Aboriginal men sometimes worked on boats and even sailed back to Indonesia on them (Mountford 1956). These painting and stone arrangements involved the depiction of new images using artistic techniques long

1 metre

Figure 14.8 Plan of the stone arrangement at Wurrawurrawoi depicting a Macassan vessel, recorded by Campbell Macknight (redrawn from Macknight and Gray 1970).

used by Aboriginal people, and symbolize one way in which they reflected upon the foreigners encroaching on their land.

Macassan goods triggered altered social and political relationships. Trade networks in coastal Arnhem Land were elaborated during the contact period, with coastal sites receiving five or six times more stone artefacts from inland regions during the post-contact period than at earlier times (Mitchell 1994b). Altered trade systems across Arnhem Land following Macassan contact is also signalled in the naming of some parts of the exchange cycle using Macassan-derived words (Thomson 1949). Changed trade networks may have been triggered by the availability of desirable metal objects such as iron axes, and facilitated by reorganized settlement systems or new transport technology, but it was sustained by the incorporation of these phenomena into reconfigured social and ideological systems. In the historical period exchange operated through the social obligations between trading partners in neighbouring groups; each giving gifts in return for the ones they received, with the ability to adequately reciprocate being crucial for maintenance of social status. Control over the acquisition and transmission of new kinds of portable goods may have created temporary inequalities among individuals and groups. The value of those new trade goods was increased by their incorporation into ritual frameworks (Berndt 1951); not only making them physically desirable but also imbuing them with status and ritual connotations. Attributing symbolic values to trade items meant that local objects could be allocated prestige and significance equivalent to that of items from Macassar, thereby maintaining reciprocal interactions between coastal groups with direct access to Macassan goods and inland groups without such access. An example of the emergence of new socially valued trade objects is the manufacture of highly prized quartzite artefacts at inland Ngilipidji, and their circulation throughout the exchange cycle that operated in the twentieth century. Much of the quarrying and artefact production at Ngilipidji probably occurred after Macassan contact, as one of many responses to enlarged exchange systems developed in the eighteenth and nineteenth centuries (Thomson 1949; Mitchell 1994a, 1994b).

Macassan contact also initiated ideological changes. Some of these may have been associated with language shifts; the languages of Aboriginal people in modern

Arnhem Land contain numerous words and associated concepts derived from Macassan language and culture (e.g. Urry and Walsh 1981; Macknight 1986). Ideology and cosmology was also sometimes reorganized in association with economic practices. For example, a number of historical coastal groups, including those on the Coburg Peninsula, carried out choreographed rituals, returning turtle and dugong bones to the sea as a way of placating spirits and ensuring future hunting expeditions (McNiven 2003). Such rituals probably arose only after the initiation of Macassan contact, when turtle and dugong hunting became an important economic activity.

Macassan-triggered ideological changes can be identified in mythology. Tony Swain (1993) observed that a number of Aboriginal myths can be interpreted as metaphors of the contested coastal landscape in which Aborigines found themselves following the arrival of the Macassans. He suggested that Aboriginal groups reflected on elements of their relationship with Macassans through the construction of myth. For instance, a song recorded by Berndt (1951) described the desire of Aboriginal people to expel light-skinned trepang harvesters called 'Baijini' from their lands. In the story the ancestral beings who create Aboriginal people expel the intruders by hiding their tools and marking the land for themselves by building sand hills and covering the shores with their footprints, thereby giving the land its form and sacredness. Swain (1993) explains that this is really a story about the tensions created by co-residence of Aboriginal and Macassan people in early historical times.

Swain (1993) interpreted historically recorded Aboriginal mythology and cosmology as reflections of historical contacts with outsiders. He argued that historically recorded stories were often narratives acknowledging and commenting on strange new people, situations or ideas; the stories notionally incorporated or reconciled these novel things into existing social and belief systems. This was not principally a recent or post-contact process; an idea that would imply a static Aboriginal pre-history giving way to an active historical period of adjustment. Archaeological research reveals that readjustments of behaviour and belief to altered circumstances were an ongoing feature of Aboriginal life stretching back into prehistory. Economic and ideological changes during the last millennium discussed here are only the latest in a long sequence of adjustments made by humans in each region.

Implications of recent transformations

These are a few examples of social and economic change in the last millennium that have been recognized and discussed by archaeologists. Changes created by the introduction of animals such as water buffalo or rabbit, alterations in the rate of soil erosion, technological and social transformations following culture contact with European explorers or Melanesian sailors have been documented (e.g. Head 1994b; Head and Fullagar 1997; Rowland 1999; David 2002, 2006; David et al. 2005). It may seem that the north of the continent bore the brunt of external contacts but this intuition is not always accurate, as the evidence for the spread of diseases such as smallpox across large portions of the continent reveals. Nor is it true that culture contact is the sole trigger of social and economic change during the last millennium. Transformed land use and ideology at Ngarrabullgan and among coastal foragers after the cessation of intensive *Anadara* harvesting, both about 600–800 years ago, was not related to culture contact as far as we know; it is more likely that those changes arose from environmental and/or local social stimuli.

Archaeological and historical evidence for economic and social changes during the last millennium gives no support for claims that there was invariably one process of change or a single prime-mover in cultural reconfigurations. Economies and settlement systems were restructured over only a few decades or less, making it impractical to disentangle causes and effects with the low chronological resolution available to archaeologists. Similar rates of culture change in the past would be so fast that the processes involved could not be observed archaeologically, especially with the lower resolution available from earlier time periods. Even more significant is the evidence that economy, political interactions and ideology were often articulated during cultural changes, reinforcing the point made above, that alterations to land use and settlement were enmeshed in social and ideological reformulations. If the interconnectedness of economic practices with those in ideological and social spheres operated frequently during pre-historic cultural transformations, and available archaeological evidence suggests it may have, then there is little basis for invoking only economic or only social factors as the principal cause for all pre-historic cultural changes. In some situations, such as economic and ideological reorganization following the cessation of shell mound building, the independence of a factor such as the disappearance of habitats suitable for large *Anadara* beds, nominates it as a likely trigger, since social and ideological change did not create that landscape change. However, in many pre-historic situations the contributions of landscape use and landscape perceptions to the initiation of cultural change are not easily assessed. Furthermore, the interpretations of recent culture change presented here indicate that there were different triggering factors in different circumstances. Hence many economic, social and ideological changes occurred during pre-history but there is no reason to allocate primacy to either economic or social factors in the initiation of all cultural changes reflected in the archaeological record.

Dynamic and changing lands; dynamic and changing peoples

Diversity and rapidity of culture change over the last millennium reinforces the picture of Aboriginal Australia as a changing, varied cultural system. Archaeological evidence indicates repeated, regionally diverse cultural transformations in the Pleistocene, revealing that economic, social and ideological change was not restricted to the historical period or even recent millennia, but occurred throughout Australian pre-history. Substantial and varied alterations of land use and perceptions of landscape in the last millennium, combined with recognition that cultural change is a long-term characteristic of human occupation in Australia, suggest that the ancient human past is not merely a simplified version of historic Aboriginal societies, the theme of the first chapter in this book. The transformation of Aboriginal societies through time is the principal reason why archaeological investigations are fundamental in charting the evolution of those societies, and the grounds for being wary of interpretations of the distant past that naively employ ethnographic and ethnohistorical information.

Ancient Aboriginal people repeatedly reorganized not only their economy but also their social life and world views. Archaeological investigations document many changes in Aboriginal occupation, over both long and short periods of time. Archaeology reveals that during Australian pre-history there were ongoing modifications to foraging practices, technology, settlement and territoriality, and to social practices and the nature of cosmology and belief.

Archaeological research creates an image of a dynamic pre-historic past, a vibrant, adaptive pre-history that is congruent with the nature of Aboriginal culture observed historically. The detailed Aboriginal knowledge of local resources and elaborate naming and cosmology of their landscapes observed historically is not the result of an unchanging, ancient way of life; on the contrary it is the result of long-term, ongoing modifications of landscape perceptions, including cosmological constructions, to accommodate, shape and mediate change in the physical and social environments in which people lived. In the dynamic physical and social landscapes of ancient as well as historical Australia, people did not inflexibly retain the cultural practices they first brought to these shores. Instead the economic, technological, social and ideological character of their lives changed regularly in conformity with alterations in their context. Throughout Australian pre-history change in belief and cosmology as well as in economy and technology was the process by which people lived.

Much remains to be learned of pre-historic human life in Australia, and for many of our questions only limited evidence has been obtained, leaving aspects of the human past uncertain and mysterious. Nevertheless, much has also been revealed, and archaeological research has now shown that since the ancestors of modern Aboriginal people colonized Australia, the history of humanity in the continent has been dynamic and ever-changing, and deserving of appreciation as such. Archaeological research encourages us to celebrate change and adaptability of human life in ancient Australia, not to demand that the past be merely the same as the present world; a view that pretends Aboriginal culture (or indeed all culture) has changed little. The dynamic reality of the human past, revealed everywhere in archaeological research, is far more interesting and challenging.

Appendix
Radiocarbon dating

Varied dating techniques are used to understand the antiquity of ancient human life in Australia. Each technique is complicated and should be interpreted carefully. This appendix describes complications of interpreting radiocarbon analyses. Measuring the carbon 14 content of bones and charcoal has been convenient and cheap, but discussions of Australian pre-history must integrate radiocarbon estimates with the results of other dating analyses such as luminescence. However, radiocarbon age-estimates are not directly comparable to those created by many other techniques, because 'radiocarbon years' are not equal to calendar or solar years. Radiocarbon estimates must therefore be converted into statements about how many solar years have passed. This conversion is called 'calibration' and it has been performed on every radiocarbon estimate in the book. Until recently calibration was rarely done in Australian archaeology and uncalibrated or 'raw' radiocarbon estimates have often been employed in describing the age of objects or events. Consequently readers may at first be surprised at ages given in this text. However, recent improvements in calibration methods make it appropriate to discuss the antiquity of human life in Australia only in terms of solar years.

Radiocarbon calibration is a complex subject, and may be performed using a number of procedures and computer programs. The transformation of radiocarbon to solar estimates is sensibly described in two parts: since different approaches are used for very old samples and more recent ones. From the present back to 26,000 calendar years a reliable and internationally agreed relationship, a 'radiocarbon calibration curve', has been established between radiocarbon estimates and solar age. Using this curve radiocarbon age-estimates for archaeological material can be reliably transformed into solar dates, and readers can have a high confidence in ages calculated for that time period. However, for the period before 26,000 years the relationship between radiocarbon estimates and solar years is very complex, there are many partly contradictory lines of evidence, and no reliable calibration curve has been identified. We have only a 'radiocarbon comparison curve' (van der Plicht et al. 2004) with which to estimate the likely age of radiocarbon samples; the result gives us a rough idea of how old samples are rather than a precise and reliable calculation. Consequently, the real age of radiocarbon estimates older than 26,000 years may be revised in the future.

Radiocarbon age-estimates less than 21,000 radiocarbon years before present were calibrated with a high resolution calibration table (Reimer et al. 2004). A summary of transformations is provided in Table A.1, which illustrates the tendency for radiocarbon estimates to understate antiquity. That tendency is exaggerated through time: discrepancies between radiocarbon and solar estimates are 500 when a sample is 5,000 years ago, 1,000 when it is 10,000 years ago, and 3,000 when it is 20,000 years old. This is the reason why calibration is so necessary. Age-ranges shown in Table A.1 are small, reflecting Reimer et al.'s (2004) statistical treatment of errors; larger age-ranges are expected from many archaeological samples, especially those older than a few thousand years and those created in the pioneering days of radiocarbon analysis. On such samples large calculated uncertainties can make it difficult to easily assign a precise age. Complex statistical treatments, such as Bayesian analysis, were not attempted but have been used where cited by other researchers.

Throughout the text radiometric age-estimates have been referred to in standard ways. Where a specific radiometric date is mentioned, the calculated age in solar years is provided, followed in brackets by an age-range representing likely minimum and maximum ages as indicated by laboratory 'error values' (calculated as two

Table A.1 Radiocarbon and solar years for terrestrial samples less than 26,000 years old, based on Reimer et al. (2004)

Radiocarbon years bp	Solar years bp	Age range (cal bp)
500	525	510–540
1,000	930	915–945
1,500	1,385	1,370–1,400
2,000	1,945	1,930–1,960
2,500	2,550	2,530–2,570
3,000	3,210	2,985–3,015
3,500	3,825	3,810–3,840
4,000	4,505	3,990–4,020
4,500	5,070	5,055–5,085
5,000	5,730	5,715–5,745
5,500	6,295	6,280–6,310
6,000	6,800	6,785–6,815
6,500	7,425	7,410–7,440
7,000	7,840	7,825–7,855
7,500	8,345	8,330–8,360
8,000	8,985	8,965–9,005
8,500	9,520	9,505–9,540
9,000	10,195	10,175–10,215
9,500	10,740	10,710–10,770
10,000	11,400	11,380–11,420
12,000	13,835	13,990–13,880
14,000	16,690	16,530–16,850
16,000	19,155	19,085–19,225
18,000	21,285	21,155–21,415
20,000	23,955	23,870–24,080

standard deviations for radiocarbon). Where more generalized ages are described, established by multiple radiometric analyses or inferred on some other basis, an age-range is not given. Uncalibrated age-estimates and laboratory or sample code are not provided – a way of making the text more digestible. Researchers desiring those details should consult the original publications.

To illustrate these conventions take a sample of charcoal from Rocky Cave North cave that was analysed for radiocarbon and reported by Jones (1971). The original radiocarbon estimate was 3,430 ± 95, but is presented in this book as 3,700 (3,500–3,900), which provides the calibrated age and calculated age-range in solar years before the present. In developing these values estimated ages have been rounded to the nearest 50 years for samples less than 10,000 years old, the nearest 100 years for samples 10,000–25,000 years old, and the nearest 500 years for older samples. This rounding serves as a way to identify broad-scale trends and represent the low resolution usually available in radiometric estimates.

The discrepancy between radiocarbon estimates and solar ages cannot be simply extrapolated for samples older than 26,000 years. From 28,000 to 50,000 years ago radiocarbon estimates of age continue to underestimate the actual solar age of samples, but by similar or smaller amounts than between 20,000–28,000 years ago. For example, at 50,000 years ago the underestimation is approximately 4,500 years (Cutler et al. 2004). Calibration for this earlier time period is still desirable but inconsistency in available evidence currently prevents calibrations from being calculated. Only a 'radiocarbon comparison curve' is possible, indicating the possible magnitude of radiocarbon underestimation. Several different curves have been offered. High resolution information from around the world was examined by van der Plicht et al. (2004), who created a curve that represents the basic relationship between radiocarbon estimates and solar ages prior to 26,000 years bp. Although this curve is not a reliable calibration it can be used as an indicator of the antiquity of radiocarbon samples (Table A.2). Another comparison curve was advocated by Miller et al. (1997), based on results of amino-acid racemization in emu eggshells. Their equation was $Solar\ age\ bp = ((-5.85 * 0.000001) * y^2) + 1.39 * y) -1807$, where y is the radiocarbon date estimate. Calculated solar ages using this method are provided in Table A.2. A comparison of the van der Plicht and Miller estimates in Table A.2 reveals differences of more than 1,000 years for some time periods, reflecting variation between sources of information (Cutler et al. 2004; Southon 2004; Van der Plicht et al. 2004). This indicates that for this period any transformations of radiocarbon estimates into solar years are rough estimates and it would be spurious to treat them as precise ages of an ancient event. Some researchers argue that the current imprecision invalidates the process, and that no attempts should be made. My position for this book is that it is still valuable to estimate the solar years represented by radiocarbon analyses; the imprecision and possible inaccuracy of calculated values should be reflected in our interpretations. Consequently, radiocarbon age-estimates greater than 26,000 years old were transformed using both the van der Plicht curve and Miller's equation; when there was agreement better than a millennium between them, an age-estimate in solar years was employed. Such estimates were rounded to represent the low

Table A.2 Possible relationship between radiocarbon and solar years for terrestrial samples greater than 26,000 years old, based on van der Plicht et al. (2004) and Miller et al. (1987)

Radiocarbon years bp	Van der Plicht et al. 2004 central value	Miller et al. 1987
25,000	30,000	29,000
30,000	34,800	34,600
35,000	40,150	39,700
40,000	44,200	44,400
45,000	47,800	48,900
50,000	—	53,000
55,000	—	57,000
60,000	—	60,500

chronological resolution. Acknowledging that this procedure yields an imprecise estimate it has been adopted to facilitate the synthesis of different data sources, such as luminescence and radiocarbon assays. Using this approach broad changes in the lives of ancient people occupying Australia have been placed in a chronological framework.

References

Adcock, G. J., Dennis, E. S., Easteal, S., Huttley, G. A., Jermiin, L. S., Peacock, W. J. and Thorne, A. (2001a) 'Mitochondrial DNA sequences in ancient Australians: implications for modern human origins', *Proceedings of the National Academy of Science* 98: 537–42.

Adcock, G. J., Dennis, E. S., Easteal, S., Huttley, G. A., Jermiin, L. S., Peacock, W. J. and Thorne, A. (2001b) 'Lake Mungo 3: a response to recent critiques', *Archaeology in Oceania* 36: 170–4.

Aitken, M. (1990) *Science-based Dating in Archaeology*, London: Longman.

Akerman, K. (1978) 'Notes on the Kimberley stone-tipped spear focusing on the point hafting mechanism', *Mankind* 11: 486–9.

Akerman, K. and Stanton, J. (1993) *Riji and Jakoli: Kimberley pearlshell in Aboriginal Australia*, Monograph Series 4, Darwin: Northern Territory Museum of Arts and Sciences.

Allen, H. (1974) 'The Bagundji of the Darling Basin: cereal gatherers in an uncertain environment', *World Archaeology* 5: 309–22.

Allen, H. (1979) 'Left out in the cold: why the Tasmanians stopped eating fish', *The Artefact* 4: 1–10.

Allen, H. (1989) 'Late Pleistocene and Holocene settlement patterns and environment, Kakadu, Northern Territory, Australia', *Bulletin of the Indo-Pacific Prehistory Association* 9: 92–116.

Allen, H. (1998) 'Reinterpreting the 1969–1972 Willandra Lakes archaeological surveys', *Archaeology in Oceania* 33: 207–20.

Allen, J. (1989) 'When did humans first colonize Australia?', *Search* 20: 149–54.

Allen, J. (1994) 'Radiocarbon determinations, luminescence dating and Australian archaeology', *Antiquity* 68: 339–43.

Allen, J. and O'Connell, J. F. (2003) 'The long and the short of it: archaeological approaches to determining when humans first colonized Australia and New Guinea', *Australian Archaeology* 57: 5–19.

Allen, J. and Porch, P. (1996) 'Warragarra Rockshelter', in J. Allen (ed.) *Report of the Southern Forests Archaeological Project, Volume 1: Site Descriptions, Stratigraphies, and Chronologies*, pp. 195–217, Melbourne: School of Archaeology, La Trobe University.

Alroy, J. (2001a) 'A multispecies overkill simulations of the end-Pleistocene megafaunal mass extinction', *Science* 292: 1893–6.

Alroy, J. (2001b) 'Did human hunting cause mass extinctions?', *Science* 294: 1459–62.

Ambrose, S. H. (1998) 'Late Pleistocene human population bottlenecks, volcanic winter, and differentiation of modern humans', *Journal of Human Evolution* 34: 623–51.

Ambrose, S. H. (2001) 'Paleolithic technology and human evolution', *Science* 291: 1748–53.

Ambrose, S. H. (2003) 'Did the super-eruption of Toba cause a human population bottleneck? Reply to Gathorne-Hardy and Harcourt-Smith', *Journal of Human Evolution* 45: 231–7.

Anderson, A. (1989) *Prodigious Birds: Moas and moahunting in prehistoric New Zealand*, Cambridge: Cambridge University Press.

Anderson, A. (2002) 'Faunal collapse, landscape change and settlement history in Remote Oceania', *World Archaeology* 33: 375–90.

Andrefsky, W. (2005) *Lithics: Macroscopic approaches to analysis*, 2nd edition, Cambridge: Cambridge University Press.

Anell, B. (1960) 'Hunting and trapping methods in Australia and Oceania', *Studia Ethnographica Upsaliensia* XVIII (Sweden).

Anker, S. A., Colhoun, E. A., Barton, C. E., Peterson, M. and Barbetti, M. (2001) 'Holocene vegetation and Paleoclimatic and Paleomagnetic history from Lake Johnston, Tasmania', *Quaternary Research* 56: 264–74.

Antón, S. C. and Weinstein, K. J. (1999) 'Artifical cranial deformation and fossil Australians revisited', *Journal of Human Evolution* 36: 195–209.

Archer, M. (1977) 'Faunal remains from the excavation at Puntutjarpa Rockshelter', in R. A. Gould (ed.) *Puntutjarpa Rockshelter and the Australian Desert Culture, Anthropological Papers of the American Museum of Natural History* 54: 158–65.

Ash, J. E. and Wasson, R. J. (1983) 'Vegetation and sand mobility in the Australian desert dunefield', *Zeitschrift für Geomorphologie NF Supplementbande* 45: 7–25.

Asmussen, B. (2003) 'An archaeological assessment of rain forest occupation in Northeast Queensland, Australia', in J. Mercader (ed.) *Under the Canopy: The archaeology of tropical rain forests*, pp. 191–216, Piscataway, NJ: Rutgers University Press.

Asmussen, B. (2005) 'Dangerous harvest revisited: taphonomy, methodology and intensification in the Central Queensland Highlands, Australia', unpublished PhD thesis, Australian National University, Canberra.

Attenbrow, V. (1982) 'The archaeology of the Upper Mangrove Creek catchment: research in progress', in S. Bowdler (ed.) *Coastal Archaeology in Eastern Australia. Proceedings of the 1980 Valla Conference on Australian Prehistory*, pp. 67–78. Canberra: Department of Prehistory, Research School of Pacific Studies, Australian National University.

Attenbrow, V. (2003) 'Habitation and land use patterns in the Upper Mangrove Creek catchment, New South Wales central coast, Australia', *Australian Archaeology* 57: 20–32.

Attenbrow, V. (2004) *What's Changing: Population size or land-use patterns? The archaeology of Upper Mangrove Creek, Sydney Basin*, Terra australis 21, Pandanus Books, Canberra: Australian National University.

Bailey, G. N. (1975) 'The role of molluscs in coastal economies: the results of midden analysis in Australia', *Journal of Archaeological Science* 2: 45–62.

Bailey, G. N. (1977) 'Shell mounds, shell middens and raised beaches in the Cape York Peninsula', *Mankind* 11: 132–43.

Bailey, G. N. (1983) 'Concepts of time in Quaternary prehistory', *Annual Review of Anthropology* 12: 165–92.

Bailey, G. N. (1991) 'Hen's eggs and cockle shells: Weipa shell mounds reconsidered', *Archaeology in Oceania* 26: 21–3.

Bailey, G. N. (1994) 'The Weipa shell mounds: natural or cultural?', in M. Sullivan, S. Brockwell and A. Webb (eds) *Archaeology in the North*, pp. 107–29, Darwin: North Australia Research Unit.

Bailey, G. N. (1999) 'Shell mounds and coastal archaeology in north Queensland', in

J. Hall and I. McNiven (eds) *Australian Coastal Archaeology*, pp. 91–103, ANH Publications, Canberra: Department of Archaeology and Natural History, Australian National University.

Bailey, G. N., Chappell, J. and Cribb, R. (1994) 'Origin of *Anadara* shell mounds at Weipa, North Queensland, Australia', *Archaeology in Oceania* 29: 69–80.

Balme, J. (1980) 'An analysis of charred bone from Devil's Lair, Western Australia', *Archaeology and Physical Anthropology in Oceania* 15: 81–5.

Balme, J. (1983) 'Prehistoric fishing in the lower Darling, western New South Wales', in J. Clutton-Brock and C. Grigson (eds) *Animals and Archaeology: Shell middens, fishes and birds*, pp. 19–32, BAR International Series 183, Oxford: British Archaeological Reports.

Balme, J. (1991) 'The antiquity of grinding stones in semi-arid western New South Wales', *Australian Archaeology* 32: 3–9.

Balme, J. (1995) '30,000 years of fishery in western New South Wales', *Archaeology in Oceania* 30: 1–21.

Balme, J. (2000) 'Excavations revealing 40,000 years of occupation at Mimbi Caves, south central Kimberley, Western Australia', *Australian Archaeology* 51: 1–5.

Balme, J. and Beck, W. (1996) 'Earth mounds in southeastern Australia', *Australian Archaeology* 42: 39–51.

Balme, J. and Morse, K. (2006) 'Some Pleistocene Australian beads and their implications for human social behaviour', *Antiquity* 80: 799–811.

Balme, J., Garbin, G. and Gould, R. A. (2001) 'Residue analysis and plaeodiet in arid Australia', *Australian Archaeology* 53: 1–6.

Barham, L. S. (2002) 'Systematic pigment use in the Middle Pleistocene of South-Central Africa', *Current Anthropology* 43: 181–90.

Barker, B. (1991) 'Nara Inlet 1: coastal resource use and the Holocene marine transgression in the Whitsunday Islands, central Queensland', *Archaeology in Oceania* 26: 102–9.

Barker, B. (1996) 'Maritime hunter-gatherers on the tropical coast: a social model for change', in S. Ulm, I. Lilley and A. Ross (eds) *Australian Archaeology* 95, pp. 31–43, Tempus 6, Brisbane: Anthropology Museum, University of Queensland.

Barker, B. (1999) 'Coastal occupation in the Holocene: environment, resource use and resource continuity', in J. Hall and I. McNiven (eds) *Australian Coastal Archaeology*, pp. 119–27, ANH Publications, Canberra: Department of Archaeology and Natural History, Australian National University.

Barker, B. (2004) *The Sea People: Late Holocene maritime specialisation in the Whitsunday Islands, central Queensland*, Canberra: Australian National University.

Barker, B. C. and Schon, R. (1994) 'A preliminary assessment of the spatial distribution of stone artefacts from the South Molle Island Aboriginal Quarry, Whitsunday Islands, central Queensland coast', *Memoirs of the Queensland Museum* 37: 5–12.

Barker, G., Barton, H., Bird, M., Daly, P., Datan, I., Dykes, A. et al. (2007) 'The "human revolution" in lowland tropical Southeast Asia: the antiquity and behavior of anatomically modern humans at Niah Cave (Sarawak, Borneo)', *Journal of Human Evolution* 52: 243–61.

Barnovsky, A. D., Koch, P. L., Feranec, R. S., Wing, S. L. and Shabel, A. B. (2004) 'Assessing the causes of late Pleistocene extinctions on the continents', *Science* 306: 70–5.

Barrows, T. T., Stone, J. O., Fifield, L. K. and Cresswell, R. G. (2001) 'Late Pleistocene glaciation of the Kosciuszko Massif, Snowy Mountains, Australia', *Quaternary Research* 55: 179–89.

Barrows, T. T., Stone, J. O., Fifield, L. K. and Cresswell, R. G. (2002) 'The timing of the last glacial maximum in Australia', *Quaternary Science Reviews* 21: 159–73.

Barrows, T. T., Stone, J. O. and Fifield, L. K. (2004) 'Exposure ages for Pleistocene periglacial deposits in Australia', *Quaternary Science Reviews* 23: 697–708.

Beaton, J. M. (1977) 'Dangerous harvest: investigations in the late prehistoric occupation of upland south-east central Queensland', unpublished PhD thesis, Australian National University, Canberra.

Beaton, J. M. (1982) 'Fire and water: aspects of Australian Aboriginal management of cycads', *Archaeology in Oceania* 17: 51–8.

Beaton, J. M. (1983) 'Does intensification account for changes in the Australian Holocene archaeological record?', *Archaeology in Oceania* 18: 94–7.

Beaton, J. M. (1985) 'Evidence for a coastal occupation time-lag at Princess Charlotte Bay (North Queensland) and implication for coastal colonization and population growth theories for Aboriginal Australia', *Archaeology in Oceania* 20: 1–20.

Beaton, J. M. (1991a) 'Wanderer's Cave and Rainbow Cave: two rockshelters in the Carnarvon Range of Central Queensland', *Queensland Archaeological Research* 8: 3–33.

Beaton, J. M. (1991b) 'Cathedral Cave: a rockshelter in Carnarvon Gorge, Queensland', *Queensland Archaeological Research* 8: 33–84.

Beck, W. (1992) 'Aboriginal preparation of Cycas seeds in Australia', *Economic Botany* 46: 133–47.

Beck, W., Fullagar, R. and White, N. (1988) 'Archaeology from ethnography: the aboriginal use of cycad as an example', in B. Meehan and R. Jones (eds) *Archaeology with Ethnography: An Australian perspective*, pp. 137–47, Canberra: Department of Prehistory, Research School of Pacific and Asian Studies, Australian National University.

Bednarik, R. G. (1994) 'A taphonomy of palaeoart', *Antiquity* 68: 68–74.

Bednarik, R. G. (1997) 'Pleistocene stone pendant from Western Australia', *Australian Archaeology* 45: 32–4.

Bellwood, P. (1997) 'Prehistoric cultural explanations for widespread language families', in P. McConvell and N. Evans (eds) *Archaeology and Linguistics: Aboriginal Australia in global perspectives*, pp. 123–34, Melbourne: Oxford University Press.

Bellwood, P. and Hiscock, P. (2005) 'Australia and the Austronesians', in C. Scarre (ed.) *The Human Past. World prehistory and the development of human societies*, pp. 264–305, London: Thames & Hudson.

Berndt, R. M. (1951) 'Ceremonial exchange in Western Arnhem Land', *Southwestern Journal of Anthropology* 7: 171–3.

Berndt, R. M. and Berndt, C. H. (1954) *Arnhem Land: Its history and its people*, Melbourne: Cheshire.

Bettinger, R. L. (1991) *Hunter-gatherers: Archaeological and evolutionary theory*, New York: Plenum Press.

Bird, C. F. M. and Frankel, D. (1991a) 'Chronology and explanation in western Victoria and south-east South Australia', *Archaeology in Oceania* 26: 1–16.

Bird, C. F. M. and Frankel, D. (1991b) 'Problems in constructing a prehistoric regional sequence: Holocene south-east Australia', *World Archaeology* 23: 179–92.

Bird, D. W. and Bird, R. B. (2005) 'Evolutionary and ecological understandings of the economics of desert societies: comparing the Great Basin USA and the Australian deserts', in P. Veth, M. Smith and P. Hiscock (eds) *Desert Peoples: Archaeological perspectives*, pp. 81–99, Oxford: Blackwell.

Bird, M. I., Turney, C. S. M., Fifield, L. K., Smith, M. A., Miller, G. H., Roberts, R. G. and Magee, J. W. (2003) 'Radiocarbon dating of organic- and carbonate-carbon in *Genyornis* and *Dromaius* eggshell using stepped combustion and stepped acidification', *Quaternary Science Reviews* 22: 1805–12.

Bird, M. K. (1992) 'The impact of tropical cyclones on the archaeological record: an Australian example', *Archaeology in Oceania* 27: 75–86.

Birdsell, J. B. (1953) 'Some environmental and cultural factors influencing the structuring of Australian Aboriginal populations', *American Naturalist* 87: 171–207.

Birdsell, J. B. (1957) 'Some population problems involving Pleistocene Man', *Cold Spring Harbor Symposia on Quantitative Biology* 22: 47–69.

Birdsell, J. B. (1967) 'Preliminary data on the trihybrid origins of the Australian Aborigines', *Archaeology and Physical Anthropology in Oceania* 2: 100–55.

Birdsell, J. B. (1977) 'The recalibration of a paradigm for the first peopling of Greater Australia', in J. Allen, J. Golson and R. Jones (eds) *Sunda and Sahul: Prehistoric studies in Southeast Asia, Melanesia and Australia*, pp. 113–67, London: Academic Press.

Bleed, P. (2002) 'Cheap, regular, and reliable: implications of design variation in Late Pleistocene Japanese microblade technology', in R. G. Elston and S. L. Kuhn (eds) *Thinking Small: Global perspectives on microlithization*, pp. 95–102, Archaeological Papers of the American Anthropological Association (AP3A) 12, Arlington, VA: American Anthropological Association.

Blumstein, D. T. (2002) 'Moving to suburbia: ontogenetic and evolutionary consequences of life on predator-free islands', *Journal of Biogeography* 29: 685–92.

Blumstein, D. T. and Daniel, J. C. (2002) 'Isolation from mammalian predators differentially affects two cogeners', *Behavioural Ecology* 13: 657–63.

Blumstein, D. T., Daniel, J. C. and Mclean, I. G. (2001) 'Group size effects in quokkas', *Australian Journal of Zoology* 49: 641–9.

Blumstein, D. T., Daniel, J. C., Mari, M., Daniel, J., Ardron, J. G., Griffin, A. S. and Evans, C. S. (2002) 'Olfactory predator recognition: wallabies may have to learn to be wary', *Animal Conservation* 5: 87–93.

Bocek, B. (1986) 'Rodent ecology and burrowing behaviour: predicted effects on archaeological site formation', *American Antiquity* 51: 589–602.

Bourke, P. (2004) 'Three Aboriginal shell mounds at Hope Inlet: evidence for coastal, not maritime Late Holocene economies on the Beagle Gulf mainland, northern Australia', *Australian Archaeology* 59: 10–22.

Bourke, P. (2005) 'Archaeology of shell mounds of the Darwin coast: totems of an ancestral landscape', in P. Bourke, S. Brockwell and C. Fredericksen (eds) *Darwin Archaeology: Aboriginal, Asian and European heritage of Australia's Top End*, pp. 29–48, Darwin: Charles Darwin University Press.

Bowdery, D. E. (1998) *Phytolith Analysis Applied to Pleistocene-Holocene Archaeological Sites in the Australian Arid Zone*, British Archaeological Reports 695, Oxford: Hedges.

Bowdler, S. (1976) 'Hook, line and dillybag: an interpretation of an Australian coastal shell midden', *Mankind* 10: 248–58.

Bowdler, S. (1977) 'The coastal colonisation of Australia', in J. Allen, J. Golson and R. Jones (eds) *Sunda and Sahul: Prehistoric studies in Southeast Asia, Melanesia and Australia*, pp. 205–46, London: Academic Press.

Bowdler, S. (1979) 'Hunter Hill, Hunter Island', unpublished PhD thesis, Australian National University, Canberra.

Bowdler, S. (1980) 'Fish and culture: a Tasmanian polemic', *Mankind* 12: 334–40.

Bowdler, S. (1981) 'Hunters in the Highlands: Aboriginal adaptations in the eastern Australian uplands', *Archaeology in Oceania* 16: 99–111.

Bowdler, S. (1984) *Hunter Hill, Hunter Island*, Terra Australis 8, Canberra: Australian National University.

Bowdler, S. (1988) 'Tasmanian Aborigines in the Hunter Islands in the Holocene: island resource use and seasonality', in G. Bailey and J. Parkington (eds) *The Archaeology of Prehistoric Coastlines*, pp. 42–52, Cambridge: Cambridge University Press.

Bowdler, S. (1990) '50,000 year-old site in Australia – is it really that old?' *Australian Archaeology* 31: 93.

Bowdler, S. (1991) 'Some sorts of dates from Malakunanja II: a reply to Roberts et al.', *Australian Archaeology* 32: 50–1.

Bowdler, S. (1999) 'Research at Shark Bay, WA, and the nature of coastal adaptations in Australia', in J. Hall and I. McNiven (eds) *Australian Coastal Archaeology*, pp. 79–84, ANH Publications, Canberra: Department of Archaeology and Natural History, Australian National University.

Bowdler, S. (2006) 'Harry Lourandos' life and work: an Australian archaeological odyssey', in B. David, B. Barker and I. McNiven (eds) *The Social Archaeology of Australian Indigenous Societies*, pp. 40–9, Canberra: Aboriginal Studies Press.

Bowdler, S. and Lourandos, H. (1982) 'Both sides of Bass Strait', in S. Bowdler (ed.) *Coastal Archaeology in Eastern Australia*, pp. 121–32, Canberra: Department of Prehistory, Research School of Pacific Studies, Australian National University.

Bowdler, S. and O'Connor, S. (1991) 'The dating of the Australian Small Tool Tradition, with new evidence from the Kimberley, W.A.', *Australian Aboriginal Studies* 1991/1: 53–62.

Bowen, G. (1998) 'Towards a generic technique for dating stone fish traps and weirs', *Australian Archaeology* 47: 39–43.

Bowler, J. M. (1983) '32 +/– 5KA – Southern Australia; Hydrologic Evidence', in J. M. A. Chappell and A. Grindrod (eds) *1983 CLIMANZ: Proceedings of the First CLIMANZ Conference, Howman's Gap, Victoria, 1981*, pp. 6–9, Canberra: Department of Biogeography and Geomorphology, Research School of Pacific Studies, Australian National University.

Bowler, J. M. (1986) 'Quaternary landform evolution', in D. N. Jeans (ed.) *The Natural Environment – A geography of Australia*, pp. 117–47, Sydney: University of Sydney Press.

Bowler, J. M. (1998) 'Willandra Lakes revisited: environmental framework for human occupation', *Archaeology in Oceania* 33: 120–55.

Bowler, J. M. and Magee, J. W. (2000) 'Redating Australia's oldest human remains: a sceptic's view', *Journal of Human Evolution* 38: 719–26.

Bowler, J. M. and Price, D. M. (1998) 'Luminescence dates and stratigraphic analyses at Lake Mungo: review and new perspectives', *Archaeology in Oceania* 33: 156–68.

Bowler, J. M. and Thorne, A. G. (1976) 'Human remains from Lake Mungo: discovery and excavation of Lake Mungo III', in R. L. Kirk and A. G. Thorne (eds) *The Origin of the Australians*, pp. 127–38, Canberra: Australian Institute of Aboriginal Studies.

Bowler, J. M. and Wasson, R. J. (1984) 'Glacial age environments of inland Australia', in J. C. Vogel (ed.) *Late Cainozoic Paleoclimates of the Southern Hemisphere*, pp. 183–208, Rotterdam: Balkema.

Bowler, J. M., Jones, R., Allen, H. and Thorne, A. G. (1970) 'Pleistocene human remains from Australia: a living site and human cremation from Lake Mungo, Western New South Wales', *World Archaeology* 2: 39–60.

Bowler, J. M., Duller, G. A. T., Perret, N., Prescott, J. R. and Wrywoll, K-H. (1998) 'Hydrologic changes in monsoonal climates of the last glacial cycle: stratigraphy and luminescence dating of Lake Woods NT, Australia', *Palaeoclimates* 3: 179–207.

Bowler, J. M., Johnston, H., Olley, J. M., Prescott, J. R., Roberts, R. G., Shawcross, W. and Spooner, N. A. (2003) 'New ages for human occupation and climatic change at Lake Mungo, Australia', *Nature* 421: 837–40.

Bradley, R. (2002) *The Past in Prehistoric Societies*, New York: Routledge.

Brandl, E. J. (1973) *Australian Aboriginal Paintings in Western and Central Arnhem Land: Temporal sequences* and elements of style in Cadell River and Deaf Adder Creek art, Canberra: Australian Institute of Aboriginal Studies.

Breen, S. (1992) 'Tasmanian Aborigines: making fire', Papers and Proceedings of the Tasmanian Historical Research Association 39: 40–3.

Brockwell, S., Meehan, B. and Ngurrabangurraba, B. (2005) 'The An-barra Archaeological Project: a progress report', Australian Aboriginal Studies 2005/1: 84–9.

Brook, B. W. and Bowman, D. M. (2002) 'Explaining the Pleistocene megafaunal extinctions: models, chronologies, and assumptions', Proceedings of the National Academy of Science 99: 14,624–7.

Brook, B. W. and Bowman, D. M. (2004) 'The uncertain blitzkrieg of Pleistocene megafauna', Journal of Biogeography 31: 517–23.

Brothwell, D. (1975) 'Possible evidence of a cultural practice affecting head growth in some late Pleistocene East Asian and Australian populations', Journal of Archaeological Science 2: 75–7.

Brown, P. (1981a) 'Sex determination of Aboriginal crania from the Murray River Valley: a reassessment of the Larnach and Freedman technique', Archaeology in Oceania 16: 53–63.

Brown, P. (1981b) 'Artificial cranial deformation: a component in the variation in Pleistocene Australian Aboriginal crania', Archaeology in Oceania 16: 156–67.

Brown, P. (1987) 'Pleistocene homogeneity and Holocene size reduction: the Australian human skeletal evidence', Archaeology in Oceania 22: 41–67.

Brown, P. (1989) Coobool Creek: a morphological and metrical analysis of the crania, mandibles and dentitions of a prehistoric Australian human population, Terra Australis 13, Canberra: Australian National University.

Brown, P. (1992a) 'Post-Pleistocene change in Australian Aboriginal tooth size: dental reduction or relative expansion?', in T. Brown and S. Molnar (eds) Human Craniofacial Variation in Pacific Populations, pp. 33–52, Adelaide: University of Adelaide.

Brown, P. (1992b) 'Recent human evolution in East Asia and Australasia', Philosophical Transactions of the Royal Society of London B 337: 235–42.

Brown, P. (1994a) 'A flawed vision: sex and robusticity on King Island', Australian Archaeology 38: 1–7.

Brown, P. (1994b) 'Human skeletons', in D. Horton (ed.) The Encyclopedia of Aboriginal Australia, Volume 1, pp. 990–1, Canberra: Australian Aboriginal Studies Press.

Brown, P. (1995) 'Still flawed: a reply to Pardoe (1994) and Sim and Thorne (1994)', Australian Archaeology 41: 26–9.

Brown, P. (2000a) 'Australian Pleistocene variation and the sex of Lake Mungo 3', Journal of Human Evolution 38: 743–9.

Brown, P. (2000b) 'The First Australians: the debate continues', Australasian Science 21(4): 28–31.

Brown, P. (2006) Peter Brown's Australian and Asian Palaeoanthropology, http://metz.une.edu.au/~pbrown3/palaeo.html.

Brown, P., Sutikna, T., Morwood, M. J., Soejono, R. P., Jatmiko, Saptomo, E. W. and Due, R. A. (2004) 'A new small-bodied hominin from the Late Pleistocene of Flores, Indonesia', Nature 431: 1055–61.

Brumm, A. and Moore, M. W. (2005) 'Symbolic revolutions and the Australian archaeological record', Cambridge Archaeological Journal 15: 157–75.

Builth, H. C. (2002) 'The archaeology and socioeconomy of the Gunditjmara: a landscape analysis from southwest Victoria, Australia', PhD thesis, Flinders University, Adelaide.

Bulbeck, D., Raghaven, P. and Rayner, D. (2006) 'Races of Homo sapiens: if not in the southwest Pacific, then nowhere', World Archaeology 38: 109–32.

Burney, D. A. and Flannery, T. F. (2005) 'Fifty millennia of catastrophic extinctions after human impacts', *Trends in Ecology and Evolution* 20: 395–401.

Burns, P. (1994) 'Mound over matter: origins of shell and earth mounds of northern Australia – an evaluation of mounds on Channel Island and Middle Arm mainland, Darwin Harbour', unpublished BA (Hons) thesis, Northern Territory University, Darwin.

Burns, P. (1999) 'Subsistence and settlement patterns in the Darwin coastal region during the late Holocene period: a preliminary report of archaeological research', *Australian Aboriginal Studies* 1999/1: 59–69.

Butlin, N. (1983) *Our Original Aggression: Aboriginal populations of south-eastern Australia 1788–1850*, Sydney: Allen & Unwin.

Butlin, N. (1985) 'Macassans and Aboriginal smallpox: the 1789 and 1829 epidemics', *Historical Studies* 21: 315–35.

Cahen, D. and Moeyersons, J. (1977) 'Subsurface movements of stone artefacts and their implications for the prehistory of central Africa', *Nature* 266: 812–15.

Cameron, D. W. and Groves, C. P. (2004) *Bones, Stones and Molecules: 'Out of Africa' and human origins*, Sydney: Academic Press.

Campbell, J. (2002) *Invisible Invaders: Smallpox and other diseases in Aboriginal Australia 1780–1880*, Melbourne: Melbourne University Press.

Capell, A. (1965) 'Early Indonesian contacts with North Australia', *Journal of the Oriental Society of Australia* 3: 69–70.

Chaloupka, G. (1984) *From Palaeoart to Casual Paintings*, Darwin: Northern Territory Museum of Arts and Sciences.

Chaloupka, G. (1985) 'Chronological sequence of Arnhem Land plateau rock art', in R. Jones (ed.) *Archaeological Research in Kakadu National Park*, pp. 269–80, Canberra: Australian National University.

Chaloupka, G. (1993) *Journey in Time: The world's longest continuing art tradition*, Sydney: Reed.

Chappell, J. (1991) 'Late Quaternary environmental changes in eastern and central Australia: their climatic interpretation', *Quaternary Science Reviews* 10: 377–90.

Chappell, J., Head, J. and Magee, J. (1996) 'Beyond the radiocarbon limit in Australian archaeology and Quaternary research', *Antiquity* 70: 543–52.

Chen, Y-S., Torroni, A., Excoffier, L., Santachiara-Benerecetti, A. S. and Wallace, D. C. (1995) 'Analyis of mtDNA in African populations reveals the most ancient of all human continent-specific haplogroups', *American Journal of Human Genetics* 57: 133–49.

Chesner, C. A., Rose, W. I., Deino, A., Drake, R. and Westgate, J. A. (1991) 'Eruptive history of earth's largest Quaternary caldera (Toba, Indonesia) clarified', *Geology* 19: 200–3.

Chippindale, C. and Taçon, P. S. C. (1998) 'The many ways of dating Arnhem Land rock-art, north Australia', in C. Chippindale and P. S. C. Taçon (eds) *The Archaeology of Rock-art*, pp. 90–111, Cambridge: Cambridge University Press.

Chippindale, C., Smith, B. and Taçon, P. S. C. (2000) 'Visions of Dynamic power: archaic rock-paintings, altered states of consciousness and 'Clever Men' in Western Arnhem Land (NT), Australia', *Cambridge Archaeological Journal* 10: 63–101.

Chivas, A. R., Garcia, A., van der Kaars, S., Couapel, M. J. J., Holt, S., Reeves, J. M. et al. (2001) 'Sea-level and environmental changes since the last interglacial in the Gulf of Carpentaria, Australia: an overview', *Quaternary International* 83–5: 19–46.

Choquenot, D. and Bowman, D. M. J. S. (1998) 'Marsupial megafauna, Aborigines and the overkill hypothesis: application of predator-prey models to the question of Pleistocene extinction in Australia', *Global Ecology and Biogeography Letters* 7: 167–80.

Clark, R. L., Guppy, J. C., Mahon, D., McBride, P. and Wasson, R. J. (1992a) 'Late Quaternary stratigraphy of the Magela plain', in R. J. Wasson (ed.) *Modern Sedimentation and Late Quarternary*

Evolution of the Magela Creek Plain, pp. 28–80, Supervising scientist for the Alligator Rivers region, Research report 6, Darwin.

Clark, R. L., Guppy, J. C., Mahon, D., McBride, P. and Wasson, R. J. (1992a) 'Late Quaternary evolution of the Magela plain', in R. J. Wasson (ed.) Modern Sedimentation and Late Quarternary Evolution of the Magela Creek Plain, pp. 81–157, Supervising scientist for the Alligator Rivers region, Research report 6, Darwin.

Clarke, A. (1994a) 'Romancing the stones. The cultural construction of an archaeological landscape in the western district of Victoria', Archaeology in Oceania 29: 1–15.

Clarke, A. (1994b) 'The winds of change: an archaeology of contact in the Groote Eylandt Archipelago, Northern Australia', unpublished PhD thesis, Australian National University, Canberra.

Clarke, A. (2002) 'The ideal and the real: cultural and personal transformations of archaeological research on Groote Eylandt, northern Australia', World Archaeology 34: 249–64.

Clarke, A. and Frederick, U. (2006) 'Closing the distance: interpreting cross-cultural engagements through indigenous rock art', in I. Lilley (ed.) Archaeology of Oceania: Australia and the Pacific islands, pp. 116–33, Oxford: Blackwell.

Clarkson, C. (2007) Lithics in the Land of the Lightning Brothers, Terra Australis 24, Canberra: Australian National University.

Clarkson, C. and David, B. (1995) 'The antiquity of blades and points revisited: investigating the emergence of systematic blade production south west of Arnhem Land, Northern Australia', The Artefact 18: 22–44.

Clarkson, C. and Wallis, L. A. (2003) 'The search for El Niño/Southern Oscillation in archaeological sites: recent phytolith analysis at Jugaliya rockshelter, Wardaman Country, Australia', in D. M. Hart and L. A. Wallis (eds) Phytolith and Starch Research in the Australian-Pacific-Asian Regions: The state of the art, pp. 137–52, Canberra: Australian National University.

Clegg, J. K. (1977) 'The four dimensions of artificial variation', in R. V. S. Wright (ed.) Stone Tools as Cultural Markers: Change, evolution and complexity, pp. 60–6, Canberra: Australian Institute of Aboriginal Studies.

Colhoun, E. A. (1992) 'Late glacial and Holocene vegetation history at Poets Hill Lake, western Tasmania', Australian Geographer 23: 11–23.

Colley, S. and Jones, R. (1987) 'New fish bone data from Rocky Cape, northwest Tasmania', Archaeology in Oceania 22: 67–71.

Collins, D. (1798) An Account of the English Colony in New South Wales, London: Cadell & Davies.

Cooper, A., Rambaut, A., Macaulay, V., Willerslev, E., Hansen, J. and Stringer, C. (2001) 'Human origins and ancient human DNA', Science 292: 1655–6.

Corbett, L. (1995) The Dingo in Australia and Asia, Sydney: University of New South Wales Press.

Cosgrove, R. (1995a) 'Late Pleistocene behavioural variation and time trends: the case from Tasmania', Archaeology in Oceania 30: 83–104.

Cosgrove, R. (1995b) The Illusion of Riches: Scale, resolution and explanation in Tasmanian Pleistocene human behaviour, BAR 608, Oxford: British Archaeological Reports.

Cosgrove, R. (1996) 'Origin and development of Australian Aboriginal tropical rainforest culture: a reconsideration', Antiquity 70: 900–12.

Cosgrove, R. (1999) 'Forty-two degrees south: the archaeology of late Pleistocene Tasmania', Journal of World Prehistory 13: 357–402.

Cosgrove, R. and Allen, J. (2000) 'Prey choice and hunting strategies in the Late Pleistocene: evidence from Southwest Tasmania', in A. Anderson, S. O'Connor and I. Lilley (eds) Histories of Old Ages: Essays in honour of Rhys Jones, pp. 397–429, Canberra: Coombs Academic Publishing, Australian National University.

Cosgrove, R. and Pike-Tay, A. (2004) 'The Middle Palaeolithic and Late Pleistocene Tasmania hunting behaviour: a reconsideration of the attributes of modern human behaviour', *International Journal of Osteoarchaeology* 14: 321–32.

Cosgrove, R. and Raymont, E. (2002) 'Jiyer Cave revisited: preliminary results from northeast Queensland rainforest', *Australian Archaeology* 54: 29–36.

Cosgrove, R., Allen, J. and Marshall, B. (1990) 'Palaeo-ecology and Pleistocene human occupation in south central Tasmania', *Antiquity* 64: 59–78.

Coutts, P. J. F., Frank, R. K. and Hughes, P. (1978) 'Aboriginal engineers of the Western District, Victoria', *Records of the Victorian Archaeological Survey 7*.

Cribb, R. (1996) 'Shell mounds, domiculture and ecosystem manipulation on Western Cape York Peninsula', *Tempus* 4: 150–74.

Cundy, B. (1989) *Formal Variation in Australian Spear and Spear Thrower Technology*, BAR International Series S548, Oxford: British Archaeological Reports.

Cundy, B. (1990) 'An analysis of the Ingaladdi assemblage: critique of the understanding of lithic technology', unpublished PhD thesis, Australian National University, Canberra.

Curnoe, D. and Thorne, A. (2006a) 'Human origins in Australia: the skeletal evidence', *Before Farming* (online version) 2006/1 article 5.

Curnoe, D. and Thorne, A. (2006b) 'The question of cranial robustness', *Before Farming* (online version) 2006/2.

Cutler, K. B., Gray, S. C., Burr, G. S., Edwards, R. L., Taylor, F. W., Cabioch, G. et al. (2004) 'Radiocarbon calibration and comparison to 50 KYR BP with paired 14C and 230TH dating of corals from Vanuatu and Papua New Guinea', *Radiocarbon* 46: 1127–60.

Cutting, W. and Elliott, K. (1994) 'Making weaning safer', *Dialogue of Diarrhoea* 56: 1.

David, B. (1991) 'Raiders of the lost axe: on macropods, phalangers, where and why – comments on Sutton's comment on Morwood and Trezise (and Pleistocene axes)', *Queensland Archaeological Research* 8: 108–11.

David, B. (1993) 'Nurrabullgin Cave: preliminary results from a pre-37,000 year old rockshelter, north Queensland', *Archaeology in Oceania* 28: 50–4.

David, B. (1998) *Ngarrabullgan: Geographical investigations in Djungan country, Cape York Peninsula*, Monash Publications in Geography and Environmental Science 51, Department of Geography and Environmental Science, Monash University, Victoria.

David, B. (2002) *Landscapes, Rock-art and the Dreaming. An archaeology of preunderstanding*, Leicester: Leicester University Press.

David, B. (2006) 'Archaeology and the dreaming: toward an archaeology of ontology', in I. Lilley (ed.) *Archaeology of Oceania: Australia and the Pacific islands*, pp. 48–68, Oxford: Blackwell.

David, B. and Chant, D. (1995) *Rock Art and Regionalisation in North Queensland Prehistory*, Memoirs of the Queensland Museum 37, Brisbane: Queensland Museum.

David, B. and Lourandos, H. (1997) '37,000 years and more in tropical Australia: investigating long-term archaeological trends in Cape York Peninsula', *Proceedings of the Prehistoric Society* 63: 1–23.

David, B. and Lourandos, H. (1998) 'Rock art and socio-demography in northeast Australian prehistory', *World Archaeology* 30: 193–219.

David, B. and Lourandos, H. (1999) 'Landscape as mind: land use, cultural space and change in north Queensland prehistory', *Quaternary International* 59: 107–23.

David, B. and Wilson, M. (1999) 'Re-reading the landscape: place and identity in NE Australia during the late Holocene', *Cambridge Archaeological Journal* 9: 163–88.

David, B., McNiven, I., Flood, J. and Frost, R. (1990) 'Yiwarlarlay 1: archaeological excavations at the Lightning Brothers site, Delamere station, Northern Territory, Australia', *Archaeology in Oceania* 25: 79–84.

David, B., McNiven, I., Attenbrow, V., Flood, J. and Collins, J. (1994) 'Of Lightening Brothers and White Cockatoos: dating the antiquity of signifying systems in the Northern Territory, Australia', *Antiquity* 68: 241–51.

David, B., Collins, J., Barker, B., Flood, J. and Gunn, R. (1995) 'Archaeological research in Wardaman country, Northern Territory: the Lightning Brothers Project 1990–91 field seasons', *Australian Archaeology* 41: 1–8.

David. B., Roberts, R., Tuniz, C., Jones, R. and Head, J. (1997) 'New optical and radiocarbon dates from Ngarrabullgan Cave, a Pleistocene archaeological site in Australia: implications for the comparability of time clocks and for the human colonization of Australia', *Antiquity* 71: 183–8.

David, B., Crouch, J. and Zoppi, U. (2005) 'Historicizing the spiritual: Bu shell arrangements on the Island of Badu, Torres Strait', *Cambridge Archaeological Journal* 15: 71–91.

Davidson, D. S. (1934) 'Australian spear traits and their derivations', *Journal of the Polynesian Society* 43: 41–72, 143–62.

Davidson, I. (1990) 'Prehistoric Australian demography', in B. Meehan and N. White (eds) *Hunter-gatherer Demography: Past and present*, pp. 41–58, Sydney: Oceania.

Davidson, I. and Noble, W. (1992) 'Why the first colonisation of the Australian region is the earliest evidence of modern human behaviour', *Archaeology in Oceania* 27: 113–19.

Dayton, L. and Woodford, J. (1996) 'Australia's date with destiny', *New Scientist* 2059: 28–31.

Dickson, F. P. (1981) *Australian Stone Hatchets*, Sydney: Academic Press.

Dodson, J. R. (2001) 'A vegetation and fire history in a subalpine woodland and rain-forest region, Solomons Jewel Lake, Tasmania', *The Holocene* 11: 111–16.

Dodson, J. R. and Wright, R. V. S. (1989) 'Humid to arid to subhumid vegetation shift on Pilliga Sandstone, Ulungra Springs, New South Wales', *Quaternary Research* 32: 182–92.

Dodson, J. R., Fullagar, R., Furby, J., Jones, R. and Prosser, I. (1993) 'Humans and megafauna in a Late Pleistocene environment from Cuddie Springs, north western New South Wales', *Archaeology in Oceania* 28: 94–9.

Dortch, C. E. (1979a) 'Devil's Lair, an example of prolonged cave use in south-western Australia', *World Archaeology* 10: 258–79.

Dortch, C. E. (1979b) '33,000 year old stone and bone artifacts from Devil's Lair, Western Australia', *Records of the Western Australian Museum* 7: 329–67.

Dortch, C. E. (1979c) 'Australia's oldest known ornaments', *Antiquity* 53: 39–43.

Dortch, C. E. (1984) *Devil's Lair, a Study in Prehistory*, Perth: Western Australian Museum.

Dortch, C. E. (1997) 'New perceptions of the chronology and development of Aboriginal fishing in south-western Australia', *World Archaeology* 29: 15–35.

Dortch, C. E. and Dortch, J. (1996) 'Review of Devil's Lair artifact classification and radiocarbon chronology', *Australian Archaeology* 43: 28–32.

Dortch, C. E. and Morse, K. (1984) 'Prehistoric stone artefacts on some offshore islands in Western Australia', *Australian Archaeology* 19: 31–47.

Dortch, C. E. and Smith, M. V. (2001) 'Grand hypotheses: palaeodemographic modeling in Western Australia's South-west', *Archaeology in Oceania* 36: 34–45.

Dortch, J. (2004) 'Archaeology at Lancefield Swamp', unpublished report.

Draper, N. (1987) 'Context for the Kartan: a preliminary report on excavations at Cape du Couedic rockshelter, Kangaroo Island', *Archaeology in Oceania* 22: 1–8.

Dunnett, G. (1993) 'Diving for dinner: some implications from Holocene middens for the role of coasts in the late Pleistocene of Tasmania', in M. A. Smith, M. Spriggs and B. Fankhauser (eds) *Sahul in Review: Pleistocene archaeology in Australia, New Guinea and Island Melanesia*, pp. 247–57, Canberra: Department of Prehistory, Research School of Pacific Studies, Australian National University.

Durband, A. C. (2004) 'A test of the multiregional hypothesis of modern human origins using basicranial evidence from Indonesia and Australia', unpublished PhD thesis, University of Tennessee.

Edwards, D. A. and O'Connell, J. F. (1995) 'Broad spectrum diets in arid Australia', *Antiquity* 69: 769–83.

Elston, R. G. and Brantingham, P. J. (2002) 'Microlithic technology in northern Asia: a risk-minimizing strategy of the Late Paleolithic and Early Holocene', in R. G. Elston and S. L. Kuhn (eds) *Thinking Small: Global perspectives on microlithization*, pp. 103–16, Archaeological Papers of the American Anthropological Association (AP3A) 12, Arlington, VA: American Anthropological Association.

Etheridge, R. (1890) 'Has man a geological history in Australia?', *Proceedings of the Linnean Society of New South Wales* 5: 259–66.

Etheridge, R. and Whitelegge, T. (1907) 'Aboriginal workshops on the coast of New South Wales, and their contents', *Records of the Australian Museum* 6: 233–50.

Fanning, P. and Holdaway, S. (2001a) 'Stone artifact scatters in western NSW, Australia: geomorphic controls on artifact size and distribution', *Geoarchaeology* 16: 667–86.

Fanning, P. and Holdaway, S. (2001b) 'Temporal limits to the archaeological record in arid Western NSW, Australia: lessons from OSL and radiocarbon dating of hearths and sediments', in M. Jones and P. Shepard (eds) *Australasian Connections and New Directions. Proceedings of the Seventh Archaeometry Conference*, pp. 85–104, Auckland: University of Auckland.

Faulkner, P. (2006) 'The ebb and flow: an archaeological investigation of late Holocene economic variability on the coastal margin of Blue Mud Bay, Northern Australia', unpublished doctoral thesis, Australian National University, Canberra.

Faulkner, P. and Clarke, A. (2004) 'Late-Holocene occupation and coastal economy in Blue Mud Bay, northeast Arnhem Land: preliminary archaeological findings', *Australian Archaeology* 59: 23–30.

Fenner, F., Henderson, D. A., Arita, I., Jezek, Z. and Ladnyi, I. (1988) *Smallpox and its Eradication*, Geneva: World Health Organization.

Ferguson, W. C. (1985) 'A mid-Holocene de-population of the Australian southwest', doctoral dissertation, Australian National University, Canberra.

Fiedel, S. and Haynes, G. (2004) 'A premature burial: comments on Grayson and Meltzer's "Requiem for overkill",' *Journal of Archaeological Science* 31: 121–31.

Field, J. and Dodson, J. (1999) 'Late Pleistocene megafauna and human occupation at Cuddie Springs, southeastern Australia', *Proceedings of the Prehistoric Society* 65: 275–301.

Field, J. and Fullagar, R. (2001) 'Archaeology and Australian megafauna', *Science* 294: 7a.

Field, J., Fullagar, R. and Lord, G. (2001) 'A large area archaeological excavation at Cuddie Springs', *Antiquity* 75: 696–702.

Field, J., Dodson, J. and Prosser, I. P. (2002) 'A Late Pleistocene vegetation history from the Australian semi-arid zone', *Quaternary Science Reviews* 21: 1023–37.

Fifield, L. K., Bird, M. I., Turney, C. S. M., Hausladen, P. A., Santos, G. M. and di Tada, M. L. (2001) 'Radiocarbon dating of the human occupation of Australia prior to 40 ka BP – successes and pitfalls', *Radiocarbon* 43: 1139–45.

Flannery, T. F. (1990) 'Pleistocene faunal loss: implications of the aftershock for Australia's past and future', *Archaeology in Oceania* 25: 45–67.

Flannery, T. F. (1994) *The Future Eaters*, Chatswood, NSW: Reed.

Flannery, T. F. (1999) 'Debating extinction', *Science* 283: 182–3.

Flannery, T. F. and Gott, B. (1984) 'The Spring Creek Site, southwestern Victoria, a late surviving megafaunal assemblage', *Australian Zoologist* 21: 385–422.

Flannery, T. F. and Roberts, R. G. (1999) 'Late Quaternary extinctions in Australia: an overview', in R. D. E. McPhee (ed.) *Extinctions in Near Time: Causes, contexts and consequences*, pp. 239–56, New York: Plenum Press.

Flenley, J. R. (1996) 'Problems of the Quaternary on mountains of the Sunda-Sahul region', *Quaternary Science Review* 15: 557–80.

Flenniken, J. J. and White, J. P. (1983) 'Heat treatment of siliceous rocks and its implications for Australian prehistory', *Australian Aboriginal Studies* 1983/1: 43–8.

Flood, J. (1974) 'Pleistocene man at Clogg's Cave – his toolkit and environment', *Mankind* 9: 175–88.

Flood, J. (1980) *The Moth Hunters*, Canberra: Australian Institute of Aboriginal Studies.

Flood, J. (1983) *Archaeology of the Dreamtime*, Sydney: Collins.

Flood, J. (1988) 'No ethnography, no moth hunters', in B. Meehan and R. Jones (eds) *Archaeology with Ethnography: An Australian perspective*, pp. 270–6, Canberra: Department of Prehistory, Research School of Pacific and Asian Studies, Australian National University.

Flood, J. (1989) *Archaeology of the Dreamtime*, Sydney: Collins.

Flood, J. (1995) *Archaeology of the Dreamtime*, Sydney: Collins.

Flood, J. (2001) *Archaeology of the Dreamtime*, Sydney: Collins.

Flood, J., David, B., Magee, J. and English, B. (1987) 'Birrigai: a Pleistocene site in the south-eastern highlands', *Archaeology in Oceania* 22: 9–26.

Florek, S. (1986) 'The archaeological variability of mound springs sites at Lake Eyre South, South Australia: work in progress', *Australian Archaeology* 24: 27–31.

Florek, S. (1993) 'Archaeology of the mound spring campsites near Lake Eyre in South Australia', unpublished PhD thesis, University of Sydney.

Foley, R. and Lahr, M. (1997) 'Mode 3 technologies and the evolution of Modern Humans', *Cambridge Archaeological Journal* 7: 3–36.

Foley, R. and Lahr, M. (2003) 'On stony ground: lithic technology, human evolution, and the emergence of culture', *Evolutionary Anthropology* 12: 109–22.

Forster, P. (2004) 'Ice Ages and the mitochondrial DNA chronology of human dispersals: a review', *Philosophical Transactions of the Royal Society of London B* 359: 255–64.

Forster, P. and Matsumura, S. (2005) 'Did early humans go North or South?', *Science* 308: 965–6.

Forster, P., Torroni, A., Renfrew, C. and Rohl, A. (2001) 'Phylogenetic star contraction applied to Asian and Papuan mtDNA evolution', *Molecular Biological Evolution* 18: 1864–81.

Frankel, D. (1986) 'Excavations in the lower southeast of South Australia: November 1985', *Australian Archaeology* 22: 75–87.

Frankel, D. (1988) 'Characterising change in prehistoric sequences: a view from Australia', *Archaeology in Oceania* 23: 41–8.

Frankel, D. (1993) 'Pleistocene chronological structures and explanations: a challenge', in M. A. Smith, M. Spriggs and B. Fankhauser (eds) *Sahul in Review: Pleistocene archaeology in Australia, New Guinea and Island Melanesia*, pp. 24–33, Canberra: Australian National University.

Franklin, N. R. (1992) 'Explorations of variability in Australian prehistoric rock engravings', unpublished PhD thesis, La Trobe University, Melbourne.

Franklin, N. R. (1996) 'An analysis of rock engravings in the Mt Isa region, Northwest Queensland', *Tempus* 4: 137–49.

Freedman, L. (1985) 'Human skeletal remains from Mossgiel, N.S.W.', *Archaeology in Oceania* 20: 21–31.

Freedman, L. and Lofgren, M. (1983) 'Human skeletal remains from Lake Tandou, New South Wales', *Archaeology in Oceania* 18: 98–105.

Friedlaender, J., Schurr, T., Gentz, F., Koki, G., Friedlaender, F., Horvat, G. et al. (2005) 'Expanding Southwest Pacific mitochondrial haplogroups P and Q', *Molecular Biology and Evolution* 22: 1506–17.

Fullagar, R. and David, B. (1997) 'Investigating changing attitudes towards an Australian Aboriginal Dreaming mountain over >37,000 years of occupation via residue and use wear analyses of stone artefacts', *Cambridge Archaeological Journal* 7: 139–44.

Fullagar, R. and Field, J. (1997) 'Pleistocene seed grinding implements from the Australian arid zone', *Antiquity* 71: 300–7.

Fullagar, R., Price, D. and Head, L. (1996) 'Early human occupation of northern Australia: archaeology and thermoluminescence dating of the Jinmium rock-shelter, Northern Territory', *Antiquity* 70: 751–73.

Fullagar, R., Field, J. and Kealhofer, L. (2007) 'Grinding stones and seeds of change: starch and phytoliths as evidence of plant food processing', in Y. M. Rowan and J. R. Ebeling (eds) *New Approaches to Old Stones: Recent studies of ground stone artifacts*, London: Equinox.

Gagan, M. K., Hendy, E. J., Haberle, S. G. and Hantoro, W. S. (2003) 'Post-glacial evolution of the Indo-Pacific Warm Pool and El Niño-Southern Oscillation', *Quaternary International* 118: 127–43.

Gathorne-Hardy, F. J. and Harcourt-Smith, W. E. H. (2003) 'The super-eruption of Toba, did it cause a human bottleneck?', *Journal of Human Evolution* 45: 227–30.

Genever, M., Grindrod, J. and Barker, B. (2003) 'Holocene palynology of Whitehaven Swamp, Whitsunday Island, Queensland, and implications for the regional archaeological record', *Palaeogeography, Palaeoclimatology, Palaeoecology* 201: 141–56.

Giddens, A. (1984) *The Constitution of Society: Outline of the theory of structuration*, Berkeley, CA: University of California Press.

Gillespie, R. and Brook, B. W. (2006) 'Is there a Pleistocene archaeological site at Cuddie Springs?' *Archaeology in Oceania* 41: 1–11.

Gillespie, R. and Roberts, R. G. (2000) 'On the reliability of age estimates for human remains at Lake Mungo', *Journal of Human Evolution* 38: 727–32.

Gillespie, R., Horton, D. R., Ladd, P., Macumber, P. G., Rich, T. H., Thorne, A. R. and Wright, R. V. S. (1978) 'Lancefield Swamp and the extinction of the Australian megafauna', *Science* 200: 1044–8.

Godfrey, M. (1989) 'Shell midden chronology in southwestern Victoria: reflections of change in prehistoric population and subsistence', *Archaeology in Oceania* 24: 65–9.

Goebel, T. (2002) 'The "Microblade Adaptation" and recolonization of Siberia during the late upper Pleistocene', in R. G. Elston and S. L. Kuhn (eds) *Thinking Small: Global Perspectives on Microlithization*, pp. 117–32, Archaeological Papers of the American Anthropological Association (AP3A) 12, Arlington, VA: American Anthropological Association.

Gollan, K. (1984) 'The Australian dingo: in the shadow of man', in M. Archer and G. Clayton (eds) *Vertebrate Zoogeography and Evolution in Australasia*, pp. 921–7, Perth: Hesperian Press.

Golson, J. (1972) 'Australian Aboriginal food plants: some ecological and culture-historical implications', in D. J. Mulvaney and J. Golson (eds) *Aboriginal Man and Environment in Australia*, pp. 196–238, Canberra: Australian National University Press.

Golson, J. (1977) 'Simple tools and complex technology', in R. V. S. Wright (ed.) *Stone Tools as Cultural Markers: Change, evolution and complexity*, pp. 154–61, Canberra: Australian Institute of Aboriginal Studies.

Gombrich, E. H. (1965) *Art and Illusion*, 2nd edition, London: Pantheon.

Gordon, J. E. (1963) 'Weanling diarrhea', *American Journal of Medical Science* 245: 345–75.

Gorecki, P., Grant, M., O'Connor, S. and Veth, P. (1997) 'The morphology, function and antiquity of Australian grinding implements', *Archaeology in Oceania* 32: 141–50.

Gott, B. (1983) 'Murnong – *Microseris scapigera*: a study of a staple food of Victorian Aborigines', *Australian Aboriginal Studies* 1983/2: 2–18.

Gott, B. (2002) 'Fire-making in Tasmania: absence of evidence is not evidence of absence', *Current Anthropology* 43: 650–6.

Gould, R. A. (1967) 'Notes on hunting, butchering, and sharing of game among the Ngatatjara and their neighbors in the Western Australian Desert', *Kroeber Anthropological Society Papers* 36: 41–66.

Gould, R. A. (1968a) 'A preliminary report on excavations at Puntutjarpa rockshelter, near the Warburton Ranges, western Australia', *Archaeology and Physical Anthropology in Oceania* 3: 162–85.

Gould, R. A. (1968b) 'Living archaeology: the Ngatatjara of Western Australia', *Southwestern Journal of Anthropology* 24: 101–22.

Gould, R. A. (1969a) 'Subsistence behaviour among the Western Desert Aborigines of Australia', *Oceania* 39: 253–74.

Gould, R. A. (1969b) *Yiwara: Foragers of the Australian Desert*, London: Collins.

Gould, R. A. (1969c) 'Puntutjarpa rockshelter: a reply to Messrs Glover and Lampert', *Archaeology and Physical Anthropology in Oceania* 4: 229–37.

Gould, R. A. (1971) 'The archaeologist as ethnographer: a case from the the Western Desert of Australia', *World Archaeology* 3: 143–77.

Gould, R. A. (1977) 'Puntutjarpa Rockshelter and the Australian desert culture', *Anthropological Papers of the American Museum of Natural History* 54.

Gould, R. A. (1978) 'James Range East Rockshelter, Northern Territory, Australia: a summary of the 1973 and 1974 investigations', *Asian Perspectives* 21: 85–125.

Gould, R. A. (1980) *Living Archaeology*, Cambridge: Cambridge University Press.

Gould, R. A. (1985) 'The empiricist strikes back: a reply to Binford', *American Antiquity* 50: 638–44.

Gould, R. A. (1991) 'Arid-land foraging as seen from Australia: adaptive models and behavioural realities', *Oceania* 62: 12–33.

Gould, R. A. (1996) 'Faunal reduction at Puntutjarpa rockshelter, Warburton Ranges, Western Australia', *Archaeology in Oceania* 31: 72–86.

Gould, R. A., O'Connor, S. and Veth, P. (2002) 'Bones of contention: reply to Walshe', *Archaeology in Oceania* 37: 96–101.

Gray, A. (1985) 'Limits for demographic parameters of Aboriginal populations in the past', *Australian Aboriginal Studies* 1985/1: 22–7.

Grayson, D. K. (1983) *The Establishment of Human Antiquity*, London: Academic Press.

Grayson, D. K. (2001a) 'Did human hunting cause mass extinction?', *Science* 294: 1459–62.

Grayson, D. K. (2001b) 'The archaeological record of human impacts on animal populations', *Journal of World Prehistory* 15: 1–68.

Grayson, D. K. and Meltzer, D. J. (2002) 'Clovis hunting and large mammal extinction: a critical review of the evidence', *Journal of World Prehistory* 16: 313–59.

Grayson, D. K. and Meltzer, D. J. (2003) 'A requiem for North American overkill', *Journal of Archaeological Science* 30: 585–93.

Grayson, D. K. and Meltzer, D. J. (2004) 'North American overkill continued?', *Journal of Archaeological Science* 31: 133–6.

Gröcke, D. R. (1997) 'Distribution of C3 and C4 plants in the Late Pleistocene of South Australia recorded by isotope biogeochemistry of collagen in megafauna', *Australian Journal of Botany* 45: 607–17.

Grootes, P. M., Stuiver, M., White, J. W. C., Johnsen, S. J. and Jouzel, J. (1993) 'Comparison of oxygen isotope records from the GISP2 and GRIP Greenland ice cores', *Nature* 366: 552–4.

Grün, R., Spooner, N. A., Thorne, A., Mortimer, G., Simpson, J. J., McCulloch, M. T. et al. (2000) 'Age of the Lake Mungo 3 skeleton, reply to Bowler and Magee and to Gillespie and Roberts', *Journal of Human Evolution* 38: 733–42.

Gutiérrez, G., Sanchez, D. and Marin, A. (2002) 'A reanalysis of the ancient mitochondrial DNA sequences recovered from Neandertal bones', *Molecular Biological Evolution* 19: 1359–66.

Haberle, S. G., Hope, G. and van der Kaars, S. (2001) 'Biomass burning in Indonesia and Papua New Guinea: natural and human induced fire events in the fossil record', *Palaeogeography, Palaeoclimatology, Palaeoecology* 171: 259–68.

Hale, H. H. and Tindale, N. B. (1930) 'Notes on some human remains in the lower Murray Valley, South Australia', *Records at the South Australian Museum* 4: 145–218.

Hall, H. J., Gillieson, D. S. and Hiscock, P. (1989) 'Platypus Rockshelter (KB:A70), Southeast Queensland: stratigraphy, chronology and site formation', *Queensland Archaeological Research* 5: 25–41.

Hall, J. (1985) 'Aboriginal–Dolphin commensalism: substantiating a traditional fishing strategy in Moreton Bay, Queensland, Australia', in A. Anderson (ed.) *Fishing in the Pacific*, pp. 3–15, Honolulu, HI: Bernice P. Bishop Museum.

Hallam, S. J. (1987) 'Coastal does not equal littoral', *Australian Archaeology* 25: 10–29.

Hanckel, M. (1985) 'Hot rocks: heat treatment at Burrill Lake and Currarong, New South Wales', *Archaeology in Oceania* 20: 98–103.

Harpending, H. C. (1994) 'Signature of ancient population growth in a low-resolution mitochondrial DNA mismatch distribution', *Human Biology* 66: 591–600.

Harris, E. (1989) *Principles of Archaeological Stratigraphy*, 2nd edition, London: Academic Press.

Harrison, S. P. (1993) 'Late Quaternary lake level changes and climates of Australia', *Quaternary Science Reviews* 12: 211–31.

Hawkes, K. (1991) 'Showing off: tests of a hypothesis about men's foraging goals', *Ethnology and Sociobiology* 12: 29–54.

Hawkes, K., O'Connell, J. F. and Blurton Jones, N. G. (2001) 'Hunting and nuclear families: some lessons from the Hadza about men's work', *Current Anthropology* 42: 681–709.

Hawks, J., Oh, S., Hunley, K., Dobson, S., Cabana, G., Dayalu, P. and Wolpoff, M. H. (2000) 'An Australasian test of the recent African origin theory using the WLH-50 calvarium', *Journal of Human Evolution* 39: 1–22.

Haynes, G. (2002) 'The catastrophic extinction of North American mammoths and mastodons', *World Archaeology* 33: 391–416.

Head, L. (1989) 'Using palaeocology to date Aboriginal fish-traps at Lake Condah, Victoria', *Archaeology in Oceania* 24: 110–15.

Head, L. (1994a) 'Both ends of the candle? Discerning human impact on the vegetation', *Australian Archaeology* 39: 82–6.

Head, L. (1994b) 'Landscapes socialized by fire: post-contact changes in Aboriginal fire use in northern Australia, and implications for prehistory', *Archaeology in Oceania* 29: 172–81.

Head, L. and Fullagar, R. (1997) 'Hunter-gatherer archaeology and pastoral contact: perspectives from the northwest Northern Territory, Australia', *World Archaeology* 28: 418–28.

Henrich, J. (2004) 'Demography and cultural evolution: how adaptive cultural processes can produce maladaptive losses – the Tasmanian case', *American Antiquity* 69: 197–214.

Henshilwood, C. S., d'Errico, F., Yates, R., Jacobs, Z., Tribolo, C., Duller, G. A. T. et al. (2002) 'Emergence of modern human behavior: Middle Stone Age engravings from South Africa', *Science* 295: 1278–80.

Hesse, P. P. (1994) 'The record of continental dust from Australia in Tasman Sea sediments', *Quaternary Science Reviews* 13: 257–72.

Hesse, P. P. and McTainsh, G. H. (1999) 'Last Glacial Maximum to Early Holocene wind strength in the mid-latitudes of the Southern Hemisphere from aeolian dust in the Tasman Sea', *Quaternary Research* 52: 343–9.

Hesse, P. P., Magee, J. W. and van der Kaars, S. (2004) 'Late Quaternary climates of the Australian arid zone: a review', *Quaternary International* 118: 87–102.

Hiscock, P. (1981) 'Comments on the use of chipped stone artefacts as a measure of "intensity of site usage"', *Australian Archaeology* 13: 20–34.

Hiscock, P. (1984) 'A preliminary report on the stone artefacts from Colless Creek Cave', *Queensland Archaeological Research* 1: 120–51.

Hiscock, P. (1986) 'Technological change in the Hunter River Valley and the interpretation of late Holocene change in Australia', *Archaeology in Oceania* 21: 40–50.

Hiscock, P. (1988a) 'Prehistoric settlement patterns and artefact manufacture at Lawn Hill, Northwest Queensland', unpublished doctoral thesis, University of Queensland, Brisbane.

Hiscock, P. (1988b) 'A cache of tulas from the Boulia District of Western Queensland', *Archaeology in Oceania* 23: 60–70.

Hiscock, P. (1990) 'How old are the artefacts at Malakunanja II?', *Archaeology in Oceania* 25: 122–4.

Hiscock, P. (1993) 'Bondaian technology in the Hunter Valley, New South Wales', *Archaeology in Oceania* 28: 64–75.

Hiscock, P. (1994) 'Technological responses to risk in Holocene Australia', *Journal of World Prehistory* 8: 267–2.

Hiscock, P. (1999) 'Holocene coastal occupation of western Arnhem Land', in J. Hall and I. McNiven (eds) *Australian Coastal Archaeology*, pp. 91–103, Canberra: Australian National University.

Hiscock, P. (2001) 'Sizing up prehistory: sample size and composition of artefact assemblages', *Australian Aboriginal Studies* 2001/1: 48–62.

Hiscock, P. (2002) 'Pattern and context in the Holocene proliferation of backed artefacts in Australia', in R. G. Elston and S. L. Kuhn (eds) *Thinking Small: Global perspectives on microlithization*, pp. 163–77, Archaeological Papers of the American Anthropological Association (AP3A) 12, Arlington, VA: American Anthropological Association.

Hiscock, P. (2003) 'Quantitative exploration of size variation and the extent of reduction in Sydney Basin assemblages: a tale from the Henry Lawson Drive Rockshelter', *Australian Archaeology* 57: 64–74.

Hiscock, P. (2006) 'Blunt and to the point: changing technological strategies in Holocene Australia', in I. Lilley (ed.) *Archaeology of Oceania: Australia and the Pacific islands*, pp. 69–95, Oxford: Blackwell.

Hiscock, P. and Allen, H. (2000) 'Assemblage variability in the Willandra Lakes', *Archaeology in Oceania* 35: 97–103.

Hiscock, P. and Attenbrow, V. (1998) 'Early Holocene backed artefacts from Australia', *Archaeology in Oceania* 33: 49–63.

Hiscock, P. and Attenbrow, V. (2002) 'Reduction continuums in Eastern Australia: measurement and implications at Capertee 3', in S. Ulm (ed.) *Barriers, Borders, Boundaries*, Tempus volume 7, pp. 167–74, Brisbane: University of Queensland.

Hiscock, P. and Attenbrow, V. (2003) 'Early Australian implement variation: a reduction model', *Journal of Archaeological Science* 30: 239–49.

Hiscock, P. and Attenbrow, V. (2004) 'A revised sequence of backed artefact production at Capertee 3', *Archaeology in Oceania* 39: 94–9.

Hiscock, P. and Attenbrow, V. (2005) *Australia's Eastern Regional Sequence Revisited: Technology and change at Capertee 3*, British Archaeological Reports, International Monograph Series 1397, Oxford: Archaeopress.

Hiscock, P. and Faulkner, P. (2006) 'Dating the dreaming? Creation of myths and rituals for mounds along the northern Australian coastline', *Cambridge Archaeological Journal* 16: 209–22.

Hiscock, P. and Kershaw, P. (1992) 'Palaeoenvironments and prehistory of Australia's tropical Top End', in J. Dodson (ed.) *The Naive Lands*, pp. 43–75, Melbourne: Longman Cheshire.

Hiscock, P. and Mowat, F. (1993) 'Midden variability in the coastal portion of the Kakadu region', *Australian Archaeology* 37: 18–24.

Hiscock, P. and O'Connor, S. (2005) 'Arid paradises or dangerous landscapes: a review of explanations for Paleolithic assemblage change in arid Australia and Africa', in P. Veth, M. Smith and P. Hiscock (eds) *Desert Peoples: Archaeological perspectives*, pp. 58–77, Oxford: Blackwell.

Hiscock, P. and O'Connor, S. (2006) 'An Australian perspective on modern behaviour and artefact assemblages', *Before Farming* (online version) 2006/1 article 5.

Hiscock, P. and Veth, P. (1991) 'Change in the Australian desert culture: a reanalysis of tulas from Puntutjarpa rockshelter', *World Archaeology* 22: 332–45.

Hiscock, P. and Wallis, L. (2005) 'Pleistocene settlement of deserts from an Australian perspective', in P. Veth, M. Smith and P. Hiscock (eds) *Desert Peoples: Archaeological perspectives*, pp. 34–57, Oxford: Blackwell.

Hofman, J. L. (1986) 'Vertical movement of artifacts in alluvial and stratified deposits', *Current Anthropology* 27: 163–71.

Holdaway, S. and Porch, N. (1995) 'Cyclical patterns in the Pleistocene human occupation of southwest Tasmania', *Archaeology in Oceania* 30: 74–82.

Holdaway, S. and Porch, N. (1996) 'Dates as data: an alternative approach to the construction of chronologies for Pleistocene sites in southwest Tasmania', in J. Allen (ed.) *Report of the Southern Forest Project, Volume 1: Site Descriptions, Stratigraphies, and Chronologies*, pp. 251–75, Melbourne: School of Archaeology, La Trobe University.

Holdaway, S., Fanning, P. C. and Witter, D. C. (2000) 'Prehistoric Aboriginal occupation of the rangelands: interpreting the surface archaeological record of far western New South Wales, Australia', *Rangelands Journal* 22: 44–57.

Holdaway, S., Fanning, P. C. and Shiner, J. (2005) 'Absence of evidence or evidence of absence? Understanding the chronology of indigenous occupation of western New South Wales, Australia', *Archaeology in Oceania* 40: 33–49.

Holdaway, S., Fanning, P. C., Jones, M., Shiner, J., Witter, D. and Nicholls, G. (2002) 'Variability in the chronology of late Holocene Australian aboriginal occupation on the arid margin of southeastern Australia', *Journal of Archaeological Science* 29: 351–63.

Hopkins, D. R. (1983) *Princes and Peasants: Smallpox in history*, Chicago, IL: University of Chicago Press.

Horsfall, N. (1983) 'Excavations at Jiyer Cave, north-east Queensland: some results', in M. Smith (ed.) *Archaeology at ANZAAS 1983*, Perth: Western Australian Mueum.

Horsfall, N. (1987) 'Living in rainforest: the prehistoric occupation of North Queensland's humid tropics', unpublished PhD thesis, James Cook University of North Queensland, Townsville, Qld.

Horsfall, N. (1996) 'Holocene occupation of the tropical rainforests of North Queensland', *Tempus* 4: 175–90.

Horton, D. R. (1979) 'Tasmanian adaptation', *Mankind* 12: 28–34.

Howells, W. W. (1973) *The Pacific Islanders*, Wellington, NZ: A. H. and A. W. Reed.

Hubbard, N. N. (1995) 'In search of regional palaeoclimates: Australia, 18,000 yr BP', *Palaeogeography, Palaeoclimatology, Palaeoecology* 116: 167–88.

Hubbard, N. N. (1996) 'An integrated method for reconstructing regional palaeoclimates: Australia (18,000 yr B.P.)', *Palaeogeography, Palaeoclimatology, Palaeoecology* 116: 141–66.

Hughes, P. J. (1977) 'A geomorphological interpretation of selected archaeological sites in southern coastal New South Wales', unpublished doctoral thesis, University of New South Wales, Sydney.

Hughes, P. J. and Hiscock, P. (2005) 'The archaeology of the Lake Eyre South Area', *Archaeology of the Lake Eyre South Region Monograph Series* 6, pp. 1–20, Adelaide: Royal Geographical Society of South Australia.

Hughes, P. J. and Lampert, R. J. (1982) 'Prehistoric population change in southern coastal Australia', in S. Bowdler (ed.) *Coastal Archaeology in Eastern Australia*, pp. 16–28, Canberra: Australian National University.

Huoponen, K., Schurr, T. G., Chen, Y-S. and Wallace, D. (2001) 'Mitochondrial DNA variation in an Aboriginal Australian population: evidence for genetic isolation and regional differentiation', *Human Immunology* 62: 954–69.

Hutton, J. (1788) 'Theory of the earth, or investigations of the laws observable in the composition, dissolution, and restoration of land upon the globe', *Transactions of the Royal Society of Edinburgh* 1: 209–304.

Huxley, T. (1864) *Evidence as to Man's Place in Nature*, London: Williams & Norgate.

Ingman, M. and Gyllensten, U. (2003) 'Mitochondrial genome variation and evolutionary history of Australian and New Guinean Aborigines', *Genome Research* 13: 1600–6.

Ingman, M., Kaessman, H., Pääbo, S. and Gyllensten, U. (2000) 'Mitochondrial genome variation and the origin of modern humans', *Nature* 408: 708–13.

Johnson, B. J., Miller, G. H., Fogel, M. L., Magee, J. W., Gagan, M. K. and Chivas, A. R. (1999) '65,000 years of vegetation change in Central Australia and the Australian summer monsoon', *Science* 284: 1150–2.

Johnson, C. N. (2002) 'Determinants of loss of mammal species during the late Quaternary "megafauna" extinctions: life history and ecology, but not body size', *Proceedings of the Royal Society of Britain* 269: 2221–7.

Johnson, C. N. (2005) 'What can the data on late survival of Australian megafauna tell us about the cause of their extinction?', *Quaternary Science Reviews* 24: 2167–72.

Johnson, C. N. and Wroe, S. (2003) 'Causes of extinction of vertebrates during the Holocene of mainland Australia: arrival of the dingo, or human impact?', *The Holocene* 13: 941–8.

Johnson, I. (1979) 'The getting of data', unpublished doctoral thesis, Australian National University, Canberra.

Johnston, H. D. (1982) 'Testing a model: an analysis of vertebrate faunal remains from Warragarra rockshelter, central Tasmania', unpublished BA (Hons) thesis, University of New England, Armidale, NSW.

Jones, R. (1969) 'Fire stick farming', *Australian Natural History* 16: 224–8.

Jones, R. (1971) 'Rocky Cape and the problem of the Tasmanians', unpublished PhD thesis, University of Sydney.

Jones, R. (1972) 'Tasmanian Aborigines and dogs', *Mankind* 7: 256–71.

Jones, R. (1974) 'Tasmanian tribes', in N. B. Tidale *Aboriginal Tribes of Australia*, pp. 321–86, Australian National University Press.

Jones, R. (1977a) 'The Tasmanian paradox', in R. V. S. Wright (ed.) *Stone Tools as Cultural Markers: Change, evolution and complexity*, pp. 189–204, Canberra: Australian Institute of Aboriginal Studies.

Jones, R. (1977b) 'Man as an element of a continental fauna: the case of the sundering of the Bassian bridge', in J. Allen, J. Golson and R. Jones (eds) *Sunda and Sahul: Prehistoric studies in Southeast Asia, Melanesia and Australia*, pp. 317–86, London: Academic Press.

Jones, R. (1978) 'Why did the Tasmanians stop eating fish?', in R. Gould (ed.) *Explorations in Ethnoarchaeology*, pp. 11–48, Albuquerque, NM: University of New Mexico Press.

Jones, R. (1979) 'The fifth continent: problems concerning the human colonization of Australia', *Annual Review of Anthropology* 8: 445–66.

Jones, R. (1990) 'Hunters of the dreaming: some ideational, economic and ecological parameters of the Australian Aboriginal productive system', in D. E. Yen and J. M. J. Mummery (eds) *Pacific Production Systems: Approaches to economic prehistory*, pp. 25–53, Occasional Papers in Prehistory 18, Canberra: Department of Prehistory, Research School of Pacific Studies, Australian National University.

Jones, R. (1993) 'A continental reconnaissance: some observations concerning the discovery of the Pleistocene archaeology of Australia', in M. Spriggs, D. E. Yen, W. Ambrose, R. Jones, A. Thorne and A. Andrews (eds) *A Community of Culture: The people and prehistory of the Pacific*, pp. 97–122, Canberra: Australian National University.

Jones, R. (1995) 'Tasmanian archaeology: establishing the sequences', *Annual Review of Anthropology* 24: 423–46.

Jones, R. and Bowler, J. (1980) 'Struggle for the savanna: northern Australia in ecological and prehistoric perspective', in R. Jones (ed.) *Northern Australia: Options and implications*, pp. 3–31, Canberra: Australian National University.

Jones, R. and Johnson, I. (1985) 'Deaf Adder Gorge: Lindner Site, Nauwalabila 1', in R. Jones (ed.) *Archaeological Research in Kakadu National Park*, pp. 165–228, Canberra: Australian National University.

Kamminga, J. (1978) 'Journey into the microcosms: a functional analysis of certain classes of prehistory Australian stone tools', unpublished PhD thesis, University of Sydney.

Kamminga, J. (1982) *Over the Edge: Functional analysis of Australian stone tools*, Occasional Papers in Anthropology 11, Brisbane: University of Queensland.

Kayser, M., Brauer, S., Weiss, G., Schiefenhovel, W., Underhill, P. A. and Stoneking, M. (2001) 'Independent histories of human Y chromosomes from Melanesia and Australia', *American Journal of Human Genetics* 68: 173–90.

Keen, I. (2004) *Aboriginal Economy and Society. Australia at the threshold of colonisation*, Oxford: Oxford University Press.

Keen, I. (2006) 'Constraints on the development of enduring inequalities in Late Holocene Australia', *Current Anthropology* 47: 7–38.

Kelly, R. L. (1995) *The Foraging Spectrum: Diversity in hunter-gatherer lifeways*, Washington, DC: Smithsonian Institution.

Kershaw, A. P. (1985) 'An extended late Quaternary vegetation record from northeastern Queensland and its implications for the seasonal tropics of Australia', *Proceedings of the Ecological Society of Australia* 13: 179–89.

Kershaw, A. P. (1986) 'The last two glacial–interglacial cycles from northeastern Australia: implications for climate change and Aboriginal burning', *Nature* 322: 47–9.

Kershaw, A. P. (1995) 'Environmental change in Greater Australia', *Antiquity* 69: 656–75.

Kershaw, A. P. and Nanson, G. C. (1993) 'The last full glacial cycle in the Australian region', *Global and Planetary Change* 7: 1–9.

Kershaw, A. P., Clark, J. S., Gill, A. M. and D'Costa, D. M. (2002) 'A history of fire on Australia', in R. Bradstock, J. Williams and M. Gill (eds) *A History of Fire in Australia*, Cambridge: Cambridge University Press.

Kershaw, P., van der Kaars, S., Moss, P., Opdyke, B., Guillard, F., Rule S. and Turney, C.

(2006) 'Environmental change and the arrival of people in the Australian region', *Before Farming* (online version) 2006/1 article 2.

Kidder, J. H., Jantz, R. L. and Smith, F. H. (1992) 'Defining modern humans: a multivariate approach', in G. Brauer and F. H. Smith (eds) *Continuity or Replacemnent? Controversies in Homo sapiens evolution*, pp. 157–77, Rotterdam: Balkema.

Kimber, R. G. (1988) 'Smallpox in Central Australia: evidence for epidemics and postulations about the impact', *Australian Archaeology* 27: 63–8.

Kimber, R. G. (1990) 'Hunter-gatherer demography: the recent past in Central Australia', in B. Meehan and N. White (eds) *Hunter-gatherer Demography: Past and present*, pp. 160–70, Sydney: Oceania.

Kimber, R. G. (1996) 'The dynamic century before the Horn expedition: a speculative history', in S. R. Morton and D. J. Mulvaney (eds) *Exploring Central Australia: Society, the environment and the 1894 Horn expedition*, pp. 91–103, Chipping Norton, UK: Surrey, Beatty and Sons.

Kohen, J., Stockton, E. and Williams, M. A. (1984) 'Shaws Creek KII rockshelter: a prehistoric occupation site in the Blue Mountains piedmont, eastern New South Wales', *Archaeology in Oceania* 19: 57–72.

Kohen, J., Stockton, E., Williams, M., Cowling, G., Glodberg, P., Scott-Virtue, L. and Sumner, C. (1981) 'Where plain and plateau meet: recent excavations at Shaws Creek Rockshelter, eastern New South Wales', *Australian Archaeology* 13: 63–8.

Kuhn, S., Stiner, M. C., Reese, D. S. and Güleç, E. (2001) 'Ornaments of the earliest Upper Paleolithic: new insights from the Levant', *Proceedings of the National Academy of Science* 98: 7641–6.

Kuper, A. (1988) *The Invention of Primitive Society*, London: Routledge.

La Blanc, S. A. and Black, B. (1974) 'A long term trend in tooth size in the eastern Mediterranean', *American Journal of Physical Anthropology* 41: 417–22.

Lahr, M. (1996) *The Evolution of Modern Human Diversity*, Cambridge: Cambridge University Press.

Lahr, M. and Foley, R. (1994) 'Multiple dispersals and modern human origins', *Evolutionary Anthropology* 3: 48–60.

Lahr, M. and Foley, R. (1998) 'Toward a theory of modern human origins: geography, demography, and diversity in recent human evolution', *Yearbook of Physical Anthropology* 41: 137–76.

Lahr, M. and Wright, R. V. S. (1996) 'The question of robusticity and the relationship between cranial size and shape in *Homo sapiens*', *Journal of Human Evolution* 31: 157–91.

Lamb, L. (1996) 'Investigating changing stone technologies, site use and occupational intensities at Fern Cave, north Queensland', *Australian Archaeology* 42: 1–7.

Lamb, L. (2005) 'Rock of ages: use of the South Molle Island Quarry, Whitsunday Islands, and the implications for Holocene technological change in Australia', unpublished PhD thesis, Australian National University, Canberra.

Lamb, L. and Barker, B. (2001) 'Evidence for early Holocene change in the Whitsunday Islands: a new radiocarbon determination from Nara Inlet 1', *Australian Archaeology* 51: 42–3.

Lambeck, K. and Chappell, J. (2001) 'Sea level change through the last Glacial Cycle', *Science* 292: 679–86.

Lambeck, K., Yokoyama, Y. and Purcell, T. (2002) 'Into and out of the Last Glacial Maximum: sea-level change during Oxygen Isotope Stages 3 and 2', *Quaternary Science Reviews* 21: 343–60.

Lampert, R. J. (1971) *Burrill Lake and Currarong*, Terra Australis 1, Canberra: Australian National University.

Lampert, R. J. (1981) *The Great Kartan Mystery*, Terra Australis 5, Canberra: Australian National University.

Lampert, R. J. (1985) 'Archaeological reconnaissance on a field trip to Dalhousie Springs', *Australian Archaeology* 21: 57–62.

Lampert, R. J. and Hughes, P. J. (1974) 'Sea level change and Aboriginal coastal adaptations in southern New South Wales', *Archaeology and Physical Anthropology in Oceania* 9: 226–35.

Lampert, R. J. and Hughes, P. J. (1987) 'The Flinders Ranges: a Pleistocene outpost in the arid zone?', *Records of the South Australian Museum* 20: 29–34.

Larnach, S. L. and Freedman, L. (1964) 'Sex determination of Aboriginal crania from Coastal New South Wales', *Records of the Australian Museum* 26: 295–308.

Larnach, S. L. and Macintosh, N. W. G. (1971) *The Mandible in Eastern Australian Aborigines*, Sydney: Oceania Monographs 17.

Law, W. B. (2004) 'Chipping away in the past: artefact reduction and Holocene systems of land use in Arid Central Australia', unpublished M.Phil. thesis, Australian National University, Canberra.

Lewis, D. (1988) *The Rock Painting of Arnhem Land, Australia: Social, ecological and material change in the post-glacial period*, BAR International Series S415, Oxford: British Archaeological Reports.

Lewis, D. (1997) 'Bradshaws: the view from Arnhem Land', *Australian Archaeology* 44: 1–16.

Libby, W. (1952) *Radiocarbon Dating*, Chicago, IL: University of Chicago Press.

Lindsell, P. (2001) 'Bergmann, Allen and Birdsell: patterns of ecogeographic adaptation in Aboriginal Australians', unpublished PhD thesis, University of New England, Armidale, NSW.

Littleton, J. (2005) 'Data quarrying in the Western Riverina: A regional perspective on post-contact health', in I. Macfarlane, M. Mountain and R. Paton (eds) *Many Exchanges: Archaeology, history, community and the work of Isabel McBryde*, pp. 199–218, Canberra: Aboriginal History Inc.

Littleton, J. and Allen, H. (2007) 'Hunter-gatherer burials and the creation of persistent places in southeastern Australia', *Journal of Anthropological Archaeology* 26: 283–98.

Longmore, M. E. and Heijnis, H. (1999) 'Aridity in Australia: Pleistocene records of Palaeohydrological and Palaeoecological change from the perched lake sediments of Fraser Island, Queensland, Australia', *Quaternary International* 57–8: 35–47.

Lorblanchet, M. and Jones, R. (1979) 'Les premieres fouilles à Dampier (Australié occidentale), et leur place dans l'ensembl Australien', *Bulletin de la Société Préhistorique Française* 76: 463–87.

Lourandos, H. (1976) 'Aboriginal settlement and land use in south western Victoria: a report of current fieldwork', *The Artefact* 1: 174–93.

Lourandos, H. (1980a) 'Forces of change: Aboriginal technology and population in Southwestern Victoria', unpublished PhD thesis, University of Sydney.

Lourandos, H. (1980b) 'Change or stability? Hydraulics, hunter-gatherers and population in temperate Australia', *World Archaeology* 11: 245–66.

Lourandos, H. (1983a) 'Intensification: a late Pleistocene-Holocene archaeological sequence from Southwestern Victoria', *Archaeology in Oceania* 18: 81–94.

Lourandos, H. (1983b) '10,000 years in the Tasmanian highlands', *Australian Archaeology* 16: 39–47.

Lourandos, H. (1984) 'Changing perspectives in Aboriginal prehistory: a reply to Beaton', *Archaeology in Oceania* 19: 29–33.

Lourandos, H. (1985a) 'Intensification and Australian prehistory', in T. D. Price and J. A. Brown (eds) *Prehistoric Hunter-gatherers: The emergence of cultural complexity*, pp. 385–423, Orlando, FL: Academic Press.

Lourandos, H. (1985b) 'Problems with the interpretation of late Holocene changes in Australian prehistory', *Archaeology in Oceania* 20: 37–9.

Lourandos, H. (1997) *Continent of Hunter-gatherers: New perspectives in Australian prehistory*, Cambridge: Cambridge University Press.

Lourandos, H. and Ross, A. (1994) 'The great "intensification debate": its history and place in Australian archaeology', *Australian Archaeology* 39: 54–63.

Lubbock, J. (1872) *Pre-historic Times: As illustrated by ancient remains, and the manner and customs of modern savages*, New York: Appleton.

Luebbers, R. (1975) 'Ancient boomerangs discovered in South Australia', *Nature* 253: 39.

Luly, J. G. (2001) 'On the equivocal fate of Late Pleistocene *Callitris* Vent. (Cupressaceae) woodlands in arid South Australia', *Quaternary International* 83–5: 155–68.

McArthur, N. (1976) 'Computer simulations of small populations', *Australian Archaeology* 4: 53–7.

Macaulay, V., Hill, C., Achilli, A., Rengo, C., Clarke, D., Meehan, W. et al. (2005) 'Single, rapid coastal settlement of Asia revealed by analysis of complete mitochondrial genomes', *Science* 305: 1034–6.

McBrearty, S. (1990) 'Consider the humble termite: termites as agents of post-depositional disturbance at African archaeological sites', *Journal of Archaeological Science* 17: 111–44.

McBrearty, S. and Brooks, A. S. (2000) 'The revolution that wasn't: a new interpretation of the origin of modern human behaviour', *Journal of Human Evolution* 39: 453–563.

McBryde, I. (1968) 'Archaeological investigations in the Graman district', *Archaeology and Physical Anthropology in Oceania* 3: 77–93.

McBryde, I. (1974) *Aboriginal Prehistory in New England*, Sydney: Sydney University Press.

McBryde, I. (1984) 'Kulin greenstone quarries: the social contexts of production and distribution for the Mt William site', *World Archaeology* 16: 267–85.

McBryde, I. (1986) 'Artefacts, language and social interaction: a case study from south-eastern Australia', in G. Bailey and P. Callow (eds) *Stone Age Prehistory: Studies in memory of Charles McBurney*, pp. 77–93, Cambridge: Cambridge University Press.

McCarthy, F. D. (1948) 'The Lapstone Creek excavation: two culture periods revealed in eastern New South Wales', *Records of the Australian Museum* 22(1): 1–34.

McCarthy, F. D. (1961) 'Regional reports: Australia', *Asian Perspectives* 5(1): 98–104.

McCarthy, F. D. (1964) 'The archaeology of the Capertee Valley, New South Wales', *Records of the Australian Museum* 26(6): 197–246.

McCarthy, L. and Head, L. (2001) 'Holocene variability in semi-arid vegetation: new evidence from *Leporillus* middens from the Flinders Ranges, South Australia', *The Holocene* 11: 681–9.

McCarthy, L., Head, L. and Quade, J. (1996) 'Holocene palaeoecology of the northern Flinders Ranges, South Australia, based on stick-nest rat (*Leporillus* spp.) middens: a preliminary overview', *Palaeogeography, Palaeoclimatology, Palaeoecology* 123: 205–18.

McConvell, P. (1996) 'Backtracking to Babel: the chronology of Pama-Nyungan expansion in Australia', *Archaeology in Oceania* 31: 125–44.

McDonald, J. (2005) 'Archaic faces to headdresses: the changing role of rock art across the arid zone', in P. Veth, M. Smith and P. Hiscock (eds) *Desert Peoples: Archaeological perspectives*, pp. 116–41, Oxford: Blackwell.

McDonald, J. and Veth, P. (2006) 'Rock art and social identity: a comparison of Holocene graphic systems in arid and fertile environments', in I. Lilley (ed.) *Archaeology of Oceania: Australia and the Pacific Islands*, pp. 96–115, Oxford: Blackwell.

McGlone, M. S., Kershaw, A. P. and Markgraf, V. (1992) 'El Niño/Southern Oscillation climate variability in Australasian and South American Paleoenvironmental records', in

H. F. Diaz and V. Markgraf (eds) El Niño: Historical and Paleoclimatic Aspects of the Southern Oscillation, pp. 435–62, Cambridge: Cambridge University Press.

Macintosh, N. W. G. (1952) 'The Talgai skull and dental arch: remeasurement and reconstruction', Oceania 23: 106–9.

Macintosh, N. W. G. (1971) 'Analysis of an Aboriginal skeleton and a pierced tooth necklace from Lake Nitchie, Australia', Anthropologie 9: 49–62.

Macintosh, N. W. G. and Larnach, S. L. (1976) 'Aboriginal affinities looked at in world context', in R. L. Kirk and A. G. Thorne (eds) The Origins of the Australians, pp. 113–26, Atlantic Highlands, NJ: Humanities Press.

Macknight, C. C. (1976) The Voyage to Marege: Macassan trepangers in northern Australia, Melbourne: Melbourne University Press.

Macknight, C. C. (1986) 'Macassans and the Aboriginal past', Archaeology in Oceania 21: 69–75.

Macknight, C. C. and Gray, W. J. (1970) Aboriginal Stone Pictures in Eastern Arnhem Land, Canberra: Australian Institute of Aboriginal Studies.

McNiven, I. J. (1994) 'Technological organization and settlement in southwest Tasmania after the glacial maximum', Antiquity 68: 75–82.

McNiven, I. J. (2000) 'Backed to the Pleistocene', Archaeology in Oceania 35: 48–52.

McNiven, I. J. (2003) 'Saltwater people: spiritscapes, maritime rituals and the archaeology of Australian indigenous seascapes', World Archaeology 35: 329–49.

McNiven, I. J., David, B. and Barker, B. (2006) 'The social archaeology of Indigenous Australia', in B. David, B. Barker and I. McNiven (eds) The Social Archaeology of Australian Indigenous Societies, pp. 2–19, Canberra: Aboriginal Studies Press.

Macumber, P. G. and Thorne, A. G. (1975) 'The Cohuna Cranium site: a re-appraisal', Archaeology and Physical Anthropology in Oceania 10: 67–72.

Magee, J. W. and Miller, G. H. (1998) 'Lake Eyre palaeohydrology from 60 ka to the present: beach ridges and glacial maximum aridity', Palaeogeography, Palaeoclimatology, Palaeoecology 144: 307–29.

Magee, J. W., Bowler, J. M., Miller, G. H. and Williams, D. L. G. (1995) 'Stratigraphy, sedimentology, chronology and palaeohydrology of Quaternary lacustrine deposits at Madigan Gulf, Lake Eyre, South Australia', Palaeogeography, Palaeoclimatology, Palaeoecology 113: 3–42.

Main, A. R. (1978) 'Ecophysiology: towards an understanding of Late Pleistocene marsupial extinction', in D. Walker and J. C. Guppy (eds) Biology and Quaternary Environments, pp. 169–83, Canberra: Australian Academy of Sciences.

Markgraf, V., Dodson, J. R., Kershaw, A. P., McGlone, M. S. and Nicholls, N. (1992) 'Evolution of late Pleistocene and Holocene climates in the circum-South Pacific land areas', Climatic Dynamics 6: 193–211.

Martin, P. S. (1973) 'The discovery of America', Science 179: 969–74.

Martin, P. S. (1984) 'Prehistoric overkill: the global model', in P. S. Martin and R. G. Klein (eds) Quaternary Extinctions: A prehistoric revolution, pp. 354–403, Tucson, AZ: University of Arizona Press.

Martin, P. S. and Steadman, D. W. (1999) 'Prehistoric extinctions on islands and continents', in R. D. E. McPhee (ed.) Extinctions in Near Time: Causes, contexts and consequences, pp. 17–56, New York: Plenum Press.

Marwick, B. (2002) 'Milly's Cave: evidence for human occupation of the inland Pilbara during the Last Glacial Maximum', Tempus 7: 21–33.

Marwick, B. (2005) 'Element concentrations and magnetic susceptibility of anthrosols: indicators of prehistoric human occupation in the inland Pilbara, Western Australia', Journal of Archaeological Science 32: 1357–68.

Maynard, L. (1976) 'An archaeological approach to the study of Australian rock art', unpublished MA thesis, University of Sydney.

Maynard, L. (1977) 'Classification and terminology in Australian rock art', in P. J. Ucko (ed.) *Form in Indigenous Art: Schematisation in the art of Aboriginal Australia and prehistoric Europe*, pp. 387–402, Canberra: Australian Institute of Aboriginal Studies.

Maynard, L. (1979) 'The archaeology of Australian Aboriginal art', in S. M. Mead (ed.) *Exploring the Visual Art of Oceania*, pp. 83–110, Honolulu, HI: University of Hawaii Press.

Meehan, B. (1982) *Shell Bed to Shell Midden*, Canberra: Australian Institute of Aboriginal Studies.

Merriwether, D. A., Hodgson, J. A., Friedlaender, F. R., Allaby, R., Cerchio, S., Koki, G. and Friedlaender, J. S. (2005) 'Ancient mitochondrial M haplogroups identified in the Southwest Pacific', *Proceedings of the National Academy of Science* 102: 13,034–9.

Miller, G. H., Magee, J. W. and Jull, A. J. T. (1997) 'Low-latitude cooling in the Southern Hemisphere from amino-acid racemization in emu eggshells', *Nature* 385: 241–4.

Miller, G. H., Magee, J. W., Johnson, B. J., Fogel, M. L., Spooner, N. A., McCulloch, M. T. and Ayliffe, L. K. (1999) 'Pleistocene extinction of *Genyornis newtoni*: human impact on Australian megafauna', *Science* 283: 205–8.

Miller, G. H., Fogel, M. L., Magee, J. W., Gagan, M. K., Clarke, S. J. and Johnson, B. J. (2005a) 'Ecosystem collapse in Pleistocene Australia and a human role in megafaunal extinction', *Science* 309: 287–90.

Miller, G. H., Mangan, J., Pollard, D., Thompson, S., Felzer, B. and Magee, J. (2005b) 'Sensitivity of the Australian monsoon to insolation and vegetation: implication for human impact on continental balance', *Geology* 33: 65–68.

Mitchell, S. (1993) 'Shell mound formation in northern Australia: a case study from Croker Island, northwestern Arnhem Land', *The Beagle* 10: 179–92.

Mitchell, S. (1994a) 'Culture contact and indigenous economies on the Coburg Peninsula, Northwestern Australia', PhD dissertation, Northern Territory University, Darwin.

Mitchell, S. (1994b) 'Stone exchange network in north-western Arnhem Land', in M. Sullivan, S. Brockwell and A. Webb (eds) *Archaeology in the North*, pp. 188–200, Darwin: North Australia Research Unit.

Morgan, L. H. (1877) *Ancient Society or Researches in the Lines of Human Progress from Savagery through Barbarism to Civilization*, New York: Henry Holt.

Morphy, H. (1990) 'Myth, totemism and the creation of clans', *Oceania* 60: 312–28.

Morphy, H. (1999) 'Encoding the dreaming – a theoretical framework for the analysis of representational processes in Australian Aboriginal art', *Australian Archaeology* 49: 13–22.

Morrison, M. (2003) 'Old boundaries and new horizons: the Weipa shell mounds reconsidered', *Archaeology in Oceania* 38: 1–8.

Morse, K. (1988) 'Mandu Mandu Creek rockshelter: Pleistocene human coastal occupation of North West Cape, Western Australia', *Archaeology in Oceania* 23: 81–8.

Morse, K. (1993a) 'New radiocarbon dates from North west Cape, Western Australia: a preliminary report', in M. A. Smith, M. Spriggs and B. Fankhauser (eds) *Sahul in Review: Pleistocene archaeology in Australia, New Guinea and Island Melanesia*, pp. 155–63, Canberra: Australian National University.

Morse, K. (1993b) 'Shell beads from Mandu Mandu Creek rock-shelter, Cape Range Peninsula, Western Australia, dated before 30,000 b.p.', *Antiquity* 67: 877–83.

Morse, K. (1996) 'Coastal shell middens, Cape Range Peninsula, Western Australia: an appraisal of the Holocene evidence', *Tempus* 4: 9–25.

Morse, K. (1999) 'Coastwatch: Pleistocene resource use on the Cape Range Peninsula', in J. Hall and I. McNiven (eds) *Australian Coastal Archaeology*, pp. 73–8, Canberra: Australian National University.

Morwood, M. J. (1981) 'Archaeology of the Central Queensland Highlands: the stone component', *Archaeology in Oceania* 16: 1–52.

Morwood, M. J. (1984) 'The prehistory of the Central Queensland Highlands', *Advances in World Archaeology* 3: 325–80.

Morwood, M. J. (2002) *Visions from the Past: The archaeology of Australian Aboriginal art*, Sydney: Allen & Unwin.

Morwood, M. J. and Hobbs, D. R. (1997) 'The Asian connection: preliminary report on Indonesian trepang sites on the Kimberley coast, N. W. Australia', *Archaeology in Oceania* 32: 197–206.

Morwood, M. J. and Trezise, P. J. (1989) 'Edge-ground axes in Pleistocene Australia: new evidence from southeast Cape York Peninsula', *Queensland Archaeological Research* 6: 77–90.

Morwood, M. J., Soejono, R. P., Roberts, R. G., Sutikna, T., Turney, C. S. M., Westaway, K. E. et al. (2004) 'Archaeology and age of a new hominin from Flores in eastern Indonesia', *Nature* 431: 1087–91.

Moser, S. (1992) 'Visions of the Australian Pleistocene: prehistoric life at Lake Mungo and Kutikina', *Australian Archaeology* 35: 1–10.

Mosimann, J. E. and Martin, P. S. (1975) 'Simulating overkill by Paleoindians', *American Scientist* 63: 304–13.

Mountford, C. P. (1956) *Records of the American-Australian Scientific Expedition to Arnhem Land*, Melbourne: Melbourne University Press.

Mowat, F. M. (1995) 'Variability in Western Arnhem Land shell midden deposits', unpublished MA thesis, Northern Territory University, Darwin.

Mulvaney, D. J. (1969) *The Prehistory of Australia*, London: Thames & Hudson.

Mulvaney, D. J. (1975) *The Prehistory of Australia*, Melbourne: Pelican.

Mulvaney, D. J. (1976) '"The chain of connection": the material evidence', in N. Peterson (ed.) *Tribes and Boundaries in Australia*, pp. 72–94, Canberra: Australian Institute of Aboriginal and Islander Studies.

Mulvaney, D. J. and Joyce, E. B. (1965) 'Archaeological and geomorphological investigations on Mt Moffatt Station, Queensland', *Proceedings of the Prehistoric Society* 31: 147–212.

Mulvaney, D. J. and Kamminga, J. (1999) *Prehistory of Australia*, Sydney: Allen & Unwin.

Murray, P. and Chaloupka, G. (1984) 'The dreamtime animals: extinct megafauna in Arnhem Land rock art', *Archaeology in Oceania* 19: 105–16.

Murray, T. (1988) 'Ethnoarchaeology or palaeoethnology?', in B. Meehan and R. Jones (eds) *Archaeology with Ethnography: An Australian perspective*, pp. 1–16, Canberra: Australian National University.

Murray-Wallace, C. V. (1996) 'Understanding "deep" time – advances since Archbishop Ussher?', *Archaeology in Oceania* 31: 173–7.

Nanson, G. C., Price, D. M., Short, S. A., Page, K. J and Nott, J. F. (1991) 'Major episodes of climate change in Australia over the last 300,000 years', in R. Gillespie (ed.) *Quaternary Dating Workshop 1990*, pp. 45–50, Canberra: Australian National University.

Nanson, G. C., Price, D. M. and Short, S. A. (1992) 'Wetting and drying of Australia over the past 300ka', *Geology* 20: 791–4.

Neal, R. and Stock, E. (1986) 'Pleistocene occupation in the southeast Queensland coastal region', *Nature* 323: 618–21.

Nilsson, S. (1868) *The Primitive Inhabitants of Scandinavia: An essay on comparative ethnography, and a contribution to the history of the development of mankind: containing a description of the implements, dwellings, tombs, and mode of living of the savages in the north of Europe during the Stone Age*, 3rd edition, London: Longmans, Green.

Nolch, G. (2001) 'Mungo man's DNA shakes the *Homo* family tree', *Australasian Science* 22(2): 29–31.

Oakley, K. P., Campbell, B. G. and Molleson, T. I. (1975) *Catalogue of Fossil Hominids*, London: British Museum.

O'Connell, J. F. and Allen, J. (1998) 'When did humans first arrive in Greater Australia and why is it important to know?', *Evolutionary Anthropology* 6: 132–46.

O'Connell, J. F. and Allen, J. (2004) 'Dating the colonization of Sahul (Pleistocene Australia – New Guinea): a review of recent research', *Journal of Archaeological Science* 31: 835–53.

O'Connor, S. (1987) 'The stone house structures of High Cliffy Island, North West Kimberley, W.A.', *Australian Archaeology* 25: 30–9.

O'Connor, S. (1989a) 'Contemporary island use in the west Kimberley, Western Australia, and its implications for archaeological site survival', *Australian Aboriginal Studies* 1989/2: 25–31.

O'Connor, S. (1989b) 'New radiocarbon dates from Koolan Island, West Kimberley, WA', *Australian Archaeology* 28: 92–104.

O'Connor, S. (1990) 'Thirty thousand years in the Kimberley', unpublished doctoral thesis, University of Western Australia, Perth.

O'Connor, S. (1992) 'The timing and nature of prehistoric island use in northern Australia', *Archaeology in Oceania* 27: 49–60.

O'Connor, S. (1994) 'A (6700) BP date for island use in the West Kimberley, Western Australia: new evidence from High Cliffy Island', *Australian Archaeology* 39: 102–7.

O'Connor, S. (1995) 'Carpenter's Gap Rock Shelter 1: 40,000 years of Aboriginal occupation in the Napier Ranges, Kimberley, W.A.', *Australian Archaeology* 40: 58–9.

O'Connor, S. (1996) 'Thirty thousand years in the Kimberley: results of excavation of three rockshelters in the coastal west Kimberley, W.A.', *Tempus* 4: 26–49.

O'Connor, S. (1999a) 'A diversity of coastal economies: shell mounds in the Kimberley region in the Holocene', in J. Hall and I. McNiven (eds) *Australian Coastal Archaeology*, pp. 37–50, Canberra: Australian National University.

O'Connor, S. (1999b) *30,000 Years of Aboriginal Occupation: Kimberley, North West Australia*, Terra Australis 14, Canberra: Australian National University.

O'Connor, S. and Fankhauser, B. (2001) 'One step closer: an ochre covered rock from Carpenters Gap Shelter 1, Kimberley region, Western Australia', in A. Anderson, I. Lilley and S. O'Connor (eds) *Histories of Old Ages: Essays in honour of Rhys Jones*, pp. 287–300, Canberra: Australian National University.

O'Connor, S. and Sullivan, M. (1994) 'Distinguishing middens and cheniers: a case study from the southern Kimberley, W.A.', *Archaeology in Oceania* 29: 16–28.

O'Connor, S. and Veth, P. (2006) 'Revisiting the past: changing interpretations of Pleistocene settlement subsistence and demography', in I. Lilley (ed.) *Archaeology of Oceania: Australia and the Pacific Islands*, pp. 31–47, Oxford: Blackwell.

O'Connor, S., Veth, P. and Hubbard, N. (1993) 'Changing interpretations of postglacial human subsistence and demography in Sahul', in M. A. Smith, M. Spriggs and B. Fankhauser (eds) *Sahul in Review: The archaeology of Australia, New Guinea and Island Melanesia*, Prehistory, pp. 95–105, Canberra: Australian National University Press.

O'Connor, S., Veth, P. and Campbell, C. (1998) 'Serpent's Glen Rockshelter: report of the first Pleistocene-aged occupation sequence from the Western Desert', *Australian Archaeology* 46: 12–22.

O'Connor, S., Veth, P. and Barham, A. (1999) 'Cultural versus natural explanations for lacunae in Aboriginal occupation deposits in northern Australia', *Quaternary International* 59: 61–70.

Odell, G. H. (2003) *Lithic Analysis*, New York: Springer.

Oppenheimer, C. (2002) 'Limited global change due to the largest known Quaternary eruption, Toba c.74kyr BP?', *Quaternary Science Reviews* 81: 1593–609.

Pack, S. M., Miller, G. M., Fogel, M. L. and Spooner, N. A. (2003) 'Carbon isotopic evidence for increased aridity in northwestern Australia through the Quaternary', *Quaternary Science Reviews* 22: 629–43.

Palanichamy, M. C., Sun, C., Agrawal, S., Bandelt, H., Kong, Q., Khan, F. et al. (2004) 'Phylogeny of Mitochondrial DNA Macrohaplogroup N in India, based on complete sequencing: implications for the peopling of South Asia', *American Journal of Human Genetics* 75: 966–78.

Pardoe, C. (1988) 'The cemetery as symbol: the distribution of prehistoric Aboriginal burial grounds in southeastern Australia', *Archaeology in Oceania* 23: 1–16.

Pardoe, C. (1990) 'The demographic basis of human evolution in southeastern Australia', in B. Meehan and N. White (eds) *Hunter-gatherer Demography: Past and present*, Sydney: Oceania.

Pardoe, C. (1991a) 'Competing paradigms and ancient human remains: the state of the discipline', *Archaeology in Oceania* 26: 79–85.

Pardoe, C. (1991b) 'Isolation and evolution in Tasmania', *Cultural Anthropology* 32: 1–21.

Pardoe, C. (1993) 'The Pleistocene is still with us: analytical constraints and possibilities for the study of ancient human remains in archaeology', in M. A. Smith, M. Spriggs and B. Fankhauser (eds) *Sahul in Review: Pleistocene archaeology in Australia, New Guinea and Island Melanesia*, pp. 59–70, Canberra: Australian National University.

Pardoe, C. (1994) 'Bioscapes: the evolutionary landscape of Australia', *Archaeology in Oceania* 29: 182–90.

Pardoe, C. (2006) 'Becoming Australian: evolutionary processes and biological variation from ancient to modern times', *Before Farming* (online version) 2006/1 article 4.

Pate, F. D. (1986) 'The effects of drought on Ngatatjara plant use: an evaluation of optimal foraging theory', *Human Ecology* 14: 95–115.

Pate, F. D. (2006) 'Hunter-gatherer social complexity at Roonka Flat, South Australia', in B. David, B. Barker and I. McNiven (eds) *The Social Archaeology of Australian Indigenous Societies*, pp. 226–41, Canberra: Aboriginal Studies Press.

Pate, F. D., Pretty, G. L., Hunter, R., Tuniz, C. and Lawson, E. M. (1998) 'New radiocarbon dates for the Roonka Flat Aboriginal burial ground, South Australia', *Australian Archaeology* 46: 36–7.

Pate, F. D., McDowell, M. M., Wells, R. T. and Smith, A. M. (2002) 'Last recorded evidence for megafauna at Wet Cave, Naracoorte, South Australia 45,000 years ago', *Australian Archaeology* 54: 53–5.

Patton, P. C., Pickup, G. and Price, D. M. (1993) 'Holocene palaeofloods of the Ross River, central Australia', *Quaternary Research* 40: 201–12.

Pearce, R. H. (1974) 'Spatial and temporal distribution of Australian backed blades', *Mankind* 9: 300–9.

Pearce, R. H. and Barbetti, M. (1981) 'A 38,000-year-old archaeological site at Upper Swan, Western Australia', *Archaeology in Oceania* 16: 173–8.

Pearson, S. and Dodson, J. R. (1993) 'Stick-nest rat middens as sources of palaeoecological data in Australian deserts', *Quaternary Research* 39: 347–54.

Peterson, N. (1971) 'Open sites and the ethnographic approach to the archaeology of hunter-gatherers', in D. J. Mulvaney and J. Golson (eds) *Aboriginal Man and Environment in Australia*, pp. 239–248, Canberra: Australian National University Press.

Peterson, N. and Lampert, R. (1985) 'A Central Australian ochre mine', *Records of the Australian Museum* 37: 1–9.

Phillip, A. (1789) *The Voyage of Governor Phillip to Botany Bay with an Account of the Establishment of the Colonies of Port Jackson and Norfolk Island*, London: John Stockdale.

Pietrusewsky, M. (1979) 'Craniometric variation in Pleistocene Australia and more recent Australian and New Guinean populations studied by multivariate procedures', *Occasional Papers in Human Biology* 2: 83–123.

Pike-Tay, A. and Cosgrove, R. (2002) 'From reindeer to wallaby: recovering patterns of seasonality, mobility, and prey selection in the Paleolithic Old World', *Journal of Archaeological Method and Theory* 9: 101–46.

Plomley, N. J. B. (1992) *The Aboriginal/Settler Clash in Van Dieman's Land 1803–1831*, Occasional Paper 3, Queen Victoria Museum and Art Gallery, Launceston, Tasmania.

Porch, N. and Allen, J. (1995) 'Tasmania: archaeological and palaeo-ecological perspectives', *Antiquity* 69: 714–32.

Presser, J. C., Deverell, A. J., Redd, A. and Stoneking, M. (2002) 'Tasmanian Aborigines and DNA', *Papers and Proceedings of the Royal Society of Tasmania* 136: 35–8.

Pretty, G. L. (1977) 'The cultural chronology of Roonka Flat', in R. V. S. Wright (ed.) *Stone Tools as Cultural Markers: Change, evolution and complexity*, pp. 288–331, Canberra: Australian Institute of Aboriginal Studies.

Pretty, G. L. and Kricun, M. E. (1989) 'Prehistoric health status of the Roonka population', *World Archaeology* 21: 198–224.

Price, G. J. (2002) '*Perameles sobbei* sp. Nov. (Marsupialia, Peramelidae), a Pleistocene bandicoot from the Darling Downs, south-eastern Queensland', *Memoirs of the Queensland Museum* 48: 193–7.

Price, G. J. (2005a) 'Fossil bandicoots (Marsupialia, Peramelidae) and environmental change during the Pleistocene on the Darling Downs, southeastern Queensland, Australia', *Journal of Systematic Palaeontology* 2: 347–56.

Price, G. J. (2005b) 'A small adult *Palorchestes* (Marsupialia, Palorchestidae) from the Pleistocene of the Darling Downs, southeast Queensland', *Memoirs of the Queensland Museum* 51: 202.

Price, G. J. and Sobbe, I. H. (2005) 'Pleistocene palaeoecology and environmental change on the Darling Downs, Southeastern Queensland', *Memoirs of the Queensland Museum* 51: 171–201.

Price, G. J., Tyler, M. J. and Cooke, B. N. (2005) 'Pleistocene frogs from the Darling Downs, southeastern Queensland, and their palaeoenvironmental significance', *Alcheringa* 29: 171–82.

Prokopec, M. (1979) 'Demographical and morphological aspects of the Roonka populations', *Archaeology and Physical Anthropology in Oceania* 14: 11–26.

Przywolnik, K. (2005) 'Long-term transitions in hunter-gatherers of coastal northwestern Australia', in P. Veth, M. Smith and P. Hiscock (eds) *Desert Peoples: Archaeological perspectives*, pp. 177–205, Oxford: Blackwell.

Quintana-Murci, L., Semino, O., Bandelt, H-J., Passarino, G., McElreavey, K. and Santachiara-Benerecetti, A. S. (1999) 'Genetic evidence of an early exit of Homo sapiens from Africa through eastern Africa', *Nature Genetics* 23: 437–41.

Radcliffe-Brown, A. R. (1926) 'The Rainbow-Serpent myths of Australia', *Journal of the Royal Anthropological Institute* 56: 19–25.

Rampino, M. R. (2002) 'Supereruptions as a threat to civilizations on Earth-like planets', *Icarus* 156: 562–9.

Rampino, M. R. and Ambrose, S. (2000) 'Volcanic winter in the Garden of Eden: the Toba super-eruption and Late Pleistocene human population crash', *Geological Society of America Special Paper* 345: 71–82.

Rampino, M. R. and Self, S. (1992) 'Volcanic winter and accelerated glaciation following the Toba supereruption', *Nature* 359: 50–2.

Rampino, M. R. and Self, S. (1993) 'Climate-volcanism feedback and the Toba eruption of 274,000 years ago', *Quaternary Research* 40: 269–80.

Rampino, M. R., Self, S. and Stothers, R. B. (1988) 'Volcanic winters', *Annual Review of Earth and Planetary Science* 16: 73–99.

Read, D. (2006) 'Tasmanian knowledge and skill: maladaptative imitation or adaptive technology', *American Antiquity* 71: 164–84.

Redd, A. J. and Stoneking, M. (1999) 'Peopling of Sahul: mtDNA variation in Aboriginal Australian and Papua New Guinean populations', *American Journal of Human Genetics* 65: 808–28.

Redd, A. J., Roberts-Thomson, J., Karafet, T., Bamshad, M., Jorde, L. B., Naidu, J. M. et al. (2002) 'Gene flow from the Indian subcontinent to Australia: evidence from the Y chromosome', *Current Biology* 12: 673–7.

Reimer, P. J., Baillie, M. G. L., Bard, E., Bayliss, A., Beck, J. W., Bertrand, C. J. H. et al. (2004) 'INTCAL04 terrestrial radiocarbon age calibration, 0–26 CAL KYR BP', *Radiocarbon* 46: 1029–58.

Relethford, J. H. (1998) 'Genetics and modern human origins and diversity', *Annual Review of Anthropology* 27: 1–23.

Relethford, J. H. (2001) *Genetics and the Search for Modern Human Origins*, New York: Wiley.

Richards, F. (1926) 'Customs and language of the western Hodgkinson Aboriginals', *Memoirs of the Queensland Museum* 8: 249–65.

Richardson, N. (1992) 'Conjoin sets and stratigraphic integrity in a sandstone shelter: Kenniff Cave (Queensland, Australia)', *Antiquity* 66: 408–18.

Rindos, D. and Webb, E. (1992) 'Modelling the initial human colonisation of Australia: perfect adaptation, cultural variability and cultural change', *Proceedings of the Australasian Society of Human Biology* 5: 441–54.

Roberts, R. G. and Jones, R. (1994) 'Luminescence dating of sediments: new light on the human colonisation of Australia', *Australian Aboriginal Studies* 1994/2: 2–17.

Roberts, R. G., Jones, R. and Smith, M. A. (1990a) 'Thermoluminescence dating of a 50,000 year-old human occupation site in northern Australia', *Nature* 345: 153–6.

Roberts, R. G., Jones, R. and Smith, M. A. (1990b) 'Stratigraphy and statistics at Malakunanja II: reply to Hiscock', *Archaeology in Oceania* 25: 125–9.

Roberts, R. G., Jones, R. and Smith, M. A. (1990c) 'Early dates at Malakunanja II: a reply to Bowdler', *Australian Archaeology* 31: 94–7.

Roberts, R. G., Jones, R. and Smith, M. A. (1993) 'Optical dating at Deaf Adder Gorge, Northern Territory, indicates human occupation between 53,000 and 60,000 years ago', *Australian Archaeology* 37: 58–9.

Roberts, R. G., Jones, R. and Smith, M. A. (1994a) 'Beyond the radiocarbon barrier in Australian prehistory: a critique of Allen's commentary', *Antiquity* 68: 611–16.

Roberts, R. G., Jones, R., Spooner, N. A., Head, M. J., Murray, A. S. and Smith, M. A. (1994b) 'The human colonisation of Australia: optical dates of 53,000 and 60,000 years bracket human arrival at Deaf Adder Gorge, Northern Territory', *Quaternary Geochronology, Quaternary Science Reviews* 13: 575–83.

Roberts, R. G., Spooner, N. A., Jones, R., Cane, S., Olley, J. M., Murray, A. S. and Head, J. (1996) 'Preliminary luminescence dating for archaeological sediments on the Nullarbor Plain, South Australia', *Australian Archaeology* 42: 7–16.

Roberts, R. G., Walsh, G. L., Murray, A., Olley, J. M., Jones, R., Morwood, M. et al. (1997)

'Luminescence dating of rock art and past environments using mud-wasp nests in northern Australia', *Nature* 387: 696–9.

Roberts, R. G., Bird, M., Olley, J., Galbraith, R., Lawson, E., Laslett, G. et al. (1998) 'Optical and radiocarbon dating at Jinmiun rock shelter in northern Australia', *Nature* 393: 358.

Roberts, R. G., Flannery, T. F., Ayliffe, L. K., Yoshida, H., Olley, J. M., Prideaux, G. J. et al. (2001) 'New ages for the last Asutralian megafauna: continent-wide extinction about 46,000 years ago', *Science* 292: 1888–92.

Roberts, R. G., Yoshida, H., Olley, J. M., Ashton, M., Lawson, E. M., Walsh, G. L. et al. (2003) 'Optical dating of fossil mud-wasp nests and associated rock art in northern Australia: implications for the antiquity of modern human behaviour', paper presented at Modern Human Origins: Australian Perspectives conference, University of New South Wales, Sydney.

Robertson, G. (2002) 'Birds of a feather stick: microscopic feather residues on stone artefacts from Deep Creek Shelter, New South Wales', in S. Ulm, C. Westcott, J. Reid, A. Ross, I. Lilley, J. Prangnell and L. Kirkwood (eds) *Barrier, Borders, Boundaries*, pp. 175–82, Brisbane: University of Queensland.

Robertson, G. (2005) 'Backed artefact use in Eastern Australia: a residue and use-wear analysis', unpublished doctoral thesis, University of Queensland, Brisbane.

Robertson, S. (2003) 'A critical evaluation of the application of cribra orbitalia in Australian archaeology as a correlate of sedentism', BA (Hons) thesis, Australian National University, Canberra.

Rogers, A. R. and Harpending, H. (1992) 'Population growth makes waves in the distribution of pairwise genetic differences', *Molecular Biology and Evolution* 9: 552–69.

Rose, D. (2006) 'A systemic functional approach to language evolution', *Cambridge Archaeological Journal* 16: 73–96.

Rose, W. I. and Chesner, C. A. (1990) 'Worldwide dispersal of ash and gases from earth's largest known eruption: Toba, Sumatra, 75 ka.', *Palaeogeography, Palaeoclimatology, Palaeoecology* 89: 269–75.

Rosenfeld, A. (1981) 'Rock engravings in the Laura area', in A. Rosenfeld, D. Horton and J. Winter (eds) *Early Man in North Queensland: Art and archaeology in the Laura Area*, Terra Australis 6, pp. 50–89, Canberra: Australian National University.

Rosenfeld, A. and Smith, M. A. (2002) 'Rock art and the history of Puritjarra rock shelter, Cleland Hills, central Australia', *Proceedings of the Prehistoric Society* 68: 103–24.

Ross, A. (1986) 'Archaeological evidence for population change in the middle to late Holocene in southeastern Australia', *Archaeology in Oceania* 20: 81–9.

Ross, A., Donnelly, T. and Wasson, R. (1992) 'The peopling of the arid zone: human–environment interactions', in J. Dodson (ed.) *The Naive Lands: Prehistory and environmental change in Australia and the South West Pacific*, pp. 76–113, Melbourne: Longman Press.

Rowland, M. (1987) 'The distribution of Aboriginal watercraft on the east coast of Queensland: implications for culture contact', *Australian Aboriginal Studies* 1987/2: 38–45.

Rowland, M. (1989) 'Population increase, intensification or a result of preservation? Explaining site distribution patterns on the coast of Queensland', *Australian Aboriginal Studies* 1989/2: 32–42.

Rowland, M. (1992) 'Climate change, sea-level rise and the archaeological record', *Australian Archaeology* 34: 29–33.

Rowland, M. (1999) 'Holocene environmental variability: have its impacts been underestimated in Australian pre history?', *The Artefact* 22: 11–40.

Ryan, L. (1996) *The Aboriginal Tasmanians*, Brisbane: University of Queensland Press.

Salmon, M. H. (1982) *Philosophy and Archaeology*, London: Academic Press.

Sattherthwait, L. D. (1980) 'Aboriginal Australia: the simplest technologies?', *Archaeology and Physical Anthropology in Oceania* 15: 153–6.

Savolainen, P., Leitner, T., Wilton, A. N., Matisoo-Smith, E. and Lundeberg, J. (2004) 'A detailed picture of the origin of the Australian dingo, obtained from the study of mitochondrial DNA', *Proceedings of the National Academy of Sciences* 101: 12,387–90.

Schiffer, M. B. (1987) *Formation Processes of the Archaeological Record*, Albuquerque, NM: University of New Mexico Press.

Schrire, C. (1972) 'Ethno-archaeology models and subsistence behaviour in Arnhem Land', in D. J. Clarke (ed.) *Models in Archaeology*, pp. 653–69, London: Methuen.

Schrire, C. (1982) *The Alligator Rivers: Prehistory and ecology in western Arnhem Land*, Terra Australia 7, Canberra: Australian National University.

Schultz, M. (2001) 'Paleohistopathology of bone: a new approach to the study of ancient diseases', *Yearbook of Physical Anthropology* 44: 106–47.

Shackleton, N. J. (1987) 'Oxygen isotopes, ice volume and sea level', *Quaternary Science Reviews* 6: 183–90.

Shackleton, N. J. and Pisias, N. G. (1985) 'Atmospheric carbon dioxide, orbital forcing, and climate', in E. T. Sunquist and W. S. Broecker (eds) *The Carbon Cycle and Atmospheric CO2: Natural variations Archean to present*, pp. 303–17, Washington, DC: American Geophysical Union.

Shawcross, W. (1998) 'Archaeological excavations at Mungo', *Archaeology in Oceania* 33: 183–200.

Sherry, S. T., Rogers, A. R., Harpending, H., Soodyall, H., Jenkins, T. and Stoneking, M. (1994) 'Mismatch distributions of mtDNA reveal recent human population size', *Genetics* 147: 1977–82.

Shulmeister, J. and Lees, B. G. (1995) 'Pollen evidence from tropical Australia for the onset of an ENSO-dominated climate at c.4000 BP', *The Holocene* 5: 10–18.

Siirainen, A. (1977) 'Rockshelters and vertical movement', *Proceedings of the Prehistoric Society* 43: 349–53.

Sim, R. (1994) 'Prehistoric human occupation in the King and Furneaux Island regions, Bass Strait', in M. Sullivan, S. Brockwell and A. Webb (eds) *Archaeology in the North*, pp. 358–74, Darwin: North Australia Research Unit.

Sim, R. (1999) 'Why the Tasmanians stopped eating fish: evidence for late Holocene expansion in resource exploitation strategies', in J. Hall and I. J. McNiven (eds) *Australian Coastal Archaeology*, pp. 263–9, Canberra: Australian National University.

Sim, R. and Thorne, A. (1990) 'Pleistocene human remains from King Island, southeastern Australia', *Australian Archaeology* 31: 44–51.

Sim, R. and Thorne, A. (1994) 'The gracile male skeleton from late Pleistocene King Island, Australia', *Australian Archaeology* 38: 8–10.

Sim, R. and Thorne, A. (1995) 'Reply to Brown', *Australian Archaeology* 41: 29–30.

Singh, G. (1981) 'Late Quaternary pollen records and seasonal palaeoclimates of Lake Frome, South Australia', *Hydrobiologia* 82: 419–30.

Singh, G. and Geissler, E. A. (1985) 'Late Cainozoic history of vegetation, fire, lake levels and climate, at Lake George, New South Wales, Australia', *Philosophical Transactions of the Royal Society of London B* 311: 379–447.

Singh, G. and Luly, J. (1991) 'Changes in vegetation and seasonal climate since the last full glacial at Lake Frome, South Australia', *Palaeogeography, Palaeoclimatology, Palaeoecology* 84: 75–86.

Slack, M. J., Fullagar, R. L. K., Field, J. and Border, A. (2004) 'New Pleistocene ages for backed artefact technology in Australia', *Archaeology in Oceania* 39: 131–7.

Smith, C. (1992) 'Colonising with style: reviewing the nexus between rock art, territoriality and the colonisation and occupation of Sahul', *Australian Archaeology* 34: 34–42.

Smith, M. (1982) 'Late Pleistocene zamia exploitation in southern Western Australia', *Archaeology in Oceania* 26: 117–21.

Smith, M. (1996) 'Revisiting Pleistocene Macrozamia', *Australian Archaeology* 42: 52–3.

Smith, M. A. (1982) 'Devon Downs reconsidered: changes in site use at a Lower Murray Valley Rockshelter', *Archaeology in Oceania* 17: 109–16.

Smith, M. A. (1985) 'A morphological comparison of Central Australian seedgrinding implements and Australian Pleistocene age grindstones', *The Beagle* 2: 23–38.

Smith, M. A. (1986a) 'The antiquity of seedgrinding in Central Australia', *Archaeology in Oceania* 21: 29–39.

Smith, M. A. (1986b) 'A revised chronology for Intirtekwerle (James Range East) rockshelter, Central Australia', *The Beagle* 3: 123–30.

Smith, M. A. (1987) 'Pleistocene occupation in arid Central Australia', *Nature* 328: 710.

Smith, M. A. (1988) 'Central Australian seed grinding implements and Pleistocene grindstones', in B. Meehan and R. Jones (eds) *Archaeology with Ethnography: An Australian perspective*, pp. 94–108, Canberra: Australian National University.

Smith, M. A. (1989a) 'Central Australian seed grinding implements and Pleistocene grindstones', in B. Meehan and R. Jones (eds) *Archaeology with Ethnography: An Australian perspective*, pp. 94–106, Canberra: Australian National University.

Smith, M. A. (1989b) 'Seed gathering in inland Australia: current evidence from seed grinders on the antiquity of the ethnohistorical pattern of exploitation', in D. R. Harris and G. C. Hillman (eds) *Foraging and Farming: The evolution of plant exploitation*, pp. 305–17, London: Unwin Hyman.

Smith, M. A. (1989c) 'The case for a resident human population in the Central Australian Ranges during full glacial aridity', *Archaeology in Oceania* 24: 93–105.

Smith, M. A. (1993) 'Biogeography, human ecology and prehistory in the sandridge deserts', *Australian Archaeology* 37: 35–50.

Smith, M. A. (1996) 'Prehistory and human ecology in central Australia: an archaeological perspective', in S. R. Morton and D. J. Mulvaney (eds) *Exploring Central Australia: Society, the environment and the 1894 Horn expedition*, pp. 61–73, Chipping Norton, UK: Surrey, Beatty and Sons.

Smith, M. A. (2005) 'Desert archaeology, linguistic stratigraphy, and the spread of Western Desert language', in P. Veth, M. Smith and P. Hiscock (eds) *Desert Peoples: Archaeological perspectives*, pp. 222–42, Oxford: Blackwell.

Smith, M. A. (2006) 'Characterising late Pleistocene and Holocene stone artefact assemblages from Puritjarra rock shelter: a long sequence from the Australian desert', *Records of the Australian Museum* 58: 371–410.

Smith, M. A. and Cundy, B. J. (1985) 'Distribution maps for flaked stone points and backed blades in the Northern Territory', *Australian Aboriginal Studies* 1985/2: 32–7.

Smith, M. A. and Sharp, N. D. (1993) 'Pleistocene sites in Australia, New Guinea and Island Melanesia: geographic and temporal structure of the archaeological record', in M. A. Smith, M. Spriggs and B. Fankhauser (eds) *Sahul in Review: Pleistocene archaeology in Australia, New Guinea and Island Melanesia*, pp. 37–59, Canberra: Australian National University.

Smith, M. A., Prescott, J. R. and Head, M. J. (1997) 'Comparison of 14C and luminescence chronologies at Puritjarra rock shelter, central Australia', *Quaternary Science Reviews* 16: 299–320.

Smith, M. A., Fankhauser, B. and Jercher, M. (1998) 'The changing provenance of red ochre at Puritjarra rock shelter, central Australia: Late Pleistocene to present', *Proceedings of the Prehistoric Society* 64: 275–92.

Smith, M. A., Bird, M. J., Turney, C. S. M., Fifield, L. K., Santos, G. M., Hausladen, P. A. and di Tada, M. L. (2001) 'New ABOX AMS-14C ages remove dating anomalies at Puritjarra rock shelter', *Australian Archaeology* 53: 45–7.

Smith, P. (2000) 'Dietary stress or cultural practice: fragmented bones at the Puntutjarpa and Serpent's Glen rockshelters', *Australian Archaeology* 51: 65–6.

Smith, P., Wax, Y., Adler, F., Silberman, D. and Heinic, G. (1986) 'Post-Pleistocene changes in tooth root and jaw relationships', *American Journal of Physical Anthropology* 70: 339–48.

Southon, J. A. (2004) 'Radiocarbon perspective on Greenland ice-core chronologies: can we use ice cores for 14C calibration?', *Radiocarbon* 46: 1239–59.

Spooner, N. A. (1998) 'Human occupation at Jinmium, northern Australia: 116,000 years ago or much less?', *Antiquity* 72: 173–8.

Stiner, M. C. (2001) 'Thirty years on the "Broad Spectrum Revolution" and paleolithic demography', *Proceedings of the National Academy of Science* 98: 6993–6.

Stiner, M. C., Munro, N. D., Surovell, T. A., Tchernov, E. and Bar-Yosef, O. (1999) 'Paleolithic population growth pulses evidenced by small animal exploitation', *Science* 283: 190–4.

Stockton, E. D. (1973) 'Shaw's Creek Shelter: human displacement of artefacts and its significance', *Mankind* 14: 112–17.

Stockton, E. D. (1981) 'Recent dates for large tool assemblages on the Central Coast, N.S.W.', *The Artefact* 6: 89–95.

Stockton, E. D. and Holland, W. (1974) 'Cultural sites and their environment in the Blue Mountains', *Archaeology and Physical Anthropology in Oceania* 9: 36–65.

Stockton, J. (1983) 'The prehistoric population of northwest Tasmania', *Australian Archaeology* 17: 67–78.

Stone, T. (1989) 'Origins and environmental significance of shell and earth mounds in northern Australia', *Archaeology in Oceania* 24: 59–64.

Stone, T. and Cupper, M. L. (2003) 'Last Glacial Maximum ages for robust humans at Kow Swamp, southern Australia', *Journal of Human Evolution* 45: 99–111.

Stringer, C. (1998) 'A metrical study of the WLH-50 calvaria', *Journal of Human Evolution* 34: 327–32.

Sullivan, M. E. (1982) 'Exploitation of offshore islands along the New South Wales coastline', *Australian Archaeology* 15: 8–19.

Sullivan, M. E. (1989) 'The recent prehistoric exploitation of edible mussel in aboriginal shell middens in southern New South Wales', *Archaeology in Oceania* 22: 97–111.

Sutton, S. (1985) 'Waragarra stone', unpublished BA (Hons) thesis, University of New England, Armidale, NSW.

Swain, T. (1993) *A Place for Strangers: Towards a history of Australian Aboriginal being*, Cambridge: Cambridge University Press.

Sweller, S. (2001) 'Vegetational and climatic changes during the last 40,000 years at Burraga Swamp, Barrington Tops, NSW', unpublished BA (Hons) thesis, University of New South Wales, Sydney.

Taçon, P. (1993) 'Regionalism in the recent rock art of western Arnhem Land, Northern Territory', *Archaeology in Oceania* 28: 112–20.

Taçon, P. (1994) 'Socialising landscapes: the long-term implications of signs, symbols and marks on the land', *Archaeology in Oceania* 29: 117–29.

Taçon, P. and Brockwell, S. (1995) 'Arnhem Land prehistory in landscape, stone and paint', *Antiquity* 69: 676–95.

Taçon, P. and Chippindale, C. (1994) 'Australia's ancient warriors: changing depictions of fighting in the rock art of Arnhem Land, N.T.', *Cambridge Archaeological Journal* 4: 211–48.

Taçon, P., Wilson, M. and Chippindale, C. (1996) 'Birth of the Rainbow Serpent in Arnhem Land rock art and oral history', *Archaeology in Oceania* 31: 103–24.

Tamisari, F. and Wallace, J. (2006) 'Towards an experiental archaeology of place: from location to situation through the body', in B. David, B. Barker and I. McNiven (eds) *The Social Archaeology of Australian Indigenous Societies*, pp. 204–23, Canberra: Aboriginal Studies Press.

Taylor, L. (1990) 'The Rainbow Serpent as visual metaphor in western Arnhem Land', *Oceania* 60: 329–44.

Thomas, J. (1999) *Understanding the Neolithic*, London: Routledge.

Thomas, M., Gilbert, P., Willerslev, E., Hansen, A. J., Barnes, I., Rudbeck, L. et al. (2003) 'Distribution patterns of postmortem damage in human mitochondrial DNA', *American Journal of Human Genetic* 72: 32–47.

Thomson, D. F. (1949) *Economic Structure and the Ceremonial Exchange in Arnhem Land*, Melbourne: Macmillan.

Thorley, P. (1998) 'Pleistocene settlement in the Austalian arid zone: occupation of an inland riverine landscape in the central Australian ranges', *Antiquity* 72: 34–45.

Thorley, P. (2001) 'Uncertain supplies: water availability and regional archaeological structure in the Palmer River catchment, central Australia', *Archaeology in Oceania* 36: 1–14.

Thorley, P. (2004) 'Rock-art and the archaeological record of Indigenous settlement in Central Australia', *Australian Aboriginal Studies* 2004/1: 79–89.

Thorne, A. G. (1971) 'Mungo and Kow Swamp: morphological variation in Pleistocene Australians', *Mankind* 8: 85–9.

Thorne, A. G. (1976) 'Morphological contrasts in Pleistocene Australia', in R. L. Kirk and A. G. Thorne (eds) *The Origin of the Australians*, pp. 95–112, Canberra: Australian Institute of Aboriginal Studies.

Thorne, A. G. (1977) 'Separation or reconciliation? Biological clues to the development of Australian Society', in J. Allen, J. Golson and R. Jones (eds) *Sunda and Sahul: Prehistoric studies in Southeast Asia, Melanesia and Australia*, pp. 187–204, London: Academic Press.

Thorne, A. G. and Curnoe, D. (2000) 'Sex and significance of Lake Mungo 3: reply to Brown "Australian Pleistocene variation and the sex of Lake Mungo 3"', *Journal of Human Evolution* 39: 587–600.

Thorne, A. G. and Macumber, P. G. (1972) 'Discoveries of Late Pleistocene man at Kow Swamp', *Nature* 238: 316–19.

Thorne, A. G. and Wilson, S. R. (1977) 'Pleistocene and recent Australians: a multivariate comparison', *Journal of Human Evolution* 6: 393–402.

Thorne, A. G. and Wolpoff, M. H. (1981) 'Regional continuity in Australasian Pleistocene hominid evolution', *American Journal of Physical Anthropology* 55: 337–41.

Thorne, A. G. and Wolpoff, M. H. (1992) 'The multiregional evolution of humans', *Scientific American* 266: 28–33.

Thorne, A. G., Grün, R., Mortimer, G., Spooner, N. A., Simpson, J. J., McCulloch, M. et al. (1999) 'Australia's oldest human remains: age of the Lake Mungo 3 skeleton', *Journal of Human Evolution* 36: 591–612.

Tindale, N. B. (1985) 'Australian Aboriginal techniques of pressure-flaking stone implements: some personal observations', in M. G. Plew, J. C. Woods and M. G. Pavesic (eds) *Stone Tool Analysis*, pp. 1–35, Albuquerque, NM: University of New Mexico Press.

Tommaseo-Ponzetta, M., Attimonelli, M., De Robertis, M., Tanzariello, F. and Saccone, C.

(2002) 'Mitochondrial DNA variability of west New Guinea populations', *American Journal of Physical Anthropology* 117: 49–67.

Tonkinson, N. B. (1991) *The Martu Aborigines: Living the dream of Australia's desert*, Fort Worth, TX: Holt, Rinehart & Winston.

Torrence, R. (1983) 'Time budgeting and hunter-gatherer technology', in G. Bailey (ed.) *Hunter-gatherer Economy in Prehistory*, pp. 11–22, Cambridge: Cambridge University Press.

Trigger, B. (1990) *A History of Archaeological Thought*, Cambridge: Cambridge University Press.

Trueman, C. N. G., Field, J. H., Dortch, J., Charles, B. and Wroe, S. (2005) 'Prolonged coexistence of humans and megafauna in Pleistocene Australia', *Proceedings of the National Academy of Science* 102: 8381–5.

Turney, C. S. M. and Hobbs, D. (2006) 'ENSO influence on Holocene Aboriginal populations in Queensland, Australia', *Journal of Archaeological Science* 33:1744–8.

Turney, C. S. M., Bird, M. I., Fifield, L. K., Roberts, R. G., Smith, M., Dortch, C. E. et al. (2001) 'Early human occupation at Devil's Lair, southwestern Australia, 50,000 years ago', *Quaternary Research* 55: 3–13.

Tylor, E. (1871) *Primitive Culture: Researches into the development of mythology, philosophy, religion, art and custom*, London: John Murray.

Ulm, S. (2004) 'Investigations towards a late Holocene archaeology of Aboriginal lifeways on the southern Curtis Coast, Australia', unpublished doctoral thesis, University of Queensland, Brisbane.

Urry, J. and Walsh, M. (1981) 'The lost Macassar language of northern Australia', *Aboriginal History* 5: 91–100.

van der Kaars, S. A. (1991) 'Palynology of eastern Indonesian marine piston cores: a late Quaternary vegetational and climatic record for Australasia', *Palaeogeography, Palaeoclimatology, Palaeoecology* 85: 239–302.

van der Plicht, J., Beck, J. W., Bard, E., Baillie, M. G. L., Blackwell, P. G., Buck, C. E., et al. (2004) 'NOTCAL04 – comparison/calibration 14C records 26–50 CAL KYR BP', *Radiocarbon* 46: 1225–38.

van Holst Pellekaan, S. and Harding, R. (2006) 'Excavating the mitochondrial genome identifies major haplogroups in Aboriginal Australians', *Before Farming* (online version) 2006/1 article 3.

van Holst Pellekaan, S. M., Frommer, M., Sved, J. A. and Boettcher, B. (1997) 'Mitochondrial D-loop diversity in Australian riverine and Australian desert Aborigines', *Electrophoresis* 618: 1538–43.

van Holst Pellekaan, S. M., Frommer, M., Sved, J. A. and Boettcher, B. (1998) 'Mitochondrial control region sequence variation in aboriginal Australians', *American Journal of Human Genetics* 62: 435–49.

van Holst Pellekaan, S. M., Ingman, M., Roberts-Thomson, J. and Harding, R. M. (2006) 'Mitochondrial genomics identifies major haplogroups in aboriginal Australians', *American Journal of Physical Anthropology* 130: 123–34.

van Huet, S., Grün, R., Murray-Wallace, C. V., Redvers-Newton, N. and White, J. P. (1998) 'Age of the Lancefield megafauna: a reappraisal', *Australian Archaeology* 46: 5–11.

Vanderwal, R. (1978) 'Adaptive technology in south west Tasmania', *Australian Archaeology* 8: 107–27.

Vanderwal, R. and Fullager, R. (1989) 'Engraved *Diprotodon* tooth from the Spring Creek locality, Victoria', *Archaeology in Oceania* 24: 13–16.

Vanderwal, R. and Horton, D. (1984) *Coastal Southwest Tasmania*, Terra Australis 9, Canberra: Australian National University.

Veitch, B. (1999) 'Shell middens on the Mitchell Plateau: a reflection of a wider phenomenon?', in J. Hall and I. McNiven (eds) *Australian Coastal Archaeology*, pp. 51–64, Canberra: Australian National University.

Veth, P. (1987) 'Martujarra prehistory: variation in arid zone adaptations', *Australian Archaeology* 25: 102–11.

Veth, P. (1989) 'Islands in the interior: a model for the colonization of Australia's arid zone', *Archaeology in Oceania* 24: 81–92.

Veth, P. (1993) *Islands in the Interior: The dynamics of prehistoric adaptations within the Arid Zone of Australia*, International Monographs in Prehistory, Archaeological Series 3.

Veth, P. (1995) 'Marginal returns and fringe benefits: characterising the prehistory of the lowland deserts of Australia', *Australian Archaeology* 40: 32–8.

Veth, P. (1996) 'Current archaeological evidence from the Little and Great Sandy Deserts', *Tempus* 4: 50–65.

Veth, P. (2000) 'Origins of the Western Desert language: convergence in linguistic and archaeological space and time models', *Archaeology in Oceania* 35: 11–19.

Veth, P. (2005) 'Cycles of aridity and human mobility risk minimization among Late Pleistocene foragers of the Western Desert, Australia', in P. Veth, M. Smith and P. Hiscock (eds) *Desert Peoples: Archaeological perspectives*, pp. 100–15, Oxford: Blackwell.

Veth, P. (2006) 'Social dynamism in the archaeology of the Western Desert', in B. David, B. Barker and I. McNiven (eds) *The Social Archaeology of Australian Indigenous Societies*, pp. 242–53, Canberra: Aboriginal Studies Press.

Veth, P. and O'Connor, S. (1996) 'A preliminary analysis of basal grindstones from the Carnarvon Range, Little Sandy Desert', *Australian Archaeology* 43: 20–2.

Veth, P., Fullagar, R. and Gould, R. (1997) 'Residue and use-wear analysis of grinding implements from Puntutjarpa Rockshelter in the Western Desert: current and proposed research', *Australian Archaeology* 44: 23–5.

Veth, P., Smith, M. and Haley, M. (2001) 'Kaalpi: the archaeology of an outlying range in the dunefields of the Western Desert', *Australian Archaeology* 52: 9–17.

Villa, P. (1982) 'Conjoinable pieces and site formation processes', *American Antiquity* 47: 276–90.

Wallis, L. A. (2001) 'Environmental history of northwest Australia based on phytolith analysis at Carpenter's Gap 1', *Quaternary International* 83–5: 103–17.

Walsh, G. L. and Morwood, M. J. (1999) 'Spear and spearthrower evolution in the Kimberley region, N.W. Australia: evidence from rock art', *Archaeology in Oceania* 34: 45–58.

Walshe, K. (1994) 'A taphonomic analysis of the vertebrate material from Allen's Cave: implications for Australian Arid Zone archaeology', unpublished PhD thesis, Australian National University, Canberra.

Walshe, K. (2000) 'Carnivores, taphonomy and dietary stress at Puntutjarpa, Serpents Glen and Intitjikula', *Archaeology in Oceania* 35: 74–81.

Walters, I. (1981) 'Why did the Tasmanians stop eating fish: a theoretical consideration', *The Artefact* 6: 71–7.

Walters, I. (1989) 'Intensified fishery production at Moreton Bay, southeast Queensland, in the late Holocene', *Antiquity* 63: 215–24.

Walters, I. (1992) 'Farmers and their fires, fishers and their fish: production and productivity in pre-European south-east Queensland', *Dialectical Anthropology* 17: 167–82.

Wang, X., van der Kaars, S., Kershaw, P., Bird, M. and Jansenc, F. (1999) 'A record of fire, vegetation and climate through the last three glacial cycles from Lombok Ridge core G6-4, eastern Indian Ocean, Indonesia', *Palaeogeography, Palaeoclimatology, Palaeoecology* 147: 241–56.

Wapler, U., Crubézy, E. and Schultz, M. (2004) 'Is cribra orbitalia synonymous with anemia? Analysis and interpretation of cranial pathology in Sudan', *American Journal of Physical Anthropology* 123: 333–9.

Ward, I. (2004) 'Comparative records of occupation in the Keep River region of the eastern Kimberly, northwestern Australia', *Australian Archaeology* 59 :1–9.

Warner, W. L. (1969) *A Black Civilization: A social study of an Australian tribe*, Gloucester, MA: Peter Smith.

Wasson, R. J. (1983) 'The Cainozoic history of the Strzelecki and Simpson dunefields (Australia), and the origin of the desert dunes', *Zeitschrift für Geomorphologie* NF 45: 85–115.

Watchman, A. (1993) 'Evidence of a 25,000-year-old pictograph in Northern Australia', *Geoarchaeology* 8: 465–73.

Watson, E., Forster, P., Richards, M. and Bandelt, H-J. (1997) 'Mitochondrial footprints of human expansion in Africa', *American Journal of Human Genetics* 61: 691–704.

Webb, C. and Allen, J. (1990) 'A functional analysis of Pleistocene bone tools from two sites in southwest Tasmania', *Archaeology in Oceania* 25: 75–8.

Webb, S. G. (1982) 'Cribra orbitalia: a possible sign of anaemia in pre- and post-contact crania from Australia and Papua New Guinea', *Archaeology in Oceania* 17: 148–56.

Webb, S. G. (1984) 'Intensification, population and social change in southeastern Australia: Tte skeletal evidence', *Aboriginal History* 8: 154–72.

Webb, S. G. (1987) 'A palaedemographic model of late Holocene Central Murray Aboriginal society, Australia', *Human Evolution* 2: 385–406.

Webb, S. G. (1989a) *The Willandra Lakes Hominids*, Canberra: Department of Prehistory, RSPacS, Australian National University.

Webb, S. G. (1989b) *Prehistoric Stress in Australian Aborigines: A palaeopathological study of a hunter-gatherer population*, BAR International Series 490, Oxford: British Archaeological Reports.

Webb, S. G. (1990) 'Cranial thickening in an Australian hominid as a possible palaeoepidemiological indicator', *American Journal of Physical Anthropology* 82: 403–12.

Webb, S. G. (1995) *Palaeopathology of Aboriginal Australians: Health and disease across a hunter-gatherer continent*, Cambridge: Cambridge University Press.

White, C. (1967) 'Early stone axes in Arnhem Land', *Antiquity* 41: 149–52.

White, C. (1971) 'Man and environment in northwest Arnhem Land', in D. J. Mulvaney and J. Golson (eds) *Aboriginal Man and Environment in Australia*, pp. 141–157, Canberra: Australian National University Press.

White, J. P. (1977) 'Crude, colourless and unenterprising? Prehistorians and their views on the Stone Age of Sunda and Sahul', in J. Allen, J. Golson and R. Jones (eds) *Sunda and Sahul: Prehistoric studies in Southeast Asia, Melanesia and Australia*, pp. 13–30, London: Academic Press.

White, J. P. (1994) 'Site 820 and the evidence for early occupation in Australia', *Quaternary Australasia* 12: 21–3.

White, J. P. and Flannery, T. (1995) 'Late Pleistocene fauna at Spring Creek: a re-evaluation', *Australian Archaeology* 40: 13–17.

White, J. P. and O'Connell, J. F. (1979) 'Australian prehistory: new aspects of antiquity', *Science* 203: 21–8.

White, J. P. and O'Connell, J. F. (1982) *A Prehistory of Australia, New Guinea and Sahul*, Sydney: Academic Press.

Williams, E. (1985) 'Estimation of prehistoric populations of archaeological sites in southwestern Victoria: some problems', *Archaeology in Oceania* 20: 73–80.

Williams, E. (1987) 'Complex hunter-gatherers: a view from Australia', *Antiquity* 61: 310–21.

Williams, E. (1988) *Complex Hunter-gatherers: A late Holocene example from temperate Australia*. BAR International Series 423, Oxford: British Archaeological Reports.

Wobst, H. M. (1978) 'The archaeo-ethnology of hunter-gatherers or the tyranny of the ethnographic record in archaeology', *American Antiquity* 43: 303–9.

Wolpoff, M. H., Thorne, A. G., Smith, F. H., Frayer, D. W. and Pope, G. G. (1994) 'Multi-regional evolution: a world-wide source for modern human populations', in M. H. Nitecki and D. V. Nitecki (eds) *Origins of anatomically modern humans*, pp. 175–200, New York: Plenum Press.

Wolpoff, M. H., Hawks, J., Frayer, D. W. and Hunley, K. (2001) 'Modern human ancestry at the peripheries: a test of the replacement theory', *Science* 291: 293–7.

Wood, B. (1977) *The Evolution of Early Man*, Melbourne: Cassell.

Wood, J. W., Miller, G. R., Harpending, H. C. and Weiss, K. M. (1992) 'The osteological paradox: problems of inferring prehistoric health from skeletal samples', *Current Anthropology* 33: 343–70.

Wood, W. R. and Johnson, D. L. (1978) 'A survey of disturbance processes in archaeological site formation', *Advances in Archaeological Methods and Theory* 1: 315–81.

Woodroffe, C. D. (2000) 'Deltaic and estuarine environments and their Late Quaternary dynamics on the Sunda and Sahul shelves', *Journal of Asian Earth Sciences* 18: 393–413.

Woodroffe, C. D., Thom, B. G. and Chappell, J. (1986) 'Development of widespread mangrove swamps in mid-Holocene times in northern Australia', *Nature* 317: 711–13.

Woodroffe, C. D., Chappell, J. and Thom, B. G. (1988) 'Shell middens in the context of estuarine development, South Alligator River, Northern Territory', *Archaeology in Oceania* 23: 95–103.

Wright, R. V. S. (1975) 'Stone artefacts from Kow Swamp with notes on their excavation and environmental context', *Archaeology and Physical Anthropology in Oceania* 10: 161–80.

Wright, R. V. S. (1977) 'Introduction and two studies', in R. V. S. Wright (ed.) *Stone Tools as Cultural Markers: Change, evolution and complexity*, pp. 1–3, Canberra: Australian Institute of Aboriginal Studies.

Wright, R. V. S. (1986) 'How old is zone F at Lake George?', *Archaeology in Oceania* 21: 138–9.

Wroe, S. and Field, J. (2001a) 'Giant Wombats and red herrings', *Australasian Science* 22: 18.

Wroe, S. and Field, J. (2001b) 'Mystery of megafaunal extinctions remains', *Australasian Science* 22: 21–5.

Wroe, S. and Field, J. (2006) 'A review of the evidence for a human role in the extinction of the Australian megafauna and an alternative interpretation', *Quaternary Science Reviews* 25: 2692–703.

Wroe, S., Field, J. and Fullagar, R. (2002) 'Lost giants', *Nature Australia* 27: 54–61.

Wroe, S., Crowther, M., Dortch, J. and Chong, J. (2003a) 'The size of the largest marsupial and why it matters', *The Royal Society of London* 271: S34–S36.

Wroe, S., Myers, T., Seebacher, F., Kear, B., Gillespie, A., Crowther, M. and Salisbury, S. (2003b) 'An alternative method for predicting body mass: the case of the Pleistocene marsupial lion', *Paleobiology* 29: 403–11.

Wroe, S., Field, J., Fullagar, R. and Jermin, L. S. (2004) 'Megafaunal extinction in the late Quaternary and the global overkill hypothesis', *Alcheringa* 28: 291–331.

Wroe, S., Field, J. and Grayson, D. K. (2006) 'Megafaunal extinction: climate, humans and assumptions', *Trends in Ecology and Evolution* 21: 61–2.

Wyrwoll, K. H. and Miller, G. H. (2001) 'Initiation of the Australian summer monsoon 14,000 years ago', *Quaternary International* 83–5: 119–28.

Yokoyama, Y., Purcell, A., Lambeck, K. and Johnston, P. (2001) 'Shore-line reconstruction around Australia during the Last Glacial Maximum and Late Glacial Stage', *Quaternary International* 83–5: 9–18.

Zielinski, G., Mayewski, P. A., Meeker, L. D., Whitlow, S. and Twickler, M. S. (1996) 'Potential impact of the Toba mega-eruption 271,000 years ago', *Geophysical Research Letters* 23: 837–40.

Index

109–11, 113–15; production methods 105; Rainbow Serpents, in 114, 261–4, 266; territoriality and 248, 252, 254–5; Therianthropes 113; weapons in 112–13; Western Desert 109; X-ray 254–5; Yam phase 112, 261–4; *see also* ochre

Aru Islands 149

Asia 13, 21, 23, 25–6, 46, 56, 83, 91, 94–5, 146–7, 150, 276

Asmussen, Brit 192, 195–7

Attenbrow, Valerie (Val) 154, 156, 229, 233–4, 236–9, 243

Aurukun 164, 270, 274

'Australian desert culture' 201

Austronesian 150

axes *see* stone tools and implements

backed artefacts *see* stone tools and implements

Badi Badi 164, 172–3

Badu Island 270, 272

Bailey, Geoff 177

Balme, Jane 122–3, 127, 189, 208, 216

Banda Sea 37

Barker, Bryce 166, 169–70

Barlambidj 270, 279–80

Bassian Plain 46

Bass Strait 129, 139, 140, 147

Bay of Fires 137

Beaton, John 152, 163, 165, 170, 179–80, 192–6, 219, 221, 243

Beck, Wendy 189

Berndt, Ronald 283

big-game hunters *see* 'overkill'

Bird, Caroline 190–1

Birdsell, Joseph 10–11, 21, 24, 49, 56, 92, 100, 146, 221, 231, 234; population change and 221; settlement and 21, 24

boats *see* watercraft

Bobadeen 147–8

Bondaian 146

Bone Cave 115, 118

bone tools 26, 116, 122, 134

Border Island 164, 169

Bowdler, Sandra 45–7, 104, 135, 148, 151–2, 184, 194

Bowler, Jim 39–41, 53, 76, 102

Bradley, Richard 259

Bidgewater Cave 190

Brockwell, Sally 273

Brown, Peter 85, 87–8, 90, 95, 98–9

Brothwell, Don 95

Budgeongutte Swamp 186

Builth, Heather 190

Bullbeck, David 94

Butlin, Noel 14

burials 8, 26, 39, 87–8, 125, 226–8, 251, 256–60; Coobool Creek 226–7; cremation 8; Katarapko 226–7; Kow Swamp 87–8, 125, 226–7, 248; Lake Victoria 226–7; Roonka 84, 226–7, 256–60; Snaggy Bend 226–7; Swanport 226–7; WLH3 125; *see also* skeletons

Burrill Lake 107, 121, 146–7, 227

Bush Peg 271

C99 46, 60

Cameron, David 87–8, 94

Capertee 146–8, 153–7, 160

Capertian 146

Cape York Peninsula 110, 147, 156, 163, 175, 177, 253–4, 265, 269, 274

carbon isotope ratios 77–8

Carnarvon Gorge 183, 192–3, 195

Carpenter's Gap 34, 46, 52–3, 125

Caselli, Giovanni 5, 6

Cathedral Cave 191–6

Cave Bay Cave 45–6, 141

cemeteries 226–7; *see also* burials

Central Australian Ranges 60

Central Queensland Highlands 229, 231, 235

ceremony and ritual 8, 16–17, 113, 125, 128, 137–8, 152, 183–4, 191, 194–5, 207, 245–8, 251–3, 265, 272, 274, 282–3; depicted in art 113; grave goods 257–8; mounds, and 178; Pleistocene 245, 251; WLH3 125; *see also* burials

Chaloupka, George 111–12

charcoal fragments 27–8, 37, 74

Cheetup Cave 195

Chinese 276

Chippindale, Christopher 113–14, 261–3, 266

Clarke, Annie 253, 273

Clarkson, Chris 273

Clear Swamp 186

Cleland Hills 47

climate change 20–22, 37, 52, 56–9, 63, 71, 76–9, 81, 98, 101, 118, 120, 139–41, 144, 158, 205, 209, 238; aridity, increase of 52, 56–9, 79, 81, 205–6, 214, 218; climatic deterioration 56–8, 77, 79, 81, 140, 205, 209, 234; effective precipitation, changes in 53,